International Law in Asia

Series Editor

Eric Yong Joong Lee, #402 Taejin Bd, YIJUN Institute of International Law, Seoul, Korea (Republic of)

This series aims to provide the latest perspectives on international law in this ever changing region of Asia. Each book of this series will address specific aspect of highly contemporary global issues such as armed conflict, maritime disputes, human rights and refugee crises, sustainable development/climate change, outer space, finance and economy, trade (WTO and FTA), investment, development, technology, intellectual property, international crime, global health, regional questions, etc.

This book series invites leading international law scholars and practitioners in Asia to contribute their expertise in interpreting a wide range of legal questions that arise in relation to the above topics through an Asian lens. This series will serve as useful guide for international lawyers, diplomats, businessmen and students to understand current and future trends of international law in Asia.

Nguyen Hong Thao · Tran Thi Kim Nguyen

Lawfulness and Lawfare in the South China Sea

Springer

Nguyen Hong Thao
Ho Chi Minh City University of Law
Ho Chi Minh City, Vietnam

Tran Thi Kim Nguyen
Faculty of Law
Ho Chi Minh City Open University
Ho Chi Minh City, Vietnam

ISSN 2731-8044 ISSN 2731-8052 (electronic)
International Law in Asia
ISBN 978-981-95-4000-6 ISBN 978-981-95-4001-3 (eBook)
https://doi.org/10.1007/978-981-95-4001-3

This Springer imprint is published by the registered company Springer Nature Singapore Pte Ltd.
The registered company address is: 152 Beach Road, #21-01/04 Gateway East, Singapore 189721, Singapore

To all who have sacrificed and fought for international law, peace, security, and prosperity in the South China Sea

Preface

In recent years, the term "lawfare" (commonly referred to as "legal warfare") has gained currency in both military and media discourse, reflecting the increasing importance of legal mechanisms as strategic tools—either as substitutes for, or in tandem with, traditional military operations. Despite its mounting relevance in contemporary geopolitics, the term "lawfare" has yet to secure an unequivocal definition within the discipline of international law, leaving its precise scope and features subject to ongoing scholarly debate. Nevertheless, the recognition of lawfare as a critical dimension of modern conflict highlights the evolving nature of warfare and underscores the growing influence of legal strategies on international relations and security.

Against this backdrop of shifting geopolitical realities, disputes in the South China Sea have taken on heightened significance. Several states in the region, most notably China, have embraced increasingly sophisticated legal tactics. Although China continues to refute the 2016 Arbitral Award, it simultaneously pursues novel interpretative approaches, selectively invoking provisions of UNCLOS that bolster its maritime claims. Yet, it also disregards the Convention's applicability to various maritime issues, calling instead for supplementary regulations. This stance not only poses immediate challenges for regional stakeholders—such as Brunei, Malaysia, the Philippines, and Vietnam—but also threatens, over time, the integrity of UNCLOS and collective efforts to uphold a rules-based maritime order. Furthermore, whereas recent Western initiatives emphasize a rules-based international order, China advances a distinct vision rooted in its domestic ideological and legal framework–namely, "the rule of law under socialism with Chinese characteristics" (坚持中国特色社会主义法治道路). In doing so, China aims to introduce an alternative framework at variance with existing international norms.

Regarding the approach and methodology, since lawfare fundamentally centers on how a state leverages the legal system, this book, **Lawfulness and Lawfare in the South China Sea**, adopts a technique-driven analytical framework. It demonstrates how these tactics operate in practice, with the understanding that a single legal issue can be approached through multiple lawfare techniques and offers a thorough analysis of legal warfare in the context of contemporary concepts like cognitive and hybrid warfare. It explores how China has operationalized these tactics in the South China Sea, alongside the responses and perspectives of Malaysia, the Philippines, and Vietnam. While Brunei is among the claimants in the Spratly Islands, its minimal involvement in lawfare-related practices places it outside the scope of this book. Moreover, the book highlights the critical distinction between genuine law implementation—termed "lawfulness"—and the strategic use of legal mechanisms as a weapon, known as "lawfare."

Organized into four chapters, the book examines China's lawfare strategies and the lawful countermeasures of other states within the context of South China Sea disputes. Chapter 1, *Lawfare and Lawfulness and an Overview of South China Sea Legal Issues*, introduces key concepts, defining lawfare, lawfulness, and the core legal issues in the South China Sea. It provides a theoretical foundation essential for understanding subsequent analysis. Chapter 2, *China's Lawfare in the South China Sea: An Overview*, analyzes China's use of lawfare, focusing on tactics from the Three Warfares strategy and, in particular, legal warfare, detailing how China employs these techniques. Chapter 3, *Lawfulness of Malaysia, Philippines, and Vietnam in the South China Sea: An Overview*, explores how Malaysia, the Philippines, and Vietnam deploy legitimate legal strategies to counter China's lawfare, emphasizing their lawful defenses. Chapter 4, *Lawfulness versus China's Lawfare in the South China Sea*, examines specific frontline instances where China unlawfully manipulates the legal system. It also details how other states respond to China's legal manipulations, highlighting the fight between lawfare tactics and lawful resistance. This structure aims to provide a clear, compelling understanding of legal conflicts in the South China Sea, emphasizing both China's aggressive tactics and the lawful responses of neighboring states.

In an era where geopolitical challenges are increasingly shaped by the interplay of military power, economic leverage, and legal argumentation, it is crucial to examine how law can be wielded both as a shield and a sword. This book presents the new initiative of "lawfulness" against lawfare, or the **3P formula**, demonstrating how legal frameworks grounded in principles of fairness can effectively balance or counteract the manipulative use of legal norms in contentious disputes. Central to this approach is the intertwined influence of Publicity, Public Opinion, and Public International Law—three elements that, when combined, have the capacity to mobilize broader support and ensure that sovereign claims remain grounded in transparent, consensus-based processes rather than mere power politics.

A significant focus of this book is the South China Sea, a region beset by overlapping territorial and maritime claims. Through detailed case studies and analyses, the book elucidates the intricate legal, historical, and strategic dimensions of disputes in this field. It aspires to present these issues with clarity and accessibility, thereby welcoming both specialists in international law and those outside of legal disciplines to engage with its core arguments. In doing so, it highlights the importance of an informed public and the global community in shaping a rules-based and equitable maritime order, as such collective awareness can exert pressure on decision-makers to adhere to principles of legality and equity.

Nevertheless, the complexity of lawfare—a term itself subject to various interpretations—calls for continued scholarly dialogue. We candidly acknowledge that our perspectives, shaped by inherent limitations of knowledge and experience, may not encompass the full extent of legal or geopolitical nuances. It is precisely for this reason that the book takes the form of an open invitation for critique and collaboration. Scholars, practitioners, and interested readers are encouraged to offer insights, corrections, and constructive views. Such collaborative engagement holds immense promise. It can inform subsequent research endeavors and stimulate international dialogues aimed at fortifying existing norms within public international law. More importantly, this process can unify voices in working toward a future where disputes are resolved through reasoned and fair legal mechanisms rather than unilateral or coercive tactics. Ultimately, this shared pursuit of a balanced legal framework in the South China Sea underscores a collective commitment to peaceful coexistence and peaceful settlement—an aspiration that transcends the immediate interests of claimant states and resonates with stakeholders worldwide.

Acknowledgments We would like to sincerely thank our colleagues Nguyen Hung Son, Nguyen Thi Lan Huong, Hoang Thanh Thao, Dinh Thi Thu, Vo Ngoc Diep, Nguyen Thu Giang, Nguyen Thuy Anh, and Nguyen Mai Huong for their initial contributions. This book would not have been possible in the Asia and International Law series without the encouragement of Professor LEE Eric Yong Joong and the superb editing skills of Anushangi Weerakoon and Anand Manimudichozhan.

Competing Interests The authors have no competing interests to declare that are relevant to the content of this manuscript.

Contents

About the Authors

Nguyen Hong Thao Member of the UN International Law Commission (2017–2022 and 2023–2027), is currently teaching as a Senior Lecturer at the Ho Chi Minh City University of Law, Diplomatic Academy of Vietnam and the National University of Hanoi. Dr. Nguyen received his LLB and PhD degrees from the University of Paris 1 Panthéon-Sorbonne (France) in 1996. His main academic specializations are in public international law, the law of the sea, international organizations and international humanitarian and environmental law. Dr. Nguyen has also authored a series of works on international law, specifically in the area of maritime dispute resolutions. His experience in maritime affairs and diplomacy includes Ambassador postings in Malaysia (2011–14) and Kuwait (2014–17). He is a member of the Asian Society of International Law and the Vietnam Society of International Law. He is the Editor-in-Chief of the Vietnamese Yearbook on International Law, and also on the advisory boards of the *Asian Yearbook of International Law* (AYBIL), the *Asian Journal of International Law* (AsianJIL), the *Asia-Africa Legal Consultative Organization Journal* (AALCO), and part of the editorial boards of the *Journal of International Law* and *Journal of East Asia and International Law*.

Tran Thi Kim Nguyen is a lecturer at the Faculty of Law, Ho Chi Minh City Open University, where she has served since 2021. She holds a Master's Degree in Law from the University of Law, Vietnam National University—Hanoi, awarded in 2020. From 2016 to 2018, she was a research fellow at the Center for the Law of the Sea and International Maritime Law (University of Law, Vietnam National University—Hanoi), and later served as a research assistant at the East Sea Institute (Diplomatic Academy of Vietnam) from 2019 to 2020. Her academic interests focus on Public International Law, with particular emphasis on the Law of the Sea and ASEAN Law.

Abbreviations

ASEAN	Association of Southeast Asian Nations
BBNJ	Biodiversity Beyond National Jurisdiction
CLCS	Commission on the Limits of the Continental Shelf
COC	Code of Conduct in the South China Sea
DOC	Declaration on the Conduct of Parties in the South China Sea 2002
EEZ	Exclusive Economic Zone
ICJ	International Court of Justice
IMO	International Maritime Organization
ITLOS	International Tribunal for the Law of the Sea
NATO	North Atlantic Treaty Organization
U.S.	United States
UN	United Nations
UNCLOS	United Nations Convention on the Law of the Sea 1982

List of Figures

List of Tables

Chapter 1
Lawfare and Lawfulness and an Overview of South China Sea Legal Issues

Chapter 1 examines the evolving concept of lawfare and contrasts it with the principle of lawfulness in international law. It traces the historical and theoretical foundations of war and law, from Grotius and Clausewitz to contemporary debates on hybrid and cognitive warfare. Various scholarly perspectives on lawfare are explored, highlighting its manifestations across international and domestic domains, including the reinterpretation of legal norms, the use of international tribunals, and national legislation. Drawing on case studies, the chapter illustrates how lawfare has become a central instrument in modern conflicts. Against this backdrop, the book advances the concept of lawfulness as a counter-strategy, emphasizing transparency, public opinion, and adherence to international law—the "3P formula." This approach underscores the distinction between lawful implementation of law and unlawful legal actions, arguing that only the latter constitutes lawfare. Ultimately, the chapter situates lawfare and lawfulness within the specific framework of the South China Sea disputes, providing a factual foundation for understanding the legal confrontations that will be further explored in the following chapters of the book.

Can Law Be a Form of War?

Since the early twenty-first century, debates have emerged over the use of law as a weapon of war or as a means of realizing a military objective in modern warfare. Initially arising within the fields of military strategy and foreign policy, these discussions have gradually gained prominence in legal scholarship. This has created an urgent need to clarify the role and position of law in maintaining

H. T. Nguyen, T. K. N. Tran, *Lawfulness and Lawfare in the South China Sea*,
International Law in Asia,
https://doi.org/10.1007/978-981-95-4001-3_1

international peace and security, as well as its function in contemporary armed conflicts.[1]

Major dictionaries typically provide concise definitions, often synthesizing elements from various perspectives. For instance, Merriam-Webster's Dictionary defines war as "a state of usually open and declared armed hostile conflict between states or nations."[2] Additionally, the Oxford Dictionary defines "war" as "hostile contention by means of armed forces, carried on between nations, states, or rulers, or between parties within the same nation or state; the employment of armed forces against a foreign power or against an opposing party within the state."[3] In contrast, Collins Dictionary offers broader definitions that encompass civil wars, internal conflicts, and metaphorical interpretations of "war," reflecting the increasingly complex nature of conflict in the modern world. It defines war as "aggressive business conflict, as through severe price-cutting in the same industry or any other means of undermining competitors" or "being in a state of strong opposition."[4] Moreover, the Cambridge Dictionary highlights metaphorical usages and broader societal impacts, offering a richer understanding of war's multifaceted nature in contemporary discourse: "any situation in which there is strong competition between opposing sides or a significant struggle against something harmful."[5]

Defining "war" is a complex undertaking, as its meaning shifts depending on the perspective applied. A Clausewitzian approach, rooted in Carl von Clausewitz's seminal work On War (1832), emphasizes the political nature of war, viewing it as "an act of violence intended to compel our opponent to fulfill our will."[6] This perspective highlights the rational calculations and inherent political objectives driving warfare, regardless of its manifestation. Mitchinson (2000)'s Marxism and War argues that understanding war from a Marxist perspective requires examining its root causes within the context of class struggle and imperialism. Rejecting both pacifism and reformist approaches, Mitchinson (2000) posits that war is fundamentally a continuation of the inherent class conflict within capitalism, manifesting in both international and intranational conflicts.[7] This approach emphasizes the prevailing power's maintenance of dominance through social institutions.

The law of war was established not to encourage warfare but to mitigate its consequences, protect human beings, and establish principles of humanitarian conduct even in armed conflicts. To gain a comprehensive understanding of the legal aspects of war, it is essential to explore the framework of war within the context of international law and international relations. This framework encompasses two primary branches of international law: *jus ad bellum*, which governs the legality of the use of force, and *jus*

[1] Kittrie (2016), pp. 40–50. See also Pinos and Hau (2024), pp. 9–11.

[2] Merriam-Webster.com dictionary website.

[3] Oxford English Dictionary website.

[4] Collins English Dictionary website.

[5] Cambridge Dictionary website.

[6] Clausewitz (1832), p. 15.

[7] Mitchinson (2000).

in bello, or International Humanitarian Law, which regulates the conduct of parties engaged in armed conflict, regardless of the legality of the conflict itself. Under international humanitarian law, the classification of a situation as an armed conflict is based on objective factual assessments rather than subjective labeling. International Humanitarian Law seeks, for humanitarian reasons, to establish rules that limit the means and methods of warfare and ensure the protection of individuals who are not, or are no longer, directly or actively participating in hostilities.[8] Additionally, it regulates the occupation and control of territory and outlines responsibilities for violations and the prosecution of such violations. Importantly, it does not serve as a tool for direct participation in warfare, nor does it directly influence the outcome of victory. The established criteria within international humanitarian law for classifying armed conflicts—centered on the intensity and nature of hostilities involving either states or organized non-state actors—serve as the essential standard for determining the applicability of international law, irrespective of the terminology employed to describe the circumstances. The emergence of new terms such as "hybrid warfare" and "gray zones,"[9] which lack precise legal definitions, may lead to misinterpretations of International Humanitarian Law principles and unintended legal consequences. Hence, a rigorous analysis grounded in the established criteria of international humanitarian law is necessary for accurately assessing the legal ramifications of various forms of conflict, ensuring that legal standards are upheld and applied consistently.

In the seventeenth century, Grotius (1625) debated the lawful aspect of war by advancing the concept of just war under a legal and moral framework to protect sovereignty and legitimate rights.[10] The just causes of war constitute a battlefield where legal arguments can serve as powerful weapons. The regulation of war and its methods finds their basis in international agreements such as The Hague Conventions of 1899 and 1907, as well as the Geneva Convention of 1949 and their Additional Protocols. These conventions establish guidelines concerning the treatment of civilians, prisoners of war, and combatants injured or ill during conflicts. In this context, war is defined as a state of armed conflict between nations, governments, societies, or even paramilitary groups, including mercenaries, insurgents, and militias. These conflicts often arise from ideological, ethnic, or religious tensions, as various factions vie for economic and political advantages. Characterized by extreme violence and aggression, warfare in international relations necessitates a declaration and imposes limitations on the use of tools and tactics that inflict significant material and human losses. War can profoundly impact the dynamics of international relations by influencing the emergence or dissolution of actors within the international system. Additionally, it can alter the relative power of these actors, either enhancing or diminishing their influence. Furthermore, war has the capacity to reshape the international system itself,

---

[8] Melzer (2019), p. 17.

[9] D'Cunha et al. (2025).

[10] Grotius (1625), pp. 32–47.

often leading to the establishment of new orders aimed at fostering security and stability in international relations.

To mitigate the devastating impacts of war, nations came together to establish a system of collective security, enshrined in the 1945 UN Charter and subsequent legal instruments. This system aims to uphold a new rules-based international order, with two primary objectives: (1) The prohibition of the use of force and the threat of force, and (2) The peaceful resolution of disputes in international relations. Exceptions to the use of force are permitted only in specific circumstances outlined by international law, such as actions authorized by the UN Security Council to maintain international peace and security, or the legitimate right of self-defense. Nations and the UN Security Council seeking to employ force must demonstrate legitimacy through legal instruments. These mechanisms also establish negotiation fora and utilize third-party assistance to peacefully resolve international disputes, as outlined in Article 33 of the 1945 UN Charter. All countries adhere to the principles of international law when asserting their positions on specific issues arising in international relations. Such applications must align with the provisions outlined in Articles 31 and 32 of the 1969 Vienna Convention on the Law of Treaties. These articles stipulate that international treaties or regulations should be interpreted in good faith, considering their context, subject matter, and intended purpose. This general rule of interpretation, widely recognized and practiced at the national and international levels, has attained customary status in international law.

Hence, international law is expected to serve inherently as a mechanism for the peaceful resolution of disputes, fostering cooperation among nations and promoting peaceful coexistence, rather than as a tool to justify or support war or as a tool to reach a military objective. However, if war is understood in a broader context, encompassing not only armed conflict or hostility but also any legal actions aimed at undermining the legitimacy of an opponent's position to achieve specific political objectives, then international law can indeed serve as a tool for waging this form of warfare.

Multiple Approaches to the Concept of Lawfare

Concepts

During the early twenty-first century, the term "lawfare," often referred to as "legal warfare," gained considerable attention and discussion within the field of international relations, particularly among military and media experts. While its roots can be traced to earlier historical periods, it has become prominent in contemporary discourse. Currently, there is no universally accepted definition of this concept; it is known by various terms such as "legal warfare," "lawfare," and as part of the broader framework of the Three Warfares. These terms are utilized by different stakeholders in diverse contexts, each tailored to their specific political, military, or economic objectives. The scope and methodologies of lawfare vary depending on the goals of individual countries or entities involved, reflecting a nuanced and multifaceted approach to achieving strategic aims. This adaptability allows for the customization of legal strategies to address the unique circumstances and challenges encountered in international relations, underscoring its continued relevance and evolution in contemporary geopolitical landscapes.

Lawfare is a portmanteau of "law" and "warfare." According to Collins English Dictionary, lawfare denotes the utilization of legal mechanisms by a nation against its adversaries, particularly through legal challenges to the legitimacy of military or foreign policies.[11] The concept of lawfare has been used in the U.S. military since 1975. John Carlson and Neville Yeomans introduced the term in an article discussing mediation,[12] advocating for the utilization of legal tactics in lieu of traditional warfare. They proposed employing legal strategies as a means of conflict resolution, emphasizing the power of words and diplomacy over weapons and violence. Subsequently, David Rivkin and Lee Casey expanded on this concept, observing a trend among U.S. allies and adversaries to use international law as a means to undermine U.S. influence.[13] They argued that as the world's foremost superpower following the Cold War, the U.S possessed a unique opportunity to leverage its dominance to shape international law and the rules-based international order in its favor.

The notion of lawfare in military circles was explored by General Colonel Charles Dunlap. Dunlap (multiple works, 2001/2009/2017) examines the intersection of international law, particularly the law of armed conflict, and modern military interventions. He challenges the prevailing notion that the law of armed conflict significantly reduces human suffering during conflicts. Dunlap (multiple works, 2001/2009/2017) argues that while the law of armed conflict's goal of minimizing harm is laudable, in practice it often falls short, and in some cases, even contributes to increased civilian casualties. He posits that the rise of lawfare—the strategic use of law as a weapon of war—exacerbates this problem. He further argues that this "hyper-legalism" is often ill-informed by the realities of modern warfare and technology. Dunlap (multiple works, 2001/2009/2017) notes that adversaries frequently exploit perceived or actual law of armed conflict violations to undermine public support for military interventions. Dunlap (multiple works, 2001/2009/2017) concludes that stronger cooperation between military leaders and legal experts, a more nuanced understanding of law of armed conflict principles within the military, and a rejection of politically motivated criticisms of military actions are all essential to preserving humanitarian values while ensuring effective military operations.[14] According to Dunlap's analysis: (i) Lawfare represents the utilization of law as a weapon in contemporary warfare, marking it as a novel form of conflict in the twenty-first century. (ii) It entails employing legal mechanisms as a means to

---

[11] "Lawfare: the use of the law by a country against its enemies, esp by challenging the legality of military or foreign policy." See Collins English Dictionary website.

[12] Yeomans (2023).

[13] Blackman (2017).

[14] Dunlap (2001). See also Dunlap (2009), pp. 34–39; Dunlap (2017), pp. 8–17.

accomplish military objectives. (iii) Lawfare involves the strategic deployment or manipulation of legal principles, often deviating from their intended purposes, to supplant traditional military strategies in achieving wartime aims. This characterization highlights a deliberate distortion of legal norms and humanitarian values.

The various definitions and interpretations of lawfare by scholars such as Goldstein (2016),[15] Mosquera (2016),[16] Logan (2017),[17] Guilfoyle (2019),[18] and Gartland (2021),[19] reveal a common thread: the strategic use of legal mechanisms to achieve specific political, military, or social objectives. Goldstein (2016) emphasizes the misuse of legal systems in the context of human rights, while Munoz Mosquera (2016) highlights the deployment of non-kinetic tools for strategic influence. Logan (2017) and Guilfoyle (2019) focus on shaping and leveraging legal frameworks to effect desired changes, illustrating the interplay between law and strategy. Additionally, Gartland (2021)'s emphasis on the creation of narratives and legal precedents underscores the innovative tactics involved in lawfare. Collectively, these perspectives illustrate a broader understanding of lawfare as a multifaceted approach that exploits legal principles to maneuver within the complex landscape of international relations and conflict.

The intersection of international law and politics is a central theme in the discussions presented by Proner and Amorim (2021),[20] Chadwick and Kolenc (2006),[21] and Scott (1994).[22] Proner and Amorim (2021) highlight lawfare as a strategic tool rooted in the manipulation of legal mechanisms to suppress political opposition, thereby underscoring the political dimensions inherent in legal frameworks. Similarly, Chadwick and Kolenc (2006) explore how nations exploit the International Criminal Court (ICC) for political and military objectives, illustrating the manner in which legal institutions can be co-opted to advance geopolitical interests. In contrast, Scott (1994) critiques the prevailing realist and positivist perspectives for their failure to recognize the interplay between compliance with international law and political motivations, arguing that such frameworks obscure the active role that states play within the international legal system. By proposing a view of international law as an ideology, Scott emphasizes its function as a set of ideas and principles that political actors use strategically to achieve their goals, reinforcing the premise that understanding international law requires a consideration of its political implications. Together,

[15] Lawfare is "the abuse of the law and our judicial systems to undermine the very principles they stand for: the rule of law, the sanctity of innocent human life, and the right to free speech." See Goldstein (2010). See also Lawfare Project Executive Director Brooke Goldstein's Outspoken premieres tonight on JBS at the Lawfare Project (2018).

[16] Muñoz (2016), pp. 63–87.

[17] Logan (2017).

[18] Guilfoyle (2019).

[19] Gartland (2021).

[20] Proner and Amorin (2021).

[21] For example, this includes exploiting the investigative process, making unfounded accusations, or manipulating the media. See Austin and Kolenc (2006), pp. 291–336.

[22] Scott (1994), pp. 313–325.

these perspectives reveal a complex and dynamic relationship wherein international law is not merely a set of rules but a vital component of the political landscape, shaping and being shaped by the interests and actions of states within the global arena.

Converging on the theme of lawfare as a strategic tool wielded within the interplay of law and politics, several scholars vary in their emphasis on the legitimate and illegitimate uses of law, the dimensions of its impact, and the essential structure of the legal frameworks at play. Dill (2017)[23] foregrounds the strategic use of international law as a means to achieve the objectives of belligerents, emphasizing that lawfare is not merely the misuse of law but entails a conscious manipulation of legal frameworks. Dill (2017) introduces a typology that differentiates between legitimate and illegitimate uses of international law, focusing on whether such uses undermine the principles underlying the legal system invoked. This perspective highlights the importance of the strategic goals of the actor, the applicable legal norms, and the context of the conflict in assessing whether an action constitutes lawfare.

In contrast, Zanin et al. (2022)[24] define lawfare as the strategic use of legal instruments to not only delegitimize but also to harm or annihilate an opponent. They argue that this concept encompasses a deliberate strategy that transcends mere legal description, suggesting that lawfare implicitly weaponizes legal norms against adversaries. Their emphasis on the distinction between strategy and tactics reinforces the methodological understanding of how legal processes can be instrumentalized. By contrasting lawfare with the "state of exception"[25] and "judicial activism,"[26] these authors further delineate lawfare's systematic nature, highlighting its broader strategies that include psychological operations and media manipulation in addition to legal means. Hsiao (2016)[27] adopts a more generalized definition of lawfare, acknowledging its dual potential to achieve both positive and negative strategic objectives in international relations. While lawfare can be employed to solidify legitimacy and advance policies or values, it can also serve to challenge an opponent's legitimacy and increase their operational costs. This duality underscores the versatile applicability of lawfare across various contexts and objectives, reinforcing the idea that it functions as a strategic tool within geopolitical dynamics. Beck (2014)[28] presents a more critical lens on lawfare, defining it through a negative framework characterized by the misuse of law to pursue military objectives. This interpretation limits the definition to contexts in which the legal framework is weakened or subverted, contrasting with the broader understandings posited by other scholars. While sharing some overlap with Dill's typology and Hsiao's observations regarding strategic ends, Beck's focus on the negative consequences of lawfare provides a more cautionary perspective on its

[23] Dill (2017), pp. 119–133.

[24] Zanin et al. (2022), pp. 4–21.

[25] Zanin et al. (2022), p. 10.

[26] Zanin et al. (2022), p. 11.

[27] Hsiao (2016), pp. 1–35.

[28] Beck (2014), pp. 306–318.

implications for the integrity of legal systems. Dill and Hsiao present more expansive views that allow for both positive and negative applications, whereas Zanin et al. and Beck emphasize the tactical and often detrimental consequences of lawfare. Together, these perspectives enrich the discourse on lawfare, illuminating the complex ways in which legal mechanisms interact with power dynamics in the international arena. Lawfare often serves dual objectives. On the one hand, it invokes international law to defend the legitimacy of a state's legal actions; on the other hand, it may involve the manipulation or misuse of international law to justify actions that are, in substance, unlawful under that same legal framework.

The evolution of science and technology has significantly transformed the role of law in international conflicts, introducing new domains such as cyberspace, environmental changes, biological and electronic warfare, and election interference. A key characteristic of future conflicts will be the increased emphasis on legal frameworks before resorting to armed force, whether traditional or nuclear. Major powers often employ lawfare to assert dominance in international relations, while smaller or weaker nations utilize legal instruments to mitigate power and size asymmetries, seeking to restore equal legal status and uphold their right to participate in international relations based on the principle of sovereign equality.

In armed conflicts, the imbalance of military power between parties is often a decisive factor. However, in the legal realm, states operate with equal legal status and share the capacity to engage in international relations, exercising the same rights and obligations under international law. In this context, law can become a powerful tool for weaker states.[29] Nevertheless, the assumption that lawfare inherently empowers weaker states to counterbalance the dominance of stronger actors can be misleading and problematic. While the strategic use of international law is a legitimate means for smaller or less influential nations to protect their interests, it is essential to distinguish between lawful and unlawful applications. The mere act of initiating legal proceedings should not automatically be labeled as "lawfare", particularly when claims remain within legal bounds. The boundary between the legitimate implementation of international law and its manipulation for strategic purposes is often blurred. Weaker states must carefully navigate this distinction to avoid undermining the core principles of justice and fairness that uphold the global legal order. Lawful conduct, even when employed to counter asymmetric power dynamics, should not be equated with lawfare. The strength of international law lies in its impartial and universal application, rather than its selective use to advance narrow national interests. Therefore, preserving this crucial distinction is fundamental to maintaining the integrity of the rule of law and fostering a more stable, just, and equitable international system.

Starting from a synthesis of multi-dimensional perspectives with regard to specific matters in the South China Sea, this book introduces the concept of lawfare as follows: Lawfare is the utilization of legal tools within international relations to assert national claims against other claimants **unlawfully**. Parties engage in applying or crafting new

[29] Guilfoyle (2023), pp. 1–36.

legal regulations, both at the international and national levels, to either to legitimize their own claims on the global stage or to challenge the legality of those made by other actors. Activities associated with lawfare can be conducted independently or in conjunction with other strategies, such as psychological or information warfare, with the aim of gaining an advantage in ongoing political-diplomatic conflicts.

In the context of this book, the concept of lawfare is defined by the following key characteristics: First, the primary actors engaged in lawfare are sovereign States or State-like entities. These actors use legal tools as instruments of geopolitical competition rather than purely for the pursuit of justice or legal order. Second, from the standpoint of the international community, lawfare carries a negative connotation. It often entails the misuse or distortion of legal norms, diverging from the foundational principles of international law. In practice, many powerful States profess commitment to the international legal order while selectively interpreting or even exploiting legal frameworks to advance their strategic interests. Third, from a national standpoint, lawfare carries an inherently dual character. On the one hand, it provides States with a proactive tool to assert and safeguard their interests through legal and normative avenues, enabling them to shape favorable legal narratives and frameworks. On the other hand, it also creates exposure to legal vulnerabilities, as their foreign, military, or domestic policies may be contested before international tribunals or through domestic proceedings initiated by external actors. Equally important are the political aims underlying its use—whether to consolidate power, weaken rivals, promote human rights, or preserve existing territorial arrangements.[30]

Manifestations

The growing use of lawfare is shaping national strategies across military, economic, political, security, human rights, and cultural domains. It has become a key instrument of national power, influencing the development and interpretation of international legal norms to advance specific policy objectives. However, lawfare differs significantly from traditional definitions of war in international law. Rather than signifying direct military conflict, it is employed metaphorically—similar to terms like "cold war" or "trade war"—to encompass non-military measures.

Drawing from Kittrie's typology, lawfare can be further classified into two main types: (i) "instrumental lawfare", which involves utilizing legal mechanisms to obtain outcomes similar to those achieved through traditional methods and is employed by both state and non-state actors; and (ii) "compliance-leverage disparity lawfare", which leverages legal instruments to gain an advantage and

---

[30] Pinos and Hau (2024), p. 90.

outmaneuver adversaries in the legal arena, primarily adopted by non-state actors.[31] The manifestations of lawfare in international relations are multifaceted, spanning various platforms such as international fora, national assemblies, published literature, newspapers, online media, visa regulations, audiovisual content, and diplomatic notes. Based on the type of instrument used (international law or national law) and the context in which it is applied (domestic or foreign), typical manifestations of lawfare can be presented as follows in Table 1.1:

These manifestations are grounded in observations of contemporary practices in international relations, aligning with the concept introduced in Section Concepts above. The increasing reliance on legal tools as a strategic instrument has become a notable trend among states in the twenty-first century due to their numerous advantages.[32] Compared to conventional warfare, lawfare requires significantly lower financial and material investment, minimizes casualties, and avoids the destruction of national infrastructure. In some cases, it may even prove more effective than kinetic warfare.

In the Israel—Iran conflict with the American engagement, lawfare has emerged as a key tactic by both sides. Israel has frequently invoked international legal principles to justify pre-emptive strikes against Iranian-linked targets, framing them as acts of self-defense under Article 51 of the UN Charter.[33] Conversely, Iran and its allies have sought to portray Israeli actions as violations of Article 2(4) of the UN Charter,[34] especially regarding genocide in Gaza.[35] Iran has also invoked Article 51 of the UN Charter to justify its actions as self-defense in response to what it describes as unprovoked attacks by Israel and later by the U.S. bombardment in June 2025.[36] Both States also leverage international institutions, media narratives, and legal accusations—such as war crimes claims—to gain strategic advantage in armed conflicts, underscoring the central role of lawfare in their broader hybrid confrontation.

Another good example is the Ukraine—Russia conflict, in which lawfare has become a central instrument in shaping international responses and advancing strategic objectives beyond the battlefield. Ukraine has actively utilized international legal mechanisms, including cases before the ICJ[37] and the International Criminal Court (ICC),[38] to hold Russia accountable for aggression, war crimes, and human rights violations.[39] By framing Russia's invasion as a breach of the UN Charter and

---

[31] Kittrie (2016), p. 10.

[32] Krisch (2005), pp. 369–408.

[33] Tsagourias (2025).

[34] See two posts of Milanovic (2025) on EJIL Talk! Blog.

[35] See Human Rights Watch (2024).

[36] Çağlar (2025), pp. 1–15.

[37] United Nations, Regional Information Centre for Western Europe (2023, September 14) International Court of Justice: Ukraine v. Russia, from https://unric.org/en/international-court-of-justice-ukraine-v-russia/, accessed on 27 July 2025.

[38] See Situation in Ukraine ICC-01/22, from https://www.icc-cpi.int/situations/ukraine, accessed on 27 July 2025.

[39] O'Flaherty (2025).

Table 1.1 Typical manifestations of lawfare

	International law	National law
International domains	– Creating new rules to diminish the opponent's advantages – Reinterpreting existing international law to exploit vulnerabilities in opponents – Employing international criminal law applications in international courts – Utilizing international law to enable investigations by international organizations – Leveraging votes within international organizations to undermine the opponents' standing – Lobbying for advisory opinions from international courts to disadvantage opponents	– Strengthening gray zone tactics to transform undisputed areas into disputed areas in order to apply national laws to international waters or maritime zones belonging to other States – Exerting influence through personnel engaged in international judicial bodies or international institutions – Influencing international legal understanding through education and publications on a global scale
National domains	– Invoking international law as a defense against criminal prosecution in national courts – Utilizing international law as the basis for the criminal prosecution of individuals and national corporations in domestic courts – Employing international law as the foundation for implementing 'universal jurisdiction' for representatives of third countries in national tribunals for war crimes – Increasing the establishment of branches of international judicial bodies within their own countries to capitalize on the benefits of the law of the seat – Influencing international legal understanding through education and publications nationwide – Leveraging its influence within international organizations to advocate for the imposition of collective sanctions on other states	– Developing new national legislation that forces foreign producers to choose between domestic and international markets – Enacting new national law to facilitate lawsuits against terrorist organizations and their supporters – Pursuing criminal prosecution of terrorist organizations – Initiating criminal and civil enforcement actions against banks that provide financial services to terrorist groups – Filing civil lawsuits against specific entities, including terrorist organizations, non-state actors engaged in activities in third countries, and banks that support terrorist financing – Utilizing national courts and domestic laws to address international disputes in areas such as investment and intellectual property

Source Authors' compilation

invoking the Genocide Convention and other treaties, Ukraine seeks not only legal redress but also global diplomatic support and sanctions enforcement.[40] Russia, meanwhile, has invoked alternative legal justifications, including the right of

[40] Hathaway (2023). See also Butchard (2022).

self-defense in response to NATO's eastward expansion, which it perceives as a threat to its national security, and the protection of ethnic Russians, in order to challenge Ukraine's legitimacy and deflect international accountability.[41] This legal contest highlights how lawfare operates as a tool of resistance and influence in modern interstate conflict.

The consequences of lawfare are varied and often unpredictable. Unlike traditional warfare, which aims to inflict human and material losses, the objective of legal warfare is to damage the national image and reputation of the opposing country while proactively protecting one's own national interests in the most effective manner. In doing so, the legal and political standing of the opponents gradually erodes.

Lawfare and Cognitive Warfare

The cognitive system has been studied by scholars in the natural sciences, psychology, and economics as early as the late 1960s, such as in experimental sociology,[42] social psychology,[43] and experimental economics.[44] It has also been explored in studies on "absurd decisions"[45] and "counterintuitive reasoning."[46] The concept gained widespread recognition through the work of Nobel laureate Daniel Kahneman and his collaborator Amos Tversky, particularly under the framework of "cognitive biases."[47] However, the cognitive term only began to enter the military and security discourse when the U.S. and NATO started to focus on the topic through a series of scientific workshops beginning in 2017. The term Cognitive Warfare has been used in the U.S. since 2017[48] to describe, in particular, the various modes of action available to a state or an influence group seeking to manipulate an adversary or its population's cognitive mechanisms in order to weaken, penetrate, influence, or even subjugate and destroy it. These modes of action are based on the application of advancements in information technology. Within NATO, cognitive warfare is defined as: "The art of using technological, psychological, and informational tools to alter how people think, act, or decide, with the aim of influencing behaviors and gaining an advantage in conflicts."[49] The cognitive domain is considered a sixth domain of military operations to be added to

41 Sari (2023), pp. 119–153. See also Tyushka (2021), pp. 115–135.
42 Zajonc (1968), pp. 1–27.
43 Goffman (1986), pp. 1–40.
44 Martinez (2010), pp. 15–23.
45 Morel (2002).
46 Berthet (2018).
47 Kahneman and Tversky (1979), pp. 313–327. See also Claverie (2022), pp. 4–17.
48 Underwood (2017).
49 Claverie et al. (2022).

the five existing ones (land, sea, air, cyber, space).[50] By NATO military staff, the cognitive warfare constitutes a three-dimensional set (information, numerical, and decision) to reach the cognitive elements of the military operator's thought as well as the strategist's, in a psychological, cybernetic, and cognitive complementarity.[51]

The rise of cognitive warfare in international military and political arenas presents unprecedented challenges to the existing framework of international law. Unlike traditional conflicts governed by established legal norms—such as the Geneva Conventions and the UN Charter—cognitive warfare operates in gray zones, blurring the lines between peace and war, coercion and persuasion, and lawful versus unlawful influence.

Cognitive warfare directly challenges fundamental principles of sovereignty, non-intervention, and human rights. Both state and non-state actors now possess the ability to manipulate foreign populations' decision-making processes, destabilizing nations without resorting to conventional military force. This raises pressing legal and ethical concerns regarding state responsibility, digital rights, and the permissible limits of influence in international relations.[52] A critical question arises: Does international law accept the use of non-kinetic but harmful technologies without accountability? Put differently, should the misuse or selective interpretation of international law, amplified by technological tools, be allowed to shape human perception in the service of narrow political goals and nationalistic ambitions? Emerging military neurotechnologies highlight the urgency of this dilemma. For instance, brain–computer interfaces (BCIs) blur the chain of accountability by translating ambiguous neural signals into military commands, making it difficult to determine whether civilian harm results from human intention, device malfunction, or flaws in algorithmic interpretation.[53] Such gaps mirror the dynamics of lawfare: powerful actors exploit legal and technological ambiguity to evade responsibility, while lawfulness demands clarity and accountability. Without clear legal definitions and robust enforcement mechanisms, Article 2(4) of the UN Charter risks losing its effectiveness in prohibiting the use of force in modern conflicts. This could create a legal vacuum, undermining sovereignty, international stability, and the broader principles of global peace and security.[54]

Cognitive warfare is characterized by its localized and tactical nature, focusing on manipulating perceptions and decision-making processes of specific targets. It operates on the premise that by seizing or distorting an opponent's perception, one can paralyze their response and achieve victory. However, this approach has inherent limitations. It often fails to account for reciprocal effects or counter-strategies employed by the opposing side and does not address the root causes of

---

[50] Le Guyader, H. (2022), pp. 3–1).

[51] Claverie (2022), pp. 4–17.

[52] Henschke A (2025).

[53] Gielas (2025).

[54] Wanyana (2025).

disputes. Moreover, its effectiveness may be temporary and localized, lacking the global and enduring impact of more comprehensive approaches.

The emergence of cognitive warfare as a military concept marks a significant evolution in the understanding of contemporary conflict. From a military standpoint, it is defined as "activities conducted in synchronization with other Instruments of Power, to affect attitudes and behaviors, by influencing, protecting, or disrupting individual, group, or population level cognition, to gain an advantage over an adversary,"[55] Cognitive warfare has been viewed by some scholars as an expansion of, a conceptual umbrella for, and potentially a replacement of China's Three Warfares strategy, which comprises Public Opinion warfare, Psychological warfare, and Lawfare. Deka (2024) argues that while seemingly novel, cognitive warfare shares significant overlaps with China's earlier Three Warfares strategy, suggesting a strategic evolution rather than a complete departure.[56] Cognitive warfare, at its core, targets the human mind. Its aim is to manipulate perceptions, beliefs, and decision-making processes to achieve strategic goals. This is achieved through various techniques, including the exploitation of information technology, social media manipulation, and the spread of disinformation. Artificial intelligence (AI) plays an increasingly significant role, enhancing the speed and sophistication of these operations.

The philosophical roots of the Three Warfares strategy and cognitive warfare can be traced back to Sun Tzu's classic military treatise, The Art of War, which emphasizes the importance of breaking the enemy's resistance without fighting—achieving victory through psychological and strategic maneuvering rather than direct confrontation.[57] This ancient wisdom has had a profound impact on the strategic thinking of modern militaries, particularly the Chinese People's Liberation Army (PLA). The Chinese People's Liberation Army (PLA)'s Three Warfares strategy, introduced in 2003, represents a formalized approach that directly foreshadows many aspects of cognitive warfare. This strategy comprises: Media or Public Opinion warfare, Psychological warfare, and Legal warfare. These three elements are intricately linked and mutually reinforcing, all working towards manipulating the cognitive landscape to favor China's objectives. Public Opinion warfare focuses on shaping domestic and international narratives to create a favorable image of China and to undermine its adversaries. This involves manipulating information flows and utilizing media outlets to disseminate pro-China messages and counter negative narratives. Psychological warfare employs a range of techniques to intimidate, demoralize, and influence the emotions of the target population, often creating an atmosphere of uncertainty and fear. Legal warfare involves leveraging legal instruments and international laws to pressure adversaries, while simultaneously shielding China's actions from criticism. The Three Warfares strategy can be considered

[55] Cognitive Warfare. Allied Command Transformation, NATO, from https://www.act.nato.int/activities/cognitive-warfare/, accessed on 27 July 2025.

[56] Deka (2024).

[57] Marma (2025).

a precursor to modern cognitive warfare. While cognitive warfare is a broader concept encompassing a wider range of technologies and techniques, the Three Warfares provide a framework for the strategic implementation of many of its key components. Both strategies emphasize indirect influence, focusing on shaping perceptions and influencing behavior rather than direct military engagement. Both leverage information technology to achieve their goals, though cognitive warfare benefits from more advanced tools such as artificial intelligence (AI) and sophisticated data analysis.[58]

However, some key differences exist. While the Three Warfares strategy may be regarded as an early iteration of cognitive warfare, the latter reflects a more technologically sophisticated and expansive approach. Cognitive warfare is built upon a three-dimensional framework–information, numerical, and decision-based domains–to achieve its objectives. These three pillars form part of an integrated process, though they do not explicitly define the specific means employed by cognitive warfare. In practice, however, cognitive warfare emphasizes psychological and media tools rather than legal instruments. Moreover, it leverages advanced technologies such as artificial intelligence (AI) and big data analytics, enabling more precise targeting, personalized messaging, and sophisticated manipulation of online narratives. Without a robust understanding of legal principles, the human mind becomes more vulnerable not only to the corrosive effects of disinformation, but also to cognitive overload caused by excessive positive stimuli. In contrast, the Three Warfares strategy is more concretely structured, treating Public Opinion Warfare, Psychological Warfare, and Lawfare as equally important, interrelated components. Strategic advantage is achieved through the effective integration of all three components. Both approaches, however, share a common core: manipulating the human mind and influencing behavior to achieve strategic goals without relying primarily on kinetic military action. Understanding the evolution and interrelationship between these strategies is crucial for comprehending the complexities of modern warfare and developing effective countermeasures.[59]

It is noteworthy that both cognitive warfare and the Three Warfares strategy use lawfare as a foundation to promote Psychological Warfare, Information Warfare, and the creation of narratives that influence the human mind. They ultimately derive arguments from interpretations of international law that are most beneficial to their proponents. The destructive lawfare contrasts with the objective interpretation methods outlined in Articles 31 and 32 of the Vienna Convention on the Law of Treaties. While cognitive warfare and related concepts like lawfare draw attention to the strategic use of legal and psychological tactics in international relations, they ultimately underscore the enduring importance of international law. Cognitive warfare remains an evolving concept within strategic discussions and still requires consistent endorsement across various levels. In contrast, the Three Warfares has been institutionalized as a concrete strategy, endorsed at the highest Chinese

[58] Deka (2024).

[59] Deka (2024).

political levels, implemented by the People's Liberation Army (PLA), and has demonstrated certain tangible outcomes in practice. Therefore, cognitive warfare cannot yet replace the Three Warfares strategy–particularly in the context of the South China Sea.

Given the doctrinal grounding and empirical application, the Three Warfares provides a more precise and authoritative lens for understanding China's coercive behavior in the region. Accordingly, this book will primarily focus on analyzing the techniques and operational methods of the Three Warfares and explore effective countermeasures against it through the concept of lawfulness.[60] This concept, with its emphasis on fairness, transparency, and universal applicability, offers a more comprehensive and ethically sound framework for addressing global challenges and maintaining international order. As nations navigate complex geopolitical landscapes, the principles of lawfulness provide a robust foundation for sustainable peace and equitable resolution of conflicts.

Lawfare and Hybrid War

The concept of lawfare can sometimes be confused with hybrid war, as both involve the use of non-military tools to achieve strategic objectives in international conflicts. Hoffman (2007) defines hybrid war as a strategy that "simultaneously"[61] employs a tailored mix of conventional weapons, irregular tactics, terrorism, and criminal activities in the same battlespace to achieve strategic goals.

The concept of hybrid warfare is not new. Like cognitive warfare, it is said to have first appeared in Sun Tzu's military doctrine around 1000 B.C., emphasizing the combination of various forms of warfare to achieve the ultimate objective: "to subdue the enemy without fighting."[62] In Vietnam, this approach took the form of the People's War—a just, prolonged resistance that integrated both regular and irregular forces, national unity, and international support, evolving from guerrilla warfare to more complex strategies and ultimately to mobile warfare for liberation and independence.[63] The strategy of hybrid war has been employed by Hezbollah and Israel in the Middle East, by the U.S. in Iran and Afghanistan, and by India against Pakistan.[64]

The emergence of advanced information and communication technologies (ICTs) has expanded the scope and effectiveness of hybrid strategies. The ongoing

---

[60] See section: Concepts.

[61] "Instead of separate challengers with fundamentally different approaches (conventional, irregular or terrorist), we can expect to face competitors who will employ all forms of war and tactics, perhaps simultaneously." See Hoffman, (2007), p. 7.

[62] Bilal (2021). See also Solen (2022).

[63] Vo (1961), pp. 21–23. See also Gates (2025).

[64] Yasin (2020), pp. 5–6.

Russia-Ukraine conflict since 2014 has further intensified debates over the definition of hybrid war. Today, hybrid war is broadly understood as a condition in which modern adversaries employ a mix of conventional and unconventional, regular and irregular, overt and covert tactics, leveraging all dimensions of warfare to challenge Western dominance in traditional military engagements.[65] In a broad sense, cognitive warfare and lawfare are both components of hybrid warfare. Lawfare can be part of a hybrid warfare strategy when used alongside other tools such as propaganda, information warfare, or economic sanctions. The tactics and tools employed in hybrid warfare are all based on leveraging one's own legal strengths while undermining or distorting the arguments of the opponent. Lawfare and hybrid war both seek to exploit the gray areas of international law and the global security environment.

However, conflating these two concepts may lead to misunderstandings about the nature of each strategy. While lawfare is primarily a legal instrument, hybrid warfare is a complex method of conflict that integrates multiple tools to achieve strategic advantages. The world is becoming overwhelmed with warfare concepts such as Three Warfares, cognitive war and hybrid war. Primarily used for military and political purposes, these terms risk obscuring the dual nature of lawfare. These debates highlight how lawfare can both reinforce the role of international law and pose challenges that may undermine it. Lawfare involves the strategic application of general legal principles and the development of specific legal norms, often in conjunction with other instruments of warfare, to gain an advantage over adversaries, bring conflicts to a favorable resolution with minimal losses, and uphold humanitarian values.

When law is used appropriately, it protects human rights, punishes and prevents war crimes, and ultimately upholds justice. Conversely, the excessive misuse of law—such as deliberately interpreting international law in a self-serving manner to isolate opponents and manipulating global public opinion to achieve military and political objectives—can result in the distortion of legal definitions to justify unlawful actions, ultimately eroding the fundamental values of international law.

Lawfare is not merely a tool of war serving a declared conventional conflict in the strict sense of The Hague Convention (III) on the Opening of Hostilities, adopted on 18 October 1907.[66] It is employed in both peacetime and wartime by state and non-state actors alike. Lawfare is not a legal concept, nor does it have a clearly defined scope or substance. It is also not bound by the interpretative mechanisms of international law as outlined in Articles 31 and 32 of the 1969 Vienna Convention on the Law of Treaties, which have been accepted as customary rules. Legal commitments made at the international level must be interpreted in

---

[65] Van Puyvelde (2015).

[66] The Hague Convention (III) on the Opening of Hostilities in 1907, Article 1: "The contracting Powers recognize that hostilities between themselves must not commence without previous and explicit warning, in the form either of a declaration of war, giving reasons, or of an ultimatum with conditional declaration of war", from https://ihl-databases.icrc.org/en/ihl-treaties/hague-conv-iii-1907/article-1, accessed on 27 July 2025.

good faith, in accordance with the governing principles of international law, and must be effectively observed and enforced within domestic and international systems. Lawfare, being inherently focused on the interests of one party, cannot replace the concept of lawful implementation of international law, which ensures the reinforcement of global order and legal accountability.

If used without control, lawfare prioritizes achieving victory at any cost, disregarding whether actions are just or unjust, legal or illegal—a mindset akin to "it does not matter whether the cat is black or white, as long as it catches mice."[67] Destructive lawfare, in effect, undermines the role of international law in protecting justice and ensuring equality among nations. Lawfare may encourage economically and politically powerful states to exploit legal systems to achieve their military or political objectives. These objectives are often limited in scope, regional in nature, and confined to specific conflicts. Lawfare operates with short-term, tactical purposes, in contrast to the long-term goal of implementing international law, which is rooted in widely accepted legal principles and representative of the collective will of the international community. Lawfare undermines the fundamental duty of states to pursue cooperation and the peaceful settlement of disputes as enshrined in international law.

Indeed, law *per se* is not a tool of warfare but a framework designed for the peaceful resolution of disputes, the regulation of state conduct, and the promotion of international cooperation. Its purpose lies in ensuring order, predictability, and fairness in relations among states, thereby fostering stability and mutual trust. To regard law as an instrument of war is to distort its essence and undermine its legitimacy. Therefore, the correct interpretation should be that there is no such thing as legal warfare in the strict sense; what exists instead is the use of law as a means of resistance (legal resistance) or the maintenance of lawfulness against unlawful encroachments. This perspective highlights the role of law as a safeguard for equality among nations, and a vehicle for advancing the noble values recognized by the international community, such as justice, equity, and peaceful coexistence. In short, the faithful implementation of law should not be mischaracterized as lawfare. Only when legal instruments are twisted, manipulated, or applied in bad faith—contrary to the spirit of international law—do they amount to lawfare.

Lawfulness in International Law

Concepts

Lawfulness, defined as adherence to established legal principles, norms, and obligations, serves as the foundation for maintaining order, resolving disputes, and fostering cooperation among states in an increasingly interconnected world. In

[67] Gosset (2020).

international law, the concept of lawfulness is rooted in the rule of law applied on a global scale. It encompasses the idea that all states, regardless of size or power, are subject to a common set of rules and standards. This notion is reflected in various international treaties, customary law, and general principles of law that collectively form the bedrock of international law. Lawfulness signifies compliance with international legal frameworks in state conduct, dispute resolution, and enforcement of rights and obligations.

The concept of lawfulness in international relations is intrinsically linked to the UN Charter of 1945. This foundational document, which established the UN and set forth its principles and structure, serves as a cornerstone for the modern international legal order. The Charter enshrines key principles of lawfulness, *inter alia*, the sovereign equality of states, the prohibition of the use of force in international relations, non-interference in internal affairs, *pacta sunt servanda*, right of self-determination, cooperation and the peaceful settlement of disputes. Article 2(4) of the Charter explicitly prohibits the threat or use of force against the territorial integrity or political independence of any state, while Article 33 mandates that parties to any dispute likely to endanger international peace and security shall first seek a solution through peaceful means. These provisions directly align with the core tenets of lawfulness, emphasizing the primacy of legal mechanisms and diplomatic approaches in resolving international conflicts. Furthermore, the Charter establishes ICJ as the principal judicial organ of the UN, underscoring the importance of legal adjudication in maintaining global order. By adhering to the principles outlined in the UN Charter, the concept of lawfulness reinforces the collective commitment of nations to uphold international law, promote justice, cooperation and maintain peace and security on a global scale. This alignment between lawfulness and the UN Charter demonstrates the enduring relevance and universal applicability of legal norms in shaping international relations and resolving disputes among nations. Lawfulness is also closely related to peremptory norms (*jus cogens*) of international law, which include the prohibition of aggression.[68] These norms provide a framework for lawful conduct among nations and serve as reference points for evaluating the legality of state actions. They embody a core set of inviolable rules that strengthen the overall structure of lawfulness in international relations. Lawfulness requires states to interpret and apply international law in a sincere and honest manner, avoiding manipulative or self-serving legal interpretations.

However, enforcing lawfulness in international law presents significant challenges. Unlike domestic legal systems, international law lacks a centralized enforcement mechanism. Compliance often relies on the willingness of states to abide by rulings and norms, which can be influenced by political, economic, and strategic considerations. This reality sometimes results in selective adherence to

[68] Draft conclusions on identification and legal consequences of peremptory norms of general international law (jus cogens). Adopted by the International Law Commission at its seventy-third session, in 2022, and submitted to the General Assembly as a part of the Commission's report covering the work of that session (A/77/10, para. 43). Available in Yearbook of the International Law Commission, 2022, vol. II, Part Two.

international law, undermining the principle of lawfulness. Additionally, the concept of state sovereignty can conflict with the universal application of international law. States may invoke sovereignty to justify actions that contravene international norms, creating tension between national interests and global legal standards. This dilemma is particularly evident in human rights issues, where international standards may clash with domestic practices or cultural norms. The rapid pace of technological advancement and global change further complicates lawfulness in international law. Emerging issues such as cyberwarfare, artificial intelligence, and climate change often outpace the development of relevant legal frameworks. This lag can create legal gray areas where the boundaries of lawful conduct are unclear, potentially leading to disputes or unilateral actions.

In the context of climate change litigation, Rogers Nicole (2013) argues that lawfulness presents a complex paradox within the established legal system.[69] The rigid nature of lawfulness often hinders successful climate change lawsuits due to precedent-bound interpretations and anthropocentric biases. Yet, this very lawfulness can paradoxically serve as a powerful tool for deconstruction and social change. Existing legal frameworks, rooted in historical contexts that may not fully address the urgency of climate change, frequently result in unsuccessful climate lawsuits, as traditional legal principles and precedent-based reasoning impede meaningful progress.[70] However, this "paradox of lawfulness"[71] highlights that the inherent contradictions within the legal system allow for strategic utilization of its tools and language by outsiders seeking to challenge the *status quo*. Surprisingly, the strict application of law can benefit those who have historically been disadvantaged or marginalized, as it provides a structured platform for articulating grievances and demanding change. This dual nature of lawfulness in climate change litigation demonstrates how the constraints of the legal system can be leveraged to drive reform, fostering a dynamic interplay between established norms and the pressing need for environmental justice.[72]

In discussing the intersection of international and domestic legal frameworks, Blay and Piotrowicz (2000) argue that the concept of lawfulness in state actions becomes particularly complex, revealing a fundamental tension between these two systems.[73] This complexity is illustrated by the ongoing debate between monism—viewing international and domestic law as a unified system—and dualism, which treats them as separate entities. Relying solely on domestic law to assess the lawfulness of state actions, particularly in relation to international human rights obligations, is inadequate and potentially misleading. This situation gives rise to what may be termed the "paradox of lawfulness,"[74] where actions deemed lawful

[69] Rogers (2013), pp. 20–24.

[70] Rogers (2013), pp. 20–24.

[71] Rogers (2013), pp. 20–24.

[72] Rogers (2013), pp. 20–24.

[73] Blay and Piotrowicz (2000), pp. 1–19.

[74] Blay and Piotrowicz (2000), pp. 1–19.

under domestic legislation can simultaneously violate international human rights standards, creating dissonance between national and international legal perspectives. This paradox underscores the need for a more nuanced and comprehensive approach to evaluating state conduct, one that considers both domestic and international legal frameworks while ultimately prioritizing international human rights standards. In essence, true lawfulness in state actions cannot be determined in isolation but must be assessed within the broader context of international obligations. This perspective challenges the traditional notion of state sovereignty and highlights the growing importance of international law in shaping domestic legal practices.[75]

Despite these challenges, the concept of lawfulness in international law continues to evolve and adapt. The international community has made significant strides in areas such as the law of the sea. A notable example is the establishment of an arbitral tribunal under UNCLOS, which allows a state to initiate a lawsuit unilaterally regarding the interpretation and application of the treaty.[76]

The concept of lawfulness in international law is far more nuanced and multifaceted than a simple binary of compliance or non-compliance. This complexity is rooted in the dynamic nature of international legal norms and their interpretation, as well as the diverse array of actors involved in shaping and responding to these norms. Howse and Teitel (2010) argue that viewing international law solely through the lens of compliance (defined as rule observance) is inadequate and oversimplifies its impact.[77] Instead, lawfulness encompasses a range of factors, including interpretive processes, the influence of diverse actors, unintended consequences, and indirect effects on state and non-state behavior. This broader understanding recognizes that international law's effectiveness extends beyond mere adherence to rules, influencing bargaining processes, shaping expectations, setting benchmarks for private actors, shifting power dynamics, and transforming policymakers' perspectives on global issues. Crucially, the meaning of international legal rules is not static but continually negotiated and contested, with interpretation playing a critical role in shaping their real-world impact. Moreover, the concept of lawfulness must account for the phenomenon of "ultra-compliance,"[78] where outcomes may exceed the initial intentions of the law's creators, as well as the indirect influence of international norms on private actors' decisions, even in the absence of formal enforcement mechanisms. This comprehensive view of lawfulness in international law provides a richer and more accurate understanding of its effectiveness and impact on global governance, moving beyond simplistic compliance-based models to capture the full complexity of how international legal norms operate and influence behavior in the international system.[79]

---

[75] Blay and Piotrowicz (2000), pp. 1–19.

[76] See UNCLOS, Part XV, Section 2. Compulsory Procedures entailing binding decisions.

[77] Howse and Teitel (2010), pp. 127–136.

[78] Howse and Teitel (2010), pp. 127–136.

[79] Howse and Teitel (2010), pp. 127–136.

Lawfulness in international law remains a critical yet complex concept. While it faces challenges in enforcement and adaptation to new global realities, it continues to serve as an essential guiding principle in international relations. Lawfulness in international law functions as a benchmark for evaluating the conduct of actors, embodying the normative expectations of the international community. The ongoing development of international legal institutions, the expansion of areas covered by international law, and the growing acceptance of universal norms all contribute to reinforcing lawfulness on the global stage. As the world becomes increasingly interconnected, the importance of upholding and evolving the concept of lawfulness in international law will only grow, playing a vital role in maintaining global order and justice.

Lawfulness as a Counter-Lawfare Strategy (3P Formula)

In the complex landscape of international relations, the concept of lawfulness has emerged as a powerful counter-lawfare strategy for nations. This approach is grounded in, and can be generalized through, three interconnected pillars: Publicity, Public Opinion, and Public International Law—collectively referred to as the "3P formula." The "3P formula" serves as a commensurate response to China's Three Warfares strategy. Together, these elements form a comprehensive framework that presents a more holistic and principled approach to global governance.

The first pillar, **Publicity**, serves as the foundation for transparency and credibility in international disputes. In an era of information warfare, the ability to present clear, factual evidence is paramount. Disputing parties must clarify their legal positions with well-founded historical and legal evidence that has stood the test of time. At the same time, they should formulate arguments to refute the opposing claims based on an objective and fair interpretation and application of international law, rather than relying on fabricated narratives. Additionally, parties should adopt appropriate policies to publicly expose unlawful activities, enabling the international and regional communities to assess, support, or oppose such actions. Media, video technology, and artificial intelligence (AI) play a crucial role in this process of public disclosure. This means meticulously documenting and disseminating evidence of its historical sovereignty and maritime rights. This includes not only archival records and cartographic materials but also contemporary data on marine activities, environmental stewardship, and consistent state practice in exercising sovereignty.

Publicity in the digital age requires a sophisticated approach to information dissemination. All concepts of Cognitive Warfare, Lawfare, and gray zone have the common characteristic of taking advantage of the ambiguity of the law to carry out measures below the threshold of war, so there needs to be publicity and explanation to the public. The power of publicity extends beyond mere information sharing. It acts as a deterrent against covert or gradual encroachment on national rights. By shining a light on unlawful activities or attempts to change the *status quo*, all states can preemptively challenge actions that might otherwise go unnoticed by the international community. This transparency also fosters domestic unity, educating citizens about the nation's heritage and the importance of defending it. Publicity emphasizes transparency and open communication in international affairs. By making legal arguments and diplomatic processes visible to the global community, nations can build credibility and foster trust. This openness stands in stark contrast to the often covert nature of cognitive warfare or lawfare tactics, promoting a more honest and accountable approach to international relations.

The second pillar, **Public Opinion**, recognizes the power of global sentiment in shaping international outcomes. By appealing to the collective conscience of the international community, lawfulness seeks to build consensus around just and equitable solutions to global challenges. This approach leverages the force of moral persuasion and collective wisdom, rather than relying on manipulation or coercion. Public Opinion generates a form of virtual enforcement that compels parties to respect international law, helping to mitigate one of its key weaknesses–the lack of a centralized enforcement mechanism or effective sanctions against illegal acts.

Cultivating favorable public opinion involves more than just presenting facts; it requires framing those facts within a compelling story of justice, historical continuity, and adherence to international norms. By highlighting the inconsistencies in expansionist claims and emphasizing the principles of equity, all states can appeal to a global sense of fairness and the rule of law. Engaging with civil society organizations, think tanks, and academic institutions can amplify the message and lend credibility to its position. These entities can provide independent analysis and advocacy, reinforcing states' stance through diverse channels. Furthermore, building coalitions with other nations facing similar challenges can create a united front against negative lawfare tactics, strengthening the collective voice for a rules-based order. Public opinion also plays a crucial role in domestic politics, influencing government policies and national resolve. By fostering a strong sense of global justice among its citizens, all states can ensure long-term support for its position, even in the face of prolonged disputes or pressure.

The third pillar, **Public International Law**, provides the foundational rules and norms that govern interactions between states. This ensures that disputes are resolved through recognized legal mechanisms, such as international courts and tribunals, rather than through force or manipulation. It sets a standard of fairness and objectivity that applies equally to all nations, regardless of their size or power. In other words, Public International Law serves as a tool to dispel the fog generated by lawfare and cognitive warfare. It offers clear answers, objective standards of comparison, and strives to fill normative gaps—ultimately advancing a fair and equitable international legal system.

The concept of lawfulness in international relations is underpinned by a robust system of public international law, which serves as a crucial pillar in this counter-lawfare strategy. The legitimacy of a legal resistance must be lawful and in accordance with international law. The foundations of public international law provide the framework and mechanisms through which the principles of lawfulness can be upheld and enforced.

At the core of public international law are the fundamental principles of sovereign equality, peaceful settlement of disputes, and the prohibition of the use of force.[80] These principles form the bedrock of lawfulness, ensuring that nations interact within a rules-based system that prioritizes justice and the peaceful resolution of conflicts. Beyond the foundational principles, international law has evolved over time to encompass a comprehensive body of treaties, customary law, and general principles of law that regulate various aspects of global affairs. This includes, but is not limited to, the laws of armed conflict, human rights law, environmental law, the law of the sea, and cyberspace law. This intricate web of legal instruments and precedents reinforces the concept of lawfulness, providing clear guidelines and procedures for the conduct of international relations. Crucially, the legitimacy of international law stems from its universal application and the principle of sovereign equality. All nations, regardless of their size, power, or political systems, are bound by the same set of rules and norms. This sense of fairness and objectivity is central to the concept of lawfulness, as it ensures that the international system operates on the basis of shared principles rather than the dictates of individual actors.

The system of international courts and tribunals, such as ICJ, the International Criminal Court (ICC), and various specialized dispute resolution mechanisms, serves as one of the subsidiary means of enforcing international law. These institutions offer impartial platforms for nations to resolve their differences through legal processes, rather than resorting to unilateral actions or force. Furthermore, international law provides a foundation for public diplomacy and the formation of global public opinion. By grounding their arguments and actions in the principles of international law, all states can build credibility and influence the collective consciousness of the international community. This, in turn, reinforces the power of public opinion as a pillar of lawfulness, as global sentiment can exert significant pressure on states to adhere to legal norms and uphold the rule of law. Public international law is a fundamental pillar of the lawfulness framework, providing the legal foundations, enforcement mechanisms, and principles of fairness that underpin this approach to international relations. By anchoring their actions and diplomacy in the rule of law, nations can not only safeguard their legitimate rights and benefits but also promote a more stable, just, and cooperative global environment.

Unlike lawfare and cognitive warfare, which may employ ethically questionable tactics to achieve short-term objectives, lawfulness aims to establish immutable principles of fairness applicable to all countries. It seeks to regulate international relations on a global scale through reason, dialogue, and adherence to established

[80] Declaration on Principles of International Law concerning Friendly Relations and Cooperation among States in accordance with the Charter of the United Nations, from https://treaties.un.org/doc/source/docs/A_RES_2625-Eng.pdf, accessed on 27 July 2025.

legal norms. This approach not only promotes peaceful resolution of disputes but also contributes to the long-term stability and predictability of the international system. While lawfare can be seen as a combative application of legal domain, lawfulness embodies a more constructive approach. It employs classical yet effective methods such as opinio juris, customary international law, and conventional law to forge common understanding and consensus. Where cognitive warfare may subjugate a person, group or nation temporarily, lawfulness seeks recognition from the entire international community, creating sustained pressure for compliance with established norms.

By embracing lawfulness, demonstrated through the **3P formula** as a counter-lawfare strategy, nations can protect their interests while simultaneously strengthening the fabric of international law. This holistic approach offers a more sustainable and ethically sound alternative to cognitive warfare, fostering a global environment where conflicts are resolved through justice and objective reasoning rather than manipulation or force. The integration of these three pillars—Publicity, Public Opinion, and Public International Law—creates a synergistic approach that is greater than the sum of its parts. The legal framework provides the structure and legitimacy that underpins both public communications and opinion-forming efforts. Publicity, in turn, shapes public opinion, generating support for the legitimacy of arguments based on international legal provisions. The implementation of public international law, when widely disseminated and publicly declared, further enhances enforcement power and oversight from the international community. The 3P formula ensures that compliance and enforcement of lawfulness are carried out in the most effective manner.

Lawfulness versus Lawfare and Cognitive Warfare

While the preceding sections have distinguished between lawfulness, lawfare, and cognitive warfare, this section aims to consolidate, reaffirm, and further clarify the conceptual distinctions among these three concepts within the analytical framework of this book.

The Distinction Between Lawfulness and Lawfare

Law has assumed a prominent role in contemporary geopolitics, particularly in the context of interstate and non-state conflicts. Lawfare and lawfulness are two facets of the same broader legal tapestry but differ in their objectives, methods, and outlook. The notions of lawfare and lawfulness both rely on legal norms and frameworks, but they diverge in their goals and methods. While lawfare leverages legal mechanisms for strategic or tactical advantages—often in political or military contexts—Lawfulness ensures the legitimate and good-faith application of international law focusing on long-term and sustainable goal of establishing, promoting, and adhering to a broad set of legally binding standards designed to maintain order and cooperation among states.

Lawfare can also be defined as the deliberate use of legal systems, principles, and arguments to further specific interests, whether to constrain an adversary's options or to defend one's own actions in a conflict. Although it can take an offensive or defensive form, it typically revolves around influencing political or military outcomes through legal pressure. Practitioners of lawfare may file lawsuits in national or international courts, appeal to international treaties to delegitimize an opponent's behavior, or level war crimes accusations against political and military leaders. By doing so, they seek either to slow down adversarial actions through procedural delays and reputational costs or to bolster their own position by appearing as the more legally compliant actor. Guilfoyle (2023) argues that litigation serves as a tool of "legal statecraft,"[81] enabling small states to achieve strategic outcomes beyond simply securing compliance with international law.[82] Litigation inflicts a "legitimacy penalty"[83] on the respondent state by framing the dispute as a violation of shared community values enshrined in international law. This mobilization of international support, along with a challenge to the respondent's legitimacy, grants small states significant political leverage. The Mauritius—United Kingdom dispute over the Chagos Archipelago[84] serves as a prime example of how a small state can effectively leverage this approach to challenge a great power.[85] Mauritius leverages legal arguments to successfully challenge the United Kingdom's actions, garnering international support and ultimately impacting the United Kingdom's political standing. Legal arguments that frame disputes as violations of community values and invoke broader legal principles are most effective for small states in this strategic context. Therefore, lawfare is not necessarily about breaking or defying international law, but rather about strategically using its mechanisms—including reinterpreting or challenging its application—to advance one's political objectives within the international system. Lawfulness, by contrast, refers to the processes and structures through which states and international organizations adopt, enforce, and observe recognized legal norms. Ideally, these mechanisms foster stability, predictability, and fairness in international relations, thereby encouraging states to cooperate and resolve disagreements in a rule-based manner rather than resorting to force or unilateral tactics.

Another compelling demonstration of lawfulness, as opposed to lawfare, is the initiative spearheaded by Vanuatu along with other small island developing states,

---

[81] Guilfoyle (2023), pp. 1–36.

[82] Guilfoyle (2023), pp. 1–365.

[83] Guilfoyle (2023), pp. 1–36.

[84] Legal Consequences of the Separation of the Chagos Archipelago from Mauritius in 1965, from https://www.icj-cij.org/case/169, accessed on 27 July 2025.

[85] Guilfoyle (2023), pp. 1–36.

which successfully navigated UN institutional processes to seek clarity on environmental duties.[86] In March 2023, during its 77th session, the UN General Assembly adopted Resolution A/RES/77/276[87] by consensus, formally requesting an advisory opinion from the ICJ under Article 96 of the UN Charter on the obligations of states "to ensure the protection of the climate system and other parts of the environment from anthropogenic emissions of greenhouse gases,"[88] and the legal consequences when states cause significant harm, especially to vulnerable communities like small island states and future generations. The ICJ delivered its advisory opinion on 23 July 2025,[89] unanimously affirming that states have binding obligations under international law to protect the climate system and prevent significant environmental harm.[90] A failure to fulfill these obligations constitutes an internationally wrongful act,[91] engaging state responsibility and potentially entailing remedies such as cessation, assurances, and reparations. The judgment also recognized a human right to a clean, healthy, and sustainable environment[92] and emphasized that inaction can command liability. This effort stands in stark contrast to lawfare tactics, because it didn't seek to block, delay, or confuse legal processes, but instead utilized them to augment legal clarity and reinforce accountability. It embodies a constructive use of legal institutions—lawfulness—in service of global environmental protection and climate justice.

Whereas lawfare focuses on leveraging legal frameworks to gain a competitive edge, lawfulness emphasizes the cooperative dimensions of legal rights and obligations. Lawfare is often more tactical, seeking to exploit or redefine norms to serve particular policy objectives and can intensify power imbalances when more resourceful states (or well-funded non-state actors) use complex legal strategies against weaker opponents. Lawfulness, however, embodies long-established legal regimes such as the Geneva Conventions or UNCLOS, which offer structured guidelines for state conduct. Nonetheless, because both rely on legal fora and

86 Kwon (2024). See also Kreft and Solmecke (2025).

87 Resolution A/RES/77/276 adopted by the General Assembly on 29 March 2023, from https://docs.un.org/en/A/RES/77/276, accessed on 27 July 2025.

88 Resolution A/RES/77/276 adopted by the General Assembly on 29 March 2023, from https://docs.un.org/en/A/RES/77/276, accessed on 27 July 2025.

89 International Court of Justice (ICJ) (2025) Obligations of States in respect of climate change, Advisory Opinion of 23 July 2025, from https://www.icj-cij.org/sites/default/files/case-related/187/187-20250723-adv-01-00-en.pdf, accessed on 27 July 2025.

90 International Court of Justice (ICJ) (2025) Obligations of States in respect of climate change, Advisory Opinion of 23 July 2025, para. 208, from https://www.icj-cij.org/sites/default/files/case-related/187/187-20250723-adv-01-00-en.pdf, accessed on 27 July 2025. See also Dugal (2025).

91 International Court of Justice (ICJ) (2025) Obligations of States in respect of climate change, Advisory Opinion of 23 July 2025, paras. 184, 202, 205, 234, 264, and 457, from https://www.icj-cij.org/sites/default/files/case-related/187/187-20250723-adv-01-00-en.pdf, accessed on 27 July 2025. See also Schaugg et al. (2025).

92 International Court of Justice (ICJ) (2025) Obligations of States in respect of climate change, Advisory Opinion of 23 July 2025, paras. 387–393, from https://www.icj-cij.org/sites/default/files/case-related/187/187-20250723-adv-01-00-en.pdf, accessed on 27 July 2025.

adjudicatory bodies, the line between genuinely maintaining international legal standards and exploiting them for political advantage can blur.

Lawfare often exploits loopholes or ambiguous legal interpretations to justify self-serving actions while Lawfulness relies on good faith (*bona fides*) and the principles of justice and fairness.

Different mechanisms underlie the enforcement and compliance in these two realms. Lawfare often depends on immediate, self-initiated legal actions like filing suits in courts with acceptable jurisdiction or rallying public opinion through media coverage of alleged legal violations. When successful, it can deter adversaries by threatening prosecutions, sanctions, or reputational harm. Lawfulness typically operates through more institutional channels, relying on the willingness of states to abide by law-based order. This system, although comprehensive and theoretically robust, sometimes falters when powerful states ignore or circumvent its requirements, exposing the limitations of a consensus-driven enforcement model.

The interplay between lawfare and lawfulness emerges in various ways. Both call upon international judicial bodies, but the motivations differ: lawfare often serves a more targeted strategic goal, whereas lawfulness is geared toward consistent application of shared standards. Occasionally, innovative legal arguments advanced through lawfare can shape or alter existing norms, leading to controversies over whether such use constitutes a distortion of international law or a necessary evolution of its interpretive scope. Public opinion and legitimacy also play important roles, as each side seeks to demonstrate fidelity to law or expose the other's transgressions in order to strengthen its political position.

Critics of lawfare argue that it manipulates legal processes and undercuts the cooperative spirit of international law by using diplomatic arena, international organizational fora and judicial bodies as battlegrounds. Proponents counter that it can avert violence by channeling disputes into judicial fora, thereby offering a less destructive alternative to armed conflict. Lawfulness, meanwhile, faces accusations of selective enforcement and ineffectiveness, especially when political incentives hamper the willingness of states to hold one another accountable. Yet its supporters maintain that consistent observance of treaties and customs remains essential for sustaining a rules-based international order, without which conflict and unilateralism might prevail.

Ultimately, lawfare and lawfulness occupy two ends of a spectrum: one emphasizes the strategic exploitation of legal instruments, while the other champions the collective, rule-based approach necessary for global stability. Constructive lawfare complements lawfulness, whereas destructive lawfare undermines it. The intersection of lawfare and lawfulness will continue shaping global politics as technology and international institutions evolve, compelling states and non-state actors alike to navigate the fine line between using the law as a tool of policy and respecting it as the bedrock of international cooperation.

The Distinction Between Lawfulness and Cognitive Warfare

The distinction between lawfulness and cognitive warfare in international relations represents a critical dichotomy in the approach to global governance and conflict resolution. Lawfulness, as a principle in international relations, is deeply rooted in the UN Charter and the broader framework of international law. It emphasizes the cooperation, the peaceful resolution of disputes, respect for sovereignty, and the prohibition of the use of force in international relations. The concept of lawfulness is predicated on the idea that nations should interact within a rules-based system, where conflicts are resolved through diplomatic channels, negotiation, and, if necessary, international judicial processes. In contrast, cognitive warfare represents a more recent and controversial approach to international conflict. It involves the systematic attempt to influence the thought processes, perceptions, and decision-making capabilities of adversaries through various psychological and informational tactics. These may include disinformation campaigns, manipulation of social media, and other forms of psychological operations designed to shape the cognitive landscape of target populations or leadership.

A critical difference lies in the ethical foundations of these approaches. Cognitive warfare may employ a range of tactics, both fair and unfair, to achieve its objectives, potentially constituting a form of force in international relations. Conversely, lawfulness explicitly prohibits all forms of force in international relations, adhering strictly to peaceful means of dispute resolution. This ethical divergence is fundamental to understanding the contrast between these two approaches.

The methods employed in cognitive warfare often operate in a gray area of international law. While not traditionally considered a form of physical force, the manipulative and potentially coercive nature of cognitive warfare tactics raises serious ethical questions. These tactics can include the spread of false information, manipulation of public opinion, and attempts to undermine the legitimacy of governments or institutions. Such actions, while not involving physical violence, can have profound impacts on national security, social stability, and democratic processes. Lawfulness, on the other hand, operates within clearly defined ethical and legal boundaries. It emphasizes transparency, fairness, and respect for international norms and institutions. The lawful approach to international relations seeks to build trust among nations, strengthen international institutions, and create a stable global order based on mutual respect and cooperation.

The implications of these divergent approaches are significant. Cognitive warfare, while potentially effective in achieving short-term objectives and localized target, can lead to increased international tension, erosion of trust between nations, and destabilization of the global order. It may provide tactical advantages but often at the cost of strategic stability and long-term international cooperation. Lawfulness, while sometimes perceived as less immediately effective, offers a more sustainable path to international stability. By adhering to established legal norms and principles, nations can build lasting relationships, resolve conflicts peacefully, and contribute to a more predictable and secure international environment.

Moreover, the rise of cognitive warfare poses new challenges to the traditional understanding of lawfulness in international relations. As these tactics become more sophisticated and widespread, there is an urgent need for the international community to adapt legal frameworks to address these emerging threats. This may involve expanding the definition of force in international law and increasing public awareness, including the development of new legal instruments to regulate the use of information and psychological tactics in international conflicts.

The distinction between lawfulness and cognitive warfare represents a fundamental choice in the approach to international relations. While cognitive warfare may offer short-term advantages, it ultimately undermines the stability and trust necessary for effective global governance. Lawfulness, with its emphasis on peaceful resolution and respect for international norms, provides a more ethical and sustainable foundation for international relations. International law, with its goal of maintaining peace and international security and promoting international cooperation, stands in complete opposition to any form of warfare, whether lawfare or cognitive warfare. As the global community faces increasingly complex challenges, the commitment to lawfulness remains crucial for maintaining international rule-based order.

An Overview of Legal Issues in the South China Sea

The South China Sea, a semi-enclosed sea,[93] within the Pacific Ocean, spans approximately 3.4 million square kilometers. It is bordered by nine coastal states (China, Vietnam, Cambodia, Thailand, Malaysia, Singapore, Indonesia, Brunei, and the Philippines), as well as one entity, Taiwan. Renowned for its crucial geostrategic location, the South China Sea is central to global maritime affairs. The region is marked by political and security complexities, primarily stemming from territorial disputes, maritime overlapping zones, and strategic competition among superpowers. These factors contribute to the region's instability (see Table 1.2 below).

The Paracel and Spratly Islands in the South China Sea are heavily contested, with various claimants occupying different features.[94] In the Paracel Islands, China has exercised full control since 1974 after expelling Republic of Vietnamese forces from the western part of the archipelago in a naval battle. In the Spratly Islands, the situation is more complex, with multiple countries maintaining a physical presence. China occupies several reefs, including Fiery Cross, Subi, and Mischief Reefs, where it has conducted large-scale land reclamation and military construction. Vietnam controls the second-largest number of features, including Spratly Island

[93] UNCLOS, Articles 122, 123.

[94] See "Territorial disputes in the South China Sea" at the Encyclopaedia Britannica website.

Table 1.2 The matrix of disputed features in the South China Sea

	China (Taiwan)	Brunei	Malaysia	The Philippines	Vietnam
Paracels	x				x
Spratlys	x	x	x	x	x
Sabah			x	x	
Scarborough shoal	x			x	
Macclesfield bank	x			x	

Source Authors' compilation

and Southwest Cay, maintaining military and civilian installations. The Philippines holds nine features, most notably Thitu Island, its largest occupied feature. Malaysia occupies at least five reefs, including Swallow Reef, while Taiwan maintains a military presence on Itu Aba, the largest naturally occurring island in the Spratlys. Brunei, while claiming part of the Spratlys, does not maintain any military outposts. The competing occupations and militarization of these islands continue to fuel regional tensions and legal disputes under international law.

The Sabah dispute is a long-standing territorial issue between Malaysia and the Philippines, rooted in historical claims over the North Borneo region.[95] Despite the Philippines' claims, Malaysia exercises full control over Sabah. The dispute remains unresolved, but Malaysia considers it a closed issue, while the Philippines has occasionally raised the matter in diplomatic and political discussions.

Scarborough Shoal and Macclesfield Bank are two contested maritime features located in the South China Sea between the Philippines and China. Scarborough Shoal, also known as Bajo de Masinloc (the Philippine name) or Huangyan Dao (the Chinese name), is claimed primarily by China and the Philippines. China asserts historical rights based on its "Nine-dash Line," while the Philippines claims sovereignty based on geographical proximity and international law, particularly under UNCLOS. Tensions escalated notably in 2012 after a standoff between Philippine and Chinese vessels led to China's *de facto* control of the area.[96] Macclesfield Bank, known as Zhongsha Qundao in Chinese, is submerged and thus not capable of generating territorial sea claims under UNCLOS, yet it remains subject to sovereignty claims primarily by China and Taiwan, based on historical arguments. The overlapping and unresolved sovereignty claims involving these maritime features continue to contribute significantly to regional tensions and broader geopolitical disputes in the South China Sea.[97]

Maritime disputes in the South China Sea can be categorized as follows[98]: (1) Disputes concerning the Nine-dash Line declared by China (including Taiwan),

[95] Malaysia, Philippines (1968, December), p. 23083.

[96] Heinzig (1976). See also Duong (2012).

[97] Heinzig (1976). See also Duong (2012).

[98] Nguyen H T and Vu H D (2024), pp. 5–35.

which encompasses approximately 80% of the South China Sea area and overlaps with EEZ and continental shelf claims of Brunei, Indonesia, Malaysia, the Philippines, and Vietnam. This dispute has evolved into China's assertion of the Four Sha and the Ten-dash Line against other countries and territories in the early twenty-first century. (2) Disputes in the waters outside the mouth of the Gulf of Tonkin between Vietnam and China. (3) Disputes in maritime areas between Vietnam and Cambodia in the Gulf of Thailand. (4) Disputes in the waters north of the island of Borneo involving China, Malaysia, Brunei, the Philippines, and Taiwan. (5) Dispute between China and Indonesia in the Natuna Sea. Notably, pure maritime delimitation disputes can be addressed under UNCLOS but are currently managed through agreements such as the 1982 Agreement on the Historical Waters between the Socialist Republic of Vietnam and the People's Republic of Kampuchea[99] and the 1992 Memorandum of Understanding between Malaysia and the Socialist Republic of Vietnam for the exploration and exploitation of petroleum in a defined area of the continental shelf involving the two countries,[100] as well as negotiations on the three overlapping areas between Vietnam, Malaysia, and Thailand in the Gulf of Thailand.[101]

The disputes in the South China Sea encompass far more than conflicting territorial claims and overlapping EEZs or continental shelf claims; they also involve a complex range of maritime activities governed by UNCLOS. These activities include fishing activities, freedom of navigation, freedom of overflight, marine scientific research, the laying of submarine cables and pipelines, the establishment and use of artificial islands, installations and structures, and the use of law enforcement forces to assert or protect maritime claims. Addressing these issues reveals their legal dimensions and implications for regional stability.

Under UNCLOS, all states are entitled to freedom of navigation and overflight on the high seas (Article 87) and in the EEZs (Article 58). However, differing interpretations regarding the boundaries of these freedoms can lead to significant disputes, particularly between coastal states with extensive maritime claims, such as China, and extra-regional powers like the U.S., India, Australia, Japan and several European nations. Disagreements often arise over whether certain waters fall within a state's territorial sea, archipelagic waters, or EEZ. Coastal states sometimes attempt to exert greater control over contiguous zones or EEZs than

[99] Agreement on the Historical Waters between the Socialist Republic of Vietnam and the People's Republic of Kampuchea, from https://maritimeindex.org/wp-content/uploads/2021/12/VN-Cambodia-agreement-on-historical-waters-South-China-Sea-unofficial-translation.pdf, accessed on 31 July 2025.

[100] The 1992 Memorandum of Understanding between Malaysia and the Socialist Republic of Vietnam for the exploration and exploitation of petroleum in a defined area of the continental shelf involving the two countries, from https://cil.nus.edu.sg/wp-content/uploads/2019/02/1992-MOU-between-Malaysia-and-Vietnam-for-the-Exploration-and-Exploitation-of-Petroleum-1.pdf, accessed on 31 July 2025.

[101] Nguyen H T (1999).

UNCLOS permits, thereby challenging the principle of free passage. In response, the U.S. and its allies frequently conduct Freedom of Navigation Operations (FONOPs) to contest what they consider excessive maritime claims, asserting that these operations are consistent with customary international law as reflected in UNCLOS.[102]

Marine scientific research in contested maritime zones can lead to diplomatic friction, particularly when it involves seismic surveys, resource exploration or the naming of undersea features.[103] Under UNCLOS, coastal states have rights and responsibilities regarding marine scientific research in their EEZs, which typically require consent from the relevant authorities for foreign nations to conduct research. Disputes may arise when a coastal state denies permission for marine scientific research based on its interpretation of national jurisdiction or when foreign vessels engage in research that the coastal state deems unauthorized. Such incidents often result in heightened tensions and mutual accusations of violating international law, complicating the pursuit of cooperation in scientific endeavors.

UNCLOS also establishes a legal framework for laying submarine cables and pipelines within the continental shelf (Article 79) and through EEZs (Article 58), granting states specific rights and obligations. However, in areas of contested or overlapping claims—such as the South China Sea—questions emerge regarding which country has the authority to authorize or prohibit such projects. Disagreements frequently arise when a coastal state seeks to impose conditions perceived as infringing on the rights to lay cables or pipelines. These matters are critically important, as submarine cables facilitate the majority of global data transmission, and pipelines are essential for energy security.[104]

The role of maritime law enforcement agencies, such as China's Coast Guard and those belonging to Southeast Asian claimants, has become increasingly prominent in the region. These agencies often patrol disputed areas to assert sovereignty or safeguard local fishing fleets. Interactions between competing enforcement forces can escalate, leading to confrontations that involve vessel rammings, blockades, or the arrest of fishermen. Such incidents raise complex legal questions about the scope of coastal-state jurisdiction in contested waters, with each party citing UNCLOS or domestic laws to justify its actions.[105]

While the central disputes involve littoral states like China, the Philippines, Vietnam, and Malaysia, the strategic importance of the South China Sea's maritime routes also attracts extra-regional powers, including the U.S., India, Australia, Japan and various European nations. These countries have significant commercial, energy, and strategic interests in maintaining freedom of navigation and a rules-based order

[102] Heriot-Darragh (2024). See also Dutton and Kardon (2017).

[103] The Diplomatic Academy of Vietnam (2023).

[104] Sun (2025), pp. 142–198. See also Yee (2023).

[105] Nguyen H K T (2023).

at sea, often conducting naval patrols, joint exercises, and operations to assert their legal and political positions.[106]

Overall, central to many disputes is the interpretation of UNCLOS, particularly its provisions concerning islands, rocks (Article 121), and low-tide elevations (Article 13) as well as the rights and obligations associated with EEZs (Part V) and continental shelves (Part VI). The absence of consensus on these interpretations, coupled with the diverse geopolitical, security, and economic stakes involved, fuels ongoing legal and diplomatic battles. Legal precedents, arbitral awards, and international legal opinions significantly influence broader maritime claims and activities worldwide. This dynamic prompts claiming states in the South China Sea to engage in lawfare or lawfulness to defend their legal positions, weaken their opponents, and establish or resist legal precedents that could impact their long-term interests in the South China Sea.

References

Books

Berthet V (2018) L'erreur Est Humaine. Aux Frontières de la Rationalité. Paris (France): CNRS Éditions, from https://www.cnrseditions.fr/catalogue/biologie-et-sante/lerreur-est-humaine/. Accessed on 27 July 2025

Clausewitz CV (1832) On war (trans: Howard M, Paret P). Princeton University Press, from https://icct.nl/sites/default/files/import/publication/On-War.pdf. Accessed on 27 July 2025

Goffman E (1986) Frame analysis: an essay on the organization of experience (New edition). Boston (MA-USA): Northeastern University Press, from https://www.academia.edu/9520207. Accessed on 27 July 2025

Grotius H (1625) The rights of war and peace, including the law of nature and of nations (trans: Original Latin of Grotius; with Notes and Illustrations from Political and Legal Writers, by Campbell AC, A.M. with an Introduction by David J Hill. M Walter Dunne, New York, 1901), Liberty Fund

Henschke A (2025) Cognitive warfare—Grey matters in contemporary political conflict. Routledge. ISBN: 978-1-003-12695-9, from https://library.oapen.org/bitstream/handle/20.500.12657/94778/9781003126959_10.4324_9781003126959-12.pdf?sequence=1. Accessed on 27 July 2025

Kittrie OF (2016) Lawfare: law as a weapon of war. Oxford University Press

Melzer N (2019) International humanitarian law: a comprehensive introduction. International Committee of the Red Cross

Morel C (2014) Les décisions absurdes (Tome 1): sociologie des erreurs radicales et persistantes. Gallimard, Paris, from https://shs.cairn.info/les-decisions-absurdes-tome-1-sociologie-des-erreurs-radicales-et-persistantes–9782070457663?lang=fr. Accessed on 27 July 2025

Nguyen HT, Vu HD (2024) Asia and UNCLOS at 30 (1994–2024). In: Nguyen HT, Vu HD (eds) Asia and UNCLOS 30 years' implementation. International law in Asia. Springer, Singapore. pp 5–35. https://doi.org/10.1007/978-981-97-1556-5_1

Pinos JC, Hau MF (2024) Lawfare: new trajectories in law, 1st edn. Routledge. https://doi.org/10.4324/9781003289869 9781032267746

[106] Bekkers et al. (2019).

Vo NG (1961) People's war, people's army (Original work titled Chiến tranh nhân dân, quân đội nhân dân). Foreign Languages Publishing House. Published online by Marxists Internet Archive in 2014, from https://www.marxists.org/archive/giap/works/1961/peoples-war-peoples-army/1961-pwpa.pdf. Accessed on 27 July 2025

Sun Z (2025) Coastal state rights and the freedom of the laying of submarine cables and pipelines. In: Finding a balance in the exclusive economic zone: conflict and stability in the law of the sea. Chapter, Cambridge University Press, pp 142–198.

Zanin C, Martins V, Valim R (2022) Lawfare: waging war through law. Routledge

Articles

Austin WC, Kolenc AB (2006) Who's afraid of the big bad wolf? the international criminal court as a weapon of asymmetric warfare. Vanderbilt J Transnatl Law. 39(2):291–336, from https://www.lawfareblog.com/about-lawfare-brief-history-term-and-site. Accessed on 27 July 2025

Beck A (2014) China's strategy in the Arctic: a case of lawfare? Polar J 4(2):306–318. https://doi.org/10.1080/2154896X.2014.954886

Blay S, Piotrowicz R (2000) The awfulness of lawfulness: some reflections on the tension between international and domestic law. Aust Yearb Int Law Online. 21(1):1–19, from https://www.austlii.edu.au/cgi-bin/viewdoc/au/journals/AUYrBkIntLaw/2000/1.html. Accessed on 27 July 2025

Çağlar B (2025) Exceptionalism and its discontents: Israel, Iran, and the crisis of global norms. Middle East Crit 1–15. https://doi.org/10.1080/19436149.2025.2535195

Dill J (2017) Abuse of law on the twenty-first-century battlefield: a typology of lawfare. In Gross ML, Meisels T (eds) Soft war: the ethics of unarmed conflict. Cambridge University Press, pp 119–133. https://doi.org/10.1017/9781316481162.009

Guilfoyle D (2023) Litigation as statecraft: small states and the law of the sea. Br Yearb Int Law 94:1–36. https://doi.org/10.1093/bybil/brad009

Howse R, Teitel R (2010) Beyond compliance: rethinking why international law really matters. Glob Policy 1:127–136. https://doi.org/10.1111/j.1758-5899.2010.00035.x

Hsiao AH (2016) China and the south china sea "Lawfare". Issues Stud 52(2):1–35. https://doi.org/10.1142/S1013251116500089

Kahneman D, Tversky A (1979) Prospect theory: an analysis of decisions under risk. Econometrica. 47(2):313–327, from https://web.mit.edu/curhan/www/docs/Articles/15341_Readings/Behavioral_Decision_Theory/Kahneman_Tversky_1979_Prospect_theory.pdf. Accessed on 27 July 2025

Krisch N (2005) International law in times of hegemony: unequal power and the shaping of the international legal order. Eur J Int Law. 16(3):369–408, from https://ejil.org/article.php?article=301&issue=16. Accessed on 27 July 2025

Martinez F (2010) L'Individu Face au Risque: l'Apport de Kahneman et Tversky. Idées Economiques et Sociales. Idees Econ Soc 161(3):15–23, from https://www.cairn.info/revue-idees-economiques-et-sociales-2010-3-page-15.html. Accessed on 27 July 2025

Muñoz MAB (2016) Lawfare in hybrid wars: the twenty-first century warfare. Int Humanit Legal Stud. 7(1):63–87, from https://brill.com/view/journals/ihls/7/1/article-p63_4.xml?language=en. Accessed on 27 July 2025

Nguyen HT (1999) Joint development in the Gulf of Thailand. IBRU Boundary and Security Bulletin, from https://www.durham.ac.uk/media/durham-university/research-/research-centres/ibru-centre-for-borders-research/maps-and-databases/publications-database/boundary-amp-security-bulletins/bsb7-3_thao.pdf. Accessed on 27 July 2025

Rogers N (2013) Climate change litigation and the awfulness of lawfulness. Altern Law J 38(1):20–24

Sari A (2023) Norm Contestation for Strategic Effect: legal Narratives as Information Advantage. ZaöRV 83:119–153. https://doi.org/10.17104/0044-2348-2023-1-119, from https://www.nomos-elibrary.de/10.17104/0044-2348-2023-1-119.pdf. Accessed on 27 July 2025

Scott SV (1994) International law as ideology: theorizing the relationship between international law and international politics Eur J Int Law 52:313–325, from https://doi.org/10.1093/oxfordjournals.ejil.a035881. Accessed on 27 July 2025

Tyushka A (2021) Weaponizing narrative: russia contesting Europe's liberal identity, power and hegemony. J Contemp Eur Stud 30(1):115–135. https://doi.org/10.1080/14782804.2021.1883561

Yasin M (2020) Hybrid warfare: countering the impending threats. Sustainable Development Policy Institute, from https://www.jstor.org/stable/resrep29111.7. Accessed on 27 July 2025

Zajonc ZB (1968) Attitudinal effects of mere exposure. J Pers Soc Psychol. 9(II, 2):1–27, from https://www.psy.lmu.de/allg2/download/audriemmo/ws1011/mere_exposure_effect.pdf. Accessed on 27 July 2025

Theses, Dissertations, and Lectures

Logan TMA (2017) International law and the use of lawfare: an argument for the U.S. to adopt a lawfare doctrine. Master's thesis, The Graduate College of Missouri State University, from https://bearworks.missouristate.edu/cgi/viewcontent.cgi?article=4156&context=theses. Accessed on 27 July 2025

Internet Materials

Bekkers F et al (2019) Geopolitics and maritime security a broad perspective on the future capability portfolioof the royal netherlands navy. The Hague Centre for Strategic Studies, from https://hcss.nl/wp-content/uploads/2021/01/Geopolitics-and-Maritime-Security-web.pdf. Accessed on 31 July 2025

Bilal A (2021, Nov 30) Hybrid warfare—New threats, complexity, and 'trust' as the antidote. NATO Review, from https://www.nato.int/docu/review/articles/2021/11/30/hybrid-warfare-new-threats-complexity-and-trust-as-the-antidote/index.html. Accessed on 27 July 2025

Blackman J (2017, Dec 26) Congress' impeachment power and the case of presidential obstruction. Lawfare, from https://www.lawfaremedia.org/article/congress-impeachment-power-and-case-presidential-obstruction. Accessed on 27 July 2025

Butchard P (2022, Mar 24) Ukraine crisis: recognition, military action, and international law, from https://researchbriefings.files.parliament.uk/documents/CBP-9470/CBP-9470.pdf. Accessed on 27 July 2025

Cambridge Dictionary website. War, from https://dictionary.cambridge.org/dictionary/english/war. Accessed on 06 Aug 2025

Claverie B (2022) What is cognition? And how to make it one of the ways of the war. In: Claverie B, Prébot B, Buchler N, Du Cluzel F (2022) (eds) Cognitive warfare: the future of cognitive dominance (pp 4–17), First NATO Scientific Meeting on Cognitive Warfare, France, from https://www.researchgate.net/publication/359991886_Cognitive_Warfare_The_Advent_of_the_Concept_of_Cognitics_in_the_Field_of_Warfare. Accessed on 27 July 2025

Claverie B, Prébot B, Buchler N, Du Cluzel F (2022) Cognitive warfare: the future of cognitive dominance. First NATO Scientific Meeting on Cognitive Warfare, France, from https://www.researchgate.net/publication/359991886_Cognitive_Warfare_The_Advent_of_the_Concept_of_Cognitics_in_the_Field_of_Warfare. Accessed on 27 July 2025

Collins English Dictionary website. War definition and meaning, from https://www.collinsdictionary.com/dictionary/english/war. Accessed on 27 July 2025

Collins English Dictionary. Lawfare, from https://www.collinsdictionary.com/dictionary/english/lawfare. Accessed on 27 July 2025.

Council of Europe Commissioner for Human Rights. (2025, July 8). Memorandum on human rights elements for peace in Ukraine. Council of Europe Commissioner for Human Rights, from https://rm.coe.int/memorandum-on-human-rights-elements-for-peace-in-ukraine-by-michael-o-/1680b678ec. Accessed on 27 July 2025

D'Cunha S, Ferraro T, Rodenhäuser T (2025, Jan 15) "Hybrid threats," "grey zones," "competition," and "proxies": when is it actually war? EJIL: talk! Blog, from https://www.ejiltalk.org/hybrid-threats-grey-zones-competition-and-proxies-when-is-it-actually-war/. Accessed on 27 July 2025

Deka BK (2024, Apr 8) The essence of cognitive warfare: focusing the lens toward Chinese strategies. Orfonline.org, from https://www.orfonline.org/expert-speak/the-essence-of-cognitive-warfare-focusing-the-lens-toward-chinese-strategies. Accessed on 27 July 2025

Dugal M (2025, July 25) ICJ advisory opinion: the world's top court has spoken unequivocally on states' climate change obligations. Earth. Org, from https://earth.org/icj-advisory-opinion-the-worlds-top-court-has-spoken-unequivocally-on-states-climate-change-obligations/. Accessed on 27 July 2025

Dunlap CJ (2001) Law and military interventions: preserving humanitarian values in twenty-first century conflicts. Paper presented at the Humanitarian Challenges in Military Intervention Conference, Carr Center for Human Rights Policy, Kennedy School of Government, Harvard University, from https://people.duke.edu/~pfeaver/dunlap.pdf. Accessed on 27 July 2025

Dunlap CJ (2009) Lawfare: a decisive element of 21st-century conflicts? Joint Force Q, 54: 34–39, from https://scholarship.law.duke.edu/faculty_scholarship/3347. Accessed on 27 July 2025

Dunlap CJ (2017, May–June) Lawfare 101: a primer. Mil Rev 97:8–17

Duong H (2012, June 18) The scarborough shoal dispute. S. Rajaratnam school of international studies, Nanyang Technological University, from https://rsis.edu.sg/rsis-publication/rsis/1764-the-scarborough-shoal-dispute/. Accessed on 31 July 2025

Dutton PA, Kardon IB (2017, June 10) Forget the FONOPs – just fly, sail and operate wherever international law allows. Lawfare, from https://www.lawfaremedia.org/article/forget-fonops-%E2%80%94-just-fly-sail-and-operate-wherever-international-law-allows. Accessed on 31 July 2025

Encyclopaedia Britannica website. Territorial disputes in the South China Sea, from https://www.britannica.com/topic/territorial-disputes-in-the-South-China-Sea. Accessed on 31 July 2025

Gartland CJ (2021, May 8) Out to sea with the CCP: a contemporary example of lawfare with China. Lawfire, from https://sites.duke.edu/lawfire/2021/05/08/out-to-sea-with-the-ccp-a-contemporary-example-of-lawfare-with-china/. Accessed on 27 July 2025

Gates JM (2025) People's war in Vietnam. Aillen Dunham University, Discover Wooster, from https://discover.wooster.edu/jgates/peoples-war-in-vietnam/. Accessed on 27 July 2025

Gielas AM (2025, Aug 21) Warfare at the speed of thought: can brain-computer interfaces comply with IHL? ICRC humanitarian law & policy blog. Centre for Global Knowledge Studies, University of Cambridge, from https://blogs.icrc.org/law-and-policy/2025/08/21/warfare-at-the-speed-of-thought-can-brain-computer-interfaces-comply-with-ihl. Accessed on 27 Aug 2025

Goldstein B (2010, Nov 5) Lawfare: real threat or illusion. The Lawfare project, from https://www.thelawfareproject.org/analysis/2010/11/5/ilawfare-real-threat-or-illusionibrthe-lawfare-project. Accessed on 27 July 2025

Gosset D (2020, Mar 3) The great escape. China Daily Global, from https://global.chinadaily.com.cn/a/202003/03/WS5e5da434a31012821727bc06.html. Accessed on 08 Aug 2025

Guilfoyle D (2019, Sep 11) Chinese lawfare, resource disputes and the law of the sea. East Asia Forum. UNSW Canberra, from https://www.eastasiaforum.org/2019/09/11/chinese-lawfare-resource-disputes-and-the-law-of-the-sea/. Accessed on 27 July 2025

Guilfoyle D (2023, July 7) Small States, Legal Argument, and International Disputes. NUS Centre for International Law, from https://cil.nus.edu.sg/blogs/small-states-legal-argument-and-international-disputes/. Accessed on 27 July 2025

Hathaway OA (2023, Apr 3) How Russia's invasion of Ukraine tested the international legal order. Brookings, from https://www.brookings.edu/articles/how-russias-invasion-of-ukraine-tested-the-international-legal-order/. Accessed on 27 July 2025

Heinzig D (1976) Disputed islands in the South China Sea: paracels - Spratlys - Pratas - Macclesfield Bank. Otto Harrassowitz Wiesbaden, from https://www.cia.gov/readingroom/docs/CIA-RDP08C01297R000300180013-8.pdf. Accessed on 31 July 2025

Heriot-Darragh K (2024, Apr 24) FONOPs send a message, but they don't speak for themselves. The Interpreter. Lowy Institute from https://www.lowyinstitute.org/the-interpreter/fonops-send-message-they-don-t-speak-themselves. Accessed on 31 July 2025

Hoffman FG (2007) Conflict in the twenty-first Century: the rise of hybrid wars, Potomac Institute for Policy Studies, from https://www.potomacinstitute.org/images/stories/publications/potomac_hybridwar_0108.pdf. Accessed on 27 July 2025

Human Rights Watch (2024, Dec 19). Israel's crime of extermination, acts of genocide in Gaza: authorities' widespread deprivation of water threatens survival, from https://www.hrw.org/news/2024/12/19/israels-crime-extermination-acts-genocide-gaza. Accessed on 27 July 2025

Kreft S, Solmecke M (2025, July 28) Delivering Climate Justice? The ICJ Advisory Opinion and its Significance for Climate Action. United Nations University, from https://unu.edu/ehs/commentary/delivering-climate-justice-icj-advisory-opinion-and-its-significance-climate-action. Accessed on 27 July 2025

Kwon S (2024, Oct 16) Vanuatu leads recent initiatives in the international push for environmental justice. Earth Law Center, from https://www.earthlawcenter.org/blog-entries/2024/10/vanuatu-leads-recent-initiatives-in-the-international-push-for-environmental-justice. Accessed on 27 July 2025

Le Guyader H (2022). Cognitive domain: a sixth domain of operations? In: Claverie B, Prébot B, Buchler N, Du Cluzel F (eds) Cognitive warfare: the future of cognitive dominance (pp 3–1), First NATO Scientific Meeting on Cognitive Warfare, France, from https://www.researchgate.net/publication/359991886_Cognitive_Warfare_The_Advent_of_the_Concept_of_Cognitics_in_the_Field_of_Warfare. Accessed on 27 July 2025

Malaysia P (1968, Dec) Keesing's record of world events (formerly keesing's contemporary archives), 14, p 23083, from https://web.stanford.edu/group/tomzgroup/pmwiki/uploads/1072-1968-12-xx-ks-a-ajg.pdf. Accessed on 31 July 2025

Marma KJS (2025, Feb 12) Cognitive warfare: the invisible frontline of global conflicts. Modern Diplomacy, from https://moderndiplomacy.eu/2025/02/12/cognitive-warfare-the-invisible-frontline-of-global-conflicts/. Accessed on 27 July 2025

Merriam-Webster.com dictionary website. War, from https://www.merriam-webster.com/dictionary/war. Accessed on 27 July 2025

Milanovic M (2025, June 13) Is Israel's use of force against iran justified by self-defence? EJIL Talk! Blog, from https://www.ejiltalk.org/is-israels-use-of-force-against-iran-justified-by-self-defence/. Accessed on 27 July 2025

Milanovic M (2025, June 23) The Illegal Israeli-American use of force against iran: a follow-up. EJIL Talk! Blog, from https://www.ejiltalk.org/the-illegal-israeli-american-use-of-force-against-iran-a-follow-up/. Accessed on 27 July 2025

Mitchinson P (2000, Sep 6) Marxism and war. Marxist.com, from https://marxist.com/marxism-and-war.htm. Accessed on 27 July 2025

Nguyen HKT (2023) Law and (Dis)order in the South China Sea: analyzing maritime law-enforcement activities in 2010–22. Asia Policy 18.2, from https://www.nbr.org/publication/law-and-disorder-in-the-south-china-sea-analyzing-maritime-law-enforcement-activities-in-2010-22/. Accessed on 31 July 2025

O'Flaherty M (2025, July 8) Memorandum on human rights elements for peace in Ukraine. Council of Europe Commissioner for Human Rights, from https://rm.coe.int/memorandum-on-human-rights-elements-for-peace-in-ukraine-by-michael-o-/1680b678ec. Accessed on 27 July 2025

Oxford English Dictionary website. War, from https://doi.org/10.1093/OED/1011940408. Accessed on 27 July 2025

Proner C, Amorin C (2021, January) Lawfare et géopolitique: focus sur l'Amérique latine, Caraïbe. Institut de Relations Internationales et Stratégiques (IRIS), from https://www.iris-france.org/wp-content/uploads/2021/01/2-Prog-Amerique-Latine-Caraibe-Janvier-2021.pdf. Accessed on 27 July 2025

Schaugg L et al (2025, July 28) Historic international court of justice opinion confirms states' climate obligations. International Institute for Sustainable Development, from https://www.iisd.org/articles/deep-dive/icj-advisory-opinion-climate-change. Accessed on 27 July 2025

Solen D (2022, March) Fight fire with fire: the PLA studies hybrid warfare. China Aerospace Studies Institute, from https://www.airuniversity.af.edu/Portals/10/CASI/documents/Research/CASI%20Articles/2022-03-23%20Fight%20Fire%20with%20Fire.pdf. Accessed on 27 July 2025

The Diplomatic Academy of Vietnam (2023). Marine scientific research in the South China Sea, from https://researchonline.ljmu.ac.uk/id/eprint/22368/1/Mariine%20Scientific%20Research%20in%20the%20South%20China%20Sea,%20Sep%2023%20%20.pdf. Accessed on 31 July 2025

The Lawfare Project (2018, June 14) Lawfare project executive director brooke Goldstein's outspoken premieres tonight on JBS, from https://www.thelawfareproject.org/releases/2018/6/14/lawfare-project-executive-director-brooke-goldsteins-outspoken-premieres-tonight-on-jbsjewish-broadcasting-service-800-pm-et. Accessed on 27 July 2025

Tsagourias N (2025, June 20) Assessing the legality of Israel's action against Iran under international law. United States Military Academy - West Point, from https://lieber.westpoint.edu/assessing-legality-israels-action-iran-international-law/. Accessed on 27 July 2025

Underwood K (2017) Cognitive warfare will be deciding factor in battle: Lt. Gen. Stewart's Remarks at DoDIIS17. Signal, The Cyber Edge, from https://www.afcea.org/content/cognitive-warfare-will-be-deciding-factor-battle; https://www.youtube.com/watch?v=Nm-lVjRjLD4. Accessed on 27 July 2025

Van Puyvelde D (2015, May 7) Hybrid war – does it even exist? NATO Review, from https://www.nato.int/docu/review/articles/2015/05/07/hybrid-war-does-it-even-exist/index.html. Accessed on 27 July 2025

Wanyana R (2025, Jan 30) Cognitive warfare: does it constitute prohibited force? EJIL:Talk! Blog, from https://www.ejiltalk.org/cognitive-warfare-does-it-constitute-prohibited-force/. Accessed on 27 July 2025

Yee WY (2023, August 4) Laying down the law under the sea: analyzing the U.S. and Chinese submarine cable governance regimes. China Brief, 23(14). The Jamestown Foundation, from https://jamestown.org/program/laying-down-the-law-under-the-sea-analyzing-the-us-and-chinese-submarine-cable-governance-regimes. Accessed on 31 July 2025

Yeomans N (2023) Whither goeth the law – humanity or barbarity, from http://www.laceweb.org.au/whi.htm. Accessed on 27 July 2025

Chapter 2
China's Lawfare in the South China Sea: An Overview

This chapter provides a comprehensive overview of China's lawfare strategy in the South China Sea, framed within the Three Warfares doctrine—Public Opinion Warfare, Psychological Warfare, and Legal Warfare—formally adopted by the Chinese Communist Party and the People's Liberation Army in 2003. It reviews the ideological development of China's lawfare, beginning with Jiang Zemin's push to instrumentalize international law and culminating in the generals Qiao Liang and Wang Xiangsui's doctrine of "unrestricted warfare." The chapter examines the mechanisms of implementation, highlighting how China coordinates military, political, diplomatic, and legal instruments to advance territorial and maritime claims while undermining adversaries.

The chapter also identifies both the strengths and weaknesses of China's lawfare. It shows how China leverages economic interdependence, centralized authority, and narrative control to legitimize its claims, while cultural legacies, divergent notions of sovereignty, and resistance from other states constrain its effectiveness. It further outlines the historical phases of China's lawfare in the South China Sea—from symbolic assertions in the 1950s to the proactive deployment of legal, political, and military instruments after the 1970s. In particular, the chapter analyzes the techniques China employs in its lawfare strategy, highlighting how international law is selectively interpreted, redefined, and instrumentalized to advance national interests. It examines China's misinterpretation of sovereignty acquisition, historical rights, innocent passage, straight baselines, and dispute settlement mechanisms, contrasting these with established rulings of the ICJ and the 2016 Arbitral Award. It also explores the use of double standards, fabricated or ambiguous historical evidence, and the "turning nothing into something" strategy as tools of legal warfare. Beyond doctrinal arguments, China's lawfare is reinforced through propaganda, education, academia, and institutional influence. By embedding legal narratives into domestic law, scientific publications, and international organizations, China seeks to normalize contested claims and constrain opposing voices. The operational dimension includes gray-zone tactics,

H. T. Nguyen, T. K. N. Tran, *Lawfulness and Lawfare in the South China Sea*,
International Law in Asia,
https://doi.org/10.1007/978-981-95-4001-3_2

deployment of the maritime militia, and the imposition of national legislation beyond recognized jurisdiction. Collectively, these strategies illustrate a comprehensive and multifaceted approach in which legal, political, and informational warfare are intertwined to sustain China's maritime claims and reshape the regional order. Finally, the chapter demonstrates how lawfare has become central to China's maritime strategy, providing a foundation for subsequent analysis of regional and international responses.

The Three Warfare (三种战法) Doctrine of China

Concepts and Characteristics of the Three Warfares

China's lawfare is centrally manifested in the 'Three Warfares' doctrine (三种战法 or 三战), approved by the Central Military Commission in 2003, which serves as a conceptual framework for information operations within the People's Liberation Army. It integrates three mutually reinforcing strategies: Public Opinion Warfare (舆论战); Psychological Warfare (心理战), and Legal Warfare (法律战).[1] The General Political Department's Liaison Department (GPD/LD)[2] is primarily responsible for implementing these strategies through various bureaus and affiliated organizations. These operations frequently target Taiwan but are increasingly focused on influencing the European Union, particularly in Central and Eastern Europe. The doctrine represents China's approach to hybrid warfare, combining non-kinetic methods to achieve strategic influence in areas of competition.[3]

In 1996, then-President of China, Jiang Zemin, articulated to a cohort of Chinese international law experts the strategic necessity for China to adeptly wield international law as a tactical instrument.[4] This strategic perspective was further expounded in 1999 by Chinese generals Qiao and Wang in their seminal publication, "Unrestricted Warfare."[5] The authors delineate an approach where non-military instruments, including international legal mechanisms, are systematically employed to fulfill strategic objectives. The text details methodologies such as crafting international legal frameworks that confer strategic advantages and the tactical use of commercial and domestic law in the global arena. They argue that

[1] 解放军报 (2004, July 16).

[2] The Liaison Department is organized into four specialized units: (1) a covert operations unit focused specifically on Taiwan, (2) a research and investigation unit dedicated to analyzing international security dynamics and engagements, (3) a foreign propaganda unit responsible for conducting psychological operations, disseminating propaganda, and undertaking legal analysis, and (4) a border protection unit tasked with managing border negotiations and treaties. See Stokes and Hsiao (2018).

[3] Raska (2015).

[4] OUP Blog (2016, May).

[5] Qiao and Wang (1999).

the efficacy of legal warfare hinges on early trend recognition to establish advantageous legal standards and regulations.[6] This integrated approach empowers nations that are comparatively less formidable or smaller to effectively challenge larger, more powerful states like the U.S., particularly in asymmetrical contexts. China's "unrestricted lawfare"[7] is highly effective due to its creativity, extensive resources, and lack of ethical constraints. They emphasize the Committee of the Communist Party of China's adeptness at leveraging legal strategies at all levels, from domestic to international spheres.

In 2003, the Central Committee of the Communist Party of China and the Central Military Commission of China officially endorsed the concept of the Three Warfares.[8] Subsequently, the General Political Department of the People's Liberation Army of China disseminated Political Work Instructions in 2003[9] and 2010,[10] which are applicable to the entire army. The Three Warfares, initially devised for military purposes and applied in the context of Taiwan, have expanded to safeguard China's core interests and counteract U.S. influence. The primary function of the Three Warfares is to bolster the political stance of the Communist Party of China both domestically and internationally. Over time, it has evolved into a doctrine within the Chinese military, serving "as a force multiplier in military operations and political and diplomatic scenarios."[11] This ideology gained public attention through a report published by the Center for a New American Security (CNAS) in 2012.[12] Subsequent research conducted by the Chinese National Defense Academy in 2013 and 2015 provided comprehensive coverage of the doctrine of the Three Warfares.[13]

(i) Public Opinion Warfare (舆论战)

Public Opinion Warfare involves leveraging public opinion as a propaganda tool across various media platforms to undermine the adversary's resolve while bolstering the morale and unity of China's populace. The objective is to shape public perception both domestically and internationally, garnering support for the Chinese

[6] Bartman (2009).

[7] Qiao and Wang (1999).

[8] Zou (2020).

[9] Central People's Government of the People's Republic of China (2005, June 28) 2003年新颁布的军事条令、条例简介 [Introduction to the Newly Promulgated Military Regulations in 2003], from https://www.gov.cn/test/2005-06/28/content_10543.htm, accessed on 15 August 2025.

[10] Central People's Government of the People's Republic of China (2010, September 13) 新修订的《中国人民解放军政治工作条例》颁布 [Newly Revised "Regulations on the Political Work of the Chinese People's Liberation Army" Promulgated], from https://www.gov.cn/jrzg/2010-09/13/content_1701725.htm, accessed on 15 August 2025.

[11] Academy of Military Science Military Strategy Research Department [军事科学院军事战略研究部] (2013), p. 131.

[12] Walton (n.d.)

[13] 2015 Science of Military Strategy—NDU SMS. See Wu [吴杰明] and Liu [刘志富] (2014), pp. 1–7, 14–20, 62–69, 121–132, 133–143, 226.

government's stance while obfuscating dissenting viewpoints. This strategy is diligently executed domestically through the coordinated efforts of mass media channels and the central government's management of open and classified information. China's contemporary military doctrine underscores the significance of achieving "information dominance" in this regard.[14]

Over the years, the media have evolved into a vital component of the political landscape, fulfilling diverse roles such as disseminating information, educating citizens, and scrutinizing authority. Initially intended as conduits for public engagement in decision-making, political communication has transformed into a powerful tool for mobilizing popular support, employing strategies that vary according to the prevailing political regime. The selection and interpretation of media are significantly influenced by individual experiences, preconceived notions, and levels of political interest.[15] Public Opinion Warfare aims to bolster domestic morale, gain international support, undermine the enemy's resolve, and alter adversarial perceptions of conflict. The effectiveness of these efforts relies on the ability to shape the narrative surrounding a conflict, preempt enemy messaging, and establish a favorable framework for one's actions, significantly impacting decision-making at both national and international levels. Key themes in Chinese Public Opinion Warfare involve a top-down approach aligned with national political and military objectives, emphasizing preemptive messaging to define the narrative and adapt strategies to specific audiences and conditions. The effective use of military and civilian resources is critical for shifting the balance of power and enhancing domestic support while undermining adversarial will.[16] Livermore (2018) has outlined this integrated approach to media warfare, which resembles the information strategies employed by Joseph Goebbels, the Propaganda Minister of Nazi Germany, who famously stated, "if you tell a lie big enough and keep repeating it, people will eventually come to believe it."[17]

(ii) Psychological Warfare (心理战)

Psychological Warfare refers to the psychological contest between opposing parties in warfare or competitive confrontations, where both sides employ various strategies to exert psychological influence and stimulation on one another. Common techniques utilized in Psychological Warfare include infiltration and differentiation, disguise and deception, psychological deterrence, emotional manipulation, and suggestion and induction. Several guiding principles inform the execution of Psychological Warfare: leveraging one's strengths to exploit the weaknesses of the adversary; launching surprise attacks to catch the opponent off guard; encouraging carelessness and complacency on the part of the adversary; applying mental pressure to create psychological burdens; and diminishing the

[14] China Military Online (2015).

[15] Mercier (2009), pp. 143–165.

[16] Cheng (2012).

[17] Livermore (2018).

enemy's morale and cohesion. The characteristics of Psychological warfare include voluntary acceptance of messages, concealed intentions, specialized tactics, and a broad scope of impact. Its effectiveness lies in its ability to achieve outcomes that conventional weapons or equipment may not accomplish. Consequently, Psychological warfare has consistently been regarded with high importance by military strategists and participants in conflict.[18]

The objective of this form of warfare is to undermine the enemy's resolve to resist. Propaganda is disseminated through various channels, including television, the Internet, and print media. Common tactics employed include intimidation via military exercises, strategic posturing, and the exhibition of advanced weaponry. These strategies are designed to mislead the adversary regarding the true intentions of the aggressor and to influence their decision-making processes. The effects of these tactics extend not only to political leaders and civilians but also permeate through to military commanders and personnel. Additionally, this approach encompasses what can be termed "psychological prevention," which aims to bolster the morale of one's own forces through methods such as encouragement and counseling. These measures are intended to mitigate the impact of the enemy's Psychological Warfare efforts, thereby reinforcing the resilience and cohesion of one's own military.[19]

In other words, Psychological Warfare aims to manipulate and disrupt an adversary's decision-making processes, fostering uncertainty, inciting discontent towards leadership, misleading opponents, and ultimately weakening their resolve to engage in combat. Psychological warfare possesses several features of cognitive warfare and can be seen as a condensed or foundational form of it. Psychological warfare employs various tactics such as diplomatic pressure, the dissemination of rumors, the propagation of false narratives, and strategic harassment to express discontent, assert dominance, and imply threats. In this context, China effectively leverages its economic power as a strategic tool. For instance, it has threatened to sell off U.S. debt, exerted pressure on American businesses with investments in the Chinese market, implemented boycotts, and restricted critical exports, such as rare minerals. Additionally, China has restricted imports and threatened aggressive practices to broaden its market share, thereby utilizing economic measures as a means of psychological leverage against its adversaries.[20]

(iii) Legal warfare (法律战)

Legal warfare is an important aspect of wartime political strategy.[21] Effective legal warfare is a powerful tool for both confronting the enemy and protecting oneself, serving as a crucial means to gain the initiative in military operations. The relevant laws encompass both international law and domestic law, particularly the law of

---

[18] 林崇德 (2003).

[19] The Strategic Research Group (2016), p. 116.

[20] China: The Three Warfares (2013), p. 12.

[21] 解放军报 (2004, May 31).

armed conflict, which includes a range of international treaties and conventions, as well as established international practices. With the deepening development of the new global military revolution, legal warfare has garnered increasing attention. When making decisions regarding military engagements, certain countries and armed forces prioritize considerations such as the legal basis for military actions, the legitimacy of those actions, and the mitigation of interference in military operations. These concerns are typically addressed through legal offensive and defensive strategies, thereby establishing a broader operational space for military engagements.[22]

The concept of "legal warfare," as exemplified by China, encompasses a range of strategic tactics. These tactics include the selective application of international treaty provisions and customary rules, intentional misinterpretation or manipulation of international law, and even the formulation of new legal frameworks. China seeks to legitimize its actions by establishing novel legal justifications, enacting domestic legislation that governs foreign conduct in a manner advantageous to its interests, and undermining the credibility of opposing viewpoints and dissenting public opinion. Such strategies aim to bolster China's competitive position and secure favorable outcomes in international relations. "Legal warfare" effectively harnesses various dimensions of law, including both domestic legal systems and international legal norms, to assert control and delegitimize adversaries. This approach enables China to curtail the operational latitude of its opponents while carving out a protected sphere for its "core interests."

Hermez (2020) analyzes China's application of lawfare within the context of the South China Sea, particularly in areas falling beyond the jurisdiction of any coastal state—referred to as the global maritime commons.[23] While China's maneuvers may superficially comply with UNCLOS, they strategically reinterpret existing laws and norms to bolster its claims, particularly regarding the establishment of baselines that effectively expand its territorial control over substantial portions of the South China Sea. This reinterpretation of international law, particularly from the perspective of customary international law, is framed as a manifestation of "legal warfare," which poses a challenge to established legal frameworks. Hermez (2020) concludes by emphasizing the importance of deeper engagement with China to enhance understanding of its legal strategies and to address the evolving governance of the oceans, with a particular focus on the South China Sea.[24]

Since the 18th Congress, the Communist Party of China has placed significant importance on "the laws of socialism with Chinese characteristics" in societal development across various domains.[25] Unlike his predecessors, Chinese

[22] 中国军事百科全书编审室 (2007).

[23] Hermez (2020), pp. 559–588.

[24] Hermez (2020), pp. 559–588.

[25] Hu, J. (2012, November 16) Firmly march on the path of socialism with Chinese characteristics and strive to complete the building of a moderately prosperous society in all respects. Report to the Eighteenth National Congress of the Communist Party of China, from http://www.china.org.cn/china/18th_cpc_congress/2012-11/16/content_27137540.htm, accessed on 31 July 2025.

President Xi Jinping has been instrumental in the advancement and refinement of the three warfare strategies, Xi Jinping frequently employs terms such as "rule of law," "in accordance with the law," "law-based governance," and "justice" in his speeches to underscore the utilization of law as a strategic tool. In his address to the 19th Congress of the Communist Party of China, Xi Jinping referenced the phrase "rule of law" 26 times.[26] Moreover, on 01 July 2021, during a speech commemorating the 100th anniversary of the Communist Party of China, General Secretary and President of China Xi Jinping highlighted the Party's utilization of law as a tool for achieving national rejuvenation and promoting its interests. The speech emphasizes the Party's role in establishing the People's Republic of China and its subsequent modernization efforts. It frames the Communist Party of China's adoption and adaptation of international law as a strategic tool to advance China's position on the global stage, contrasting this with the country's earlier history of subjugation under unequal treaties.[27] The narrative underscores the Communist Party of China's commitment to a path of "socialism with Chinese characteristics," which involves utilizing law and legal institutions as tools for achieving national strength and prosperity.

On 16 August 2021, the Publicity Department of the Communist Party of China Central Committee and China's foreign ministry released the "An outline for studying Xi Jinping Thought on Diplomacy," which underscores Xi Jinping Thought on Socialism with Chinese Characteristics for a New Era in the arena of foreign affairs. This initiative emphasizes a comprehensive and systematic approach to study, including timely reviews, in-depth reflection, and practical application. The goal is to continuously strengthen understanding of Xi Jinping's new era of socialism with Chinese characteristics, which serves to inform practices and advance initiatives. This approach aims to usher in a new chapter of major-country diplomacy with distinct Chinese characteristics, aligning with the broader Chinese Dream and reinforcing efforts towards the comprehensive modernization of a socialist society and the realization of the great rejuvenation of the Chinese nation.[28] Beyond viewing the Three Warfares solely as a military tactic, China has actively expanded this doctrine into its international relations and political directives, leveraging both international and national law as instruments to counter Western influence and suppress dissent.

Following the 20th Party Congress, held on 23 October 2022, Xi Jinping was reaffirmed as General Secretary for a third consecutive 5-year term by the newly

---

[26] Xi, J. (2017, October 18) Secure a decisive victory in building a moderately prosperous society in all respects and strive for the great success of socialism with Chinese characteristics for a new era. Report to the 19th National Congress of the Communist Party of China, from http://www.xinhuanet.com/english/download/Xi_Jinping's_report_at_19th_CPC_National_Congress.pdf, accessed on 31 July 2025.

[27] Xi, J. (2021, July 1) Speech by Xi Jinping at a ceremony marking the centenary of the Communist Party of China, from http://lv.china-embassy.gov.cn/eng/xwdt/202107/t20210702_8990960.htm, accessed on 31 July 2025.

[28] People.com.cn. (2021). See also Tianjin High-end Equipment Research Institute (2021).

elected Central Committee of the Communist Party of China. The resolution amending the Party Charter highlighted the necessity for party members to diligently study and strictly adhere to the Party Charter. It emphasized the comprehensive construction of modern socialism, with Xi Jinping serving as the core of the Party Central Committee and the entire Party.[29] In his address to the Congress, Xi Jinping underscored the importance of strengthening legal frameworks in key areas, emerging sectors, and foreign affairs, advocating for coordinated efforts to promote the rule of law both domestically and internationally.[30]

The Three Warfares have become an essential element of China's strategic approach in its relations with neighboring countries, and are characterized by the following features:

1. Continuity: The Three Warfares are employed consistently in both wartime and peacetime, maintaining an unbroken application.
2. Coordination: China's strategy involves the close coordination of the Three Warfares—psychological, public opinion, and legal[31]—with the objective of "using public opinion to suppress public opinion," controlling ongoing debates, and shaping perceptions in China's favor while undermining its opponents' ability to respond.[32] Legal Warfare serves as the spearhead, establishing the foundation for the development of Psychological and Public Opinion Warfare. Psychological Warfare leverages legal bases as weapons to influence and psychologically assail opponents, fostering doubt and undermining the credibility of their arguments. Public Opinion Warfare lays the groundwork for the implementation and success of Psychological and Legal Warfare, triggering widespread reactions in domestic and international public opinion supportive of China's legal assertions. Legal Warfare and Public Opinion Warfare typically operate at the strategic level, while Psychological Warfare is often deployed at tactical, campaign, and potentially strategic levels, targeting the leadership ranks of the opponent.
3. Non-military influence (soft power): The Three Warfares are regarded as crucial tactics for bolstering China's soft power on a global scale. Their applicability extends beyond national boundaries, affording China the means to pursue its objectives without relying on military interventions. This strategic approach creates favorable conditions for the Chinese military to gain an advantage in future conflicts or political and diplomatic endeavors.

[29] Xinhua (2022, October 23).

[30] 习近平 (2022) 高举中国特色社会主义伟大旗帜 为全面建设社会主义现代化国家而团结奋斗—在中国共产党第二十次全国代表大会上的报告. 中国政府网, from http://www.gov.cn/xinwen/2022-10/25/content_5721685.htm, accessed on 31 July 2025.

[31] "[…] the 'tight connection' of three warfares as an 'integrated whole' that should be utilized synthetically." See China Military Online (2015).

[32] Kania (2016).

4. Victory without resorting to armed force or with limited use of armed force; rather, it involves fostering support and creating favorable conditions for military operations that can hasten the achievement of victory.
5. Comprehensiveness and synchronization: The strategies of the Three Warfares are implemented across all areas of social life, extending beyond the military domain to encompass leadership at all levels and reaching the general populace. This approach spans from multilateral international conferences to bilateral relations, aiming to instill public confidence in the validity and legality of China's positions in each specific field.
6. Gray zone tactics involve exploiting loopholes or gaps in international law, where actors proactively initiate actions to gauge public opinion reactions, adjust strategies, and determine levels of conflict. These actions are conducted below the threshold of war and are advantageous to the actor. Beijing has introduced concepts such as "red lines,"[33] "core interests,"[34] "four respects,"[35] and others to shape public opinion and normalize *de facto* actions, irrespective of their alignment with international law. China's "gray zone" tactics are employed both on land and at sea, seeking to obscure the distinctions between legal and illegal claims, regular and irregular forces, the intention to resolve disputes peacefully versus through force, and the application of international versus domestic legal standards.
7. Up–to-date and adaptable: China demonstrates a willingness to adapt and evolve its arguments in response to challenges. In the face of setbacks, China swiftly introduces new claims, complicating matters for its opponents while simultaneously maintaining previous assertions. For instance, following the rejection of the U-shaped line (dotted line) claim in the South China Sea by the Arbitration in 2016, China asserted the Four Sha claim,[36] later introduced a Standard Map featuring a Ten-dash Line in 2023,[37] renamed some islands and reefs in the South China Sea in 2024[38] and announced baselines for determining the territorial sea width of the Scarborough Shoal in 2024.[39] Additionally, in response to the U.S.'s launch of the Asia Maritime Transparency Initiative (AMTI), China

---

[33] Montemayor (2025, February 17).

[34] Yoshihara and Holmes (2011), pp. 45–59.

[35] Ministry of Foreign Affairs People's Republic of China (2014, September 07) Wang Yi: Sticking to "Four Respect" on the South China Sea Issue, from https://www.fmprc.gov.cn/eng/gjhdq_665435/3265_665445/3271_664430/3273_664434/202406/t20240611_11419613.html, accessed on 12 August 2025. See also Kim (2016).

[36] Ministry of Foreign Affairs of the People's Republic of china (2016, July 13). China Adheres to the Position of Settling Through Negotiation the Relevant Disputes Between China and the Philippines in the South China Sea, from https://www.fmprc.gov.cn/mfa_eng/wjdt_665385/2649_665393/201607/t20160713_679474.html, accessed on 31 July 2025.

[37] Ma (2023).

[38] Global Times (2024, November 10).

[39] Strangio (2024).

promptly established the South China Sea Strategic Situation Probing Initiative (SCSPI).[40]

While Chinese coast guard and naval vessels continue to use water cannons to suppress Philippine and Vietnamese boats at sea,[41] China declares that "throughout history, China has never sought to pursue 'regional hegemony',"[42] and quickly introduces the new "4C" principle,[43] including Consultation, Co-management, Cooperation, and Constructiveness, which in essence represents a renewed form of the "shelving disputes and pursuing joint development"[44] approach, aimed at lulling the claimant states. The so-called "4C" principle emphasizes bilateral consultation with claimant states, interim arrangements to prevent conflict, and selective cooperation in areas such as fisheries, energy exploration, and environmental protection.[45]

Consequently, as legal or territorial disputes intensify, China simultaneously deploys its Three Warfares strategy with increased frequency. In this approach, China meticulously constructs narratives designed to transform falsehoods into perceived truths through persistent repetition. It employs Psychological Warfare techniques to intimidate and deter adversaries and engages in ambiguous or subjective interpretations that obscure the true nature of events. Furthermore, China actively seeks to introduce new regulations under international law to achieve private gains, capitalizing on the mechanisms of Legal Warfare. It is crucial to acknowledge that Legal Warfare is intricately linked to the domains of Psychological Warfare and the influence of public opinion. The integration and synergy of these Three Warfares confer significant strategic advantages upon China. China's Three Warfares directly exemplifies its approach to cognitive warfare. This strategy leverages a blend of Sun Tzu-inspired principles to subtly influence perceptions and erode the West's will to resist.

Organizations and Implementation of the Three Warfares

To effectively execute the Three Warfares, China institutes a strict division of tasks among central and local agencies, as well as between the military, scientific community, representative bodies, and the Ministry of Foreign Affairs. This strategy leverages the research strength of Chinese institutes while garnering

[40] See the website of South China Sea Strategic Situation Probing Initiative (SCSPI): http://www.scspi.org/en.

[41] See section "Lawfare in the Disruption of Maritime Economic Activities in the South China Sea".

[42] Xinhua News Agency Research Institute [新华社研究院] (2025), pp. 10–11.

[43] Xinhua News Agency Research Institute [新华社研究院] (2025), pp. 10–14.

[44] Xinhua News Agency Research Institute [新华社研究院] (2025), p. 4.

[45] Xinhua News Agency Research Institute [新华社研究院] (2025), pp. 10–14.

support from domestic and international research institutions, publishers, and scholars. The Liaison Department—General Political Department of the People's Liberation Army serves as the coordinating agency for the Three Warfares within the People's Liberation Army. Additionally, the 311th Base in the Nanning Military Region maintains close ties with organizations promoting Chinese culture, such as the Chinese Association for Cultural Development (CAPCC), China International Friendly Contact Association, China-U.S. Exchange Foundation (CUSEF), China Center for Peace and Development Studies (CPDS), Foreign Propaganda Bureau (EPB), and China Energy Fund Committee (CEFC).[46]

China strategically assigns and promotes ministries and branches to actively engage in various international organizations across political, technical, and judicial domains. These organizations include the International Maritime Organization (IMO), International Hydrographic Organization (IHO), UPI, World Health Organization (WHO), World Intellectual Property Organization (WIPO), ICJ, and ITLOS. By participating in and assuming leadership roles in these organizations, China aims to shape public opinion and utilize professional expertise to obscure its intentions in Legal Warfare. Furthermore, China's involvement partly influences countries' reluctance to resort to judicial agencies and international organizations for peaceful dispute resolution. China's legal warfare initiatives are strategically deployed through Track 1, Track 2, or Track 1.5, mobilizing a significant number of domestic forces, overseas Chinese, and private organizations.

Historically and politically, China advocates resolving disputes through bilateral negotiations and, to a certain extent, through regionally controlled mechanisms, in order to maintain decision-making authority without third-party intervention. As for ICJ, China's engagement with ICJ has been notably limited, characterized by a marked absence of participation in contentious cases. Historically, China viewed the ICJ with suspicion, associating it with past instances of Western imperialism and the imposition of unequal treaties. Although this historical distrust has lessened considerably in recent decades, owing to China's greater integration within the international legal order, it still informs China's approach to the ICJ. Strategically, China's consistent reservations regarding the ICJ's compulsory jurisdiction and its avoidance of submitting disputes through special agreements reflect a calculated effort to avoid potential challenges to its core national interests, particularly concerning territorial sovereignty in regions like the South China Sea and Taiwan. A similar attitude is also applied to the compulsory mechanisms of UNCLOS. However, China may be more open to participating in non-binding fora, as demonstrated by its greater willingness in recent years to engage in advisory opinion proceedings, evident in its participation in the Kosovo and Chagos Archipelago cases. Ultimately, China's approach to the ICJ reflects a complex interplay of historical perceptions, strategic considerations, and evolving policy priorities.[47]

---

[46] Raska (2015).

[47] Rasilla and Hao (2024), pp. 498–501.

Strengths and Weaknesses of China in Implementing the Three Warfares

China's Strengths in Deploying the Three Warfares

Over the past several decades of reform and opening up, China has experienced profound transformation and growth. This developmental trajectory has enabled China to expand its presence in international relations, establishing itself as a key economic and political actor in various countries and regions around the globe. There is a widespread expectation that China's rise will persist throughout the twenty-first century, solidifying its status as a formidable competitor in both economic and political arenas on the global stage. With its international position as a rapidly emerging power, China boasts numerous strengths on the international legal front. The 20th Congress of the Communist Party of China was instrumental in cementing China's trajectory toward becoming a modern socialist power by the mid-twenty-first century, aiming to achieve the objectives set forth for "the Second Centenary Goal" (commemorating the 100th anniversary of the founding of the People's Republic of China).[48]

Economically, China is strategically positioned for significant expansion driven by innovation in high-tech sectors. Massive investments in "new quality productive forces" target industries like semiconductors, electric vehicles, artificial intelligence, and advanced manufacturing, aiming to create a technologically independent and resilient economy less reliant on traditional export-driven models. This proactive approach aims to secure China's future economic dominance.[49] Furthermore, as the second-largest economy globally, China boasts a substantial GDP per capita of US$13,303.1 as of 2024.[50] China's substantial engagement in the global economy, coupled with its market of over 1.4 billion individuals,[51] renders it nearly indispensable in shaping the economic strategies of other nations. As a result, there has been a marked increase in global dependence on the Chinese market.[52] Given its immense economic strength, China is well-equipped to invest in legal battles and leverage Legal Warfare strategies effectively.

China's economic leverage over other small states, stemming from their extensive economic interdependence, presents a complex and multifaceted strategic tool. While offering significant potential influence, its effectiveness is contingent upon various political and domestic factors among countries. Beijing's attempts to convert economic influence into political leverage have been met with challenges,

[48] See all documents adopted at the 20th National Congress of the Communist Party of China, from https://english.www.gov.cn/2022special/20thcpccongress/63310431c6d0a757729e0852, accessed on 31 July 2025.

[49] Asia Society Policy Institute's Center for China Analysis (2024).

[50] See GDP per capita (current US$)—China. World Bank Data.

[51] See China population. Worldometers.

[52] Armstrong (2020).

as evidenced by Taiwan's efforts to mitigate its economic dependence and Beijing's own difficulties in consistently applying economic pressure effectively. The interplay of economic interdependence and political objectives highlights the inherent complexities and risks associated with utilizing economic leverage as a primary tool in international relations.[53] Recent data highlights a growing trade imbalance between ASEAN and China, with China consolidating its position as the region's dominant trading partner. In 2023, ASEAN imported 23.9% of its total goods from China—surpassing intra-ASEAN trade, which stood at 22.1%—underscoring ASEAN's increasing dependence on Chinese products.[54] According to HSBC Global Banking and Markets (GBM), ASEAN's trade deficit with China has widened by approximately US $35 billion since 2019, even as the region improved its trade balance with other partners.[55] Preliminary figures for the first half of 2025 show that China's exports to ASEAN surged by 16.8% year-over-year, contributing to a record monthly trade surplus of US $114.7 billion in June 2025.[56] Economic instruments are employed to cultivate support for China's positions on a myriad of issues, frequently transcending the scope of direct bilateral concerns.

Politically, Xi Jinping's centralized authority enables swift decision-making and the execution of complex reforms, providing a framework for ambitious development goals. This strong leadership ensures stability and continuity in policy implementation. The party-state's robust control mechanisms and sophisticated domestic security apparatus maintain order and suppress dissent.[57] In a society marked by centralized authority under the governance of the Chinese Communist Party, strategies for shaping public opinion can be systematically and consistently executed at various levels throughout the nation. China's comprehensive approach includes initiatives across both Track 1 and Track 2 diplomacy, notably in the context of educating successive generations of Chinese citizens to misinterpret international law concerning its excessive claims in the South China Sea. Furthermore, despite participating in fora that may be disadvantageous to its interests, China remains actively engaged, seeking to transform perceptions of 'wrong' into 'right' through persistent reiteration of its positions. In addition, China benefits from its vast population. This demographic advantage makes Chinese one of the most widely spoken languages worldwide. The large population serves as a valuable human resource for China, providing strength in disseminating information through the technique of repeating falsehoods in Legal Warfare.

---

[53] Tanner (2007), pp. 135–144.

[54] See ASEAN Statistical Highlights 2024.

[55] See ASEAN perspectives: Bucking the global trend in trade. HSBC Global Banking & Markets.

[56] Cash and Wang (2025, July 14).

[57] Asia Society Policy Institute's Center for China Analysis (2024).

China's Weaknesses in Deploying the Three Warfares

Despite its ambition, the Three Warfares doctrine is not without vulnerabilities. A central weakness lies in its dependence on information control and narrative dominance. While effective domestically, such control is far harder to sustain abroad, where open media environments, independent scholarship, and competing state narratives can dilute or discredit Beijing's messaging.

Firstly, Chinese culture places greater emphasis on Li (礼, rites) than on rationality, as Li (礼, rites) is one of its key concepts.[58] Rites prescribe the proper position of each individual, thereby fostering harmony among people and between humanity and the natural world. By contrast, the character Fa (法),[59] which originally meant "penalty,"[60] came to denote the legal system of laws, decrees, and regulations. In ancient China, Li (礼) and Fa (法) worked in tandem: Li rewarded virtue, while Fa punished vice. Only the sovereign possessed the authority to enact and promulgate laws, everyone was bound to obey them.[61] Yet, because moral order was thought to be maintained primarily through rites rather than adjudication, this cultural orientation manifests in a comparatively diminished emphasis on the rule of law and the application of legal precedents for dispute resolution, as observed in Western legal traditions. The transition toward a more developed legal mindset necessitates considerable time for the accumulation of quantitative experience to yield qualitative change. Judge Xue Hanqin articulates that the culture of law in China is profoundly influenced by its historical and traditional context, which prioritizes harmony and mutual respect.[62] Historically, Confucian principles have significantly shaped dispute resolution practices in China, favoring compromise and persuasion over coercive legal measures, thereby promoting negotiation as opposed to litigation. Although China now actively engages with the international legal system, its historical experiences—particularly the era of foreign imperialism—continue to inform its perspective on international law. In matters concerning sovereignty and territorial integrity, China emphasizes direct negotiations, reflecting a preference for contextual understanding of disputes rather than reliance on third-party mechanisms, which are often viewed with skepticism regarding their impartiality and fairness. Moreover, China's unique developmental trajectory, coupled with its strong emphasis on national sovereignty and non-interference in domestic affairs, further influences its approach to international law. Therefore, a comprehensive understanding of China's perspective on international law necessitates an examination of not only its legal framework but also its historical experiences and deeply entrenched cultural values.[63]

[58] See Key concepts in Chinese thought and culture website, Li (Rites / Social Norms/ Propriety).

[59] See Key concepts in Chinese thought and culture website, Law/ Dharma.

[60] See Key concepts in Chinese thought and culture website, Law/ Dharma.

[61] See Key concepts in Chinese thought and culture website, Law/ Dharma.

[62] Xue (2016).

[63] Xue (2016).

Seo (2024) analyzes the South China Sea dispute from the perspective of international law and politics, highlighting the divergent legal interpretations of China and the West.[64] China prioritizes its historical rights and adopts a restrictive interpretation of UNCLOS, while Western nations advocate for a broader *mare liberum* approach that emphasizes freedom of navigation. This divergence extends to their respective views on sovereignty; China maintains an absolute perspective that underscores its historical claims and resolutely rejects external interference. In contrast, the Western viewpoint emphasizes the role of international law in defining and limiting state sovereignty. Furthermore, while the philosophical foundations of Confucianism, with its focus on harmony, and Legalism, which emphasizes strict governance, shape the social order and stability within China, there remains a profound cultural skepticism toward the law itself. This skepticism, rooted in historical experiences and traditional values, indicates that, despite the influence of these philosophical systems on engagement with international law, a significant lack of confidence in legal frameworks persists, affecting China's perspective on these issues.[65] Additionally, the concept of lawfare, defined as the strategic use of legal arguments and processes to achieve political objectives, is employed by both China and the U.S. in the South China Sea context. This involves contrasting approaches to interpreting UNCLOS provisions and law of the sea, leveraging public opinion, and utilizing legal mechanisms such as arbitration. Such dynamics underscore the complexities and tensions that characterize the ongoing dispute, revealing how legal frameworks are manipulated to serve national interests.

Secondly, China's distinct interpretation of sovereignty makes its claims that run counter to international norms. China's understanding of sovereignty is nuanced and context-dependent, as it is fundamentally intertwined with the nation's nationalism and underpins much of the geopolitical tension in its neighboring regions. This interpretation is rooted in the political philosophy of "monism," a concept articulated by Confucian and Legalist thinkers between 475 and 221 BC, which posits that legitimate international order cannot be established among sovereign equals. In this view, sovereignty is perceived as indivisible; the existence of equals undermines true sovereignty.[66] This stark contrast between China's notion of sovereignty and the Westphalian model established in 1648 is a primary driver of China's skepticism towards the existing international legal frameworks that have governed global relations for the past two centuries. Beijing especially criticizes the structures developed in the aftermath of World War II, including institutions such as the UN, the ICJ, the World Bank. From leading G77 countries during the Third UN Conference on the Law of the Sea (UNCLOS III) to BBNJ negotiation, Beijing has shifted to questioning the integrity of UNCLOS, arguing that the convention does not address all international maritime issues.[67]

---

[64] Seo (2024), pp. 57–113.

[65] He and Sun (2020), p. 107.

[66] China: The Three Warfares (2013), p. 14.

[67] Liu and Scott (2024), pp. 1–20.

China's objective is to not only challenge but to overhaul the prevailing global legal system, advocating for a framework that aligns more closely with its own principles and characteristics.[68] On the other hand, differing interpretations of legal principles often place China at a disadvantage in disputes. This is exemplified by China's propensity to maintain ambiguity and repetitively employ outdated rhetorical strategies, which frequently elicits opposition from a variety of nations. Moreover, China's decision to abstain from participating as a defendant in the South China Sea arbitration case highlights its perceived lack of confidence in its legal position in the context of impartial adjudication.

Thirdly, China's actions have, to some extent, undermined the current international legal order, eliciting responses from countries such as the U.S. and its allies who are committed to upholding this order. China's increasing influence in East Asia poses a threat to international maritime law. To counter this trend, countries like the U.S. must exert continuous efforts to persuade China that its interests are better served by preserving maritime rights and freedoms rather than challenging them. Moreover, China fails to garner support from middle-range countries that traditionally rely on international law for dispute resolution. Despite close economic ties with China, countries like Indonesia, Australia and New Zealand, Japan and European states such as Germany, France and the United Kingdom are willing to engage in disputes such as the 2009–2011 and 2019–2025 note battles on the expanded continental shelf in the South China Sea to safeguard their legitimate interests. While China also relies on the law to legitimize its claims, viewing legal arguments as instrumental in garnering support from other countries or, at the very least, minimizing objections to its stance.

Fourthly, while China often utilizes international law strategically to advance its interests, it also recognizes the inherent value and limitations of the system. China's pragmatic approach allows it to benefit from the international order while simultaneously seeking to shape its norms and rules. This necessitates a robust and effectively enforced international legal framework capable of addressing the challenges posed by a rising China.[69] China's political and legal demands are often contradictory. While it aims to portray itself as a "peaceful rise," advocating for responsible behavior as a major power and seeking a peaceful and stable regional environment with the support of neighboring countries to sustain its economic growth, it also seeks to uphold its territorial claims to appease nationalist sentiments. Consequently, China faces challenges in deploying consistent and synchronized messaging in both domestic and foreign political discourse.

China's lawfare in the South China Sea have projected a dual and often contradictory image onto the world stage. On the one hand, its meticulously crafted legal arguments, presented through official statements, white papers, and scholarly publications, demonstrate a sophisticated understanding of international law and a willingness to engage in legal discourse. This showcases China's growing

[68] China: The Three Warfares (2013), p. 14.

[69] Williams (2020), pp. 5–6.

confidence in its ability to articulate and defend its positions within the established international legal framework. Conversely, China's outright rejection of the Arbitral Tribunal's Ruling and its consistent emphasis on bilateral negotiations, rather than multilateral dispute resolution mechanisms, highlight a more assertive and less conciliatory approach. This tension between legal engagement and assertive unilateralism underscores the complex interplay of legal strategies, power politics, and nationalistic sentiment driving China's response to the South China Sea disputes. This duality creates ambiguity concerning its long-term approach to international law and its role within the existing global order.[70]

The issue for the China is that, as mentioned previously, no nation possesses "exclusive rights" in the use of legal tools or in employing lawfare.[71] It can be considered "a weapon of the weak" in asymmetric lawfare.[72] China is deeply concerned about its international reputation should it outright disregard international law. The cost of maintaining an image of a responsible actor abiding by international norms is likely to remain significant in the eyes of China's leadership. However, China also finds itself in a quandary as direct confrontation with international law could undermine its international standing, while complete adherence to international norms risks portraying its leaders as weak and compromising national interests in the eyes of the Chinese populace. Whether motivated by an attempt to exploit loopholes in international law or a desire to mitigate the reputational costs of non-compliance with international norms, Beijing often behaves in a manner that implicitly recognizes the legitimate function of international law. Even China's persistent refusal to clarify its nine or Ten-dash Line and its Four Sha claim can be interpreted as tacit acknowledgment that these assertions lack transparency and are considered illegal by countries such as the Philippines, Vietnam, and the U.S.[73]

The Three Warfares doctrine is eliciting significant pushback as its opponents become more cooperative and strategic in countering Chinese objectives. With the long-standing War on Terror no longer a primary focus, Western nations have strengthened alliances through multilateral security agreements like QUAD (comprising Australia, India, Japan, the U.S.)[74] and AUKUS (involving Australia, the United Kingdom, and the U.S.).[75] Consequently, there is a growing emphasis on the threat presented by China the potential economic fallout from China's legal strategies, combined with growing international opposition, could lead to significant setbacks for China in the coming years.[76]

---

[70] Hsiao (2016), pp. 1–35. See also Schultheiss (2023).

[71] Pinos and Hau (2024), p. 16.

[72] Pinos and Hau (2024), p. 74.

[73] Williams (2020), pp. 5–6.

[74] Stiftung Wissenschaft und Politik (2023).

[75] AUKUS, from https://www.asa.gov.au/aukus, accessed on 31 July 2025.

[76] Nash and Guzel (2024), pp. 55–58.

Phases of Establishing and Implementing China's Lawfare in the South China Sea

China's approach to lawfare is shaped by a combination of traditional cultural factors, domestic imperatives, and international dynamics. These same factors guide China's use of "legal warfare" tactics in the South China Sea. Before examining China's lawfare objectives tactics, this section provides an overview on the key phases and events of China's legal warfare in the region, from the establishment of the People's Republic of China to the present day.[77]

Phase 1 (1949–1972): Biding Time and Hiding Capabilities. During this period, despite facing international isolation and grappling with internal challenges, China remained focused on establishing a legal framework to assert its sovereignty over key territories in the South China Sea, including the Pratas Islands, Paracel Islands, Spratly Islands, and the Macclesfield Bank. Despite its limited international engagement, China continued to advance its claims in the region, setting the stage for future developments. China's focus on maritime matters was limited, exemplified by its Declaration of 12-nautical-mile territorial waters in 1958. China regarded areas beyond the 12-nautical-mile limit as high seas, shared by all nations. While the dash-line claim was occasionally referenced, it did not feature prominently in international fora.

The establishment of the People's Republic of China (PRC) in 1949 marked a new era in its approach to these territories. While the preceding Nationalist government had already asserted sovereignty, often through symbolic acts like renaming islands and raising flags, the People's Republic of China (PRC) embarked on a more assertive strategy, building on existing claims and incorporating them within its newly established national identity.[78] Chinese Prime Minister Zhou Enlai solidified China's stance on 15 August 1951, prior to the San Francisco Conference convened by the U.S. to sign the Peace Treaty with Japan.[79] In his declaration, Zhou Enlai emphasized that:

> [...] whether or not the United States-British Draft Treaty contains provisions on this subject and no matter how these provisions are worded, the inviolable sovereignty of the People's Republic of China over Nan Wei Island (Spratly Islands) and Si Sha Islands (Paracel Islands) will not be in any way affected.[80]

---

[77] The phrases and segments in this section are adapted, with adjustments and updates, from the work: Nguyen (2023), pp. 61–85.

[78] Shen (2002), pp. 145–152.

[79] Foreign Minister Chou En-lai's Statement on the U.S.-British Draft Peace Treaty with Japan and the San Francisco Conference, August 15, 1951, Supplement to Peoples China Vol. IV, No. 5, September lt 195, from https://www.massline.org/PeoplesChina/PC1951/PC1951-V4-05-Sup1-OCR-sm.pdf, accessed on 31 July 2025.

[80] Foreign Minister Chou En-lai's Statement on the U.S.-British Draft Peace Treaty with Japan and the San Francisco Conference, August 15, 1951, Supplement to Peoples China Vol. IV, No. 5, September lt 195, from https://www.massline.org/PeoplesChina/PC1951/PC1951-V4-05-Sup1-OCR-sm.pdf, accessed on 31 July 2025. See also Zhou Enlai, Minister of Foreign Affairs of

On 4 September 1958, the Government of the People's Republic of China issued the Declaration on the Territorial Sea, establishing a 12-nautical-mile territorial sea applicable to all its territories, including the mainland, Taiwan, the Penghu Islands, the Dongsha Islands, the Xisha Islands, the Zhongsha Islands, the Nansha Islands and other affiliated islands.[81] This was a unilateral declaration that contained several provisions misaligned with the law of the sea at the time, reflecting China's attempt to shape regional maritime law according to its own interpretations. Beyond defining the breadth of its territorial sea, the declaration explicitly included the Xisha (Paracel) and Nansha (Spratly) Islands within China's territorial waters, reinforcing claims over archipelagos that remain central to ongoing disputes with Vietnam, the Philippines, and other nations. It is important to note that, at that time, China had illegally occupied only the western part of the Paracel Islands. Additionally, the declaration rejected the right of innocent passage for foreign military vessels by stipulating that such vessels and aircraft were prohibited from entering China's territorial sea and airspace without prior permission. Furthermore, the declaration included provisions establishing straight baselines to enclose the larger areas of Bohai Bay and the Qiongzhou Strait as internal waters.[82] China has consistently prioritized lawfare as a means to establish a legal foundation for its expansive activities in subsequent stages.

However, it is necessary to underscore that, through this declaration, China affirms its stance that its maritime claims do not extend beyond a 12-nautical-mile territorial sea and that waters beyond this claimed territorial sea are considered the high seas.

Phase 2 (1972—Present): Proactive implementation of the Three Warfares Strategy. This phase is proposed to be divided into four segments based on key political, diplomatic, and legal factors, as well as the extent of China's shift from passive or occasional use to active deployment of lawfare in the South China Sea region.

Segment 1 (1972–1992): Establishing a pretext for the use of force, carrying out actual occupation, and introducing the concept of "setting aside disputes and pursuing joint development" (搁置争议、共同开发).[83]

---

the Central People's Government of the People's Republic of China (1951, August 16). 中华人民共和国中央人民政府外交部部长周恩来关于美英对日和约草案及旧金山会议的声明 [Statement by Zhou Enlai, Minister of Foreign Affairs of the Central People's Government of the People's Republic of China, on the Draft Peace Treaty with Japan by the U.S. and the United Kingdom and the San Francisco Conference]. People's Daily, p. 1, from https://cn.govopendata.com/renminribao/1951/8/16/1/, accessed on 15 August 2025.

[81] Declaration of the Government of the People's Republic of China on China's Territorial Sea, on September 4, 1958, from https://www.s3.documentcloud.org/documents/1341822/declaration-of-the-government-of-the-prc-on.pdf, accessed on 31 July 2025.

[82] Shen (2002), pp. 145–146.

[83] The idea of "set aside dispute and pursue joint development" was advanced by Deng Xiaoping. Set aside dispute and pursue joint development, from https://www.mfa.gov.cn/eng/zy/wjls/3604_665547/202405/t20240531_11367540.html, accessed on 31 July 2025.

This segment witnessed China's military actions to seize and control the Paracel Islands (in 1974) and subsequent advances into the Spratly Islands. In 1988, China occupied Subi Reef, Fiery Cross Reef, Hugh Reef, Cuarteron Reef, and Johnson Reef. Gaven Reef was occupied in 1989, followed by the occupation of Mischief Reef in 1995. China utilized international law to justify its use of force, often citing defense against perceived threats to its fishermen. This period also marked the beginning of China's implementation of the "gray zone" and "salami-slicing" strategies.

On 30 January 1980, China published a document concerning the Paracel and Spratly Islands, entitled "China's Indisputable Sovereignty over the Xisha and Nansha Islands".[84] China's legal rationale for its sovereignty claims over the Paracel and Spratly Islands is based on three pillars: historical rights, sovereign inheritance rights, and longstanding sovereign rights. Regarding historical rights, China asserts its claims based on the following arguments: (i) The claim that the Chinese people were the first to discover the Paracel and Spratly Islands. (ii) The naming of numerous islands in the South China Sea by China. (iii) Early exploration and commercial activities conducted by the Chinese in these archipelagos. (iv) The assertion that the Chinese government exercised management and sovereignty over these islands from the earliest opportunities. In terms of sovereign inheritance rights, China argues that: (i) Sino-French Boundary Conventions of 1887 and 1895 can be interpreted as recognizing Chinese sovereignty over certain islands. (ii) Title to these territories was inherited from Japan, as recognized by international agreements following World War II. Concerning longstanding sovereign rights, China claims: (i) The lack of objection from the French government when Admiral Li Zhun landed on the Paracels. (ii) Recognition of China's sovereignty over the Paracel and Spratly Islands in international documents following World War II. (iii) Alleged acknowledgment by the Vietnamese government of China's sovereignty over these islands.[85] (iv) The inclusion of the Paracel and Spratly Islands as part of Chinese territory on global maps. (v) Recognition of China's sovereignty over these islands at various international conferences. (vi) Comments from foreign scholars supporting China's claims.

---

[84] Ministry of Foreign Affairs of the People's Republic of China (1980) China's Indisputable Sovereignty over the Xisha and Nansha Islands. Foreign Languages Press Beijing, from https://www.bannedthought.net/China/MaoEra/Vietnam/China%27sIndisputableSovereignty-1980.pdf, accessed on 31 July 2025.

[85] China's interpretation of Prime Minister Pham Van Dong's September 14, 1958, Diplomatic Note as evidence that Vietnam recognized China's sovereignty over the Paracels and Spratlys is highly biased and misrepresents the note's content and intent. This interpretation is entirely inconsistent with Vietnam's legal foundation and international law. The 1958 Diplomatic Note does not contain any language addressing issues of territory or sovereignty, nor does it declare Vietnam's renunciation of sovereignty over the Paracels and Spratlys, contrary to China's claims. See 1958 Diplomatic Note with Vietnam's Sovereignty over Hoang Sa and Truong Sa, Vietnam Government Electronic Newspaper, from https://baochinhphu.vn/cong-ham-1958-voi-chu-quyen-hoang-sa-truong-sa-cua-viet-nam-102164331.htm, accessed on 31 July 2025.

In 1982, China established the Hainan Administrative Region. Following this, in 1988, the government announced that the islands and reefs of the Xisha (Paracel) archipelago, the Nansha (Spratly) archipelago, the Zhongsha archipelago, and the surrounding seas would fall under Hainan's jurisdiction.[86] On 12 May 1988, the Chinese government issued a "Memorandum on the Xisha and Nansha Islands Issues", stating that disputes over the Nansha (Spratly) Islands could be set aside and resolved at a later date (以后可以商谈).[87]

The policy of "set aside dispute and pursue joint development" (搁置争议、共同开发)[88] originated from Deng Xiaoping's pragmatic approach to managing territorial and maritime disputes around the Senkaku Islands in the late 1970s. It was later proposed for application to the South China Sea disputes in the early 1980s.[89] Deng believed that a rigid insistence on immediately resolving sovereignty questions could hinder productive relations between China and its neighbors. Instead, he advocated a strategy that would defer contentious arguments over ownership while allowing cooperative economic activities—such as resource exploration and development—to proceed in disputed areas.[90] This policy essentially consists of three components: "Sovereignty belongs to us, set aside disputes, and pursue joint development," later reflected in Beijing's 12 May 1988 memorandum indicating Nansha disputes could be discussed later. The policy's purpose is to defer sovereignty questions while enabling cooperative resource activity—functioning as legal-narrative leverage within broader information operations. However, in external propaganda, China places greater emphasis on the aspect of joint development. If other parties agree to joint development, it implies an acceptance of China's sovereignty and recognition of the South China Sea as a disputed maritime area.

This strategy represents a combination of lawfare and informative war, aimed at promoting China's narrative on a broad scale. By continuously disseminating its legal arguments, China seeks to shape a common perception among involved parties and test their willingness to accept dispute resolution models based on joint development frameworks proposed by China.

Segment 2 (1992–2009): Leveraging domestic laws and bilateral negotiations.

The year 1992 is regarded as the starting point of this segment, marked by the adoption of the Law on the Territorial Sea and the Contiguous Zone of the People's

---

[86] Lo (1989), p. 93.

[87] 新华社 (2012) 中华人民共和国外交部发表关于西沙群岛、南沙群岛问题的备忘录 [Memorandum on the Xisha and Nansha Islands Issue]. 新华社, from https://subsites.chinadaily.com.cn/SouthChinaSea/2016-06/28/c_52677.htm, accessed on 31 July 2025.

[88] The idea of "set aside dispute and pursue joint development" was advanced by Deng Xiaoping. Set aside dispute and pursue joint development, from https://www.mfa.gov.cn/eng/zy/wjls/3604_665547/202405/t20240531_11367540.html, accessed on 31 July 2025.

[89] Ministry of Foreign Affairs People's Republic of China (n.d.) Set aside dispute and pursue joint development. from https://www.mfa.gov.cn/eng/zy/wjls/3604_665547/202405/t20240531_11367540.html, accessed on 16 August 2025.

[90] Phan (2018), pp. 30–49.

Republic of China and by China's focus on developing domestic legislation as a basis to justify its territorial and maritime claims in the South China Sea. The endpoint of this segment is 2009, when China circulated the nine-dash line map at the United Nations. In this segment, the regional and international context witnessed significant changes. The entry into force of UNCLOS on 16 November 1994, marked a milestone in international law since the World War II. However, rather than easing tensions, the South China Sea issue became increasingly complex. Disputes between China and Southeast Asian countries remained intertwined with no signs of resolution. Additionally, China adopted a strategy of unilaterally promulgating domestic laws concerning the South China Sea and prioritizing bilateral negotiations with disputing countries, further complicating the situation.

During this period, China actively pursued the development of maritime laws to justify and support its maritime strategy. Several significant legal documents related to the sea were promulgated, including the Law on Territorial Sea and Contiguous Zones on 25 February 1992, and the Declaration of Ratification of UNCLOS on 15 May 1996, which included the geographical coordinates of the 1996 baseline and the application of the archipelagic baseline for the Paracel Islands. Additionally, the Law on Exclusive Economic Zones and Continental Shelf was enacted in 1998. These documents assert China's sovereignty over island groups such as the Pratas Islands, Paracel Islands, Spratly Islands, and the Macclesfield Bank, as well as historical rights.

The Law on Territorial Sea and Contiguous Zones, enacted on 25 February 1992, by the Standing Committee of the National People's Congress of China, consists of 17 articles. Article 2 delineates the scope, stating that "The People's Republic of China's territorial land includes the mainland and its offshore islands, Taiwan and the various affiliated islands including Diaoyu Island, Penghu Islands, Dongsha Islands, Xisha Islands, Nansha (Spratly) Islands and other islands that belong to the People's Republic of China."[91] Article 3 specifies that "The extent of the People's Republic of China's territorial sea measures 12 nautical miles from the baseline of the territorial sea. The People's Republic of China's baseline of the territorial sea is designated with the method of straight baselines, formed by joining the various base points with straight lines."[92] China asserts that this baseline system is not yet complete, and the Chinese Government will continue to announce baselines in areas where they have not yet been determined in the future. While this statement may initially appear to align with the law of the sea, there are at least two contradictions in the interpretation and application of maritime law: (i) China

[91] 1992年2月25日第七届全国人民代表大会常务委员会第二十四次会议通过 [Law on Territorial Sea and Contiguous Zones of China], from http://www.gov.cn/ziliao/flfg/2005-09/12/content_31172.htm or https://www.un.org/depts/los/LEGISLATIONANDTREATIES/PDFFILES/CHN_1992_Law.pdf, accessed on 31 July 2025.

[92] 1992年2月25日第七届全国人民代表大会常务委员会第二十四次会议通过 [Law on Territorial Sea and Contiguous Zones of China], from http://www.gov.cn/ziliao/flfg/2005-09/12/content_31172.htm or https://www.un.org/depts/los/LEGISLATIONANDTREATIES/PDFFILES/CHN_1992_Law.pdf, accessed on 31 July 2025.

unilaterally establishes its baseline system for maritime zones, including the Paracel and Spratly Islands, which are subject to territorial sovereignty disputes with countries including Vietnam; (ii) China does not permit foreign warships to exercise the right of innocent passage as stipulated by UNCLOS but requires prior notification.

On 15 May 1996, China announced the baseline for measuring the breadth of the territorial sea for mainland China and the baseline for the Paracel Islands simultaneously with its ratification of UNCLOS.[93] The straight baseline designated for the Paracel Islands encompasses the 29 most prominent points of the entities surrounding the Islands, accompanied by specific coordinates adhering to the archipelagic baseline model outlined in UNCLOS, which is typically applicable to archipelagic states. China deliberately adopts the method of delineating archipelagic baselines prescribed by UNCLOS for archipelagic nations to define baselines for offshore archipelagos under the jurisdiction of coastal states.[94]

On 26 June 1998, China enacted the Exclusive Economic Zone and Continental Shelf Act, comprising 16 articles aimed at governing the legal framework of China's EEZ and continental shelf.[95] Article 2 stipulates that:

> The EEZ of the People's Republic of China is an area beyond and adjacent to the territorial sea of the People's Republic of China extending to a distance of 200 nautical miles from the baselines from which the breadth of the territorial sea is measured. The continental shelf of the People's Republic of China comprises the seabed and subsoil of the submarine areas that extend beyond its territorial sea throughout the natural prolongation of its land territory to the outer edge of the continental margin, or to a distance of 200 nautical miles from the baselines from which the breadth of the territorial sea is measured where the outer edge of the continental margin does not extend up to that distance.

In addition, Articles 5, 7, 8, 9, and 11 outline regulations for foreign international organizations, entities, or individuals seeking entry into China's EEZ or continental shelf for activities such as fishing, resource exploration, exploitation, marine scientific research, and the establishment of artificial islands, construction of infrastructure, installation of equipment, and laying of pipelines. Permission for such activities must be obtained from the relevant Chinese authorities. This grants China several advantages, including: (i) The ability to take necessary measures for resource preservation and environmental protection; (ii) Jurisdiction to enforce Chinese law within the EEZ and continental shelf, including investigation, arrest, search, and pursuit measures; (iii) Enjoyment of rights in accordance with both international law and Chinese law; (iv) Article 14, in particular, stipulates that this law does not affect China's historical rights. This provision is intended to preserve

---

[93] The 1996 China's baselines, from https://www.un.org/Depts/los/ LEGISLATION ANDTREATIES/PDFFILES/DEPOSIT/chn_mzn7_1996.pdf, accessed on 31 July 2025.

[94] Dzurek (1996), pp. 84–85.

[95] 中华人民共和国专属经济区和大陆架法 [Exclusive Economic Zone and Continental Shelf Law of the People's Republic of China], from http://www.law-lib.com/law/law_view.asp?id=384 or https://www.un.org/Depts/los/LEGISLATIONANDTREATIES/PDFFILES/chn_1998_eez_ act.pdf, accessed on 31 July 2025.

the possibility for China to claim historical rights not explicitly covered by the law or UNCLOS provisions.

In addition, China has issued a series of other maritime legal documents and systems, including: (i) Fisheries Law of the People's Republic of China, enacted on 20 January 1986[96]; (ii) Marine Environment Protection Law of the People's Republic of China on 25 December 1999[97]; (iii) Law of the People's Republic of China on the Administration of Sea Areas,[98] effective from 01 January 2002; (iv) Registration of geographical coordinates of points, in accordance with Articles 16 (2), 74(2), and 84(2) of UNCLOS, issued on 27 September 2004[99]; (v) later, National Security Law of the People's Republic of China, enacted on 01 July 2015.[100] Those national laws and regulations extend their scope of application over the waters claimed by China in the South China Sea.

During this period, China engaged in negotiation activities aimed at binding countries to common legal principles, interpreting and applying UNCLOS according to its own intentions, and closely linking sovereignty issues with maritime disputes. This approach fostered division and resistance to the internationalization of disputes, while simultaneously promoting China's image as a peacefully rising power adhering to international law. It served as a foundation for psychological warfare and media manipulation.

China prioritized bilateral negotiations with relevant countries, particularly focusing on the Philippines and Vietnam, while strongly opposing the internationalization of the disputes.

With the Philippines. This period is marked by the dispute between China and the Philippines over Mischief Reef and Huangyan Island, which became a significant aspect of China's South China Sea policy in the 1990s. Through numerous bilateral consultations, China and the Philippines issued a joint statement on the Nansha issues on 10 August 1995, outlining a policy framework known as the eight-point principle for peaceful and friendly dispute resolution, aimed at establishing a general version of a code of conduct (referred to as the Philippine-China

[96] Fisheries Law of the People's Republic of China, from http://www.china.org.cn/china/LegislationsForm2001-2010/2011-02/14/content_21917138.htm, accessed on 31 July 2025.

[97] Marine Environment Protection Law of the People's Republic of China, from https://www.english.www.gov.cn/archive/press_briefing/2014/08/23/content_281474983042445.htm, accessed on 31 July 2025.

[98] Law of the People's Republic of China on the Administration of Sea Areas, from http://www.ajne.org/sites/default/files/document/laws/6842/law-of-the-peoples-republic-of-china-on-the-administration-of-sea-areas.pdf, accessed on 31 July 2025.

[99] Registration of geographical coordinates of points under Articles 16(2), 74(2) and 84(2) UNCLOS dated September 27, 2004, from https://www.un.org/Depts/los/LEGISLATIONANDTREATIES/PDFFILES/mzn_s/mzn51.pdf, accessed on 31 July 2025.

[100] 中华人民共和国国家安全法(主席令第二十九号) [National Security Law of the People's Republic of China], from http://www.gov.cn/c16762/2015-07/01/content_2893902.htm or https://govt.chinadaily.com.cn/s/201812/11/WS5c0f1b56498eefb3fe46e8c9/national-security-law-of-the-peoples-republic-of-china-2015-effective.html, accessed on 31 July 2025.

COC version).[101] The key points of this framework include: (i) Resolving territorial disputes through peaceful consultation based on principles of peace, friendship, equality, and mutual respect without affecting bilateral relations' normal development; (ii) Building mutual trust and confidence to consolidate peace and stability, refraining from using or threatening to use force to resolve disputes; (iii) Adopting a progressive approach to cooperation and negotiating final dispute resolutions while expanding consensus and narrowing differences; (iv) Agreeing to resolve disputes in accordance with recognized principles of international law, including UNCLOS; (v) Being open to constructive proposals for multilateral cooperation in the South China Sea; (vi) Promoting cooperation in various marine-related fields such as marine environment protection, maritime safety, anti-piracy efforts, marine scientific research, disaster mitigation and prevention, search and rescue operations, meteorology, and marine pollution control, as well as engaging in multilateral cooperation on these topics; (vii) Emphasizing the cooperation of all relevant countries in protecting marine resources in the South China Sea; (viii) Resolving disputes directly involved by the countries concerned without affecting freedom of navigation.

In November 1996, the leaders of China and the Philippines reached a mutual understanding and established a consultation mechanism to address cooperation in the South China Sea, encompassing three key working groups: (i) Fisheries: Focused on addressing fisheries-related issues, such as management, conservation, and sustainable utilization of marine resources in the region; (ii) Conservation and Environmental Protection: Aimed at promoting environmental conservation efforts and addressing environmental challenges in the South China Sea, including pollution control and habitat preservation; (iii) Confidence-Building Measures: Geared towards fostering trust and confidence between the two countries through collaborative initiatives aimed at enhancing maritime security, promoting dialogue, and preventing conflicts in the region.[102]

While signing cooperation agreements with the Philippines, China simultaneously carried out occupation activities and constructed a military base at Mischief Reef. In response to protests, China claimed that it was establishing search and rescue support facilities for both Chinese and Philippine fishermen on Mischief Reef.[103] However, Mischief Reef has since evolved into a significant military installation for China in the South China Sea.

With Vietnam. Following the normalization of Vietnam-China relations in November 1991, a conflict arose between the two nations from 1992 to 1994 over an oil and gas block adjacent to Vietnam's *Bãi Tư Chính* (Vanguard Bank),

---

[101] Republic of the Philippines and People's Republic of China. Joint Statement of the Republic of the Philippines and the People's Republic of China on the South China Sea and on Other Areas of Cooperation. 10 August 1995, from https://www.scribd.com/document/61125477/Joint-Statement-PRC-and-RP, accessed on 31 July 2025.

[102] Dongfang Zaobao [东方早报] (2014).

[103] Liu (2019).

which China refers to as "Wan'an Tan" (万安滩).[104] Despite this conflict, the two countries established negotiation mechanisms on border and territorial disputes, including the Joint Working Group on Land Border, the Joint Working Group on the Demarcation of the Gulf of Tonkin, and the Group of Experts on Maritime Issues between China and Vietnam. Through extensive bilateral negotiations, significant progress was made. On 30 December 1999, China and Vietnam signed the Land Border Delimitation Treaty.[105] This was followed by the signing of an Agreement on the Delimitation of Territorial Waters, Exclusive Economic Zones, and Continental Shelves in the Gulf of Tonkin,[106] along with an Agreement on Fisheries Cooperation in the Gulf of Tonkin on 25 December 2000.[107] These agreements effectively resolved two out of the three historical territorial border issues between the two countries. While both nations expressed a mutual desire to resolve bilateral disputes, China often cites these cases as models of peaceful dispute resolution, portraying itself as making concessions. However, China remains steadfast in its refusal to negotiate sovereignty over the Paracel Islands.

Segment 3 (2009–2016): Official Announcement of the Nine-dash Line as a Legal Claim and the Increasing Framing of the South China Sea as a Core National Interest. This segment reflects the struggle to clarify the nature of the nine-dash line claim, beginning with its public circulation at the United Nations. It culminated in the 2016 ruling of the Arbitral Tribunal in Philippines v. China (PCA Case No. 2013-19), constituted under Annex VII of UNCLOS, which concluded that the claim was null and void.

On 07 May 2009, China officially introduced the Nine-dash Line map to the international community through the Note Verbale CML/17/2009 from China to the UN. This Note Verbale was made in response to the submissions by Vietnam and Malaysia to the Commission on the Limits of the Continental Shelf on 06–07 May 2009, regarding the outer limits of their continental shelves beyond 200 nautical miles. This Note Verbale marked the first time in over 60 years since its establishment that China had formally articulated its position on the Nine-dash Line, also known as the U-shaped Line claim. In the note, China unequivocally stated:

> The People's Republic of China has indisputable sovereignty over the islands in the South China Sea and adjacent waters, and enjoys sovereign rights and jurisdiction over relevant

---

[104] Kivimäki (2002), p. 56.

[105] Nguyen (2000), 87–89.

[106] Agreement between the People's Republic of China and the Socialist Republic of Viet Nam on the delimitation of the territorial seas, exclusive economic zones and continental shelves of the two countries in Beibu gulf/Bac Bo gulf, from https://maritimeindex.org/wp-content/uploads/2021/12/VN-China-agreement-on-delimitation-of-territorial-seas-EEZs-and-continental-shelves-of-Bac-Bo-Gulf-South-China-Sea-adopted-from-UN-Treaty-Series.pdf, accessed on 31 July 2025.

[107] Vietnam—China Agreement on Fisheries Cooperation in the Gulf of Tonkin, from https://maritimeindex.org/wp-content/uploads/2021/12/VN-China-agreement-on-fishery-cooperation-in-Gulf-of-Tonkin-South-China-Sea.pdf, accessed on 31 July 2025.

> water areas as well as the seabed and subsoil thereof […]. The above position is consistently held by the Chinese Government, and is widely known by the international community.[108]

The Cow Tongue Line, U-shaped line, Nine-dash Line, and Ten-dash Line are various terms used by international scholars to refer to China's territorial claims depicted on maps, which run in close proximity to the coastlines of countries bordering the South China Sea. However, China has never provided specific coordinates for the line and has ambiguously linked it to historical rights as a means of propaganda and legal warfare. The legal nature of this line will be analyzed in the following sections.

On 14 April 2011, the Chinese Permanent Mission to the UN issued a Note, marking the first time it used the term "invasion" to accuse the Philippines.[109] Additionally, China publicly declared for the first time that the Paracel and Spratly Islands have EEZs and continental shelves in accordance with UNCLOS.[110] Specifically, China emphasized the following two points: Firstly, China affirms its indisputable sovereignty over the islands in the South China Sea and adjacent waters, along with the enjoyment of sovereign rights and jurisdiction over the relevant waters, seabed, and subsoil beneath. China's claims to sovereignty, rights, and jurisdiction in the South China Sea are backed by ample historical and legal evidence. Secondly, since the 1930s, the Chinese Government has consistently delineated the geographical scope of the Spratly Islands and assigned names to their components. Moreover, in accordance with the relevant provisions of UNCLOS and the laws of the People's Republic of China, including the Law on the Territorial Sea and Contiguous Zone of 1992 and the Law on the Exclusive Economic Zone and Continental Shelf of 1998, the Spratly Islands were recognized as having full territorial waters, EEZs, and continental shelves.[111]

On 9 June 2014, the Note from the Permanent Mission of the People's Republic of China to the UN, addressed to the Secretary-General of the UN, protested against Vietnam's actions in obstructing the operation of the HD-981 oil rig.[112] China contends that, although the maritime area between the Paracel Islands and the Vietnamese coast remains undelimited, it asserts that, regardless of the

[108] The Note Verbale CML/17/2009 dated 07 May 2009 of the Permanent Mission of China to the UN, from https://www.un.org/depts/los/clcs_new/submissions_files/mysvnm33_09/chn_2009re_mys_vnm_e.pdf, accessed on 31 July 2025.

[109] 乌元春 (2011).

[110] The Note Verbale CML/8/2011 dated April 14, 2011 of the Permanent Mission of the People's Republic of China to the UN, from http://www.un.org/Depts/los/clcs_new/submissions_files/mysvnm33_09/chn_2011_re_phl_e.pdf, accessed on 31 July 2025.

[111] The Note Verbale CML/8/2011 dated April 14, 2011 of the Permanent Mission of the People's Republic of China to the UN, from http://www.un.org/Depts/los/clcs_new/submissions_files/mysvnm33_09/chn_2011_re_phl_e.pdf, accessed on 31 July 2025.

[112] The Note Verbale from the Permanent Mission of China to the United Nations to the UN Secretary-General protesting Vietnam's actions in obstructing the operation of the HD-981 drilling rig, from https://undocs.org/A/68/907, accessed on 31 July 2025.

delimitation method used, this area does not fall under Vietnam's EEZ or continental shelf. Additionally, China presented historical evidence to support its sovereignty over the Paracel Islands.

The HD-981 oil rig incident was merely a diversion, aimed at deflecting international attention from China's concurrent land reclamation campaign on seven submerged features in the Spratly Islands. The initial justification offered by China for these activities was that "the construction work China is undertaking on relevant islands is mainly for the purpose of improving the working and living conditions of people stationed on these islands."[113] However, just one year later, on 09 April 2015, Chinese Foreign Ministry spokesperson Hua Chunying officially confirmed that China's activities were "mainly for civilian purposes," but also intended to serve "necessary military defense requirements."

On 7 December 2014, the Chinese government released the Position Paper of the Government of the People's Republic of China on the Matter of Jurisdiction in the South China Sea Arbitration Initiated by the Republic of the Philippines, pointing out that the Philippines' initiation of arbitration breaches the agreement between the two states, violates UNCLOS, and goes against the general practice of international arbitration, and that the Arbitral Tribunal has no jurisdiction.[114] The document consists of six sections and 93 articles, focusing on four main topics. Section 2 underscores that "The essence of the subject-matter of the arbitration is the territorial sovereignty over several maritime features in the South China Sea, which does not concern the interpretation or application of the Convention." Section 3 emphasizes that "There exists an agreement between China and the Philippines to settle their disputes in the South China Sea through negotiations, and the Philippines is debarred from unilaterally initiating compulsory arbitration." Section 4 highlights that even if arbitration is initiated by the Philippines on matters related to the interpretation or application of the Convention, it remains a component of maritime delimitation and is precluded by China's 2006 Declaration, thus ineligible for submission to the Arbitral Tribunal. Section 5 asserts that China's right to freely choose the means of dispute settlement must be fully respected, and its rejection of and non-participation in the present arbitration is solidly grounded in international law. The arguments presented in the Position Paper were analyzed and rejected by the Arbitral Tribunal in its 2016 Ruling. The ongoing conflict between lawfulness and lawfare, as reflected in the positions of the parties involved in the ruling, will be explored in the following sections. During this period, it is evident that China's stance has fluctuated: at times asserting territorial and maritime claims over the Paracels and Spratlys within the Nine-dash Line, and at other times claiming that these islands possess EEZs and continental shelves, regardless of the scope of the Nine-dash Line.

---

[113] Statement of Chinese Foreign Ministry spokesperson Hua Chunying on September 9th 2014. See Glaser (2015).

[114] The Position Paper of the Government of the People's Republic of China on the Matter of Jurisdiction in the South China Sea Arbitration Initiated by the Republic of the Philippines, issued on December 7, 2014, from https://english.www.gov.cn/archive/press_briefing/2014/12/07/content_281475020441708.htm, accessed on 31 July 2025.

Segment 4 (2016—present): From Deng's "Biding Time" and Hiding capabilities to Xi's "Periphery Security" and the "Cautious Shaper of a New Order": Proactively Shaping the South China Sea through China's Selective Interpretation of International Law.

During this period, China took assertive actions, including efforts to reinterpret or amend UNCLOS to align with its interests and strong opposition to the 2016 South China Sea Arbitration ruling. China employed various tactics, such as issuing diplomatic protests and introducing new concepts like the Four Sha, Nanhai Zhudao, and the Solid U-shaped Line.[115] In his statement on "Four Respects on the South China Sea Issue" on 06 August 2021, Foreign Minister Wang Yi reiterated China's stance, criticizing countries for misinterpreting the significance of the Nine-dash Line. According to him, the line merely asserts sovereignty over maritime features, while the delineation of the surrounding waters would follow China's evolving legal framework, particularly its newly introduced Four Sha claim.[116]

These new concepts were deliberately vague, allowing China to expand its maritime claims, including encroachments into areas like Indonesia's Natuna region, which the international community still considers to be non-disputed waters. Furthermore, China forcefully reiterated its position on the Nine-dash Line and the Four Sha concept, engaging in a diplomatic note exchange from 2019 to 2021 and again in 2024–2025 in response to submissions by other countries regarding the outer limits of their continental shelves in the South China Sea, reinforcing its legal warfare strategy in the region. On 10 November 2024, China announced the baselines of its territorial sea around Scarborough Shoal,[117] aiming to strengthen its claim over the South China Sea feature, which lies within the Philippines' EEZ according to the 2016 Arbitral Tribunal Ruling.[118]

Additionally, China continued to refine new national laws, such as the Coast Guard Law of China (2021)[119] and the Maritime Traffic Safety Law of the People's Republic of China (2021),[120] to regulate the behavior of foreign ships, boats, and construction activities in "sea areas under Chinese jurisdiction."[121] This move

---

[115] See section "China's Maps".

[116] Wang, Y. (2021, August 6). "Four Respect" on the South China Sea issue. Ministry of Foreign Affairs, from http://eng.chinamil.com.cn/view/2021-08/06/content_10071930.htm, accessed on 31 July 2025.

[117] Ministry of Foreign Affairs of the People's Republic of China (2024, November 10). 外交部发言人就中国政府公布黄岩岛领海基点基线答记者问 [Foreign Ministry Spokesperson Answers Reporter's Questions on the Chinese Government's Announcement of the Baseline of the Territorial Sea Baseline of Huangyan Island], from https://www.mfa.gov.cn/wjdt_674879/zcjd/202411/t20241110_11524097.shtml, accessed on 15 August 2025.

[118] Chi (2024).

[119] Law on Coast Guard of China (2021) [海警法], from https://www.chinajusticeobserver.com/law/x/coast-guard-law-of-china20210122/chn, accessed on 31 July 2025.

[120] Maritime Traffic Safety Law of the People's Republic of China, from http://www.en.npc.gov.cn.cdurl.cn/2021-04/29/c_846012.htm, accessed on 31 July 2025.

[121] Maritime Traffic Safety Law of the People's Republic of China, from http://www.en.npc.gov.cn.cdurl.cn/2021-04/29/c_846012.htm, accessed on 31 July 2025.

aimed to assert control over disputed territories and maritime areas and challenge the authority of UNCLOS, undermining its unity and integrity. China also took a leading role in negotiating a Code of Conduct (COC) in the South China Sea, aiming to divide ASEAN countries and manipulate the COC to its advantage. This approach was intended to create a Code that lacks substance and effectiveness, serving as a tool to bind ASEAN nations to China's strategic interests, rather than addressing the regional disputes effectively.

On 09 April 2025, at the Party Central Committee's Conference on Relations with Neighboring Countries, President Xi Jinping officially announced that China had entered a new strategic phase—one defined by "Periphery Security" and the role of a "Cautious Shaper of a New Order."[122] The South China Sea, Taiwan, and Hong Kong are no longer viewed merely as peripheral hotspots or components of a broader security buffer,[123] but as core geopolitical spaces vital to China's national survival. China has effectively transitioned away from Deng Xiaoping's doctrine of "biding time and hiding capabilities" and the principle of "befriend those far, contend with those near (近攻远交)."[124] It has entered a new era focused on strategic assertiveness, proactive control, and redefining regional security structures in its favor. The 9 April 2025 Declaration is not merely a policy statement; it is a clear signal that China will not back down from efforts to expand and entrench its influence in its immediate neighborhood. In August 2025, Beijing further codified this approach by unveiling the "4C" principle of Consultation, Co-management, Cooperation, and Constructiveness.[125] Although framed as a cooperative framework and presented as a continuation of earlier formulas such as "shelving disputes and pursuing joint development,"[126] the "4C" principles effectively served to legitimize China's expanding influence and provide a diplomatic veneer to its assertive strategy. Together, the April Declaration and the August "4C" principle illustrate how China pairs hardened security doctrines with soft-power narratives, combining assertive control with claims of constructive engagement.

Within this shifting strategic environment, lawfare has emerged as a central instrument in China's neighborhood diplomacy. It exemplifies the deliberate implementation of the Three Warfares doctrine—encompassing Public Opinion warfare, Psychological warfare, and Legal warfare—as Beijing seeks to assert maritime dominance and protect its broader strategic interests in the South China Sea.

[122] South China Morning Post (2025, April 9).

[123] "When dealing with neighboring countries and related issues, we need a multidimensional perspective that extends beyond the immediate confines of time and space". See Xi (2014), p. 326. See also Des Garets Geddes (2023); Smith (2019), pp. 56–84.

[124] "Befriend those far, contend with those near" (远交近攻) is a Chinese proverb. For further explanation, see 远交近攻 at OMGChinese, from https://www.omgchinese.com/dictionary/chinese/%E8%BF%9C%E4%BA%A4%E8%BF%91%E6%94%BB, accessed on 31 July 2025.

[125] Xinhua News Agency Research Institute [新华社研究院] (2025), pp. 10–14.

[126] Xinhua News Agency Research Institute [新华社研究院] (2025), p. 4.

Objectives of China's Lawfare in the South China Sea

From the main activities summarized in the section above, it is noted that China's ambition to dominate the South China Sea is driven by several key objectives. First, it seeks to assert control over approximately 80% of the South China Sea through the Nine-dash Line and Four Sha claims, extending over a large part of the continental shelf and the EEZs of neighboring countries in the region (see Fig. 2.1)[127]. Second, it aims to occupy and control all maritime features in the South China Sea, preventing foreign countries from using these features, which could pose a threat to China's security. Third, the exercise of authority over crucial sea trade routes and the assertion of control over freedom of navigation and aviation are integral to this Chinese strategy. Finally, China focuses on securing resources for itself and applying measures to enhance its ability to exploit both living and non-living resources in the South China Sea. Collectively, these objectives underscore China's strategic efforts to expand its influence and secure its geopolitical and economic interests in the region.

Apparently, because UNCLOS provides limited legal space for China's expansive claims, Beijing has increasingly turned to lawfare. Lawfare serves as a strategic tool for China, particularly in the context of its actions in the South China Sea. One of the primary objectives of employing lawfare is to shape public opinion in a manner that gradually legitimizes legal assertions which diverge from established international law. This includes claims to maritime zones based on historical rights, represented by the controversial dash lines (often referred to as the nine dotted or ten dashes line), as well as claims to islands, rocks, reefs and low-tide elevations collectively known as the Four Sha. Through lawfare, China aims to strengthen contested legal arguments and interpret UNCLOS in a way that aligns more closely with its national interests.

Another critical objective of China's use of lawfare involves establishing a legal foundation for conducting law enforcement operations in disputed maritime areas. This entails issuing justifications for actions that could restrict freedom of navigation, prohibiting military exercises by other nations, and curtailing maritime activities within waters that China perceives as under its jurisdiction. These justifications have been highlighted in recent reforms, such as the revised Coast Guard Law of China (2021) and the Maritime Traffic Safety Law of the People's Republic of China (2021). By creating a semblance of legal basis for its enforcement actions, China seeks to bolster its claims and strengthen its position in the contested waters of the South China Sea.

Moreover, managing international public opinion forms a significant aspect of China's lawfare strategy, as it aims to gain leverage in diplomatic negotiations and enhance its propaganda efforts. This multitiered approach is characterized by a dual

[127] The Note Verbale CML/17/2009 dated 07 May 2009 of the Permanent Mission of the People's Republic of China to the UN, from https://www.un.org/depts/los/clcs_new/submissions_files/mysvnm33_09/chn_2009re_mys_vnm_e.pdf, accessed on 31 July 2025.

Fig. 2.1 Map attached to the note verbale CML/17/2009 of the permanent mission of the People's Republic of China to the United Nations on 07 May 2009. *Source* UN Division for Ocean Affairs website

focus: on the one hand, China endeavors to preserve its image as a "peaceful rising" global power that promotes regional stability and fosters economic growth; on the other hand, it seeks to expand its control over the South China Sea, particularly within the scope of the disputed Nine-dash Line claim. However, these objectives often stand in opposition, necessitating the implementation of nuanced strategies comparable to the metaphorical expression of "crossing the river by feeling the stones (摸着石头过河)",[128] China thus proceeds with caution, intentionally avoiding direct confrontations while incrementally shifting the *status quo* to its advantage in the region.

These broad objectives translate into six operational directions, which combine legal, administrative, diplomatic, and coercive measures: (i) Making excessive sovereignty and maritime claims; (ii) Imposing internal regulations and administrative measures to assert sovereignty and jurisdiction over the South China Sea; (iii) Implementing control, domination, and occupation of maritime features; (iv) Utilizing diplomatic and propaganda measures to coerce and attract countries with limited interests in the South China Sea, as well as some international scholars, to support its stance; (v) Being prepared to use or threaten the use of force to prevent the activities of other countries in areas within the scope of the Nine-dash Line and Four Sha claims; and (vi) Pressuring countries with territorial claims in the South China Sea to cooperate in ways that benefit China.

Techniques of China's Lawfare in the South China Sea

China has maintained a consistent and systematic approach to lawfare in the South China Sea, utilizing both Track 1 and Track 2 diplomacy in a structured manner. Every technique employed in its legal warfare strategy is designed to reinforce China's position. This level of consistency is so pronounced that it is nearly impossible to find dissenting voices within China on issues related to the South China Sea.

In general, it is evident that China has employed multiple techniques to generate and disseminate fraudulent legal arguments. This section will examine China's lawfare techniques, categorizing them by their operational contents, forms of legal warfare, the substitution of national law for international law, and the strategic integration of legal warfare with psychological and media warfare. As this section's analytical framework is technique-driven, each subsection below may revisit the same legal issue to illustrate how different tactics have been exercised in practice.

[128] Balderton (2019).

Lawfare Techniques in Generating Fraudulent Legal Arguments

Misinterpretation of International Law Provisions and Rules

Zoppolato and Farah (2025) highlight that the political and legal institutions shaping China's distinct trajectory have focused on maintaining Chinese foundations while integrating Western knowledge, a concept encapsulated by the phrase "中体西用."[129] In the South China Sea context, China's legal warfare has interpreted certain provisions of international law in ways that serve its interests, notably in several key areas: (1) modes of acquiring territorial sovereignty, (2) historical rights, (3) the right of innocent passage for foreign military vessels in territorial waters, (4) straight baselines, and (5) dispute settlement mechanisms.

China's Interpretation and Application of Territorial Title and Modes of Acquisition

China asserts its sovereignty over island groups in the South China Sea based on the principle of discovery. The 1980 Chinese White Paper, China's Indisputable Sovereignty over the Xisha and Nansha Islands, consistently claims that Chinese fishermen were the first to discover, name, and manage the islands in the South China Sea as early as the second century BC.[130]

Regarding the initial discovery of the Paracel Islands, while there is no consensus on whether it occurred during the Xia or Han dynasties, China's argument emphasizes its earliest historical influence over the archipelago. China contends that, according to international law and historical practice dating back approximately 2100 years, sovereignty belongs to the first discoverer—namely, Chinese fishermen. On this basis, China asserts its legitimate sovereignty over the region.[131] International law recognizes discovery as an inchoate title to sovereignty; however, it requires concrete acts of state authority to establish and maintain sovereignty, which must be reinforced by subsequent acts of administration and control.[132]

The rules of law stipulate that legal provisions take effect only from the time of their establishment and cannot be applied retroactively. The 'right of discovery' theory emerged with the development of international law on territorial acquisition around the fifteenth century. However, China attempts to retroactively apply this

[129] Zoppolato and Farah (2025), pp. 1–36.

[130] "As early as the second century B.C, at the time of Emperor Wu Di of the Han dynasty, Chinese people began sailing the South China Sea. After long years of navigation, they discovered succes sively the Xisha and Nansha Islands." See Ministry of Foreign Affairs of the People's Republic of China (1980) China's Indisputable Sovereignty over the Xisha and Nansha Islands. Foreign Languages Press Beijing, p. 2, from https://www.bannedthought.net/China/MaoEra/Vietnam/China%27sIndisputableSovereignty-1980.pdf, accessed on 31 July 2025.

[131] Nguyen (2022), pp. 229–272.

[132] Pedrozo (2014), p. 8.

concept to maritime features in the South China Sea, dating back to the Qin and Han dynasties—nearly 2000 years before the concept's inception. As a result, this application lacks credibility and is unconvincing. Moreover, international law does not recognize individual actions as sufficient to establish territorial sovereignty. Additionally, historical evidence shows that various communities, including Vietnamese fishermen, the Champa people, and Filipinos, were active in the South China Sea, further undermining China's claim to exclusive rights based solely on the 'right of discovery' by Chinese fishermen.[133]

Furthermore, case law concerning territorial sovereignty disputes underscores the principle of 'effective acquisition,' emphasizing the exercise of effective control in establishing sovereignty rather than solely relying on the 'right of first discovery.' Several notable cases adjudicated by ICJ involving sovereignty disputes over archipelagos or island groups include:

1. In the case of Land, Island, and Maritime Frontier Dispute between El Salvador and Honduras (1986–1992), the contested territories included maritime features as El Tigre, Meanguera, and Meanguerita. The Chamber observed that effective possession by one of the states could constitute post-colonial *effectivité*, shedding light on the legal situation. Based on evidence of 'effective acquisition' presented by both parties, the Court awarded sovereignty over El Tigre to Honduras. Meanwhile, Meanguerita, being very small, uninhabited, and contiguous to Meanguera, was considered a "dependency" of Meanguera. Consequently, both Meanguera and Meanguerita were granted to El Salvador.[134]
2. In the case of Sovereignty over Pulau Ligitan and Pulau Sipadan (Indonesia/Malaysia) (1998–2002), the contested entities were Pulau Ligitan and Pulau Sipadan. The Court rejected Indonesia's arguments based on its *effectivités*, considering that "activities by private persons [could] not be seen as *effectivités* if they [did] not take place on the basis of official regulations or under governmental authority." In contrast, the Court found that 'the activities relied upon by Malaysia (such as the collection of turtle eggs and the construction of lighthouses on Ligitan and Sipadan in 1962–1963—author added) … [we]re modest in number but … they [we]re diverse in character and include[d] legislative, administrative and quasi-judicial acts. They cover[ed] a considerable period of time and show[ed] a pattern revealing an intention to exercise State functions in respect of the two islands in the context of the administration of a wider range of

[133] Nguyen (2022), pp. 229–272.

[134] International Court of Justice (n.d.). Land, Island and Maritime Frontier Dispute (El Salvador/Honduras: Nicaragua intervening), Overview of the case, from https://www.icj-cij.org/en/case/75, accessed on 31 July 2025.

islands.' Based on the above-mentioned *effectivités*, the Court concluded that "sovereignty over Pulau Ligitan and Pulau Sipadan belonged to Malaysia."[135]

3. In the case of Territorial and Maritime Dispute between Nicaragua and Honduras in the Caribbean Sea (Nicaragua v. Honduras) (1999–2007), the contested entities were the islands of Bobel Cay, Savanna Cay, Port Royal Cay, and South Cay. In seeking to identify any post-colonial *effectivités*, the Court determined that sovereignty over these islands belonged to Honduras. The ruling was based on evidence that Honduras had consistently applied and enforced its criminal and civil laws, regulated immigration and fisheries activities, overseen building developments, and exercised authority over public works in the area.[136]
4. In the case of Sovereignty over Pedra Branca/Pulau Batu Puteh, Middle Rocks, and South Ledge (Malaysia/Singapore) (2003–2008), the Court first recognized that the Sultanate of Johor (the predecessor of Malaysia) originally held title to Pedra Branca/Pulau Batu Puteh, a granite island where the Horsburgh Lighthouse is located. However, the Court concluded that by the time the dispute crystallized in 1980, sovereignty had passed to Singapore. This conclusion was based on the conduct of both parties, particularly Singapore's acts *à titre de souverain* and Malaysia's failure to contest Singapore's actions. Consequently, the Court awarded sovereignty over Pedra Branca/Pulau Batu Puteh to Singapore, while Middle Rocks was awarded to Malaysia. Regarding South Ledge, which lies within overlapping territorial waters of Pedra Branca/Pulau Batu Puteh and Middle Rocks, the Court determined that sovereignty belongs to the state whose territorial sea encompasses it, as it lacked authority from the parties to delimit the territorial sea."[137]
5. The case of Territorial and Maritime Dispute (Nicaragua v. Colombia) (2001–2012) concerned sovereignty over several maritime features in the Caribbean Sea—Alburquerque Cays, East-Southeast Cays, Roncador, Serrana, Quitasueño, Serranilla, and Bajo Nuevo. The Court determined that these features, being above water at high tide, qualified as islands capable of appropriation under international law. In its analysis, the ICJ assessed the parties' arguments based on *effectivités*. The Court found that Colombia had continuously and consistently exercised acts of sovereignty (*à titre de souverain*) over these maritime features for many decades. These sovereign acts were public, and there was no evidence that Nicaragua had protested them prior to 1969,

[135] International Court of Justice (n.d.). Sovereignty over Pulau Ligitan and Pulau Sipadan (Indonesia/Malaysia), Overview of the case, from https://www.icj-cij.org/en/case/102, accessed on 31 July 2025.

[136] International Court of Justice (n.d.). Territorial and Maritime Dispute between Nicaragua and Honduras in the Caribbean Sea (Nicaragua v. Honduras), Overview of the case, from https://www.icj-cij.org/en/case/120, accessed on 31 July 2025.

[137] International Court of Justice. (n.d.). Sovereignty over Pedra Branca/Pulau Batu Puteh, Middle Rocks and South Ledge (Malaysia/Singapore), Overview of the case, from https://www.icj-cij.org/en/case/130, accessed on 31 July 2025.

when the dispute crystallized. Furthermore, Colombia's administrative actions regarding the islands stood in stark contrast to Nicaragua's lack of any demonstrated *effectivités*. Based on this reasoning, the Court concluded that sovereignty over Alburquerque, Bajo Nuevo, East-Southeast Cays, Quitasueño, Roncador, Serrana, and Serranilla belonged to Colombia, not Nicaragua.[138]

Overall, all Court rulings have been consistent in recognizing *effectivités* as the decisive factor in determining territorial sovereignty (*à titre de souverain*) disputes. There has been no ruling that acknowledges discovery alone as a basis for establishing territorial sovereignty.

China's Misuse of Historical Rights in Maritime Claims[139]

China's interpretation of historical rights has evolved over time. Initially, it focused solely on sovereignty over disputed islands, later expanding to claim EEZs and continental shelves stemming from these islands. However, these zones did not fully cover the South China Sea. Subsequently, China shifted its strategy to assert "historic rights" via the Nine-dash Line claim, without specifying whether it pertained to islands, waters, or both. Following the rejection of the Nine-dash Line by the Arbitral Award in 2016, China introduced the concept of Four Sha or Nanhai Zhudao,[140] claiming all features in the South China Sea and demanding a 200-nautical-mile boundary from them. This aligns with the archipelagic baseline theory, which extends to offshore island groups. Chinese scholars also advocate for a continuous boundary line based on the Nine-dash Line or Ten-dash Line theory, treating it as a maritime border from which to expand into other sea areas.[141]

From the perspectives of Chinese Scholars, both China's old claim (Nine-dash Line) and its new claim (Four Sha), emphasize the historical aspect. However, the Chinese government has never provided a clear explanation of the concept behind the Nine-dash Line or the Four Sha, leaving ambiguity about whether it claims islands, waters, or both. Chinese scholars have been mobilized to construct arguments for legal and media warfare. China asserts that it holds historical rights in the South China Sea, which it argues are "recognized" under general international law, rather than under UNCLOS. As a result, China believes it has the right to claim resources in the South China Sea, alongside other maritime regulations outlined in UNCLOS. To align with political objectives, Chinese scholars offer varying explanations of the meaning behind the Nine-dash Line and "historical rights", which can be categorized into three main arguments:

---

[138] International Court of Justice. (n.d.). Territorial and Maritime Dispute (Nicaragua v. Colombia), Overview of the case, from https://www.icj-cij.org/en/case/124, accessed on 31 July 2025.

[139] See section "The Strategy of "Turning Nothing into Something" (化无为有): A Legal and Political Art of War".

[140] See section "China's Maps".

[141] Wood (2021). See section "Legal Confrontation on Maps and the Rectification of Information".

The first argument posits that China's primary objective is to establish sovereignty over maritime features within the Nine-dash Line, using this as the foundation to claim relevant maritime areas in accordance with the provisions of UNCLOS. Scholars such as Li Jinming and Li Dexia (2003) argue that over several decades, the Chinese government has consistently asserted its domestic laws regarding the islands situated within the Nine-dash Line as part of Chinese territory. Over this prolonged period, China may have acquired historical rights over these islands.[142] This argument focuses solely on the Nine-dash Line's claim to sovereignty over specific features and does not extend to maritime areas beyond them.

The second argument highlights that the notion of "historical rights" differs from that of historical waters or historical bays, asserting that the waters encompassed by the Nine-dash Line constitute China's historical EEZ. As such, proponents argue that these waters should be subject to regulations akin to those governing EEZs under UNCLOS. This argument primarily pertains to maritime claims within the Nine-dash Line.[143]

The third argument is articulated by a faction of scholars who emphasize the historical foundation of China's rights in the South China Sea. However, they do not explicitly specify whether these rights pertain to maritime features, maritime zones, or both. For instance, Hao (2011) asserts, "China's claim to rights and interests in the South China Sea is based on historical rights and international law."[144] Similarly, Pan (1996) posits that "The Nine-dash Line drawn on China's map is a sign that defines China's historical title."[145] Gao and Jia argue that it is essential to understand that it would be reasonable to conclude the Nine-dash Line represents a claim to sovereignty over all maritime features within it, all rights under UNCLOS attaching to those features, and in addition, "historic rights … in respect of fishing, navigation, and exploration and exploitation of resources'."[146]

China's propaganda strategy seeks to reconcile historical rights claims with UNCLOS regulations, attempting to fuse these two concepts despite their contradictory implications. This represents a significant challenge for China, as it attempts to reconcile these differing legal frameworks while advancing its territorial ambitions.

The interpretation of "historic rights" must meet two criteria to be considered valid: firstly, China must have established legal historical rights in waters beyond the 12-nautical-mile zone of the disputed islands before UNCLOS was enacted; secondly, these historical rights must align with the principles outlined in the Convention. Even if traditional fishing practices contribute to the establishment of some historical rights, it is important to note that China is not the sole claimant

142 Li and Li (2003), p. 209.

143 Zou (2021), p. 160.

144 Su (2011).

145 Pan (1996), p. 61.

146 Gao and Jia (2013), pp. 98–124.

to such rights. The Arbitration Tribunal rejected the historicity of the Nine-dash Line, arguing that even if China had established historical rights, they would be superseded by the provisions of the Convention.[147] In a Note Verbale written in 2021 New Zealand observed that, "There is no legal basis for states to claim 'historic rights' with respect to maritime areas in the South China Sea, as confirmed in the 2016 South China Sea Arbitral Award."[148] As a member of UNCLOS, China is bound by its provisions. Consequently, the Tribunal dismissed China's Nine-dash Line claim in the South China Sea.

The Right of Innocent Passage and China's Stance on Foreign Military Vessels in Its Territorial Waters[149]

Under UNCLOS, foreign vessels, including warships, enjoy the right of innocent passage through a coastal state's territorial sea. This right is recognized as customary international law. Foreign vessels can exercise innocent passage within the territorial sea of a coastal state without requiring prior permission or the need to justify their passage. ITLOS also clarified this provision in its Provisional Measures Order issued in the Case Concerning the Detention of Three Ukrainian Naval Vessels (2019), stating that: "Under the Convention, passage regimes, such as innocent or transit passage, apply to all ships."[150]

However, China's 1992 Law on Territorial Sea and Contiguous Zone Article 5 stipulates that foreign military ships must obtain prior permission from the Chinese government before entering its territorial waters.[151] Some Chinese scholars justify this regulation by arguing that coastal states have the right to safeguard national security interests and regulate innocent passage, including requiring notification or permission from foreign military vessels before entering territorial waters, or suspending passage when necessary, in accordance with Articles 19, 25, and 30

---

[147] "The Tribunal concludes that, as between the Philippines and China, China's claims to historic rights, or other sovereign rights or jurisdiction, with respect to the maritime areas of the South China Sea encompassed by the relevant part of the 'nine-dash line' are contrary to the Convention and without lawful effect to the extent that they exceed the geographic and substantive limits of China's maritime entitlements under the Convention. The Tribunal concludes that the Convention superseded any historic rights or other sovereign rights or jurisdiction in excess of the limits imposed therein." See PCA Case No. 2013-19, the matter of the South China Sea Arbitration (Philippines v. China), Award of 12 July 2016, paras. 277–278, from https://pcacases.com/web/sendAttach/2086, accessed on 31 July 2025.

[148] The Note Verbale No. 08/21/02 dated 3 August 2021 from the Permanent Mission of New Zealand to the United Nations addressed to the Secretary-General of the United Nations, from https://www.un.org/depts/los/clcs_new/submissions_files/mys_12_12_2019/20210803NzNote.pdf, accessed on 31 July 2025.

[149] See also section "The Tactic of Double Standards in China's Lawfare".

[150] ITLOS, Case Concerning the Detention of Three Ukrainian Naval Vessels (Ukraine v. Russian Federation), Provisional Measures Order, May 25, 2019, para. 68.

[151] "Foreign ships for military purposes shall be subject to approval by the Government of the People's Republic of China for entering the territorial sea of the People's Republic of China." See Article 5 of China's 1992 Law on Territorial Sea and Contiguous Zone, from https://faolex.fao.org/docs/pdf/chn11830.pdf, accessed on 31 July 2025.

of UNCLOS. In addition, the revised Maritime Traffic Safety Law of the People's Republic of China, which came into effect on 01 September 2021, introduces new reporting requirements for five categories of ships, mandating them to notify the Chinese Maritime Administration upon entering China's territorial waters. Notably, Article 2 of the Maritime Traffic Safety Law expands the law's scope from "coastal waters" to "sea areas under the jurisdiction of the People's Republic of China." However, this term is not explicitly defined in the legislation, leaving its meaning deliberately ambiguous. It is likely intended to encompass all waters and seabed areas: (1) within the Nine-dash Line in the South China Sea, (2) extending to the Okinawa Trough in the East China Sea, and (3) beyond Ieodo (Socotra Rock) in the Yellow Sea.[152] In China's Note of Objection to New Zealand's Note (August 2021), China acknowledged that countries can exercise freedom of navigation and the right of innocent passage in a coastal state's territorial sea and other seas. However, China strongly opposes any actions by States that violate a coastal state's sovereignty or national security under the pretext of 'freedom of navigation' or the 'right of innocent passage'.[153]

China's Interpretation of "Straight Baseline"

China, as a continental State, has the option to employ two methods for determining the baselines from which the breadth of its territorial sea is measured: (i) the normal baseline, as defined in Article 5 of UNCLOS, and (ii) straight baselines, as provided under Article 7 of UNCLOS, subject to specific conditions stipulated by the Convention. In its Declaration of the Government of the People's Republic of China on China's Territorial Sea, issued on 4 September 1958, China reserved the right to use the straight lines joining each of the base points on the mainland coast and on the outermost of its coastal islands as the baselines for measuring the breadth of the territorial sea of the mainland and its coastal islands.[154] However, in its Declaration of the Government of the People's Republic of China on the Baselines of the Territorial Sea, dated 15 May 1996, China shifted its approach and applied the method of delineating archipelagic-style baselines to the Paracel Islands (see Fig. 2.2).[155] The Paracel Islands comprise about a dozen small islands and reefs scattered over an area approximately 120 miles by 100 miles. The largest islands in the Paracels, Woody Island and Pattle Island, are only 1.62 km^2 (400 acres) and

---

[152] Pedrozo (2021), pp. 956–957.

[153] The Note Verbale CML/32/2021 dated 16 August 2021 of the Permanent Mission of the People's Republic of China to the UN, from https://www.un.org/depts/los/clcs_new/submissions_files/mys_12_12_2019/20210816ChnNvUNen.pdf, accessed on 31 July 2025.

[154] Declaration of the Government of the People's Republic of China on China's Territorial Sea, 4 September 1958, from https://www.s3.documentcloud.org/documents/1341822/declaration-of-the-government-of-the-prc-on.pdf, accessed on 31 July 2025.

[155] Declaration of the Government of the People's Republic of China on the baselines of the territorial sea, 15 May 1996, from https://www.un.org/Depts/los/LEGISLATIONANDTREATIES/PDFFILES/CHN_1996_Declaration.pdf, accessed on 31 July 2025.

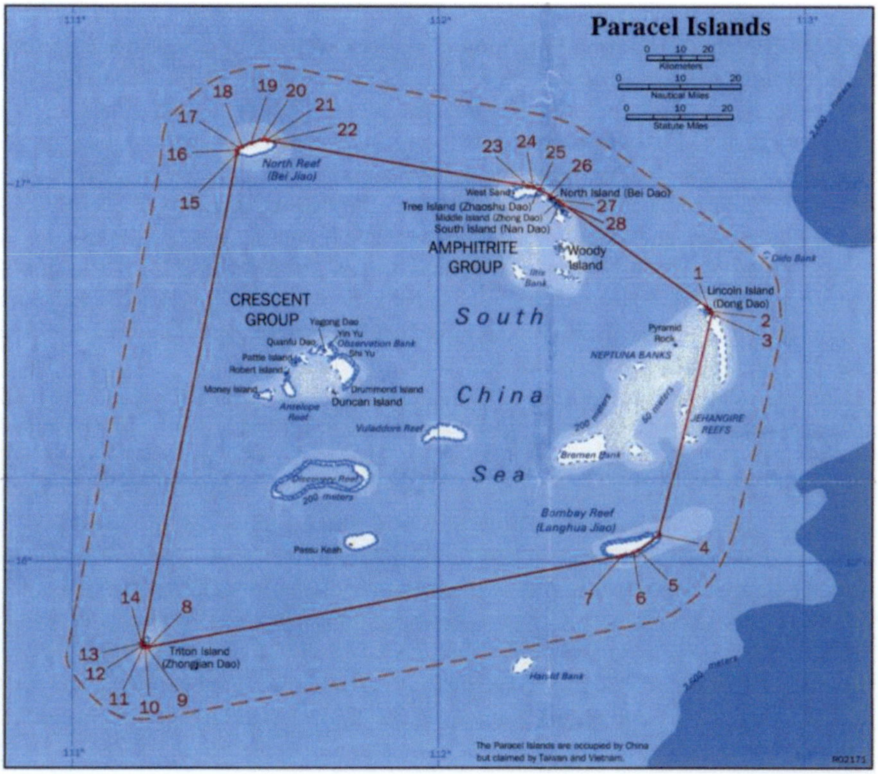

Fig. 2.2 The Chinese baseline (in red) around Paracel Islands. *Source* The U.S. Department of State, Limits in the Sea No. 117—Straight baseline: China, p. 18[158]

0.26 km^2 (64 acres), respectively.[156] China employed 28 base points connecting the outermost points of the outermost islands and features of the offshore archipelago, thereby enclosing a maritime area of approximately 17,000 km^2. This approach was applied unilaterally, treating the offshore archipelago as if it were part of an archipelagic State, regardless of whether it conformed to established international legal practices concerning archipelagic or continental States.[157]

Even if China were to draw such baselines, it would not satisfy the ratio requirement for water to land area as stipulated in Article 47(1) of UNCLOS. This provision permits an archipelagic State to draw straight archipelagic baselines connecting the outermost points of the outermost islands and drying reefs of an archipelago, provided that the baselines enclose the main islands and the ratio of the area of

[156] U.S. Department of State (2020). Limits in the Sea No. 117—Straight baselines: China (p. 8), from https://www.state.gov/wp-content/uploads/2020/01/LIS-117.pdf, accessed on 31 July 2025.

[157] Nguyen (2020), pp. 77–104.

[158] The U.S. Department of State, Limits in the Sea No. 117—Straight baseline: China, p. 18, from https://www.state.gov/wp-content/uploads/2020/01/LIS-117.pdf, accessed on 31 July 2025.

water to the area of land—including atolls—falls between 1:1 and 9:1. In the case of the Paracel Islands, the total land area does not exceed 10 km^2, dispersed over a maritime area of approximately 17,000 km^2. As such, China's claim fails to meet the legal criteria for drawing archipelagic baselines under UNCLOS.[159] China has previously revealed its intention to potentially apply the archipelagic baseline method to the Four Sha island groups. On 10 November 2024, the Chinese government delimited and announced the baselines of the territorial sea adjacent to Scarborough Shoal (Huangyan Dao) (see Fig. 2.3).[160] This move is widely viewed as a response to the Philippine Maritime Zones Act, enacted on 07 November 2024.[161] A similar strategy may be applied to the Spratly Islands. It should be recalled that the total land area of the islands in the Spratlys is no more than 10 km^2, scattered across a maritime area of approximately 1,60,000 km^2.

Chinese scholars have prominently featured the argument that an international customary law exists allowing mainland countries to draw straight baselines toward offshore archipelagos, as discussed in numerous domestic and international scholarly works. Notably, the Chinese Society of International Law (CSIL) presented this argument in South China Sea: A Critical Study (2018).[162] To bolster their position, the Chinese Association of International Law cited 17 instances where it claimed countries had drawn special baselines for offshore archipelagos. Following this, the Chinese Government has supported the assertion that such a customary law exists. In the Note CML/63/2020, dated 18 September 2021, in response to protests from France, Germany, and the UK, China explicitly affirmed that "the long established practice in international law related to continental States' outlying archipelagos shall be respected. The drawing of territorial sea baselines by China on relevant islands and reefs in the South China Sea conforms to UNCLOS and general international."[163]

However, this argument is flawed. The number of continental states that have applied the archipelagic baseline method to such island groups is exceedingly limited, with most of these practices occurring prior to UNCLOS coming into force and since undergoing revision. Furthermore, during the UNCLOS negotiation process, the possibility of applying archipelagic baselines to island groups of

[159] Dzurek (1996), pp. 77–87.

[160] Ministry of Foreign Affairs of the People's Republic of China (2024, November 10). Foreign Ministry Spokesperson's remarks on China's release of the baselines and base points of the territorial sea adjacent to Huangyan Dao, from https://www.fmprc.gov.cn/eng/xw/fyrbt/202411/t20241110_11524122.html, accessed on 31 July 2025.

[161] Republic of the Philippines (2024, November 7) Republic Act No. 12064—An Act declaring the maritime zones under the jurisdiction of the Republic of the Philippines, from https://www.lawphil.net/statutes/repacts/ra2024/ra_12064_2024.html, accessed on 31 July 2025.

[162] Chinese Society of International Law (2018) South China Sea: A Critical Study. Oxford University Press, from https://www.mfa.gov.cn/eng/wjb/zzjg_663340/bianhaisi_eng_665278/plpbo/202406/P020240606690256291745.pdf, accessed on 31 July 2025.

[163] The Note Verbale CML/63/2020 dated 18 September 2020 of The Permanent Mission of the People's Republic of China to the UN on, from https://www.un.org/Depts/los/clcs_new/submissions_files/mys_12_12_2019/2020_09_18_CHN_NV_UN_009_e.pdf, accessed on 31 July 2025.

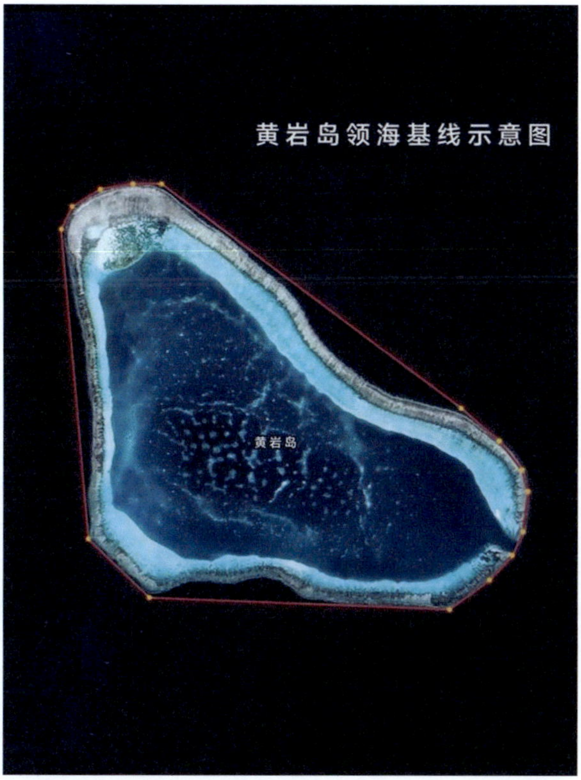

Fig. 2.3 The Chinese baseline (in red) around Scarborough Shoal in the South China Sea. *Source* China Central Television via BenarNews[164]

continental states was considered but ultimately rejected. This argument has been met with opposition from other nations. When China declared the establishment of straight baselines around the Paracel Islands in 1996 and the Senkaku Islands in 2012, countries with vested interests, such as Vietnam and Japan, promptly lodged protests. The U.S., a non-regional state, also objected.[165]

Notably, certain countries such as the United Kingdom, France, and Australia (referenced in China's cited list) have strongly opposed such purported customary

[164] RFA Staff (2024, November 12) Beijing draws baselines around shoal in Manila's jurisdiction to fortify claims. The Jakarta Post, from https://www.thejakartapost.com/world/2024/11/12/beijing-draws-baselines-around-shoal-in-manilas-jurisdiction-to-fortify-claims.html, accessed on 16 August 2025.

[165] The U.S. Department of State, Limits in the Sea No 117—Straight baseline: China, p.8, from https://www.state.gov/wp-content/uploads/2020/01/LIS-117.pdf, accessed on 31 July 2025. See also The U.S. Department of State, Limits in the Sea No 150 People's Republic of China: Maritime Claims in the South China Sea, from https://www.state.gov/wp-content/uploads/2022/01/LIS150-SCS.pdf, accessed on 31 July 2025.

international rules in diplomatic notes exchanged during the 2019–2022 note battle.[166] In actual fact, the 2016 South China Sea Arbitral Award noted that "in the Tribunal's view, any application of straight baselines to the Spratly Islands in this fashion would be contrary to the Convention."[167] Accordingly, the application of the archipelagic baseline method to offshore islands constitutes a misinterpretation of UNCLOS provisions and does not give rise to international customary law, contrary to China's assertions.

China's Interpretation of Dispute Resolution Mechanisms

China's interpretation of dispute resolution mechanisms in the South China Sea reflects a deliberate effort to reframe international legal obligations in ways that align with its strategic interests.

China consistently reiterates that disputes in the South China Sea should be resolved through "bilateral friendly consultations"[168] with the states directly concerned. In Beijing's view, this approach represents the most appropriate mechanism for addressing maritime differences, as it avoids the involvement of outside actors. China argues that any form of "external intervention"[169] only "complicates matters,"[170] creating unnecessary tensions, hardening positions, and undermining the prospects of compromise. By advancing this narrative, China frames itself as a responsible power committed to peace while simultaneously steering the process toward a forum where the asymmetry of power favors its position. In this discourse, China stresses that it and the "relevant countries"[171] possess both the capability and the confidence to properly manage their disputes, thereby guaranteeing "long-term peace and stability in the South China Sea."[172] Yet behind this rhetoric lies a strategic purpose: by promoting "bilateral friendly consultations"[173] and rejecting third-party adjudication or multilateral mechanisms, China seeks to shape the rules of engagement, marginalize international law institutions, and maintain control over the trajectory of dispute settlement.

In the South China Sea case, China consistently maintained its stance of non-participation and non-recognition of the jurisdiction of the Arbitral Tribunal established under Annex VII of UNCLOS, despite being a member of the convention.[174] However, UNCLOS is considered a "package" Convention, encompassing

---

166 Nguyen (2020), pp. 77–104.

167 PCA Case No. 2013-19, the matter of the South China Sea Arbitration (Philippines v. China), Award, para. 575, from https://www.docs.pca-cpa.org/2016/07/PH-CN-20160712-Award.pdf, accessed on 31 July 2025.

168 Xinhua News Agency Research Institute [新华社研究院] (2025), p. 15.

169 Xinhua News Agency Research Institute [新华社研究院] (2025), p. 15.

170 Xinhua News Agency Research Institute [新华社研究院] (2025), p. 15.

171 Xinhua News Agency Research Institute [新华社研究院] (2025), p. 15.

172 Xinhua News Agency Research Institute [新华社研究院] (2025), p. 15.

173 Xinhua News Agency Research Institute [新华社研究院] (2025), p. 15.

174 The Position Paper of the Government of the People's Republic of China on the Matter of Jurisdiction in the South China Sea Arbitration Initiated by the Republic of the Philippines, issued

a mandatory dispute resolution mechanism. Article 300 of the Convention mandates that States Parties shall fulfill in good faith the obligations assumed under this Convention and shall exercise the rights, jurisdiction and freedoms recognized in this Convention in a manner which would not constitute an abuse of right. Accordingly, China's aforementioned arguments were dismissed by the Arbitral Tribunal in two rulings on 29 October 2015,[175] and 12 July 2016.[176]

The Tactic of Double Standards in China's Lawfare

China consistently interprets the same provisions of law to maximize its rights while minimizing its obligations towards other countries. This approach is evident in various legal issues, including: (1) the legal status of islands deemed uninhabitable; (2) the right of innocent passage for warships in territorial waters; and (3) foreign military activities in the EEZ of a coastal state.

First, legal status of uninhabitable features.[177] In disputes with Japan, China acknowledges Okinotorishima as merely a rock, devoid of the characteristics of an island, and thus contends it has no EEZ or continental shelf.[178] Consequently, China rejects Japan's assertion of such zones around Okinotorishima.[179] Conversely, in the South China Sea, China claims EEZs and separate continental shelves for the Paracel and Spratly Islands, despite their comparable size to or smaller than Okinotorishima, and their inability to sustain economic life.[180] Furthermore, China asserts sovereignty over submerged features in Macclesfield Bank, contending that even these formations warrant EEZs and continental shelves.

Second, the right of innocent passage of warships in territorial waters. China mandates that foreign military vessels seek permission when entering its territorial waters, yet Chinese military vessels enter other countries' territorial waters without seeking such permission. For instance, in 2015, five Chinese navy ships traversed the territorial waters of the Aleutian Islands near Alaska, USA, without prior approval from the US, as required by China in its own territorial waters in the South China Sea.[181] Likewise, the Chinese Navy has frequently conducted innocent

on December 7, 2014, from https://english.www.gov.cn/archive/press_briefing/2014/12/07/content_281475020441708.htm, accessed on 31 July 2025.

[175] See Table 4.1 in Section "China's Lawfare Strategy in Response to the 2016 Award". PCA Case No. 2013-19, the matter of the South China Sea Arbitration (Philippines v. China), Judgment on Jurisdiction and Admission of Case dated 29 October 2015, from https://pcacases.com/web/sendAttach/2579, accessed on 31 July 2025.

[176] PCA Case No. 2013-19, South China Sea Arbitration, Award of 12 July 2016, from https://docs.pca-cpa.org/2016/07/PH-CN-20160712-Award.pdf, accessed 30 March 2025.

[177] UNCLOS, Article 121(3).

[178] Herbert Smith Freehills (2012). See also Song (2009), p. 145.

[179] Global Times (2012).

[180] Nguyen (2011), p. 26.

[181] Page and Lubold (2015).

passage through the English Channel without obtaining prior permission from either the United Kingdom or France. Another example is the enactment of the revised Maritime Traffic Safety Law in 2021, as previously discussed. Beijing has leveraged the pretext of maritime safety to impose additional obligations on foreign vessels exercising the right of innocent passage through its territorial waters—obligations that go beyond what is stipulated in UNCLOS.

Third, regarding foreign military activities in the EEZ of a coastal state, while China has not explicitly addressed the necessity for permission regarding such activities, its stance has been evident through past responses. For instance, in the case of the U.S. ship USNS Impeccable operating in the South China Sea in 2009, Chinese Foreign Ministry's spokesperson Ma Zhaoxu stated:

> China has lodged a protest to the United States as the USNS Impeccable conducted the activities [...] without China's permission, [...] We demand that the United States immediately stop such activities and take effective measures to prevent similar acts from recurring.[182]

Meanwhile, the U.S. firmly believes that China's attempts to restrict foreign military activities and the right of innocent passage of foreign warships in the South China Sea violate the principles of maritime freedom under international law.[183] China frequently criticizes the activities of U.S. military ships when operating within what China considers its "EEZ".[184] However, in the EEZs of other countries, China still invokes international law to justify its right to conduct military activities. For instance, in 2017 and 2018, the Chinese navy deployed a Type 815 Auxiliary General Intelligence vessel for surveillance and reconnaissance in the Talisman Saber region of Australia. And since 2017, the U.S. Coast Guard has released several photos showing Chinese navy ships frequently entering the U.S. EEZ near the Aleutian Islands in the state of Alaska.[185]

In December 2016, a Chinese naval vessel seized a U.S. Navy unmanned underwater vehicle (UUV) being operated by the USNS Bowditch approximately 50 nautical miles northwest of Subic Bay in the Philippines' EEZ. The U.S. immediately protested, emphasizing that the unmanned underwater vehicle (UUV) was a "sovereign immune vessel"[186] conducting lawful oceanographic research in

---

[182] Li (2009).

[183] Buckley (2009).

[184] Ministry of Foreign Affairs of the People's Republic of China (2002, September 26). Foreign Ministry Spokeswoman's Press Conference on September 26, 2002, from https://www.fmprc.gov.cn/ce/cegr/eng/ztlm/lxjzzdh/zdh2002/zdh200209/t145965.htm, accessed on 31 July 2025.

[185] Nelson (2024).

[186] Cook, P. (2016, December 20). Statement by Pentagon Press Secretary Peter Cook on Return of U.S. Navy Unmanned Underwater Vehicle. U.S. Department of Defense, from https://www.pacom.mil/Media/News/News-Article-View/Article/1035113/statement-by-pentagon-press-secretary-peter-cook-on-return-of-us-navy-unmanned/, accessed on 31 July 2025.

international waters and demanding its prompt return. China, while later agreeing to return the drone, framed its action as a response to navigational safety concerns and criticized U.S. close-in reconnaissance activities in the South China Sea.[187] The incident underscored the divergent legal positions of the two states: Washington invoked sovereign immunity under UNCLOS, while Beijing sought to legitimize its actions by portraying the seizure as defensive and precautionary.[188]

Then, in January-February 2023, the two nations encountered another incident involving a Chinese hot air balloon flying in the skies above the U.S.[189] On 04 February 2023, a Chinese hot air balloon was shot down off the coast of the U.S. state of South Carolina. The U.S. contends that the Chinese balloon, suspected of being deployed for reconnaissance purposes, "clearly violated" U.S. sovereignty as well as international law. However, in response to U.S. criticism, China asserted that the balloon was merely a "civilian" craft that accidentally drifted into U.S. airspace.[190]

The Strategy of "Turning Nothing into Something" (化无为有): A Legal and Political Art of War

"Turning nothing into something" (化无为有) is indeed one of the 36 strategies outlined in Sun Tzu's ancient treatise The Art of War, dating back to 512 B.C. Beyond its military applications, China has adapted this strategy to legal battles, demonstrating a willingness to assert novel claims, amalgamate them intricately, surpass conventional international legal frameworks, and at times even fabricate evidence to bolster its sovereignty arguments.

China's fraudulent or fabricated evidence. The majority of historical documents cited by China in support of its maritime claims are unofficial in nature. These sources primarily consist of scattered accounts from sea voyages and compilations by private individuals, rather than formal state records.[191] Frequently cited

[187] Xinhua (2016, December 18). See also U.S. Confronts China over Seizure of Unmanned Drone in the South China Sea (2017), pp. 513–517.

[188] Ku (2016). See also Kraska and Pedrozo (2016).

[189] BBC News (2023, February 3).

[190] Al Jazeera & News Agencies (2023, February 4).

[191] China has a long tradition of systematically collecting and organizing its historical records. The official dynastic histories, often called the Standard Histories (正史), detail the recognized dynasties in Chinese history and have served as authoritative references for scholarly study and imperial examinations. Foremost among these works are the "Twenty-Four Histories" (二十四史), beginning with Sima Qian's Records of the Grand Historian (史记) and continuing through later texts such as the History of Ming (明史). In addition, there are thirteen supplementary histories, which expand upon or refine the narratives found in the Standard Histories. See Pham H Q (2014). See also Regencia (2020).

unofficial texts by Chinese scholars.[192] Although these texts occasionally mention offshore features such as "magnetic stones" or "exotic things" in the sea, they lack precise geographic references or measurable distances from the mainland. As such, they offer no solid scientific or legal basis for asserting that the locations described are indeed the Paracel Islands, Spratly Islands, or Macclesfield Bank, or that these areas have been under Chinese sovereignty for over two millennia.[193] These unofficial records have nonetheless been extrapolated and retroactively interpreted to form legal arguments, often in at least three problematic ways: first, by arbitrarily matching ancient place names with modern geographical features; second, by treating mentions of maritime activity as evidence of continuous state administration; and third, by overlooking the absence of formal state authority or official cartographic documentation at the time of the original recordings.

Place names cited in support of China's maritime claims often vary considerably and lack consistency, rendering their annotation both forced and devoid of verifiable authenticity. Terms such as *Jiurulozhou*, *Wanlizhitang*, *Wanlichengsha*, *Qianlishitang*, *Qizhouyang*, and *Qizhousan* appear inconsistently across historical sources, making it difficult for foreign researchers to interpret their meaning or verify their geographic relevance. Chinese authors have frequently failed to provide precise coordinates or consistent nomenclature for the islands in question. For example, a comprehensive compilation edited by Han Zhenhua extensively cites quotations to support the historical assertions made in China's 1980 White Paper. However, this document significantly diverges from original historical texts and reflects selective interpretation of the sources.[194] The resulting lack of clarity has led to ongoing variations in translation and considerable scholarly disagreement regarding the identification and meaning of these terms. Moreover, many of the place names have been shown to be later inventions—translations, transliterations, or names derived from ships or explorers—thereby undermining their value as reliable historical evidence.[195] Ultimately, vague and inconsistent references to ancient place names cannot serve as a legitimate basis for establishing sovereignty under contemporary standards of international law.

---

[192] Nan Zhou Yi Wu Zhi [Strange Things of the South, Jin Dynasty (265–419 A.D)] by Wan Zhen Fu Nan Zhuan [Phu Nam Story] by Kang Tai, from the Three Kingdoms—Wu (220–280 A.D) Yi Wu Zhi [Memories of Marvellous Things] by Yang Fu (Eastern Han period, 25–220 A.D.) Ling Wai Dai Da [Information on What is Beyond the Passes] by Zhou Chufei (Song Dynasty, 1178) Zhu Fan Zhi [Notes on Foreigners] by Zhao Ruguo (Song Dynasty, 1225) Dao Ji Zhi Lue [General Survey of the Islands] by Wang Dayuan (Yuan Dynasty, 1349) Dong Xi Yang Kao [Study of the Eastern and Western Oceans] by Zhang Xie (1618) Wu Bei Zhi [Treatise on Armament Technology] by Mao Yuanyi (1628), referencing Zheng He's voyages (1405–1433) Haiguo Wenjian Lu [Things Seen and Heard in Overseas Countries] by Chen Lunjiong (1730, Qing Dynasty) Hai Lu [Notes on Sea Voyages] by Yang Bingnan (1820) Haiguo Tuzhi [Illustrated Treatise on the Maritime Kingdoms] by Wei Yuan (1841–1852) Yinghuan Zhilue [Brief Survey of the Maritime Circuit] by Xu Jishe (1848).

[193] Phan et al. (2020). See also Wood (2021); Grady (2016).

[194] 韩振华 (1988).

[195] Hayton (2018). See also Jacobs (2014).

Descriptions and calculations of navigation time mentioned in historical documents are unlikely to refer to the Paracel Islands but may pertain only to islands along the coast of Hainan Island.[196] This discrepancy could be attributed partly to limitations in contemporary science and technology, which made it challenging to accurately identify and delineate places mentioned in the documents.

Moreover, descriptions found in historical Chinese documents often refer to neighboring "barbarian" territories without offering a clear delineation of China's sovereign borders. Several titles explicitly suggest that, even if the Paracel Islands are referenced, these areas were still perceived as "foreign" in the context of the Chinese empire.[197] According to Li Zhun, a Chinese researcher, as early as 1933, he acknowledged that "the territorial sea was not a prime concern in Chinese history. Consequently, China has neither the nautical charts nor the knowledge of foreign invasions of nearby islands for thousands of years."[198] Such references highlight the lack of any formal or effective administration over the Paracels and Spratlys, undermining China's sovereignty claims.[199] French legal scholar Chemillier-Gendreau (1996) emphasizes that these documents merely reflect a general awareness of distant places, without providing the kind of evidence necessary to substantiate territorial sovereignty under international law.[200]

While the ICJ permits parties in a dispute to submit any evidence they consider pertinent, it remains vigilant in preserving the integrity of proceedings by rejecting fraudulent submissions. A telling example is the case Maritime Delimitation and Territorial Questions between Qatar and Bahrain (Qatar v. Bahrain),[201] where Qatar submitted 82 documents that were later exposed as false and promptly withdrawn when Bahrain challenged their authenticity, in response, the Court excluded them from consideration, underscoring that procedural openness does not extend to fabricated evidence.[202]

Hainan Island as the Chinese southernmost point in official Chinese historiography. The territorial borders of countries are constantly evolving over time, and China is no exception, having undergone changes across various dynasties. However, a consistent element in China's official historical records concerning territorial boundaries is the assertion that the southernmost point of the country is

---

[196] Pedrozo (2014), p. 67.

[197] For example, texts such as A Record of Strange Things in Jiaozhou (交州异物志), attributed to Yang Fu (杨孚) of the Eastern Han Dynasty; A Record of Strange Things in the Southern Region (南州异物志), attributed to Wan Zhen (万震) of the Three Kingdoms period; and A Treatise on the Various Barbarians (诸蕃志) by Zhao Rushi (赵汝适) of the Song Dynasty, primarily describe territories outside the authors' own domains. These sources indicate that the islands in question were regarded as lying "beyond the borders" of Chinese territory.

[198] Li (1933), pp. 1–8.

[199] Nguyen (2012), pp. 165–211.

[200] Chemillier-Gendreau (1996), pp. 58–62.

[201] Maritime Delimitation and Territorial Questions between Qatar and Bahrain, Merits, Judgment, ICJ Reports 2001, p. 64–65, para 200–204.

[202] Rose (2016), pp. 329–332.

Hainan Island (see Fig. 2.4). Official historical texts[203] all describe the southernmost border of China as extending only to Hainan Island, with no mention of offshore archipelagos like the Paracel or Spratly Islands as part of its administrative territory.[204] It was not until the twentieth century that the southernmost point of China began to shift in accordance with its newly asserted territorial claims.[205] It should be noted that it was only in 1935–1936 that the names "Nansha" (南沙) and "Tuansha" (團沙) first appeared on Chinese maps. At that time, "Nansha", meaning "southern sands", referred to the Macclesfield Bank, while "Tuansha", loosely translated as "area of sand", was used for the Spratly Islands. From 1939 onwards, the designation "Nansha" began to be used for Vietnam's Truong Sa (Spratly Islands). The name "Tuansha" disappeared from usage, and the Macclesfield Bank was subsequently renamed "Zhongsha" (中沙).[206]

Over approximately 2000 years, Chinese political history has maintained persistent and continuous documentation of the geographical landscape within the nation and its surrounding regions, presenting a significant advantage. These historical records exhibit a remarkable degree of stability and consistency, with distinct sections dedicated to different aspects. While the quantity of records may vary across different periods, there exists a cohesive framework in terms of administrative geography. Importantly, historical documentation reveals that the Chinese state has historically administered lands and territories up to Yai County, Hainan island.

According to the Book of Han (汉书), during the Han Dynasty's peak, its territory extended to encompass Vietnam, with the region along the South China Sea divided into seven districts, two of which were situated north of Hainan Island. However, the unique manner in which these two Hainan Island districts were recorded is noteworthy—they were not included in the Geography section detailing the areas governed directly by the Han Dynasty's central government. Instead, they were documented separately within the section detailing Vietnamese customs.[207] This distinction suggests that while the dynasty exerted control over mainland territories along the South China Sea, Hainan Island remained beyond its direct administration, despite being recognized. Consequently, this historical context adds complexity to China's efforts to assert sovereignty over smaller islands further south, such as the Paracels. Furthermore, the Book Later Han indicates that the Eastern Han Dynasty's management of land was less extensive than that of

[203] Such as the Book of Han (汉书), Xin Tang Shu (新唐书), Yuan Shi (元史), and Ming Shi (明史), as well as maps from various Chinese feudal periods such as Qīng Huìdiǎnzhī Huángdiǎn Yútú 1899 (清会典之皇舆全图 1899, Complete Imperial Map of the Qīng 1899, Huángcháo Zhíshěng Dìyǔ Quántú (皇朝直省地舆全圖, Complete Map of All Provinces of the Empire) published by the Qīng Dynasty in 1904.

[204] Kurz (2019). See also Li (2016), p. 452; Phan et al (2020).

[205] Triton Island in the Paracels is fixed as the southern border of Chinese territory. Chen (2001), p. 19.

[206] Hayton (2018), p. 31.

[207] Pham (2014).

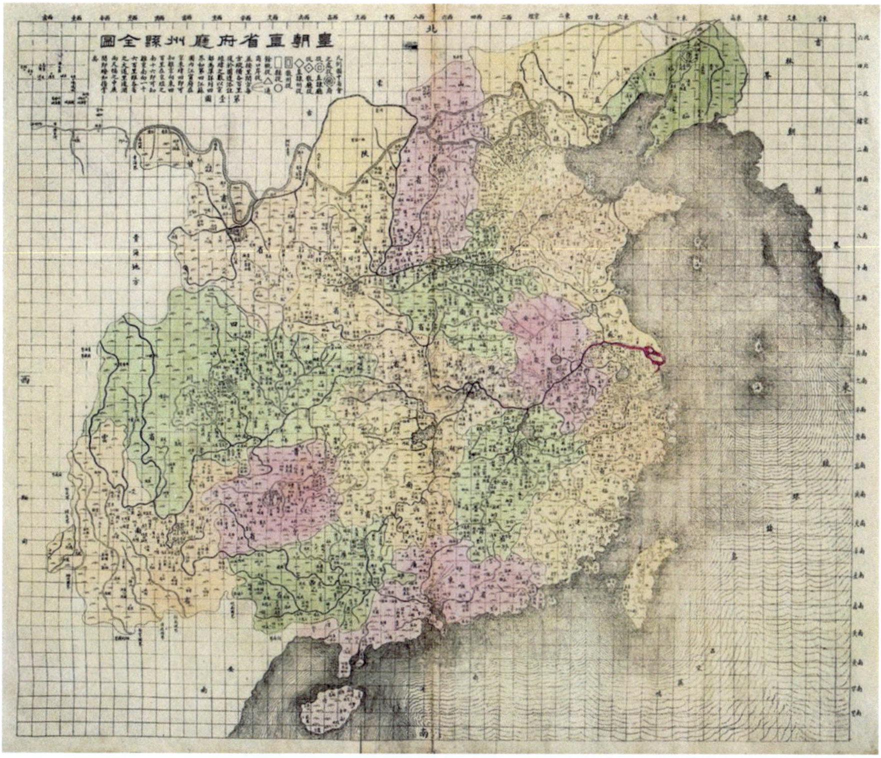

Fig. 2.4 皇朝直省地與全圖 [complete map of all provinces of the empire]. *Source* 中文百科全書 [Chinese Encyclopedia][208]

the Western Han Dynasty, and it did not exercise full control over the entirety of Qiongzhou Island (琼州) (the ancient name for Hainan Island). Notably, the book records numerous tribute voyages from southern countries, likely conducted by sea through the South China Sea.[209]

Indeed, historical documents from this period often document more instances of foreign sea voyages to China than records of China actively asserting control over the surrounding sea areas. Many official Chinese historical maps also delineate the country's territory as extending only to Hainan Island. One such example is the 386 × 456 cm map of the Ming Dynasty and neighboring countries, drawn on silk

[208] Huángcháo Zhíshěng Dìyǔ Quántú (皇朝直省地與全圖, Complete Map of All Provinces of the Empire) published by the Qīng Dynasty in 1904 shows that the southernmost part of China's territory in 1904 is Qióngzhōufǔ (瓊州府) that is now on Hǎinán Island, from https://www.newton.com.tw/wiki/皇朝直省地輿全圖/10232162 or https://www.newton.com.tw/img/4/80a/cGcq5CNkZGM3E2M0QjMmBzMiZDMlNjN3kjM5gDZjZTZhZWNzcDM0QmYyYTOv0WZ0l2LjlGcvU2apFmYv02bj5SdklWYi5yYyN3Ztl2LvoDc0RHa.jpg, accessed on 31 July 2025.

[209] Pham (2014).

Fig. 2.5 Map of the Ming Dynasty and neighboring countries in 1389. *Source* Beijing Museum of History[210]

in 1389, which is preserved at the Beijing History Museum (see Fig. 2.5). This map serves as tangible evidence of China's territorial demarcation, illustrating its boundaries as extending to Hainan Island during that era. From this analysis, it can be concluded that, based on historical data, China's claim to longstanding sovereignty lacks substantial evidence.

Establishing an astronomical observatory to measure the Four Seas, including the South China Sea. The 1980 Chinese White Paper dates back to 1279 during the Yuan Dynasty when Kublai Khan ordered Guo Shou Jing to establish an observatory (see Fig. 2.6) to measure the four seas at 27 points across the country, including the South

[210] A Ming Dynasty map of China and neighboring countries, dated 1389, measuring 386 × 456 cm and painted on silk, is currently preserved at the Beijing Museum of History. This map is also featured in the collection Ancient Chinese Maps, available at: https://www.viewofchina.com/ancient-chinese-maps/ or https://i0.wp.com/www.viewofchina.com/wp-content/uploads/2019/04/map-great-ming.jpg?w=880&ssl=1, accessed on 31 July 2025.

Fig. 2.6 Guo Shoujing established the astronomical observatory at Dengfeng, Gaocheng, Henan, in the Yuan Dynasty in the thirteenth century. *Source* 大河网 [dahe.Cn][213]

Sea point. However, Chinese scholars disagree on the location of this observatory, sometimes suggesting it was in Xi Sha (Paracels) and other times in Scarborough or Nan Sha (Spratly), depending on their intention to expand China's claims.[211]

Hayton (2018) discovered evidence of a thirteenth-century observatory, linking it to claims by some Chinese officials that Guo Shoujing established it on Scarborough Shoal or the Paracel Islands.[212] However, Hayton argued that placing such a large observatory on a small rock in the South China Sea seems implausible. He also provided compelling evidence to challenge China's sovereignty markers in the

[211] Bill Hayton believes that the name Nansha was only used in 1947: "The Chinese names were revised in 1947 by the Republic of China government. Spratly Island, which had previously been known as Si-ba-la-tuo (the transliteration of the English name) became 'Nanwei' (Noble South, an obviously artificial name) and Scarborough Shoal was changed from Si-ge-ba-luo (the transliteration) to Min-zhu Jiao (Democracy Reef). In 1983 China revised the names again and Min-zhu Jiao became Huangyang, the less threatening-sounding 'Yellow Rock'. See Hayton (2018). The full list of Chinese names and their evolution can be found in 陈克勤 (1996).

[212] See Antiokhos [@AntiokhosE] (2021, June 22). [Tweet]. X (formerly Twitter), from https://twitter.com/AntiokhosE/status/1407229477357166595, accessed on 31 July 2025. See also Hayton, B. [@bill_hayton]. (2021, June 22). [Tweet]. X (formerly Twitter), from https://twitter.com/bill_hayton/status/1407240082516500481, accessed on 31 July 2025.

[213] See 大河网 (2022, February 19) The Dengfeng Observatory, from https://5g.dahe.cn/en/20220219968911 or https://img.henan.gov.cn/bbcf7ad5b6cea51b0aa3e9a5da95585d?p=0, accessed on 31 July 2025.

Paracels, suggesting they were initially made on the mainland and then transported to the islands to bolster China's claims. Additionally, Bill Hayton recently shared on Twitter a letter from the Ministry of Foreign Affairs during the Qing Dynasty, which stated that Paracels are merely a sea area and not subject to Chinese sovereignty.[214]

China's propaganda on the international recognition of its sovereignty over maritime features in the South China Sea. China consistently propagates the notion that international conferences following World War II all affirmed that the islands in the South China Sea belonged to China. In July 2020, the Chinese Ambassador to the Philippines, Huang Xilian, reiterated that: "China recovered and exercised sovereignty over the Nansha Islands after the war in accordance with the Cairo Declaration, the Potsdam Proclamation, and other post-war documents."[215] The Cairo Declaration confirmed that:

> The Three Great Allies are fighting this war to restrain and punish the aggression of Japan. They covet no gain for themselves and have no thought of territorial expansion.
>
> It is their purpose that Japan shall be stripped of all the islands in the Pacific which she has seized or occupied since the beginning of the First World War in 1914, and that all the territories Japan has stolen from the Chinese, such as Manchuria, Formosa, and the Pescadores, shall be restored to the Republic of China. Japan will also be expelled from all other territories which she has taken by violence and greed.[216]

The Potsdam Declaration of 26 July 1945, reiterated the implementation of the provisions outlined in the Cairo Declaration.[217] However, neither the Cairo nor the Potsdam Declaration explicitly mentioned that the Paracel, Spratly Islands or Scarborough Shoal belong to China or must be returned to China. These islands were situated within territories that Japan forcibly occupied, including Vietnam. Consequently, Article 2 of the San Francisco Peace Treaty, signed between the Allied countries and Japan on 8 September 1951, addressed the separation of Taiwan and Penghu, which Japan had occupied from China, from the Spratly and Paracel Islands: "(b) Japan renounces all right, title and claim to Formosa and the Pescadores. […] (f) Japan renounces all right, title, and claim to the Spratly Islands and to the Paracel Islands."[218]

---

[214] Hayton, B. [@bill_hayton]. (2021, August 26). [Tweet]. X (formerly Twitter), from https://twitter.com/bill_hayton/status/1430844688689414149, accessed on 31 July 2025.

[215] Hayton (2021).

[216] U.S. Department of State (1961) Foreign relations of the U.S.: Diplomatic papers–The conferences at Cairo and Teheran, 1943 (pp. 448–449). Washington, D.C.: U.S. Government Printing Office. See also U.S. Department of State. (1943). Foreign relations of the U.S.: Diplomatic papers–The Conferences at Cairo and Tehran, 1943. Washington, D.C.: U.S. Government Printing Office, from https://digital.library.wisc.edu/1711.dl/G5OAT7XT7HRHX84, accessed on 31 July 2025.

[217] U.S. Department of State (1960) Foreign relations of the U.S.: Diplomatic papers–The conferences of Berlin (The Potsdam Conference), 1945 (Vol. II, pp. 1474–1476). Washington, D.C.: U.S. Government Printing Office.

[218] Ministry of Foreign Affairs of Japan. (n.d.). San Francisco Peace Treaty, from https://www.mofa.go.jp/region/europe/russia/territory/edition92/period4.html, accessed on 31 July 2025.

The San Francisco Peace Treaty 1951 obligated Japan to renounce its rights, title, and claims to the islands, without granting Japan the authority to assign territories as it sees fit. Therefore, it cannot be inferred that Japan returned the Paracel and Spratly Islands to China.[219] Moreover, historical records indicate that during the San Francisco conference on 7 September 1951, Prime Minister and Foreign Minister *Trần Văn Hữu*, representing the Associated State of Vietnam, declared: "In order to eliminate all sources of discord, we hereby affirm our country's sovereignty over the Paracel and Spratly Islands, which have long been integral parts of Vietnam's territory." This declaration did not elicit objections or reservations from any country, including China.[220]

Until 1943, China did not assert its claim over the Spratly Islands, despite being a signatory to the Cairo Declaration. Hayton (2021) presented evidence in the book China Handbook 1937–1945 published by Ministry of Information under the National Government of the Republic of China, which served as a comprehensive source of data encompassing geography, history, politics, and China's economy. On the first page of the book, it states: "Chinese territory extends from the Sayan Mountains Plateau in the north to … Triton Island of the Paracel Island group."[221] This demonstrates that the Chinese government did not administer the archipelagos since the second century BC, as claimed in the 1980 White Paper published by the Chinese Ministry of Foreign Affairs. Instead, China expanded its claim to the Paracel Islands before World War II and to the Spratly Islands after World War II.

Challenging international norms. In recent years, an increasing number of scholars and strategists on both sides of the Pacific have asserted that China is challenging the international order both regionally and globally. As noted by Mira Rapp-Hooper and others: "China's approach to the international order is complex, often appearing to support the rules-based system while simultaneously undermining it in specific contexts."[222] Chinese strategists clearly hold a vision of international order that diverges from the Western liberal model. Many Chinese scholars continue to argue that the idea of a single, "liberal international order" is illusory. In discussing the regional order, they often emphasize the need to build a more just, equal, fair, democratic, and representative economic and political international system—a vision in which China plays a leading role.

China's position is clearly reflected in a speech by General Secretary Xi Jinping at a seminar jointly organized by the Chinese Society of International Law and Hainan University on 22–23 May 2021, under the theme "Xi Jinping Thought on Legalism (Rule by Law) and International Law." In the speech, Xi stated that "improving international law is an important means of reforming the unfair and unreasonable aspects of the global governance system and promoting the

[219] Chen (2014), pp. 169–196.

[220] Chemillier-Gendreau (1996), p. 115.

[221] Hayton (2021).

[222] Rapp-Hooper et al. (2019).

establishment of a more just and rational international order and system."[223] He further emphasized that "all States should oppose the distortion of international law and have the right to resist actions that violate the legitimate rights and interests of other States and undermine peace and stability in the name of the 'rule of law.'"[224]

In the field of the Law of the Sea, China argues that all parties must interpret and apply the rules of the law of the sea, including UNCLOS, in a comprehensive, objective, and fair manner, asserting that selective or biased interpretations are unlawful and politically motivated.[225] However, in practice, China has consistently interpreted UNCLOS in ways that serve its national interests—particularly in areas such as so-called "historic rights", the establishment of straight baselines, restrictions on the innocent passage of military vessels, and heightened security requirements in the contiguous zone.[226]

China further maintains that UNCLOS does not fully regulate all aspects of the maritime order, and frequently invokes Paragraph 8 of its preamble, which states: "matters not regulated by this Convention continue to be governed by the rules and principles of general international law." As evidence of what it perceives as the Convention's limitations, China pointed to the negotiation process for a legally binding international instrument on the conservation and sustainable use of marine biological diversity in BBNJ.[227] However, it is important to highlight that the UN General Assembly has explicitly reaffirmed that the BBNJ negotiations and outcomes must remain fully consistent with UNCLOS.[228]

Regarding the regional security order, there is growing evidence that China is actively challenging the existing rules-based framework in Asia. Beijing has consistently contested or undermined established legal norms and institutional mechanisms, particularly in the context of regional security. Through the selective and unorthodox interpretation of UNCLOS and the construction of artificial islands in the South China Sea, China has engineered strategic stalemates and disrupted ASEAN's dispute resolution mechanisms, notably the negotiation process

---

[223] Zhang (2018)

[224] Zhang (2018)

[225] Sakamoto (n.d.)

[226] Article 13 of the Law on the Territorial Sea and the Contiguous Zone 1992 stipulates that "The People's Republic of China has the authority to exercise powers within its contiguous zone for the purpose of preventing or punishing infringement of its security, customs, fiscal sanitary laws and regulations or entry-exit control within its land territories, internal waters or territorial sea." China has added "security" to the beginning of the list provided by Article 33 of UNCLOS that states, the "infringements of customs, fiscal, immigration or sanitary laws." In this manner, China has extended the right to exercise control concerning security to the contiguous zones. See Sakamoto (n.d.)

[227] The Note Verbale CML/32/2021 dated 16 August 2021 of the Permanent Mission of the People's Republic of China to the UN, from https://www.un.org/depts/los/clcs_new/submissions_files/mys_12_12_2019/20210816ChnNvUNen.pdf, accessed on 31 July 2025.

[228] The Note Verbale No. 08/21/02 dated 03 August 2021 of The Permanent Mission of New Zealand to the UN, from https://www.un.org/depts/los/clcs_new/submissions_files/mys_12_12_2019/20210803NzNote.pdf, accessed on 31 July 2025.

surrounding the Code of Conduct for the South China Sea. Rather than seeking to dismantle the existing international legal regime altogether, China adopts a revisionist strategy, targeting specific rules and norms to secure and promote its.[229]

China is unwilling—or perhaps unable—to completely transform international law, as the existing framework of principles and norms continues to serve important functions. Specifically, international law acts as a tool for achieving strategic objectives, a source of legitimacy, and a constitutive element of China's national interest.[230] This indicates that China adopts a pragmatic and functional approach to international law—one that enables it to benefit from and exploit the existing global order without necessarily advocating for sweeping legal changes across most areas.

Operational Applications of Lawfare Techniques

Lawfare Through Expert Formation and Institutional Influence in South China Sea Disputes

The development of international law in China has been shaped by shifting government attitudes since its introduction. Although notable progress has been made—especially following the 1978 reform and opening-up policy—the field still lacks true professionalism and international integration. At the undergraduate level, international law remains marginalized in legal education, where curricula tend to prioritize business-oriented subjects. While graduate programs offer greater variety, they often emphasize practical skills at the expense of theoretical depth. This educational gap is exacerbated by limited textbook diversity, a lack of case-based learning, and low English proficiency among both students and faculty. These structural weaknesses hinder the cultivation of legal professionals capable of operating effectively in international settings.[231]

The post-1978 evolution of international law in China began with leading universities establishing dedicated programs, which later expanded to include broader research and training components. While the field has since grown rapidly and attracted global attention, existing literature has not fully captured its depth and dynamism.[232]

President Xi Jinping has explicitly highlighted the need for a stronger cadre of professionals versed in international law to protect China's expanding global interests, calling the current shortage a national "security risk."[233] Much of

[229] Rapp-Hooper et al. (2019).

[230] Williams (2020).

[231] Kong (2017).

[232] Zhang and Zhang (2017), pp. 427–445.

[233] Mai (2021).

China's foreign-related legal work is still outsourced to international law firms, placing the country at a disadvantage in high-stakes disputes, such as the 2016 South China Sea arbitration or recent litigation involving TikTok in the U.S.

To realize President Xi Jinping's directive, China has embraced a multidimensional strategy that revolves around three main axes. Central to this approach is the deployment of lawfare—the strategic use of legal mechanisms in international disputes—not only as a tactical tool in foreign relations but also as a means to safeguard national sovereignty and advance core interests. As China continues to refine its legal expertise, it increasingly leverages international legal tools to assert influence in vital domains such as trade, technology, sovereignty, and maritime disputes.[234]

In addition to cultivating a new generation of legal professionals, the Chinese government actively mobilizes nationalist sentiment and constructs compelling narratives that prioritize Chinese interests—often at the expense of established international legal norms. A key component of this effort is the long-term conditioning of public perception, particularly regarding the South China Sea. Generations of Chinese citizens have been taught to view the South China Sea as inherently belonging to China, a perception deeply embedded through state-controlled education and media systems. In Chinese schools and universities, textbooks emphasize historical claims over the region by referencing ancient maps, dynastic records, and maritime history. This educational framing fosters a strong sense of national pride and historical continuity, reinforcing China's maritime claims within the national consciousness.

Beyond the classroom, the state-controlled media plays a crucial role in reaffirming these narratives. Patriotic messaging and carefully curated historical accounts are frequently disseminated—especially during periods of diplomatic tension—to justify assertive foreign policy moves and rally domestic support. Studies of media framing reveal how historical memory, nationalism, and strategic storytelling are used to consolidate national consensus and deflect international criticism.[235]

This interplay between education, media control, and national identity is central to understanding China's evolving approach to international law and the South China Sea. Influenced by its Confucian heritage, which emphasizes harmony and order, and shaped by past experiences with unequal treaties, China's legal worldview is undergoing a transformation. Its rejection of the 2016 Arbitral Tribunal Award on the South China Sea exemplifies how lawfare is used not as mere legal dissent, but as a deliberate strategic maneuver to protect territorial claims and uphold national legitimacy.

Additionally, China has intensified efforts to build internal legal capacity and expand its footprint within international legal institutions. A core component of this strategy involves the deliberate placement of Chinese legal professionals within

---

[234] Rasilla and Hao (2024), pp. 513–521.

[235] Sandy (2020).

international adjudicative bodies. Since 1977, China has maintained a continuous presence in key judicial institutions, notably ITLOS since 1996, and has steadily broadened its influence across other multilateral legal fora. Prominent examples include the appointments of Judge Xue Hanqin to ICJ and Judge Duan Jielong to ITLOS.[236] China has leveraged the reputations of judges to justify its positions on the East and South China Seas. Gao, notably a judge at ITLOS and the predecessor of Judge Duan Jielong, has written extensively on the legal nature of the Nine-dash Line. Although he acknowledged that China had never clearly defined the legal entitlements it was asserting within the Nine-dash Line, he nonetheless attempted to justify its existence. He suggested that the Nine-dash Line might also represent a claimed maritime boundary between China and neighboring states, based on the 'nascent notion of the continental shelf' at the time of its emergence in the 1930s or 1940s."[237]

China's ambitions extend beyond courtroom representation. It has systematically sought leadership roles in international organizations to shape legal norms and standards. Chinese nationals currently lead more UN agencies than any other country, including the Food and Agriculture Organization (FAO), the International Telecommunication Union (ITU), the International Civil Aviation Organization (ICAO), and the UN Industrial Development Organization (UNIDO). The elevation of Liu Zhenmin, former Vice Foreign Minister, to UN Deputy Secretary-General exemplifies this institutional integration.

This increasing institutional presence enables China to exercise normative influence over the rule-making processes in key global sectors such as air travel, telecommunications, and agriculture. It also facilitates Beijing's long-term objective of reforming the international legal and organizational architecture—often perceived as Western-centric—to better reflect and accommodate Chinese values, legal philosophies, and strategic preferences.

Chinese commentators often cite a 1985 International Maritime Organization (IMO) arrangement as proof that China, together with Hong Kong, was assigned responsibility for maritime search and rescue in the northern sector of the South China Sea.[238] Rear Admiral Yin Zhuo, for instance, has argued that the IMO determined China's authority extended to waters north of 10° North latitude and west of 124° East longitude, presenting this as "undisputed responsibility"[239] for maritime search and rescue in the region. Yet official documentation from the Hong Kong Maritime Rescue Coordination Centre describes its search and rescue region as bounded by 10° North latitude and 120° East longitude,[240] and IMO

236 Sugandha (2020, August 27).

237 Gao and Jia (2013), pp. 98–124.

238 Glaser (2015).

239 Glaser (2015).

240 The Hong Kong Maritime Rescue Co-ordination Centre, from https://www.mardep.gov.hk/en/public-services/port-services/search-and-rescue/index.html or https://www.info.gov.hk/gia/general/200010/17/1017207.htm, accessed on 31 July 2025.

records acknowledge unresolved overlaps and the absence of clearly defined responsibility between China and the Philippines.[241] This contrast suggests that Yin Zhuo's assertion should be understood not as a settled legal fact, but as a Chinese claim, one that exceeds the parameters reflected in formal IMO arrangements.

Another example is China's strategic engagement with the International Hydrographic Organization (IHO) and its General Bathymetric Chart of the Oceans (GEBCO)—Sub-Committee on Undersea Feature Names (SCUFN), particularly following the release of a list of 80 undersea features in the South China Sea—most of which lie within the EEZs and continental shelves of coastal states such as Vietnam and the Philippines. While General Bathymetric Chart of the Oceans—Sub-Committee on Undersea Feature Names is specifically mandated to standardize the naming of undersea features located in international waters (i.e., beyond the limits of the territorial sea) for use in General Bathymetric Chart of the Oceans products, the International Hydrographic Organization charts, and regional bathymetric compilations (IBCs), China has actively submitted naming proposals even for features clearly situated within the maritime zones of other states.[242]

Vietnam, Malaysia, and the Philippines strongly objected, arguing that coastal states should have the *prior right* to name undersea features located within their EEZs or continental shelves, as established by international law, including UNCLOS. They emphasized that if other states wish to propose names for features within these maritime zones, consultations with the concerned coastal states must be conducted. Moreover, they reaffirmed their sovereign right to name features within their own EEZs and continental shelves and objected to the so-called "older names" proposed by China. These states contended that since such names were not reviewed and accepted by Sub-Committee on Undersea Feature Names—the sole international authority on this matter—Sub-Committee on Undersea Feature Names must treat all proposals submitted by coastal states with sovereign rights in a fair and equal manner.[243]

Despite these objections, China has maintained its position and strategically prolonged the process by advocating for a procedural freeze under the guise of

[241] The 1979 International Convention on maritime search and rescue, from https://treaties.un.org/doc/publication/unts/volume%201405/volume-1405-i-23489-english.pdf, accessed on 31 July 2025. See also The IMO Maritime Search and Rescue Regions, from https://www.dco.uscg.mil/Portals/9/CG-5R/nsarc/IMO%20Maritime%20SAR%20Regions.pdf, accessed on 31 July 2025.

[242] General Bathymetric Chart of the Oceans—Sub-Committee on Undersea Feature Names (SCUFN), from https://iho.int/en/scufn, accessed on 31 July 2025.

[243] Sub-Committee on Undersea Feature Names 37 on 26 June 2024. See also Ministry of Foreign Affairs of Vietnam (2024, June 26). Statement of Vietnam, from https://iho.int/uploads/user/Inter-Regional%20Coordination/GEBCO/SCUFN/SCUFN37/SCUFN37_Statement_Viet_Nam_26%20JUNE%202024.pdf, accessed on 31 July 2025; Department of Foreign Affairs of the Philippines. (2024, June 25). Philippine statement on naming of undersea features in the South China Sea, from https://iho.int/uploads/user/Inter-Regional%20Coordination/GEBCO/SCUFN/SCFUN37%20the%20PHL%20statement%2025%20June%202024.pdf, accessed on 31 July 2025.

consensus-building. At the 36th session of Sub-Committee on Undersea Feature Names (2023), China supported a motion "to freeze" all naming proposals in the South China Sea until a joint proposal is submitted by all interested parties,[244] as stipulated in Sub-Committee on Undersea Feature Names Rules of Procedure 2.10 (SCUFN36/04.6/01). This move, adopted by a narrow vote of 7–5, has been criticized as politically motivated rather than grounded in legal justification. It effectively delays recognition of names proposed by coastal states and allows China to maintain a *status quo* that benefits its broader strategic agenda in the region.

By embedding its personnel in key legal and regulatory institutions, China seeks not merely to participate in, but to actively shape, the development, interpretation, and application of international law in a manner that aligns with and promotes its national interests.

Lawfare by Numbers: Leveraging Quantity Over Quality in Global Legal Fora

China's lawfare strategy increasingly extends beyond traditional legal and political arenas, penetrating academic publishing as a subtle yet strategic means of legitimizing its claims in the South China Sea. A key manifestation of this approach involves embedding the contested Nine-dash Line into scientific articles—often in disciplines unrelated to territorial or maritime studies. This tactic reflects an effort to normalize China's sovereignty narrative under the guise of scientific objectivity. It marks a "non-traditional frontline" in the South China Sea disputes, where international science journals become inadvertent platforms for disseminating contested claims.

A China National Knowledge Infrastructure (CNKI.net) search from 2020 to December 2024 identified 2336 Chinese-language legal publications on the South China Sea, representing 3.6% of the total publications on the topic across all fields (65,660) (see Fig. 2.7).[245] This excludes non-Chinese language publications.

Beyond isolated cases, a broader trend has emerged that reveals the scale and sophistication of China's strategy. A preliminary survey by Vietnamese legal scholar *Nguyễn Thùy Anh* found that as of mid-2019, at least 260 articles containing the Nine-dash Line had appeared across 20 leading international scientific journals, published by well-known houses such as Springer Nature, Science, Elsevier, and MDPI. The growth in frequency is particularly striking: while only 10 such articles were found in 2010, the number rose to 60 in 2018 and then 90 in

[244] Government of the People's Republic of China (2024, June 26). China's statement on undersea feature naming in the South China Sea, from https://iho.int/uploads/user/Inter-Regional%20Coordination/GEBCO/SCUFN/SCUFN37/SCUFN%2037%20Statement-China.pdf, accessed on 31 July 2025.

[245] China National Knowledge Infrastructure, from https://cnki.net/kns/defaultresult/index, accessed on 31 July 2025.

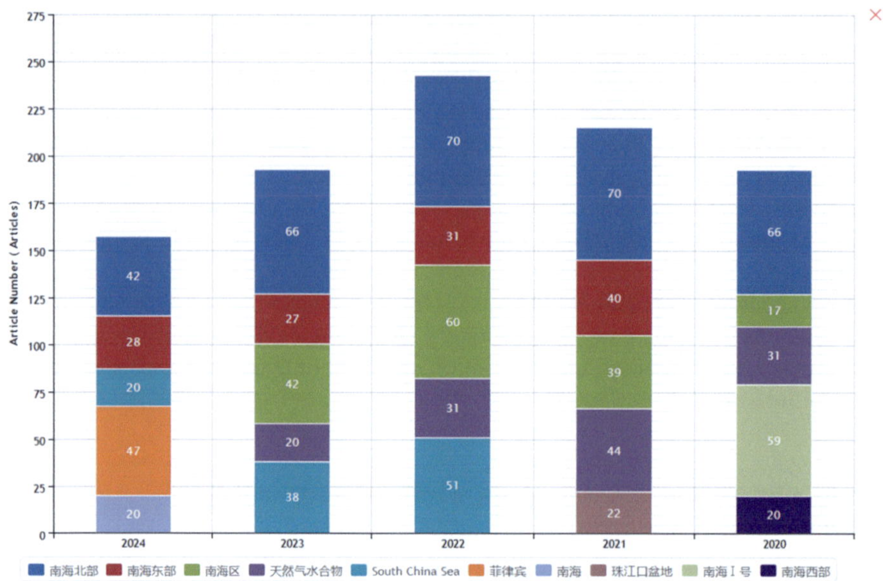

Fig. 2.7 Trends in publication of articles about the South China Sea in Chinese over the years 2020–2024. *Source* China National Knowledge Infrastructure website[246]

just the first half of 2019—with the trend continuing upward in the following years. These maps were embedded not in political or legal discourse, but in articles covering a wide range of hard-science disciplines, including climate change, hydrography, archaeology, agriculture, bioenergy, waste management, and public health.[247]

One striking example is a 2011 article published in Science, titled "China's Demographic History and Future Challenges" by Professor Xizhe Peng.[248] Although the article focused on population trends, it originally included a map featuring the Nine-dash Line, prompting strong objections from Vietnamese scholars and raising alarms about the politicization of scholarly work. In the same year, Nature published two articles[249] confirming that China intended to "use scientists' publications to promote the country's territorial claims."[250] Since then, Nature has added a Publisher's Note[251] to each article illustrated with the Nine-dash Line, stating that "Springer Nature remains neutral with regard to jurisdictional claims in

[246] China National Knowledge Infrastructure, from https://cnki.net/kns/defaultresult/index, accessed on 31 July 2025.

[247] Nguyen (2020).

[248] Peng (2011), pp. 581–587.

[249] Cyranoski (2011). See also Uncharted territory (2011).

[250] Nguyen (2020).

[251] Jiang et al. (2019).

published maps and institutional affiliations."[252] In 2018, Elsevier issued a clearer and stronger response through a Publisher's Note[253] after the Journal of Hydrology published 13 articles with maps featuring the Nine-dash Line, declaring: "the legal correctness … of the China 9-dash line … is disputed in international law, diplomacy and politics."[254]

This quantitative surge suggests a calculated use of academic publishing to normalize disputed territorial claims through repeated exposure. By saturating scholarly output with depictions of the Nine-dash Line, China is not only seeking to influence international perception, but also to embed its narrative into the global knowledge infrastructure in a way that is difficult to contest retroactively.

These examples illustrate that China is employing a propaganda technique akin to *repetition for truth*—whereby a claim, though controversial, gains perceived legitimacy through repeated exposure. Whitton and Larson discuss how states use defamatory propaganda against one another and consider it distinct from subversive or war-mongering forms. They highlight the difficulty of determining whether such propaganda is genuinely intended to harm or whether it simply produces harmful consequences. International treaties have had limited success in controlling defamatory propaganda, given problems with enforcement and the varying interpretations of defamation law among different countries.[255]

China's domestic and international propaganda efforts often present the nation as having legitimate sovereignty over the contested South China Sea. By strategically utilizing various fora, China communicates its position while frequently limiting the opportunity for other countries to respond effectively. This approach can sway audiences who may not fully understand the complexities of the South China Sea issue, leading them to accept China's narrative without critical analysis. In its media strategies, China distorts information regarding the South China Sea to gain advantages both domestically and internationally. Beijing's propaganda generally revolves around two main themes. First, it emphasizes its claims, based on historical rights and the Nine-dash Line, as "indisputable," portraying the demands of neighboring countries like the Philippines and Vietnam as unreasonable. Any allegations of aggression against China are dismissed as false and groundless. Second, China highlights its preference for bilateral negotiations with regional states while accusing third-party nations, including the U.S., Australia, Japan, and the European Union, of disregarding international law and further inflating tensions in the region.

Additionally, China leverages historical narratives to support its claims in the South China Sea. Historians are tasked with crafting narratives that highlight China's historical presence in the area, seeking to counter competing claims and

---

[252] Jiang et al. (2019).

[253] See Publisher's note, from https://www.sciencedirect.com/science/article/pii/S0025326X14006298, accessed on 31 July 2025.

[254] Nguyen (2020).

[255] Whitton and Larson (1964), pp. 104–132.

reinforce its position. This strategy involves promoting specific interpretations of history while minimizing unfavorable events, ultimately strengthening China's credibility both internationally and domestically. The construction of artificial islands also serves as a tangible representation of these claims, reinforcing China's assertions. Collectively, these tactics illustrate the deliberate shaping of historical narratives for propaganda purposes, underscoring the necessity for critical evaluation of China's claims regarding its sovereignty in the South China Sea dispute.

The disparity in media influence and the limited capacity for rebuttal in international fora have allowed China's position—despite its contested nature—to dominate global public perception, particularly among audiences unfamiliar with the legal and historical complexities of the South China Sea disputes.

Academic Lawfare: How China Internationalizes Disputed Claims Through Scholarly Influence

In addition to mobilizing domestic academia, China also leverages the expertise of international scholars as well as think tanks to produce research that supports its maritime claims and to influence global perception. In the South China Sea, ideas have emerged as tools of power when China leverages a network of state-aligned think tanks and academic institutions to shape global perceptions of its maritime claims.[256] Think tanks such as the China Institute of International Studies (CIIS), the Charhar Society,[257] the Huayang Center, and the Grandview Institution[258] play a central role in this effort, acting both as buffers and as instruments for amplifying Chinese strategic interests.[259] These entities promote a narrative framing China's actions as defensive, historically justified, and consistent with international law. Through publications and international fora, they help legitimize Beijing's stance, test legal arguments, and diffuse criticism under the guise of neutral research. Functioning as intermediaries between strategic objectives and public perception, these institutions perform three key roles: Nexus, which is linking knowledge production with policymaking; Network, which is bringing together domestic and international experts to harmonize narratives; and Narrative, which is disseminating China's maritime claims through diverse media channels.

A prominent example is the 500-page publication titled *South China Sea: A Critical Study*, released in June 2018 by the China Society of International Law. Authored by over 50 Chinese scholars and legal experts, the work is meticulously

[256] Borton and Chen (2025).

[257] This organization elevates China's maritime messaging into civilizational discourse, framing actions harmoniously and historically.

[258] This institution distinguishes itself through tactical agility in narrative projection, co-hosting fora and presenting China's claims as restrained and law-bound.

[259] Borton and Chen (2025).

crafted, featuring detailed annotations, citations, and academic language. It was published through a prestigious journal associated with Oxford University's publishing system.[260] The publication advances China's positions on contentious legal concepts such as the "archipelagic baseline" and the "Four Sha," and these arguments are disseminated across academic and official platforms at multiple times and in various formats. Notably, the study references and incorporates views from foreign legal experts like Professor Stefan Talmon, co-director of the Institute of International Law at the University of Bonn, Germany.[261]

Beyond publications, China has ramped up its efforts to co-opt international scholars sympathetic to its maritime claims. Scholars such as Mark J. Valencia, affiliated with the East-West Center in Hawaii, have shifted from earlier criticism to now frequently writing in support of China's position in international fora. China has also recruited numerous foreign experts to work with institutions like the National Institute for South China Sea Studies [中国南海研究院],[262] capitalizing on their international reputations. Some of the prominent names affiliated with this institute include Rommel C. Banlaoi, Hasjim Djalal, Lee Seok-woo, Stein Tønnesson, B.A. Hamzah, Vivian Louis Forbes, Zheng Yongnian, Zou Keyuan, Phillip M. Saunders, or Gordon Houlden.[263] For example, Mark J. Valencia, an American scholar originally known for his relatively objective perspective in works such as Sharing Resources in the South China Sea, has shifted his stance in recent years. He has increasingly published articles that defend China's maritime activities and legal positions. Notably, Valencia has not only supported China's claims but also frequently criticized Vietnam. Shortly after Chinese Foreign Minister Wang Yi's official visit to Vietnam in September 2021, Valencia published an article in Asia Times accusing Vietnam of violating international law and deliberately provoking tensions with China.[264] This claim was quickly rebutted by legal experts from Vietnam.[265] Similarly, Australian scholar Austin has argued that Vietnam, not China, is the primary aggressor in the South China Sea dispute, although this view has also faced broad academic rejection.[266]

China's strategic legal campaign encompasses the publication of legal documents, diplomatic notes, and the promotion of legal expertise at both domestic and international levels. What is notable in recent years is not just the persistence of these activities, but their increased frequency, expanded scope, and sophistication. The growing collaboration with international publishers and foreign academics

---

[260] Chinese Society of International Law (2018).

[261] Talmon (2016), p. 309.

[262] See https://www.nanhai.org.cn/ for more details on the National Institute for South China Sea Studies [中国南海研究院].

[263] Adjunct Research Professor, from http://en.nanhai.org.cn/index/survey/team_i/cid/3/t/3.html, accessed on 31 July 2025.

[264] Valencia (2021).

[265] Tran et al. (2021).

[266] Nguyen (2015).

underscores China's intention to legitimize its claims and shape global narratives through legal and scholarly means. This trend is poised to continue and intensify in the near future.

Personal Attacks in the Name of Legal Standards: China's Tactics Against the Arbitral Tribunal in the South China Sea Case

China's consistent rejection of the jurisdiction of the Arbitral Tribunal in the South China Sea case has involved efforts to delegitimize the tribunal by discrediting its judges, particularly through accusations of bias. One prominent tactic was to emphasize the nationality of certain judges, notably Mr. Shunji Yanai, a Japanese national who was serving as President of ITLOS at the time. By focusing on Yanai's nationality, Chinese officials aimed to undermine the perceived impartiality of the tribunal and question the legitimacy of its procedures and rulings—especially those that were unfavorable to China's maritime claims. This strategy resonates with what Zaffaroni et al. (2023) describe as a "drop-by-drop coup,"[267] in which the cumulative effect of repeated accusations and media narratives produces the "legal and political death"[268] of the target. In Latin America, such techniques discredited political leaders; in the South China Sea, they work to erode confidence in international adjudicatory institutions. Each accusation of bias, while limited in isolation, contributes to a broader campaign that gradually delegitimizes the tribunal itself, aiming at the "legal death"[269] of its authority in disputes over maritime entitlements.

Under Annex VII of UNCLOS, a five-member tribunal panel is normally constituted with each party selecting one judge and the two jointly appointing the remaining three. If one party refuses to participate, the President of ITLOS steps in to appoint judges on that party's behalf. In the South China Sea case, China's decision to abstain from participation meant it forfeited its right to appoint judges. As a result, Mr. Yanai, in accordance with procedural rules, selected the tribunal members for both sides.

China objected to this process on the grounds of Yanai's nationality, citing Japan's ongoing maritime dispute with China in the East China Sea. Chinese sources argued that Yanai's national background constituted a conflict of interest—even though he played no active role in the proceedings themselves. These objections first surfaced in 2013 and were amplified in later years. For example, an editorial published in the People's Daily on 11 May 2016, under the pseudonym "Zhong Sheng" (often used to signal the China's Communist Party's official stance), claimed that Yanai had "clearly violated procedural justice requirements"

[267] Zaffaroni et al. (2023), p. 9.

[268] Zaffaroni et al. (2023), p. 6.

[269] Zaffaroni et al. (2023), p. 6.

by participating in the selection process and should have recused himself. Notably, the editorial failed to cite any specific provision of law that was allegedly violated.

The criticism was echoed by Chinese diplomats as well. On 8 June 2016, China's ambassador to Indonesia, Xie Feng, wrote an op–ed in the Jakarta Post, accusing the tribunal's president of being biased due to his Japanese nationality and criticizing the composition of the tribunal as lacking global representation—since it included four European judges and one from Ghana.[270]

In addition, Wu Shicun, President of the National Institute for South China Sea Studies in Hainan, China's southernmost island province, claimed in an email to Foreign Policy that there was evidence of bias on the part of Mr. Shunji Yanai in favor of the Philippines. "In April 2013, Mr. Yanai appointed Mr. Chris Pinto as the President of the Arbitral Tribunal. Although Mr. Pinto is a Sri Lankan national, his wife is Filipino," Although Mr. Pinto proactively rejected this proposal to be in the jury, but Mr. Wu still believes there was a personal connection influencing the case proceedings. Wu further argued that the ruling against China in the Philippines' arbitration case could also serve Japan's strategic interests. According to him, "Japan, by contributing to China's defeat in the tribunal, could portray itself as a 'good guy' in East Asia."[271]

Such nationality-based attacks, however, run counter to established principles of international law. The impartiality and integrity of international judges are evaluated based on their qualifications, judicial conduct, and adherence to legal standards, rather than their country of origin.[272] Consequently, China's attempts to dismiss the tribunal's authority through these arguments have drawn significant criticism from the international community. Legal scholars and commentators have labeled these efforts as unfounded and inconsistent with procedural fairness.[273]

China's Strategic Deployment of Lawfare: Legal Instruments and Unofficial Channels as Tools of Influence in the South China Sea Disputes

China's use of lawfare in maritime and international disputes—particularly in the South China Sea—has evolved into a comprehensive and multi-layered strategy that extends beyond traditional statecraft. Beyond its public rejection of international rulings, China exploits both foreign legal systems and unofficial channels as instruments of strategic influence, aiming to shape legal narratives, exhaust adversaries, and legitimize its contested claims.

[270] Allen-Ebrahimian (2016).

[271] Allen-Ebrahimian (2016).

[272] "[...] attacking tribunal members individually is transparently the argument of a sore loser. The tactic is particularly without merit given that China voluntarily forfeited its opportunity to participate in the process of selecting arbitrators, leaving the President of ITLOS to fill the vacancies on the ad hoc panel". See Guilfoyle (2016).

[273] The Guardian (2016, July 12). See also Beckman and Davenport (2021).

A key tactic involves initiating lawsuits in European and American jurisdictions through prominent international law firms. These legal offensives often target governments, corporations, and individuals, entangling them in prolonged litigation intended to drain resources, deter future resistance, and coerce settlements. This method mirrors China's broader strategy of "law as a weapon," where legal instruments are not only defensive shields but also offensive tools to weaken rivals through procedural and reputational attrition.[274]

At the same time, China has become increasingly assertive in seeking to influence major international arbitration institutions, while also strengthening its domestic legal system as a parallel venue for resolving international investment and intellectual property disputes. Recent moves to adjudicate international intellectual property cases in Chinese courts signal an effort to recenter legal authority within its own jurisdiction, while discouraging foreign entities from pursuing claims through international mechanisms perceived as biased against Beijing.

Furthermore, lawfare is not limited to formal judicial avenues. China actively uses Track 2 diplomacy—involving academics, research institutions, and think tanks—to propagate legal narratives that align with state policy. These narratives are often embedded in academic publications, expert fora, and media commentaries, which subtly embed controversial claims—such as the legitimacy of the Nine-dash Line—into broader international discourse. This coordinated messaging effort lends the appearance of scholarly legitimacy to Beijing's stance, thereby shaping perceptions over time.

In essence, China's lawfare strategy blends hard and soft tactics, merging assertive legal postures with diplomacy and information warfare. It seeks to reshape legal interpretations, delegitimize opposing claims, and establish new norms of regional order—often under the guise of multilateralism and cooperation. For affected states, this presents a complex challenge: they must navigate a battlefield where law, politics, and propaganda are intricately intertwined.

China's Gray Zone Tactics

In recent years, a growing number of scholars and strategists across the Pacific have contended that China is not merely rising within the international order but actively seeking to reshape it—particularly in the Asia-Pacific region. China's behavior reflects a broader pattern of exploiting the flexibility and ambiguity of international law to gain legitimacy for contested actions, especially in maritime contexts. Nowhere is this more apparent than in its selective interpretations of UNCLOS, its island-building activities in the South China Sea, and its opposition to dispute resolution mechanisms such as arbitration. China has skillfully exploited legal ambiguities and gaps in the law of armed conflict and the law of the sea—to effectively implement its gray zone strategy.[275]

---

[274] Zumbrun (2021). See also The Economist (2021).

[275] Lin (2022).

According to the principle of distinction in international humanitarian law, only lawful combatants may engage in hostilities, while civilians must remain protected from military operations. However, China has taken advantage of the legal ambiguity surrounding the status of maritime militia, which exists in a gray zone between civilians and state armed forces. This ambiguity enables China to deploy these forces for coercive activities—such as patrols, harassment, and presence operations—particularly in the South China Sea, without triggering clear legal consequences. These operations are deliberately conducted below the threshold of armed conflict, yet they are sufficient to intimidate, undermine sovereignty, and erode the jurisdictional rights of coastal states.[276] By using fishing vessels and disguised militia rather than regular naval ships—which would be more easily categorized as acts of militarization or escalation—China is able to operate in legally contested zones where international responses are constrained by the lack of legal clarity. These actions not only undermine regional stability but subvert existing legal mechanisms from within, gradually eroding the authority of rules-based frameworks without formally rejecting them.

A striking development in China's recent rhetoric is its attempt to delegitimize the very concept of "gray zone" operations. While Western analysts, including the U.S. Department of Defense and the Center for Strategic and International Studies (CSIS), have consistently labeled China's maritime militia and coercive patrols as "gray zone tactics,"[277] Beijing now inverts the narrative by claiming that the term itself was fabricated by the U.S. to tarnish China's image. According to a 2025 report by Xinhua Research Institute, China's actions in the South China Sea are "open, transparent, reasonable and lawful," and it is the Philippines—encouraged by Washington—that engages in genuine "gray zone provocations." As evidence, Beijing points to the 2024 incident at Sabina Shoal (仙宾礁), where a Philippine Coast Guard vessel (BRP Teresa Magbanua, 9701) remained illegally for more than four months in an effort to replicate the Sierra Madre grounding strategy at Second Thomas Shoal. Chinese officials contend that the vessel's activities amounted to "seeking actual control," and portray China's coast guard response —radio warnings, shadowing, and regulatory enforcement—as normal law-enforcement actions rather than coercion.[278] This rhetorical reversal exemplifies how China reframes lawfare accusations as part of its broader strategy to claim lawfulness while simultaneously undermining its opponents' legitimacy.

---

[276] Poling et al. and Center for Advanced Defense Studies (2021). See also Ratner (2022); Kraska (2020).

[277] Poling et al. and Center for Advanced Defense Studies (2021).

[278] 新华社研究院 [Xinhua News Agency Research Institute] (2025), pp. 3–5.

Lawfare Techniques Through the Imposition of Domestic Law on the International Arena

China diligently seeks to assert its national laws within the context of international disputes, establishing a legal and propaganda framework that justifies the use of force and coercive measures when deemed necessary. This strategic approach encompasses several key tactics: First, China promulgates national laws that claim maritime zones extending beyond its recognized jurisdiction. Second, it enacts legislation that expands the jurisdiction and authority of maritime law enforcement agencies, enabling greater control over these areas. Third, it is the enactment of national laws expanding administrative control and civilian involvement to support gray zone tactics. Collectively, these strategies reflect China's effort to integrate domestic legal frameworks into its international maritime operations and assert its interests within contested regions.

Promulgation of National Laws to Assert Maritime Claims Beyond Recognized Jurisdiction

A review of the historical trajectory reveals that China has systematically expanded its maritime claims in the South China Sea through a series of unilateral statements and national legal instruments.[279] This progression began with the 1951 declaration of sovereignty over the islands, followed by the 1958 Declaration on the Territorial Sea, which established a 12-nautical-mile territorial sea around these features. The trajectory continued with the promulgation of the 1992 Law on the Territorial Sea and Contiguous Zone, the 1996 announcement of baselines for the Paracel Islands, and the 1998 Law on the Exclusive Economic Zone and the Continental Shelf. Subsequent developments include the Four Sha claim in 2019 and the 2024 declaration of baselines around Scarborough Shoal. These assertions are reinforced by domestic legislation such as the China Coast Guard Law (2021) and the Maritime Traffic Safety Law (2021), both of which embed strategic ambiguity into Chinese maritime governance. A key feature of these laws is the undefined term "the sea areas under the jurisdiction of the People's Republic of China," which introduces legal uncertainty regarding the geographic scope of Chinese jurisdiction. This ambiguity potentially extends the application of Chinese domestic law far beyond the country's internationally recognized maritime zones, especially within the South and East China Seas.

By adopting expansive interpretations and vague legal language, China facilitates the projection of state control over contested waters.[280] These laws not only enable administrative regulation and law enforcement operations in disputed areas

[279] See section "Phases of Establishing and Implementing China's Lawfare in the South China Sea".

[280] Tsuruta (2024).

but also authorize the use of force in defense of perceived violations of Chinese sovereignty—thereby blurring the line between civilian enforcement and military action. Such a legal approach undermines the right of innocent passage, challenges the rules-based international order, and complicates diplomatic and operational responses by other coastal states.

In response, several regional and extra-regional actors have strengthened maritime law enforcement capabilities through enhanced international cooperation. China's persistent reliance on ambiguous legal justifications underscores the urgent need for a robust, transparent, and universally respected international legal framework to govern maritime activities in contested regions.

Enacting National Laws that Broaden the Jurisdiction and Authority of Maritime Law Enforcement Agencies

China has gradually expanded the authority of its maritime law enforcement forces into disputed waters, exemplified by unilateral fishing bans in the South China Sea issued from 1998 to the present, the "Blue Sea Strategy 2020", the Coast Guard Law and the Maritime Traffic Safety Law (2021).

The annual fishing bans from May 1 to September 16, covering waters north of the South China Sea up to 12 degrees north latitude, including areas within Vietnam's sovereignty such as the Tonkin Gulf and the Paracel Islands.[281] China justifies these measures under the pretext of protecting marine resources and promoting sustainable development in line with the UN's Millennium Development Goals (SDGs). However, these bans blatantly contravene international law, including UNCLOS and related legal instruments. They also violate the DOC, infringe upon the sovereignty and sovereign rights of other nations, and impede the normal activities of foreign fishing vessels and fishermen. Such actions increase the risk of clashes between foreign law enforcement vessels and China's coast guard, given that the South China Sea is a semi-enclosed sea where long-distance resource management activities should be carried out cooperatively and in compliance with Article 123 of UNCLOS.

The 2020 Blue Sea Strategy is part of China's broader efforts to extend its jurisdiction over disputed waters, particularly in environmental matters. Under this strategy, China asserts its authority to enforce environmental regulations on maritime activities conducted by other countries.[282] Additionally, China has expanded "patriotic" tours to the Paracel Islands for Chinese citizens, aiming to bolster national sentiment and reinforce its sovereignty claims.[283] Furthermore, China utilizes visa stamps on passports to assert its territorial control over areas that it

[281] Li (2023). See also Maulaya (2022).

[282] Xinhua (2020, April 1).

[283] Huang (2022).

has occupied by force. These measures serve to assert China's dominance in the region and strengthen its territorial claims in the South China Sea.[284]

Beijing has emphasized that the 2021 Coast Guard Law represents a routine legislative process undertaken by the National People's Congress. Chinese scholars have further argued that comparable laws exist in other coastal states such as Vietnam, Malaysia, and the Philippines, where maritime law enforcement agencies are empowered to maintain maritime order and security. However, the enactment of this Chinese law has raised significant concerns among neighboring countries and the broader international community. While the authority to legislate within a sovereign jurisdiction is a recognized prerogative of any state, the application of the Coast Guard Law extends beyond China's legitimate maritime zones under UNCLOS. It encompasses areas that are disputed or recognized as part of the high seas or other states' EEZs. This expansive scope of jurisdiction raises serious questions about the law's conformity with international law and has triggered apprehension over its potential ramifications for regional peace, stability, and maritime security.

Firstly, the Coast Guard Law establishes the coastal police force as a significant element of China's armed forces, elevating it from a conventional law enforcement agency to a constituent part of the regular armed forces. This transition raises concerns, particularly when the coast guard operates in encounters with vessels from other nations exercising freedom of navigation. Such a move could potentially escalate tensions and increase the risk of maritime incidents in disputed waters.

Secondly, the Coast Guard is now positioned as a frontline force alongside the maritime militia and self-defense units to assert China's sovereignty claims in the East and South China Seas. Supported by the Chinese Navy, these entities collaborate to enforce China's claims, adhering to a strategy of "winning without fighting." By blurring the lines between civil and military functions, China strategically positions its coast guard ships in a gray area, avoiding direct accusations of violating international law on armed conflict. This approach allows China to assert its interests while minimizing the risk of direct confrontation.

Thirdly, Articles 3 and 12 of the China Coast Guard Law outline the responsibilities of the China Coast Guard, which include guarding key islands and reefs, managing and protecting maritime boundaries, and preventing, stopping and eliminating activities that endanger national sovereignty, security and maritime rights and interests. This law does not clearly define the sea areas under China's jurisdiction or their boundaries. If the Nine-dash Line boundary, without specific coordinates, is considered China's national border, then all activities within this range by other countries could be subject to interception or even attack by the Chinese coast guard. Without clear delineation, the law sets a precedent for using national legislation to resolve international disputes within maritime areas claimed by China. This approach contradicts the principles of international law, particularly

[284] VnExpress (2017, March 3). See also Callahan (2020).

Article 27 of the Vienna Convention on the Law of Treaties, which prohibits parties from invoking their internal laws to justify non-compliance with treaty obligations.[285]

Fourthly, the China Coast Guard Law risks legitimizing the unlawful actions of the Chinese Coast Guard, including firing upon, ramming, and sinking fishing vessels from other nations that are operating lawfully within their own EEZs as defined by UNCLOS.

Fifthly, the China Coast Guard Law provides legal justification for the Chinese Coast Guard to escort and safeguard resource exploration and exploitation activities conducted by Chinese companies, even in maritime areas that lie within the continental shelf of other coastal states. Article 20 of the Law establishes a domestic legal foundation for Chinese law enforcement to obstruct or prevent the construction and installation of fixed or floating infrastructure by other nations within their own lawful maritime zones. This provision effectively enables coercive practices aimed at compelling other states to acquiesce to China's proposal of "setting aside disputes and pursuing joint development," even in areas that, under international law, fall squarely within the sovereign rights of other coastal states as defined by UNCLOS.

Sixthly, the China Coast Guard Law authorizes the Chinese Coast Guard to obstruct the exercise of lawful freedoms of navigation and overflight, including Freedom of Navigation Operations (FONOPs) regularly conducted by the U.S. and its allies in the South and East China Seas. Article 17 of the Law permits the use of coercive enforcement measures—such as detention, forced removal, and towing of foreign vessels—that are deemed to have "unlawfully" entered China's territorial waters. However, the legislation fails to clearly define what constitutes an unlawful entry, creating significant legal ambiguity. This lack of clarity grants Chinese authorities broad discretion in enforcing maritime claims, even in areas that may lie beyond China's internationally recognized jurisdiction. Furthermore, the 2021 amendments to the Maritime Traffic Safety Law have introduced additional restrictions on the right of innocent passage for foreign vessels, further tightening China's control over maritime access and raising concerns over the erosion of navigational freedoms protected under international law, particularly UNCLOS and the regulatory frameworks of IMO.

Notably, Articles 54 and 55 of China's 2021 Maritime Traffic Safety Law introduce requirements that regarding the right of innocent passage, particularly with respect to certain categories of vessels. These provisions mandate that foreign vessels falling into specific classifications—submersibles, nuclear-powered vessels, ships carrying radioactive or other hazardous materials, and any vessel deemed to potentially endanger China's maritime traffic safety—must report to the Chinese maritime safety administration when entering or exiting the territorial

285 "A party may not invoke the provisions of its internal law as justification for its failure to perform a treaty". Vienna Convention on the Law of Treaties, Article 27—Internal law and observance of treaties, from https://legal.un.org/ilc/texts/instruments/english/conventions/1_1_1969.pdf, accessed on 31 July 2025.

sea. The vessels must also comply with Chinese laws and accept supervision from maritime authorities.

Supplementing these legal requirements, the China Maritime Administration issued detailed operational instructions on 27 August 2021, requiring these ships to report comprehensive information, including name, call sign, satellite phone number, IMO number, current position, last and next ports of call, estimated times of arrival and departure, and whether dangerous or noxious cargo is onboard.[286]

While such measures may be justified from a security standpoint, coastal states must still ensure that any requirements imposed on foreign vessels exercising the right of innocent passage align with international law. Specifically, Article 20 of UNCLOS mandates that submarines must navigate on the surface and show their flags, while Article 21(2) allows coastal states to regulate passage for certain categories of hazardous vessels but requires that routes be coordinated with the International Maritime Organization (IMO). In the absence of designated traffic separation schemes or safety corridors, such vessels still retain the right of innocent passage under Article 23 of UNCLOS, provided they carry valid safety certificates and observe international regulations.

While Article 25 of UNCLOS permits coastal states to temporarily suspend innocent passage in designated areas of their territorial sea for security reasons, such suspensions must be duly announced, geographically limited, and of a temporary nature. In contrast, Article 92 of China's 2021 Maritime Traffic Safety Law authorizes maritime administrative agencies to order the immediate departure of foreign vessels deemed to pose safety threats within China's internal waters and territorial sea. It further grants these agencies the authority to exercise the right of hot pursuit in cases involving violations of domestic laws governing maritime traffic safety and marine environmental protection.

Such regulatory measures might be justifiable if applied strictly within areas recognized under international law as Chinese territorial waters. However, the persistent ambiguity surrounding the scope of "sea areas under Chinese jurisdiction" in multiple Chinese legal instruments—particularly when potentially extended to areas within the Nine-dash Line—has raised serious concerns. If foreign vessels are regarded as violating the 2021 Maritime Traffic Safety Law in these contested areas, they may be subjected to coercive enforcement measures, including the use of force as permitted under the 2021 Coast Guard Law. This legal ambiguity risks undermining the principle of innocent passage, challenges the integrity of UNCLOS, and increases the likelihood of confrontation in disputed maritime regions.

Article 22 of China's Coast Guard Law authorizes the Chinese Coast Guard to "use all necessary measures, including weapons, to stop the infringement and eliminate danger" in maritime zones claimed by China—even if these waters are

---

[286] See detailed instructions on requirements for foreign vessels entering and leaving the territorial waters of the People's Republic of China from https://www.msa.gov.cn/html/xxgk/tzgg/thgl/20210827/F56A3BCA-7AA 9–4E12- 8D3D-2DCE3F8BABC9.html, accessed on 31 July 2025.

internationally recognized as falling within another state's maritime areas. This provision raises significant concerns regarding its compatibility with fundamental principles of international law. Specifically, it appears to contravene Article 2(4) of the UN Charter, which prohibits the threat or use of force against the territorial integrity or political independence of any state. Moreover, Article 22 undermines the obligation to settle international disputes by peaceful means, as mandated by Article 279 of UNCLOS and reaffirmed in Article 33 of the UN Charter.

The inclusion of such expansive enforcement powers, particularly in disputed or contested waters, can be viewed as a legal instrument aimed at legitimizing China's non-compliance with the 2016 South China Sea Arbitral Award. This posture further undermines the authority of UNCLOS as the foundational legal framework for maritime entitlements and dispute resolution. Moreover, it risks eroding mutual trust among regional stakeholders and impeding ongoing negotiations, such as those surrounding the Code of Conduct of parties (COC) in the South China Sea. Instead of contributing to a peaceful settlement, these provisions heighten the potential for confrontation and destabilization. As such, they not only escalate tensions but also challenge the integrity of the rules-based international maritime order.

Enactment of National Laws Expanding Administrative Control and Civilian Involvement to Support Gray Zone Tactics

In 1988, China incorporated the Xisha (Paracels) and Nansha (Spratlys) into Hainan province. Subsequently, on 18 April 2020, China announced the establishment of two administrative districts, Xisha and Nansha, in the South China Sea.[287] The creation of the Xisha (Paracel) and Nansha (Spratly) Districts introduces new district governments and party committees, further strengthening China's administrative capabilities and potentially leading to new policymaking dynamics in the region. This expansion of governance is part of a long-term strategy to solidify China's presence and control in the South China Sea.[288]

In addition to its political and administrative maneuvers, China has intensified efforts to assign names to various geographical features in the South China Sea, including submerged entities. This practice began in 1983, when China designated names for 287 features in the region. On 19 April 2020, Beijing announced standardized names for 25 islands, shoals, and rocks, along with 55 underwater features. Among these 80 newly designated entities, 10 shoals and 02 minor rocks are located within the Paracel Islands, while 13 smaller features—referred to as "entities"—are situated near West London Reef, an area currently occupied by Vietnam. Most recently, on 10 November 2024, China's Ministry of Natural Resources and Ministry of Civil Affairs jointly released another set of standardized

[287] CGTN (2020, April 18).

[288] Haver (2020).

names for islands and reefs in the South China Sea. This latest batch included 64 features, such as Houteng Xidao, Ren'ai Nanjiao, and Ren'ai Beijiao, highlighting China's continued efforts to consolidate its claims and administrative control over contested maritime zones.[289] Furthermore, China has sought to internationalize these standardized names by proposing their inclusion in global naming systems, such as those managed by the Sub-Committee on Undersea Feature Names (SCUFN), thereby advancing its narrative and influence in the region.

Gregory Poling, Director of the Asia Maritime Transparency Initiative (AMTI), characterized the decision to assign names to these features as an uncommon step that may contravene international law.[290] A similar view was expressed by Jay Batongbacal, who heads the University of the Philippines College of Law's Institute for Maritime Affairs and Law of the Sea. He emphasized that conducting surveys and naming underwater features during marine scientific research does not, in itself, confer any legal basis for asserting rights over any part of the marine environment. This interpretation aligns with the provisions of UNCLOS, which makes clear that sovereignty over an underwater feature can only be claimed if it lies within 12 nautical miles of a land feature.[291] In response, Ms. Yan Yan, Director of the Chinese Research Centre of Oceans Law and Policy at the National Institute for South China Sea Studies, defended the action by asserting that Beijing was "merely exercising its sovereign right."[292] These contrasting positions underscore a fundamental legal principle in the settlement of territorial disputes: actions by a state to assert sovereignty over an area carry no legal weight if that area is under dispute with another state. This long-established norm of international law is intended to prevent unilateral acts—such as the ones currently undertaken by China—from altering the legal status of contested territories.[293]

China has implemented regulations related to construction, training, and preferential subsidy policies that formalize the establishment of a maritime militia force. This force is primarily focused on maritime coercion rather than fishing activities. Operating under a unique structure, the militia is composed of personnel officially designated as "civilians," yet it is directly managed by local authorities and indirectly overseen by the Central Military Commission through the National Defense Mobilization Board system at both national and provincial levels. These militia vessels are equipped with weaponry, and their hulls are reinforced with steel, enabling them to confront both foreign fishing vessels and law enforcement forces.[294]

According to the Taiwan Institute for National Defense and Security Research (INDSR), China's maritime militia is a key component of its "gray zone"

---

[289] Global Times (2024, November 10).
[290] Pong (2020). See also Huang (2020).
[291] Pong (2020). See also Huang (2020).
[292] Pong (2020). See also Huang (2020).
[293] Guilfoyle (2019), pp. 911–929.
[294] Luo and Panter (2021).

strategy.[295] This approach allows Beijing to assert territorial claims and provoke neighboring countries without crossing the threshold into open warfare. The militia has been repeatedly deployed for this purpose in notable incidents: in 1956 and 1974 at the Paracel Islands, in 1995 at Mischief Reef, in 2012 at Scarborough Shoal, during the HD-981 oil rig standoff in 2014, and at Whitsun Reef between 2019 and 2021. From 2022 to 2025, China also utilized paramilitary forces alongside coast guard units to obstruct the delivery of supplies and construction materials to Second Thomas Shoal, where Philippine troops are stationed.[296] Similar actions occurred at Whitsun Reef and Sabina Shoal.[297]

The Asia Maritime Transparency Initiative (AMTI), in its February 2024 report, noted a significant increase in the presence of China's maritime militia throughout 2023 compared to the previous year, with an average of 195 vessels observed daily across nine key locations. A particularly notable spike occurred at Mischief Reef in July 2023, where more than 180 militia vessels were detected. Although this surge coincided with heightened tensions at Second Thomas Shoal, the analysis suggests that the two events were largely unrelated. The report highlights the growing visibility and coordination between the maritime militia and the Chinese Coast Guard, emphasizing the importance of remote sensing data as a critical tool for monitoring these otherwise covert operations.[298]

The deployment of the maritime militia enables China to advance its strategic interests while avoiding direct military confrontation and potential international backlash.[299] By employing militia forces to harass foreign vessels in contested waters, China maintains plausible deniability, portraying these operations as civilian-led and independent of state control. This tactic reduces the risk of military escalation while facilitating the unlawful occupation of disputed territories.[300]

Combining Legal Warfare with Psychological Warfare and Public Opinion Warfare

China closely integrates the dissemination of unfounded legal arguments with psychological tactics to influence its opponents, their allies, and the broader international community, aiming to undermine cooperation. This strategy is frequently manifested in the South China Sea through a combination of intimidation, false promises, deception, and the deliberate sowing of confusion—targeted at individual coastal states—with the broader objective of dividing ASEAN.

---

[295] See also section "China's Gray Zone Tactics".

[296] Calupitan and Favila (2024).

[297] Pham (2021). See also Mistreanu and Gomez (2024).

[298] Asia Maritime Transparency Initiative (2024, February 28).

[299] Luo and Panter (2021).

[300] Tran (2020), p. 63.

Lawfare in the Disruption of Maritime Economic Activities in the South China Sea

China's assertive tactics in the South China Sea represent a calculated application of lawfare—the use of legal claims and quasi-legal instruments as strategic tools—to disrupt the maritime economic activities of neighboring states.

Vietnam: Energy Development Under Pressure
A prominent example is the Blue Whale (*Cá Voi Xanh*) gas field, Vietnam's largest planned offshore natural gas project. Discovered in 2011 by ExxonMobil in partnership with PetroVietnam, it is projected to supply 9–10 billion cubic meters of gas annually, supporting Vietnam's Power Development Plan 8 (PDP8).[301] Despite being clearly within Vietnam's EEZ under UNCLOS, the project has stalled for years. Beijing's objections to "disputed waters" have deterred ExxonMobil from making a final investment decision, while Chinese Coast Guard patrols near the site are viewed as signals of possible interference.[302]

China's coercive tactics have already inflicted substantial financial costs on Vietnam. In 2020, under direct threats from Beijing, Hanoi was compelled to cancel exploration contracts with Repsol and Mubadala for Blocks 07/03 and 135–136/03, incurring compensation costs estimated at $1 billion.[303] Around the same time, Rosneft and the Noble Clyde Boudreaux drilling rig also suspended operations in Block 06–01, citing similar intimidation.[304] The pressure has not abated. In February 2024, the Chinese Coast Guard vessel CCG 5901 entered Vietnamese waters near Vanguard Bank, directly challenging Vietnam's PDP8 ambitions to expand domestic gas production.[305] This incident occurred against the backdrop of Beijing's promotion of "joint development" schemes in disputed waters, framed as cooperative but widely seen as a lawfare tactic to erode the EEZ rights of coastal states under UNCLOS. Faced with these mounting geopolitical risks, Vietnam must balance its growing energy demands with the challenges of operating in contested maritime zones. One promising path to reduce dependence on fossil fuel development in sensitive areas is the strategic expansion of renewable energy, particularly offshore wind power, which offers both energy security and environmental sustainability.[306]

Malaysia: The Haiyang Dizhi 8 Standoff
China has also projected power beyond Vietnam's EEZ. In August 2023, the survey vessel Haiyang Dizhi 8, escorted by Coast Guard and maritime militia, entered the vicinity of Malaysia's West Capella oil platform, after conducting

[301] Mentor (2018). See also Guarascio and Vu (2023).

[302] Pitlo (2019). See also Guarascio and Vu (2023).

[303] Hayton (2020).

[304] Radio Free Asia (2020, July 13).

[305] Daiss (2024).

[306] Daiss (2024).

similar activities in Vietnamese waters.[307] While Malaysia acknowledged the vessel's presence within its EEZ, its official response was restrained, emphasizing peaceful resolution. Analysts note that Beijing exploited global distractions such as the COVID-19 pandemic to conduct such "routine" incursions simultaneously across multiple EEZs.

The August 2023 standoff followed a separate diplomatic protest by Vietnam, which alleged that a Chinese maritime surveillance vessel had rammed a Vietnamese fishing boat. Although Malaysia acknowledged the presence of the Haiyang Dizhi 8 within its EEZ, its response remained restrained, emphasizing a continued commitment to peaceful dispute resolution. Nonetheless, the incident underscores an ongoing pattern of Chinese assertiveness that not only raises regional tensions but also poses a direct challenge to the international legal framework governing maritime entitlements, especially as set forth under UNCLOS.

Indonesia's Natuna Seas

Although Indonesia is often regarded as a non-claimant state in the South China Sea disputes, it has increasingly faced challenges in countering China's assertive activities, particularly those involving Chinese coast guard and survey vessels. Between December 2019 and January 2020, tensions escalated when a Chinese coast guard vessel, escorting several Chinese fishing boats, entered Indonesia's EEZ near the Natuna Islands. In response, Jakarta lodged a formal protest and summoned the Chinese ambassador. Demonstrating a firm stance, Indonesia deployed four fighter jets to the region—underscoring its commitment to defending national sovereignty and deterring further incursions.[308]

The Philippines: From Scarborough Shoal to Sandy Cay

The Scarborough Shoal incident in 2012 highlighted a significant inconsistency between China's rhetoric and its actions.[309] In April of that year, Philippine authorities discovered Chinese fishing vessels engaged in illegal fishing activities at Scarborough Shoal and attempted to apprehend them. However, their efforts were obstructed by the presence of Chinese vessels. The U.S intervened as a mediator, facilitating an agreement for both China and the Philippines to withdraw their ships from the area. Despite the agreement, after the Philippines complied in June 2012 and withdrew its vessels, believing that China would follow suit, China denied that any such agreement existed. Instead, it continued to deploy additional Coast Guard ships to effectively assert control over Scarborough Shoal. China framed its actions as defensive measures, attempting to position itself as a nation protecting its interests rather than intimidating a smaller country. Nevertheless, these maneuvers appeared designed to provoke the Philippines by feigning withdrawal while unilaterally occupying the area. This incident mirrors the earlier 1995

[307] Ananthalakshmi and Latiff (2023).

[308] The Straits Times (2020).

[309] Lohman (2012). See also De Castro (2014), p. 124).

Mischief Reef event, during which China reassured the Philippines by establishing a base that it claimed was meant to assist fishermen. However, once the Philippines sought to benefit from the resources in that area, China restricted access and militarized the reef.[310]

Following the Arbitral Tribunal's ruling on 12 July 2016, which invalidated China's extensive claims in the South China Sea, Chinese efforts to influence President Duterte's administration became apparent. China sought to dissuade the Philippine government from emphasizing the tribunal's findings, promising increased economic cooperation and substantial investments in return for this restraint. Despite these assurances, the anticipated investments and cooperation from China have largely failed to materialize. Instead, China has escalated its pressure on the Philippines regarding territorial claims in the South China Sea. This heightened pressure has manifested in the deployment of paramilitary and military forces, including Coast Guard vessels, aimed at obstructing shipments of supplies and construction materials to Thitu Island. Thitu Island is a strategically significant location for the Philippines, as it maintains a military presence and has a rudimentary airstrip that the country intends to upgrade. This situation underscores the ongoing complexities and challenges faced by the Philippines in asserting its rights in the contested waters of the South China Sea, particularly in light of China's aggressive tactics.[311]

On 25 January 2025, the Philippines suspended a scientific survey in the South China Sea after two of its fisheries vessels were harassed by Chinese coast guard and navy vessels near Sandy Cay, a feature claimed by both countries. This incident is the latest in a series of escalating confrontations between the Philippines and China in the disputed waters of the South China Sea. China's coast guard asserted its "indisputable sovereignty" over the area, claiming that the Philippine vessels entered Chinese waters illegally and attempted to land on Sandy Cay to collect samples. The Philippines countered that the Chinese vessels engaged in aggressive maneuvers, including deploying small boats to harass the Philippine vessels and a navy helicopter hovering at an unsafe altitude. Despite a recent agreement between Manila and Beijing to seek common ground, the incident highlights the persistent tensions and the challenges to peaceful resolution in the strategically vital South China Sea. The incident comes after an international tribunal ruled in 2016 that China's claims to the area, based on historical precedent, lacked a basis in international law, a ruling that Beijing does not recognize. This ongoing dispute underscores the complex geopolitical dynamics and the challenges to maintaining stability in this crucial maritime region.[312]

---

[310] Meyer (1996).

[311] Bogusz (2024).

[312] Reuters (2025, January 25).

U.S. Response: Freedom of Navigation

In 2016, Chinese President Xi Jinping assured U.S. President Barack Obama that China would not militarize the South China Sea.[313] However, this promise has been broken, as evidenced by China's escalating militarization efforts in the region. China has constructed ammunition depots, deployed missiles, and installed various military equipment on structures it unlawfully occupies in the South China Sea. This breach of trust has elicited a stronger response from the U.S., both in rhetoric and in actions related to the South China Sea. The U.S. has conducted freedom of navigation operations (FONOPS) in the region to affirm its commitment to preserving freedom of navigation and to challenge China's attempts to impose its own rules. These operations signal to China that its unilateral efforts to dictate terms in the South China Sea will not be tolerated by the international community. In particular, the U.S. State Department has vocally condemned China's interference with Vietnam's oil and gas exploration activities in its EEZ.[314] A notable incident occurred in August 2019, when China deployed a government-owned survey vessel, escorted by armed vessels, near Vanguard Bank. The U.S. characterized this escalation as an intimidation tactic aimed at Vietnam and other smaller claimant nations in the South China Sea. Furthermore, this aggressive behavior is part of a wider Chinese strategy to pressure ASEAN countries into limiting their cooperation with non-Chinese firms, raising serious concerns about China's commitment to regional stability and adherence to international maritime law. In light of these developments, the U.S. has reiterated its support for Vietnam, underscoring the significant economic repercussions that Southeast Asian nations may face due to China's obstruction of access to critical hydrocarbon resources.[315]

Dealing with Individual Southeast Asian Countries Over the ASEAN Bloc

China strategically focuses on engaging with individual Southeast Asian countries rather than addressing the ASEAN bloc as a whole. This approach leverages China's greater power relative to each Southeast Asian nation, aligning interactions more closely with China's interests. China has skillfully employed its Three Warfares doctrine through four primary tactics: **intimidation**, **promises**, **deception**, and **confusion**. These methods are strategically used to influence individual Southeast Asian countries and, more critically, to undermine ASEAN unity on the South China Sea issue. By tailoring its approach to each state's political and economic vulnerabilities, Beijing seeks to create divisions within the bloc and weaken collective regional responses to its maritime claims.

The first measure, **intimidation**, involves China's assertive military presence and aggressive maneuvers in the contested waters, such as conducting frequent patrols

---

313 The Straits Times (2019, May 30).

314 Taylor (2019).

315 Taylor (2019).

and engaging in confrontational incidents with vessels from neighboring countries. These actions serve to instill fear and uncertainty in nations like the Philippines and Vietnam, thereby discouraging them from pursuing their territorial and maritime claims vigorously. In a notable development, China's coast guard has commenced patrols along a segment of its self-declared Nine-dash Line in the South China Sea for the first time.[316] These operations are being carried out by large coast guard vessels, including the CCG 5901, which is recognized as the largest coast guard cutter in the world. The patrols have brought these vessels within approximately 55 nautical miles of Philippine shores, marking a significant escalation in China's assertion of control over the region. The Chinese coast guard has defended its actions by asserting that they are in line with China's enforcement of its laws within its claimed territory. However, this assertion directly encroaches upon the Philippines' EEZ, thereby challenging Philippine sovereignty claims and raising concerns in Manila about China's expansive maritime activities. In response to this situation, the Philippine Coast Guard has deployed the BRP Teresa Magbanua to monitor Chinese activities closely and counter the assertion of jurisdiction by the Chinese coast guard. The observed patrol patterns of the Chinese vessels, which follow a north-south trackline closely correlating with the disputed Nine-dash Line, indicate a strategic effort by China to normalize such excursions and gradually establish a new *status quo* in the contested waters. The Philippine Coast Guard perceives this behavior as a deliberate attempt by China to incrementally assert control over the area. In light of this, the Philippines is actively working to counter China's actions by raising awareness about the illegality of these maneuvers within the international community. This includes efforts to draw attention to China's disregard for established international maritime laws and norms, which the Philippines argues undermine its sovereign rights in the South China Sea. The situation underscores the escalating tensions in the region and the complex interplay of national interests as both nations navigate their claims in these contested waters.[317]

The second measure revolves around **promises**, wherein China offers economic incentives, aid, or investment opportunities to countries in the region. These overtures are designed to foster dependency and encourage cooperation with China, often at the expense of collective regional responses to Chinese assertiveness. By positioning itself as a benefactor, China seeks to influence the decisions of neighboring states and reduce the likelihood of coordinated resistance against its territorial claims. For instance, in 2012, under Cambodia's chairmanship, the 45th ASEAN Foreign Ministers' Meeting marked a significant turning point in the organization's history by failing to produce a Joint Declaration—a rare incident in ASEAN's diplomatic engagements. This setback was reportedly influenced by discussions between Cambodian officials and Chinese representatives, highlighting China's strategy of fostering disunity within ASEAN. In April 2025, facing increased U.S. tariffs, China and Indonesia signed a significant Memorandum of

[316] The Maritime Executive (2025).

[317] The Maritime Executive (2025).

Understanding during President Xi Jinping's visit to Jakarta.[318] This was part of Xi's strategic tour of Southeast Asia, which also included stops in Vietnam, Malaysia, and Cambodia from 14 to 18 April 2025. This move is believed to consolidate China's solidarity with ASEAN against the unilateral tariffs imposed by the U.S., but it also has another, subtler objective: to weaken ASEAN unity by using economic incentives. This approach strengthened bilateral relationships while simultaneously diminishing ASEAN's ability to present a united front against China's maritime assertiveness.[319]

Deception serves as the third measure in China's strategy, characterized by the manipulation of information and narratives related to its activities in the South China Sea. This includes employing misleading legal arguments to justify its expansive territorial claims and portraying its military buildup as defensive rather than aggressive. Through these actions, China aims to create an appearance of legality and legitimacy surrounding its ambitions, potentially misleading other nations and undermining their ability to adopt a unified stance against its assertive policies.[320] A notable example of this deception is the presence of military point-defense capabilities—such as anti-aircraft guns and close-in weapon systems—on Chinese-controlled artificial islands in the Spratly Islands. This development directly contradicts President Xi Jinping's 2015 assertion that China would not pursue the militarization of these islands. Subsequently, the Chinese Ministry of Defense has openly acknowledged the deployment of "necessary military facilities," marking a significant departure from Xi's previous commitments and confirming a breach of his earlier promise. This inconsistency further illustrates the complexities and challenges faced by other nations in responding to China's actions in the region.[321]

Confusion, the fourth measure, results from China's strategic communication and fluctuating assertions regarding its intentions and rights in the South China Sea. By utilizing ambiguous language and shifting positions on various maritime issues, China complicates the ability of neighboring countries and ASEAN members to formulate coherent responses. This tactic can lead to misinterpretation and hesitation among regional actors, ultimately undermining collective security efforts. China has employed tactics aimed at influencing certain ASEAN member states, creating divisions within the ASEAN community and instilling a sense of fear that discourages these nations from openly expressing their views on the South China Sea issue. China's efforts have even extended to enticing some countries to lend their support to China's stance on the South China Sea matter. Prior to the 2016 South China Sea Arbitration, Mr. Liu Zhenmin, representing the Chinese delegation at the annual ASEAN-China senior diplomatic officials dialogue in

[318] This Indonesia–China MOU centers on expanded Chinese imports of Indonesian goods and deeper cooperation across sectors like energy and agriculture, signaling to ASEAN that close alignment with China could buffer them against U.S. economic pressure. See Reuters (2025, April 21).

[319] Mingjiang et al. (2025). See also Guarascio and Vu (2025).

[320] Ortagus (2020).

[321] Panda (2016).

Singapore,[322] emphasized the significance of DOC. He asserted that adherence to the DOC is crucial for maintaining peace and stability in the region, and any actions deviating from the DOC would yield negative consequences. This statement was perceived as implying that the Philippines' decision to pursue legal action against China was a violation of the DOC.

Together, these measures of intimidation, promises, deception, and confusion represent an encompassing strategy employed by China to assert its influence in the South China Sea while seeking to dominate the narrative surrounding the region's territorial disputes. By carefully calibrating its approach to the unique situations of each bordering country, China aims to achieve its geopolitical objectives while minimizing opposition and fostering a sense of inevitability regarding its claims. The differing perspectives among ASEAN member states on the South China Sea issue can be attributed to external pressures and diverse national interests, highlighting the complexities that surround this contentious topic within the ASEAN framework. This situation underscores the challenges ASEAN faces in maintaining unity and effectively addressing regional security concerns in light of external influences, particularly from China.[323]

Propaganda by Design: Normalizing the Nine-Dash Line

China's strategy to embed the Nine-dash Line into both tangible and symbolic domains underscores a sophisticated fusion of symbolic propaganda and legal posturing. By saturating passports, apparel, technological tools, and media with this cartographic assertion, Beijing normalizes its expansive maritime claims, making them appear quotidian rather than controversial. Such propagation serves dual purposes: domestically reinforcing national unity and sovereignty, and internationally subtly shaping global perceptions before legal mechanisms can challenge the claim.

China has institutionalized the Nine-dash Line as more than a declarative map; it is a ubiquitous symbol of sovereignty. In 2012, Beijing began issuing passports emblazoned with the Nine-dash Line,[324] prompting swift backlash—Vietnam and the Philippines officially protested, and in some cases, refused to stamp the passports, seeing them as direct infringements on national sovereignty.[325] In a similar vein, a group of Chinese tourists arriving at Cam Ranh airport in May 2018 wearing T-shirts with the Nine-dash Line were ordered to change attire or risk denial of entry—an incident that went viral and sparked national outrage in

[322] Ministry of Foreign Affairs, the People's Republic of China (2016, April 29). Eleventh Senior Officials Meeting on the Implementation of the Declaration on the Conduct of the Parties in the South China Sea Held in Singapore. MFA News, from https://www.fmprc.gov.cn/nanhai/eng/wjbxw_1/201605/t20160504_8523279.htm, accessed on 15 August 2025.

[323] Tran (2013).

[324] 人民网 (2012, November 23).

[325] See section "The Rectification of Information on the South China Sea Issues".

Vietnam.[326] Beyond documents and tourist apparel, the line has permeated digital and consumer domains. In October 2019, Vietnamese authorities mandated the removal of navigation software displaying the line from Chinese-made vehicles and even confiscated a Volkswagen SUV shown at a motor show because its built-in maps included the disputed demarcation.[327] These actions reflect how cartographic propaganda infiltrates everyday technology—normalizing territorial claims across borders—eliciting regulatory responses as a form of counternarrative.

This multi-pronged normalization campaign is deliberate. It saturates both physical and digital spaces with the disputed boundary, reinforcing the line's ubiquity while making resistance appear pedantic. From passports to pop culture, and from in-car display units to consumer electronics, the Nine-dash Line has been positioned as a default representation of Chinese territory. By doing so, China attempts to shift public perception from questioning the map's legality to accepting it as a given, even as international community and arbitration assert its illegitimacy.

The fusion of legal maneuvers and propaganda tactics is exemplified in China's approach, which extends to various aspects of its territorial claims, notably the contentious "Nine-dash Line." China mandates the inclusion of the Nine-dash Line on passports carried by travelers and even prints the map on the apparel of Chinese tourists. An incident in May 2018 vividly illustrates this strategy when a group of Chinese tourists, adorned in T-shirts bearing the Nine-dash Line map, attempted to enter Vietnam via Cam Ranh airport. Vietnamese authorities promptly intervened, requesting the tourists to change their attire before proceeding into the country. Furthermore, China amplifies its territorial narrative by incorporating the Nine-dash Line into navigation software installed in vehicles destined for export to other nations. This deliberate inclusion of the disputed maritime boundary on mapping systems serves to assert China's claims and influence perceptions beyond its borders. These instances underscore China's multifaceted approach in advancing its territorial assertions through a combination of legal mandates and strategic propaganda efforts.

Implications of China's Lawfare in the South China Sea

The lawfare strategy initiated by China has had varying degrees of impact on smaller countries, particularly those engaged in maritime disputes in the South China Sea. A notable example is the Philippines, the state that initiated the landmark arbitration case against China.

During President Rodrigo Duterte's administration, the Philippines adopted a China-friendly approach, prioritizing economic cooperation and investment opportunities. As part of this strategy, the Duterte government deliberately downplayed the significance of the 2016 Arbitral Award, despite its favorable legal implications

[326] Ma (2018).

[327] Bloomber (2019).

for the Philippines. As Duterte remarked, the arbitration victory was "just a piece of paper."[328] This posture can be partly attributed to China's lawfare strategy, which sought to delegitimize the Award through diplomatic pressure, legal reinterpretations, and influence operations.

However, President Ferdinand Marcos Jr. has decisively rejected his predecessor's conciliatory stance. Since taking office, Marcos has reasserted the value of the Arbitral Award and acknowledged the broader implications of China's legal manipulation efforts. As he pledged, the Philippines will uphold the landmark ruling and defend its maritime rights in accordance with UNCLOS.[329]

Consequently, tensions in Philippine-China relations have escalated, as Manila adopts a firmer stance on defending its sovereignty and maritime entitlements.

China's increasing use of lawfare—the strategic deployment of legal instruments to pursue geopolitical aims—poses a significant challenge to the modern international order. Through unilateral interpretation of legal terms, the dissemination of disinformation, and the introduction of so-called "red lines" based on its core interests, China creates confusion and shapes public opinion, particularly among those lacking a solid understanding of international law. This lawfare strategy is reinforced by the implementation of domestic laws related to sensitive regions such as Xinjiang, Tibet, Taiwan, the East and South China Sea, which serve as legal justifications for escalating border disputes and intensifying maritime tensions.

Although China has not yet established a distinct school of international law, scholars anticipate that, through its lawfare strategies, it may develop one within the next 10–20 years to support its strategic ambitions.[330] The incremental nature of these actions—"accumulating small gains"—poses a long-term risk to the stability of the existing international legal order.

China also leverages cultural narratives to shape legal perceptions. As Judge Xue Hanqin has observed, cultural elements increasingly influence legal reasoning in a globalized world. She underscores that historical experiences, societal values, and philosophical traditions play a critical role in how states interpret and apply international law—particularly in non-Western legal systems such as China's.[331] In China's case, this cultural influence is reflected in its strong preference for bilateral negotiations and its reluctance to engage in third-party dispute settlement. This approach—negotiating from a position of strength to compel the other party into consensus—illustrates how China strategically leverages its advantages to shape outcomes in its favor.

In response, regional states and the international community must adopt a coordinated legal and diplomatic strategy to counter these moves. This includes reaffirming UNCLOS, upholding the 2016 Arbitral Ruling, resisting unlawful maritime claims, and advocating for a substantive Code of Conduct (COC) in the South China Sea.

---

[328] Halim (2021).

[329] Strangio (2022).

[330] Rühlig (2018).

[331] Xue (2016).

References

Books

Academy of Military Science Military Strategy Research Department [军事科学院军事战略研究部] (2013) The science of military strategy [战略学]. Military Science Press

Chemillier-Gendreau M (1996) La souveraineté sur les archipels Paracels et Spratleys. L'Harmattan

Chinese Society of International Law (2018) South China Sea: A Critical Study. Oxford University Press, from https://www.mfa.gov.cn/eng/wjb/zzjg_663340/bianhaisi_eng_665278/plpbo/202406/P020240606690256291745.pdf. Accessed on 31 Jul 2025

Hayton B (2018) Writing the History of the South China Sea Disputes. In: Spangler J, Karalekas D, Lopes de Souza M (eds) Enterprises, Localities, People, and Policy in the South China Sea. Critical Studies of the Asia-Pacific. Palgrave Macmillan, Cham, https://doi.org/10.1007/978-3-319-62828-8_1, Accessed on 31 Jul 2025

He Z, Sun L (2020) A Chinese theory of international law. Law Press China and Springer

Kurz J (2019) The South China Sea and how it turned into "historically" Chinese territory in 1975. In: China and the world—the world and China: a transcultural perspective (Vol 3). Ostasien Verlag, pp 133–160

Li WT [黎蝸藤] (2016) 被扭曲的南海史: 二十世紀前的南中國海 [Distorted history of the South China Sea: The South China Sea before the twentieth century]. 五南 [Wǔnán Press]

Lin B (2022) Understanding and countering China's gray zone tactics. RAND Corporation, from https://www.rand.org/content/dam/rand/pubs/research_briefs/RBA500/RBA594-1/RAND_RBA594-1.pdf. Accessed on 31 Jul 2025

Lo CK (1989) China's position towards territorial disputes: the case of the South China Sea islands. Routledge. ISBN 978-041-50-0927-0

Mercier A (2009) The media and searching for political information. In: Perrineau P, Rouban L (eds) Politics in France and Europe. Europe in transition: the Nyu European Studies Series. Palgrave Macmillan, New York. https://doi.org/10.1057/9780230101890_10

Nash PS, Guzel D (2024) Total lawfare: new defense and lessons from China's unrestricted lawfare program. Routledge. ISBN 978-103-27-1020-4

Nguyen HT (2022) Vietnam's position on sovereignty over the Paracels and the Spratlys: Its maritime claims. In E. Y. J. Lee (ed), ASEAN international law. Springer, pp 229–272. https://doi.org/10.1007/978-981-16-3195-5_14

Nguyen HT et al (2023) Chiến tranh pháp lý và thực tiễn áp dụng ở Biển Đông [Lawfare and Application in the South China Sea]. NXB Chính trị quốc gia. ISBN 978-604-57-9101-1

Nguyen HT (2024) Indonesia–Vietnam maritime delimitation: From single-line to double-line. In Nguyen H. T. & Vu. H. D. (eds), Asia and UNCLOS: 30 years' implementation—An assessment. Springer. https://doi.org/10.1007/978-981-97-1556-5_12

Pan S (1996) Spratly Islands, oil politics, and international law. Hong Kong Economics Herald Press

Pham HQ (2014) Hoàng Sa, Trường Sa – Nghiên cứu từ sử liệu Trung Quốc [Paracel, Spratly Islands – A study from Chinese historical sources]. Văn hóa - Văn nghệ Publishing House

Pinos JC, Hau MF (2024) Lawfare: new trajectories in law (1st edn). Routledge. https://doi.org/10.4324/9781003289869 ISBN 978-103-22-6774-6

Qiao L, Wang X (1999) Unrestricted warfare. PLA Literature and Arts Publishing House, from https://www.c4i.org/unrestricted.pdf. Accessed on 31 Jul 2025

Rasilla I de la, Hao Y (2024) China and international dispute settlement by adjudicative and other means. In: de la Rasilla I and Cai C (eds) The Cambridge handbook of China and international law. Cambridge University Press. https://doi.org/10.1017/9781009041133.026

Seo Y (2024) The South China Sea dispute as international law and politics: Discovering the role of law in times of power shift. Brill | Nijhoff

Song YH (2009) Okinotorishima: a "rock" or an "island"? Recent maritime boundary controversy between Japan and Taiwan/China. In: Hong SY, Van Dyke JM (eds) Maritime boundary disputes, settlement processes, and the law of the sea. Martinus Nijhoff, pp 145–175. https://doi.org/10.1163/ej.9789004173439.i-308.56
Wu J [吴杰明], Liu Z [刘志富] (2014) An introduction to public opinion warfare, psychological warfare, [and] legal warfare [舆论战心理战法律战概论]. National Defense University Press
Xi J (2014) The governance of China. Foreign Languages Press
Xinhua News Agency Research Institute [新华社研究院] (2025) Making the South China Sea a Sea of Peace, Friendship and Cooperation: China's Actions. Xinhua News Agency Research Institute. https://f3.xhinst.net/group1/M00/00/B4/CgoMnGhE_VCEDchGAAAAACwCuCM703.pdf, Accessed on 22 Aug 2025
Zaffaroni ER et al (2023) Lawfare: the criminalization of democratic politics in the Global South. Brill. https://doi.org/10.1163/978-90-04535-15-2
中国军事百科全书编审室 (2007) 中国大百科全书·军事 [Chinese Encyclopedia of Military Affairs]. 中国大百科出版社
新华社研究院 [Xinhua News Agency Research Institute] (2025) 挑拨 威胁 谎言——域外势力插手南海问题的事实真相 [provocation, threats, lies—the truth about external forces interfering in the South China Sea issue]. Xinhua News Agency Research Institute, from https://f1.xhinst.net/group2/M00/00/BF/CgoMnmilaq-EOl2IAAAAABctSm4300.pdf. Accessed on 25 Aug 2025
林崇德 (2003) 心理学大辞典(下卷) [Encyclopaedia of Psychology 2. 上海教育出版社, from https://baike.baidu.com/item/%E5%BF%83%E7%90%86%E6%88%98/1698051. Accessed on 31 Jul 2025
陈克勤 (主编) (1996) 中国南海诸岛 [China's Southern Sea Islands]. 海口: 海南国际新闻出版中心. ISBN 7806091955
韩振华 (1988) 我国南海诸岛史料汇编 [Compilation of historical materials on the islands in the South China Sea of our country]. 东方出版

Articles

Chen H (2014) Territorial disputes in the South China Sea under the San Francisco Peace Treaty. Issues Stud 50(3):169–196. https://core.ac.uk/download/pdf/225236036.pdf
Chen HC (2001) La réponse chinoise à l'occupation française des Îles Spratly en 1933. Guerres mondiales et conflits contemporains, 199, pp 5–24. http://www.jstor.org/stable/25732693
Cheng D (2012) Winning without fighting: Chinese public opinion warfare and the need for a robust American response. Backgrounder, 2745. The Heritage Foundation
Cyranoski D (2011) Angry words over East Asian seas. Nature 478:293–294. https://doi.org/10.1038/478293a
Dzurek Daniel J (1996) The People's Republic of China straight baseline claim. IBRU Bound Secur Bull 4(2):77–87, from https://www.durham.ac.uk/media/durham-university/research-/research-centres/ibru-centre-for-borders-research/maps-and-databases/publications-database/boundary-amp-security-bulletins/bsb4-2_dzurek.pdf. Accessed on 31 Jul 2025
Gao Z, Jia BB (2013) The nine-dash line in the South China Sea: history, status, and implications. Am J Int Law 107(1):98–124
Guilfoyle D (2019) The rule of law and maritime security: Understanding lawfare in the South China Sea. Int Aff 95(5):911–929. https://doi.org/10.1093/ia/iiz141
Hayton B (2018) The modern origins of China's South China Sea claims: maps, misunderstandings, and the maritime geobody. Mod China 44(6):571–597. https://doi.org/10.1177/0097700418771678. Accessed on 31 Jul 2025

Hermez M (2020) Global commons and the law of the sea: China's lawfare strategy in the South China Sea. Int Comm Law Rev 22(2):559–588, from https://doi.org/10.1163/18719732-12341447. Accessed on 31 Jul 2025

Hsiao AH (2016) China and the South China Sea "Lawfare". Issues Stud 52(2):1–35. https://doi.org/10.1142/S1013251116500089. Accessed on 31 Jul 2025

Huang Y (2022) Consuming geopolitics and feeling maritime territoriality: The case of China's patriotic tourism in the South China Sea. Polit Geogr 98:102669. https://doi.org/10.1016/j.polgeo.2022.102669

Jiang Z, Liu B, Wang Y et al (2019) Tree ring phototropism and implications for the rotation of the North China Block. Sci Rep 9, 4856. https://doi.org/10.1038/s41598-019-41339-2

Kivimäki T (2002) War or peace in the South China Sea? Nordic Institute of Asian Studies (NIAS), from https://www.academia.edu/82799237/War_or_Peace_in_the_South_China_Sea. Accessed on 31 Jul 2025

Kong Q (2017) International law teaching in China. Cambridge J China Stud 12(1). https://doi.org/10.17863/CAM.21524, from https://www.repository.cam.ac.uk/bitstreams/1a1c7e03-b82e-4d20-8ac4-bcc60a4c1b27/download. Accessed on 31 Jul 2025

Li J, Li D (2003) The dotted line on the Chinese map of the South China Sea: a note. Ocean Develop Int Law 34(3–4):287–295

Li Z (李準) (1933 Aug) 李準巡海記 [On Li Zhun's patrol of the sea]. 國聞周報 10(33):1–8

Liu N, Scott SV (2024) China in the UNCLOS and BBNJ negotiations, yesterday once more? Leiden J Int Law:1–20. https://doi.org/10.1017/S0922156524000347

Livermore D (2018) China's "three warfares" in theory and practice in the South China Sea. Georgetown Secur Stud Rev, from https://georgetownsecuritystudiesreview.org/2018/03/25/chinas-three-warfares-in-theory-and-practice-in-the-south-china-sea/. Accessed on 31 Jul 2025

Luo S, Panter JG (2021 Jan–Feb) China's maritime militia and fishing fleets: a primer for operational staffs and tactical leaders. In: Military Review. Army University Press, from https://www.armyupress.army.mil/Journals/Military-Review/English-Edition-Archives/January-February-2021/Panter-Maritime-Militia. Accessed on 16 Aug 2025

Meyer SE (1996 Jan 8) Incident at mischief reef: implications for the Philippines, China, and the United States (Strategic Research Paper). United States Army War College, Strategy Research Project, from https://apps.dtic.mil/sti/tr/pdf/ADA309432.pdf. Accessed on 31 Jul 2025

Nguyen HT (2000) The China-Vietnam land border delimitation treaty of 30 December 1999. IBRU Bound Secur Bull 8(1):87–90, from https://durham.ac.uk/media/durham-university/research-/research-centres/ibru-centre-for-borders-research/maps-and-databases/publications-database/boundary-amp-security-bulletins/bsb8-1_thao.pdf. Accessed on 31 Jul 2025

Nguyen HT (2011) Khả năng sử dụng Tòa Trọng tài quốc tế về Luật biển trong tranh chấp Biển Đông [The possibility of using the International Tribunal for the Law of the Sea in South China Sea disputes]. Nghiên cứu Lập pháp 17(202)

Nguyen HT (2012) Vietnam's position on the sovereignty over the Paracels and the Spratlys: its maritime claim. J East Asia Int Law 5(1):165–211

Nguyen TLH (2020) Offshore outlying archipelagoes of continental states: Chinese perspectives and counter-arguments. Int Stud 43(2):77–104

Pedrozo R (2014) China versus Vietnam: an analysis of the competing claims in the South China Sea. A CNA Occasional Paper, CNA Corporation, from https://www.cna.org/reports/2014/iop-2014-u-008433.pdf. Accessed on 31 Jul 2025

Pedrozo R (2021) China's revised Maritime Traffic Safety Law. Int Law Stud 97:956–957, from https://digital-commons.usnwc.edu/cgi/viewcontent.cgi?article=2976&context=ils. Accessed on 31 Jul 2025

Peng X (2011) China's demographic history and future challenges. Science 333(6042):581–587. https://doi.org/10.1126/science.1209396

Phan TNM (2018) Vietnamese position regarding China's South China Sea policy of "set aside dispute and pursue joint development. Int J Soc Sci Manage Rev 1(1):30–49, from https://ijssmr.org/uploads/ijssmr01_03.pdf. Accessed on 31 Jul 2025

Publisher's note, from https://www.sciencedirect.com/science/article/pii/S0025326X14006298. Accessed on 31 Jul 2025
Rose C (2016) Fraudulent evidence at the international court of justice. Proc Ann Meet (Am Soc Int Law) 110:329–332. https://doi.org/10.1017/S0272503700103374
Shen J (2002) China's sovereignty over the South China Sea: a historical perspective. Chinese J Int Law 1(1):94–157. https://doi.org/10.1093/oxfordjournals.cjilaw.a000432
Smith SN (2019) Harmonizing the periphery: China's neighborhood strategy under Xi Jinping. Pac Rev 32(5):56–84. https://doi.org/10.1080/09512748.2019.1651383
Talmon S (2016) The South China Sea arbitration: observations on the award on jurisdiction and admissibility. Chin J Int Law 15
Tanner MS (2007) China's economic leverage: a powerful weapon, but Tricky to use. In: Chinese economic coercion against Taiwan: a Tricky weapon to use, 1st edn. RAND Corporation, from http://www.jstor.org/stable/10.7249/mg507osd.14. Accessed on 31 Jul 2025
Uncharted Territory (2011) Nature 478, 285. https://doi.org/10.1038/478285a
United States Confronts China over Seizure of Unmanned Drone in the South China Sea (2017) Am J Int Law, 111(2): 513–517. https://doi.org/10.1017/ajil.2017.33
Whitton JB, Larson A (1964) Propaganda towards disarmament in the war of words. Oceana Publications, Dobbs Ferry, NY, pp 104–132
Wood AS (2021 Mar 8) Historically mine: the (potentially) legal basis for China's sovereignty claims to land in the South China Sea. J Indo-Pacific Aff, Air University Press, from https://www.airuniversity.af.edu/JIPA/Display/Article/2528218/historically-mine-the-potentially-legal-basis-for-chinas-sovereignty-claims-to/. Accessed on 31 Jul 2025
Yoshihara T, Holmes JR (2011) Can China Defend a "Core Interest" in the South China Sea? Wash Q 34(2):45–59. https://doi.org/10.1080/0163660X.2011.562082, from https://csis-website-prod.s3.amazonaws.com/s3fs-public/legacy_files/files/publication/twq11springyoshiharaholmes.pdf. Accessed on 12 Aug 2025
Zou K (2021) Historic Rights in International Law and in China's Practice. Ocean Develop Int Law 32(2):149–168. https://doi.org/10.1080/00908320151100280, from https://www.researchgate.net/publication/248922015_Historic_Rights_in_International_Law_and_in_China%27s_Practice. Accessed on 31 Jul 2025
Zhang L, Zhang L (2017) Research and teaching of international law in contemporary China: a landscape sketch. J East Asian Int Law 2(2):427–445
Zoppolato DG, Farah PD (2025) China's path to modernization and legal pluralism: transplants and the belt and road initiative. Asian J Law Soc 1:1–36. https://doi.org/10.1017/als.2025.7. Accessed on 31 Jul 2025
解放军报 (2004 Jul 16) 中国人民解放军开始"三战"的研究和训练, from https://mil.news.sina.com.cn/2004-07-16/1738210714.html. Accessed on 31 Jul 2025

Theses, Dissertations, and Lectures

Bartman CS (2009) Lawfare: use of the definition of aggressive war by the Soviet and Russian governments. Doctoral dissertation, Bowling Green State University, from https://etd.ohiolink.edu/apexprod/rws_etd/send_file/send?accession=bgsu1241726718&disposition=inline. Accessed on 31 Jul 2025
Sandy JM (2020) Chinese nationalism and the South China Sea. Master's thesis, Wright State University, from https://corescholar.libraries.wright.edu/etd_all/2364. Accessed on 31 Jul 2025
Tran TKN (2020) The use of force in Bien Dong (South China Sea) under the light of international law (Master's thesis, School of Law, Vietnam National University, Hanoi)

Xue H (2016 May 5) Cultural element in international law. University of Manchester—Melland Schill Lecture, from https://www.library.manchester.ac.uk/media/services/library/usingthelibrary/serviceweprovide/digitisation/Judge-Xue-speaker-notes.pdf. Accessed on 31 Jul 2025

Internet Materials

Adjunct Research Professor, from http://en.nanhai.org.cn/index/survey/team_i/cid/3/t/3.html. Accessed on 31 Jul 2025

ASEAN perspectives: Bucking the global trend in trade. HSBC Global Banking & Markets, from https://www.gbm.hsbc.com/en-gb/insights/global-research/asean-perspectives-bucking-the-global-trend-in-trade. Accessed on 31 Jul 2025

Allen-Ebrahimian B (2016 June 21) Beijing: Japanese judge means South China Sea tribunal is biased. Foreign Policy, from https://foreignpolicy.com/2016/06/21/beijing-japanese-judge-means-south-china-sea-tribunal-is-biased-china-philippines-maritime-claims/. Accessed on 31 Jul 2025

Armstrong S (2020 Mar 18) Are we too reliant on Chinese trade? East Asia Forum, from https://www.openforum.com.au/are-we-too-reliant-on-chinese-trade/. Accessed on 31 Jul 2025

Antiokhos [@AntiokhosE] (2021 June 22) [Tweet]. X (formerly Twitter), from https://twitter.com/AntiokhosE/status/1407229477357166595. Accessed on 31 Jul 2025

Al Jazeera & News Agencies (2023 Feb 4) China condemns US military strike on suspected spy balloon. Al Jazeera, from https://www.aljazeera.com/news/2023/2/4/biden-says-us-will-take-care-of-suspected-chinese-spy-balloon. Accessed on 31 Jul 2025

Ananthalakshmi A, Latiff R (2023 Aug 25) Chinese and Malaysian ships in South China Sea standoff, sources say. Reuters, from https://www.reuters.com/article/world/chinese-and-malaysian-ships-in-south-china-sea-standoff-sources-idUSKBN21Z2IW. Accessed on 31 Jul 2025

Asia Maritime Transparency Initiative (2024 Feb 28) Wherever they may roam: China's militia in 2023, from https://amti.csis.org/wherever-they-may-roam-chinas-militia-in-2023. Accessed on 31 Jul 2025

ASEAN Statistical Highlights (2024), from https://www.aseanstats.org/wp-content/uploads/2024/10/ASH-2024-v1-1.pdf. Accessed on 31 Jul 2025

Asia Society Policy Institute's Center for China Analysis (2024) China 2025: What to watch. Asia Society Policy Institute, from https://asiasociety.org/sites/default/files/inline-files/China2025_report%20fin%20web%20Dec6.pdf. Accessed on 31 Jul 2025

Balderton (2019) Engaging with China – Cross the river by feeling for stones, from https://www.balderton.com/news/engaging-with-china-cross-the-river-by-feeling-the-stones/. Accessed 27 Aug 2025

Borton J, Chen S (2025) Beijing's battle of ideas in the South China Sea: how Chinese think tanks deliver maritime strategy. South China Sea NewsWire, from https://southchinaseanewswire.com/wp-content/uploads/2025/07/Beijings-Battle-of-Ideas-in-the-South-China-Sea_FINAL.pdf. Accessed on 31 Jul 2025

Buckley C (2009) China says U.S. naval ship broke the law. Reuters, from https://www.reuters.com/article/us-usa-china-idUSPEK9458120090310. Accessed on 31 Jul 2025

Bloomber (2019 Oct 23) Vietnam orders car importer to ditch navigation maps showing 'nine-dash line' in South China Sea. South China Morning Post, from https://www.scmp.com/news/asia/southeast-asia/article/3034207/vietnam-orders-car-importer-ditch-china-map-app-over-nine. Accessed on 31 Jul 2025

Beckman R, Davenport T (2021 Jul 30) South China Sea arbitral award is not 'a piece of waste paper'. Straits Times, from https://www.straitstimes.com/opinion/south-china-sea-arbitral-award-is-not-a-piece-of-waste-paper. Accessed on 31 Jul 2025

BBC News (2023 Feb 3) Chinese spy balloon: US tracks suspected surveillance device, from https://www.bbc.com/news/world-us-canada-64507225. Accessed on 31 Jul 2025

Bogusz M (2024 Oct 25) China's pressure on the Philippines: the risk of an escalating conflict. OSW Comm Cent East Stud, from https://www.osw.waw.pl/en/publikacje/osw-commentary/2024-10-25/chinas-pressure-philippines-risk-escalating-conflict. Accessed on 31 Jul 2025

Borton J, Chen S (2025 Jul 18) China's war of ideas in the South China Sea. Nikkei Asia, from https://asia.nikkei.com/Opinion/China-s-war-of-ideas-in-the-South-China-Sea. Accessed on 31 Jul 2025

Callahan WA (2020) Map-fare: a cartographic photo-essay. Sens Pol, from https://sensiblepolitics.net/map-fare. Accessed on 31 Jul 2025

China Military Online (2015), from http://english.chinamil.com.cn/news-channels/2015-05/26/content_6507716.htm. Accessed on 31 Jul 2025

China National Knowledge Infrastructure, from https://cnki.net/kns/defaultresult/index. Accessed on 31 Jul 2025

China population. Worldometers, from https://www.worldometers.info/world-population/china-population. Accessed on 31 Jul 2025

China: The Three Warfares (2013), from https://www.esd.whs.mil/Portals/54/Documents/FOID/Reading%20Room/Litigation_Release/Litigation%20Release%20-%20China-%20The%20Three%20Warfares%20%20201305.pdf. Accessed on 31 Jul 2025

CGTN (2020 Apr 18) China's Sansha City establishes Xisha, Nansha districts in major administrative move, from https://news.cgtn.com/news/2020-04-18/China-s-Sansha-City-establishes-Xisha-Nansha-districts-PN5hyJkgFy/index.html. Accessed on 31 Jul 2025

Chi C (2024 Dec 13) Philippines rebukes China's claims over Scarborough Shoal at UN, from https://www.philstar.com/headlines/2024/12/13/2407141/philippines-rebukes-chinas-claims-over-scarborough-shoal-un. Accessed on 31 Jul 2025

Calupitan J, Favila A (2024 Mar 7) China coast guard flexes its might against the Philippines in disputed waters as journalists watch. AP News, from https://apnews.com/article/south-china-sea-philippines-disputed-second-thomas-shoal-5fec2d298151891d79cc077ff02f3a74. Accessed on 31 July 2025

Cash J, Wang E (2025 Jul 14) China's exporters rush to beat Trump's next big tariff deadline. Reuters, https://www.reuters.com/world/china/chinas-exports-imports-pick-up-trump-tariff-deadline-looms-2025-07-14. Accessed on 31 Jul 2025

De Castro RC (2014) The 2012 Scarborough Shoal stand-off. In: The South China Sea maritime dispute, from https://www.researchgate.net/publication/345611834_The_2012_Scarborough_Shoal_stand-off. Accessed on 31 Jul 2025

Dongfang Zaobao [东方早报] (2014) 当代中国南海政策的演变 [The evolution of contemporary China's South China Sea Policy]. Dagongbao [大公报], from http://news.takungpao.com/history/dongjian/2014-05/2472653_4.html. Accessed on 31 Jul 2025

Des Garets Geddes T (2023 Dec 3) China's grand strategy in Asia and beyond according to Shi Yuanhua. Signification, from https://www.sinification.com/p/chinas-grand-strategy-in-asia-and. Accessed on 31 Jul 2025

Daiss T (2024 Apr 9) China thwarts Vietnam's gas production targets in South China Sea. Gas Outlook, from https://gasoutlook.com/analysis/china-thwarts-vietnams-gas-production-targets-in-south-china-sea/. Accessed on 31 Jul 2025

GDP per capita (current US$)—China 2025 World Bank Data, from https://data.worldbank.org/indicator/NY.GDP.PCAP.CD?locations=CN. Accessed on 31 Jul 2025

GEBCO Sub-Committee on Undersea Feature Names (SCUFN) (2025), from https://iho.int/en/scufn. Accessed on 31 Jul 2025

Global Times (2012) China welcomes UN decision on Okinotorishima, from https://www.globaltimes.cn/content/709913.shtml. Accessed on 31 Jul 2025

Glaser BS (2015 Apr 20) On the defensive? China explains purposes of land reclamation in the South China Sea. Asia Maritime Transp Initiat, from https://amti.csis.org/on-the-defensive-china-explains-purposes-of-land-reclamation-in-the-south-china-sea/. Accessed on 31 Jul 2025

Guilfoyle D (2016 Jul 13) South China Sea decision "simply historic": law of the sea expert. Monash University, from https://www.monash.edu/law/news/archive/archive/south-china-sea-decision-simply-historic-assoc-prof-douglas-guilfoyle. Accessed on 31 Jul 2025

Grady J (2016 Sept 23) Geographer: China's claim to South China Sea not rooted in history. USNI News, from https://news.usni.org/2016/09/23/geographer-chinas-claim-south-china-sea-not-rooted-history-british-geographer-journalist-described-chinas-claims-large-swaths-seas-land-formations-off-co. Accessed on 31 Jul 2025

Guarascio F, Vu K (2023 Oct 5) Vietnam sees no gas from Exxon, Gazprom projects for years. Reuters, from https://www.reuters.com/business/energy/vietnam-sees-no-gas-exxon-gazprom-projects-years-draft-govt-document-2023-10-05. Accessed on 16 Aug 2025

Global Times (2024 Nov 10) China announces standard names of some islands and reefs in the South China Sea, from https://www.globaltimes.cn/page/202411/1322772.shtml. Accessed on 31 Jul 2025

Guarascio F, Vu K (2025 Apr 14) China, Vietnam sign deals as Xi visits Hanoi amid US tariff tensions. Reuters, from https://www.reuters.com/world/asia-pacific/chinas-xi-meet-vietnam-leaders-kick-off-southeast-asia-tour-amid-us-tariffs-2025-04-14. Accessed on 31 Jul 2025

Herbert SF (2012) A rock or an island? In: The significance of Okinotorishima and its status under the international law of the sea, from https://www.herbertsmithfreehills.com/notes/arbitration/2012-07/a-rock-or-an-island-the-significance-of-okinotorishima-and-its-status-under-the-international-law-of-the-sea. Accessed on 31 Jul 2025

Huángcháo Zhíshěng Dìyǔ Quántú (皇朝直省地與全圖, Complete Map of All Provinces of the Empire), from https://www.newton.com.tw/wiki/皇朝直省地輿全圖/10232162. Accessed on 31 Jul 2025

Huang K (2020 Apr 25) Beijing could face ASEAN's wrath over 'naming and claiming' of South China sea features, observers say. S China Morn Post, from https://www.scmp.com/news/china/diplomacy/article/3081275/beijing-could-face-aseans-wrath-over-naming-and-claiming-south. Accessed on 12 Aug 2025

Haver Z (2020 May 12) Sansha and the expansion of China's South China Sea administration. Asia Maritime Transp Initiat, from https://amti.csis.org/sansha-and-the-expansion-of-chinas-south-china-sea-administration/. Accessed on 31 Jul 2025

Hayton B (2020 Jul 22) China's pressure costs Vietnam $1 billion in the South China Sea. Diplomat, from https://thediplomat.com/2020/07/chinas-pressure-costs-vietnam-1-billion-in-the-south-china-sea/. Accessed on 31 Jul 2025

Halim D (2021 May 6) Arbitration win over China just a piece of paper: Philippines president. Anadolu Agency, from https://www.aa.com.tr/en/asia-pacific/arbitration-win-over-china-just-a-piece-of-paper-philippines-president/2231477. Accessed on 31 Jul 2025

Hayton B (2021 May 27) Did the allies promise the sea to China? Philippine Strategic Forum, from https://www.stratforumph.com/post/did-the-allies-promise-the-sea-to-china. Accessed on 31 Jul 2025

Hayton B [@bill_hayton] (2021 June 22) [Tweet]. X (formerly Twitter), from https://twitter.com/bill_hayton/status/1407240082516500481. Accessed on 31 Jul 2025

Hayton B [@bill_hayton] (2021 Aug 26) [Tweet]. X (formerly Twitter), from https://twitter.com/bill_hayton/status/1430844688689414149. Accessed on 31 Jul 2025

Hu J (2012 Nov 16) Firmly march on the path of socialism with Chinese characteristics and strive to complete the building of a moderately prosperous society in all respects. Report to the Eighteenth National Congress of the Communist Party of China, from http://www.china.org.cn/china/18th_cpc_congress/2012-11/16/content_27137540.htm. Accessed on 31 July 2025

Instructions on requirements for foreign vessels entering and leaving the territorial waters of the People's Republic of China, from https://8D3D-2DCE3F8BABC9.html. Accessed on 31 Jul 2025

Jacobs JB (2014 June 26) China's frail historical claims to the South China and East China Seas. Am Enterp Inst, from https://www.aei.org/research-products/report/chinas-frail-historical-claims-to-the-south-china-and-east-china-seas/. Accessed on 31 Jul 2025

Kania E (2016) The PLA's latest strategic thinking on the three warfares. China Brief, from https://jamestown.org/program/the-plas-latest-strategic-thinking-on-the-three-warfares/. Accessed on 31 Jul 2025

Key concepts in Chinese thought and culture website, Li (Rites/Social Norms/ Propriety), from https://www.chinesethought.cn/EN/shuyu_show.aspx?shuyu_id=2274. Accessed 27 Aug 2025

Key concepts in Chinese thought and culture website, Law/Dharma, from https://www.chinesethought.cn/EN/shuyu_show.aspx?shuyu_id=3959. Accessed 27 Aug 2025

Kim J (2016) China's diplomacy towards the South China Sea disputes. ISA-HK, from https://web.isanet.org/Web/Conferences/AP%20Hong%20Kong%202016/Archive/81673df0-1a83-4288-80f8-4365d18def22.pdf. Accessed on 12 Aug 2025

Ku J (2016 Dec 16) The Nonexistent legal basis for China's Seizure of the U.S. Navy's Drone in the South China Sea. Lawfare, from https://www.lawfaremedia.org/article/nonexistent-legal-basis-chinas-seizure-us-navys-drone-south-china-sea. Accessed on 31 Jul 2025

Kraska J, Pedrozo R (2016 Dec 16) China's capture of U.S. underwater drone violates law of the Sea. Lawfare, from https://www.lawfaremedia.org/article/chinas-capture-us-underwater-drone-violates-law-sea. Accessed on 31 Jul 2025

Kraska J (2020 Jul 7) China's maritime militia vessels may be military objectives during armed conflict. Diplomat, from https://thediplomat.com/2020/07/chinas-maritime-militia-vessels-may-be-military-objectives-during-armed-conflict/. Accessed on 31 Jul 2025

Luo S, Panter JG (2021 Apr 9) How organized is China's maritime militia. Maritime Execut, from https://www.maritime-executive.com/editorials/how-organized-is-china-s-maritime-militia. Accessed on 31 Jul 2025

Li X (2009 Mar 11) Protest lodged against US incursion. China Daily, from https://www.chinadaily.com.cn/china/2009-03/11/content_7565717.htm. Accessed on 31 Jul 2025

Lohman W (2012 May 14) Scarborough Shoal and safeguarding American interests. The Heritage Foundation, from https://www.heritage.org/asia/report/scarborough-shoal-and-safeguarding-american-interests. Accessed on 31 Jul 2025

Liu Z (2019) China builds rescue centre on artificial Spratly island in South China Sea. South China Morning Post. https://www.scmp.com/news/china/diplomacy/article/2184351/china-builds-rescue-centre-artificial-spratly-island-south. Accessed on 31 Jul 2025

Lin B (2022) Understanding and Countering China's Gray Zone Tactics. RAND Corp, from https://www.rand.org/content/dam/rand/pubs/research_briefs/RBA500/RBA594-1/RAND_RBA594-1.pdf. Accessed on 31 Jul 2025

Li L (2023 May 4) Annual summer sea fishing moratorium begins. China Daily/Xinhua, from https://www.chinadaily.com.cn/a/202305/04/WS645305c2a310b6054fad0ebc.html. Accessed on 31 Jul 2025

Ma N (2018 May 24) When Chinese tourism is unfashionable in Vietnam. Asia Times, from https://asiatimes.com/2018/05/when-chinese-tourism-is-unfashionable-in-vietnam/. Accessed on 31 Jul 2025

Mentor (2018 Jul 27) Nine dash line and the blue whale project—what will happen?, from https://www.mentorimcgroup.com/2018/07/27/blue-whale-project-ca-voi-xanh-exxonmobil/. Accessed on 16 Aug 2025

Mai J (2021) Xi Jinping says China has a legal problem: finding the lawyers to defend its interests abroad. South China Morning Post, from https://www.scmp.com/news/china/politics/article/3123130/xi-jinping-says-china-has-legal-problem-finding-lawyers-defend?module=perpetual_scroll_0&pgtype=article. Accessed on 31 Jul 2025

Maulaya M (2022 June 24) The truth behind China's fishing ban in the South China Sea: Is China sharing its catch, or just baiting its adversaries? Policy Forum, from https://www.policyforum.net/the-truth-behind-chinas-fishing-ban-in-the-south-china-sea/. Accessed on 31 Jul 2025

Ma Z (2023 Aug 28) 2023 Edition of national map released. China Daily, from https://www.chinadaily.com.cn/a/202308/28/WS64ec91c2a31035260b81ea5b.html. Accessed on 31 Jul 2025

Mistreanu S, Gomez J (2024 Aug 19) Chinese and Philippine ships collide again in disputed waters, and the countries are trading blame. AP News, from https://apnews.com/article/china-philippines-sabina-shoal-collision-fd76fcfcbcfcfdce5eb81c9422e8216c. Accessed on 31 Jul 2025

Montemayor MT (2025 Feb 17) PH, China argue over South China Sea row in global security conference. The Philippine News Agency, from https://www.pna.gov.ph/articles/1244284. Accessed on 12 Aug 2025

Mingjiang L et al (2025 Apr 24) How Southeast Asia sees Xi Jinping's regional push amid US–China tensions. Carnegie Endowment for International Peace, from https://carnegieendowment.org/research/2025/04/how-southeast-asia-sees-xi-jinpings-regional-push-amid-us-china-tensions?lang=en. Accessed on 31 Jul 2025

Nguyen HT (2015) The truth about who is biggest aggressor in the South China Sea. Vietnam Law and Legal Forum Magazine, from https://vietnamlawmagazine.vn/the-truth-about-who-is-the-biggest-aggressor-in-the-south-china-sea-3796.html. Accessed on 31 Jul 2025

Nguyen TA (2020) Science journals: a new frontline in the South China Sea disputes. Center Strat Int Stud, from https://amti.csis.org/science-journals-a-new-frontline-in-the-south-china-sea-disputes/. Accessed on 31 Jul 2025

Nelson M (2024 Jul 16) Coast Guard crews spot 4 Chinese warships near Aleutian Islands. Alaska Pub Media, from https://alaskapublic.org/news/2024-07-16/coast-guard-crews-spot-4-chinese-warships-near-aleutian-islands. Accessed on 31 Jul 2025

OUP Blog (2016 May) The emerging of lawfare, from https://blog.oup.com/2016/05/emergence-of-laawfare-infographic/. Accessed on 31 Jul 2025

Ortagus M (2020 Sept 27) China's empty promises in the South China Sea. U.S. Department of State, from https://2017-2021.state.gov/chinas-empty-promises-in-the-south-china-sea/. Accessed on 31 Jul 2025

Page J, Lubold G (2015 Sept 4) Chinese Navy ships came within 12 nautical miles of U.S. coast. Wall Street J, from https://www.wsj.com/articles/chinese-navy-ships-off-alaska-passed-through-u-s-territorial-waters-1441350488. Accessed on 31 Jul 2025

Panda A (2016 Dec 16) It's official: Xi Jinping breaks his non-militarization pledge in the Spratlys. The Diplomat, from https://thediplomat.com/2016/12/its-official-xi-jinping-breaks-his-non-militarization-pledge-in-the-spratlys/. Accessed on 31 Jul 2025

Pitlo LB III (2019 Oct 8) Drivers and risks of China's pressure on Vietnam. Asia Maritime Transp Initiat, from https://amti.csis.org/drivers-and-risks-of-chinas-pressure-on-vietnam. Accessed on 31 Jul 2025

Pong A (2020 May 1) China's naming of geographical features in the South China Sea escalates territorial disputes with Vietnam and Malaysia. Org World Peace, from https://theowp.org/chinas-naming-of-geographical-features-in-the-south-china-sea-escalates-territorial-disputes-with-vietnam-and-malaysia. Accessed on 31 Jul 2025

Phan VS et al (2020 June 16) Examining the "historical evidence" for China's sovereignty over the South China Sea islands (Part 2). US-VN History, from https://usvietnam.uoregon.edu/en/examining-chinese-historical-evidence-of-sovereignty-over-the-south-china-sea-islands-part-2-chinese-official-maps-and-historical-geographical-books-against-chinas-claim-i/. Accessed on 31 Jul 2025

People.com.cn (2021) 《习近平外交思想学习纲要》出版发行 [Xi Jinping's diplomatic thought learning outline published], from https://cpc./shipin/n1/2021/0817/c243247-32195936.html. Accessed on 31 Jul 2025

Pham L (2021) Presence of China vessels in Whitsun Reef: critical hype. Hanoi Times. from http://hanoitimes.vn/presence-of-china-vessels-in-whitsun-reef-critical-hype-316889.html. Accessed on 31 Jul 2025

Poling GB et al (2021 Nov 18) Center for Advanced Defense Studies. Pulling back the curtain on China's maritime militia. CSIS, from https://www.csis.org/analysis/pulling-back-curtain-chinas-maritime-militia. Accessed on 31 Jul 2025

Raska M (2015) Hybrid warfare with Chinese characteristics. RSIS Comm, from https://www.rsis.edu.sg/wp-content/uploads/2015/12/CO15262.pdf. Accessed on 31 Jul 2025

Rühlig T (2018) How China approaches international law: implications for Europe. EUAsia at a Glance, from https://www.eias.org/wp-content/uploads/2016/03/EU_Asia_at_a_Glance_Ruhlig_2018_China_International_Law.pdf. Accessed on 31 Jul 2025

Rapp-Hooper M et al (2019) Responding to China's complicated views on international order. Carnegie Endowment Int Peace, from https://carnegieendowment.org/posts/2019/10/responding-to-chinas-complicated-views-on-international-order?lang=en. Accessed on 31 Jul 2025

Radio Free Asia (2020 Jul 13) Oil company pulls out of Vietnamese oil field as China puts pressure, from https://www.rfa.org/news/oil-china-07132020173206. Accessed on 31 Jul 2025

Regencia T (2020 Jul 16) China's own records debunk 'historic rights' over disputed seas. Al Jazeera, from https://www.aljazeera.com/news/2020/7/16/chinas-own-records-debunk-historic-rights-over-disputed-seas. Accessed on 31 Jul 2025

Ratner E (2022 Aug 2) PRC is using its military, maritime militia, and state-owned enterprises to intimidate the Indo-Pacific region. Global Strat View, from https://www.globalstratview.com/dr-ely-ratner-prc-is-using-its-military-maritime-militia-and-state-owned-enterprises-to-intimidate-the-indo-pacific-region/. Accessed on 31 Jul 2025

RFA Staff (2024 Nov 12) Beijing draws baselines around shoal in Manila's jurisdiction to fortify claims. The Jakarta Post, from https://www.thejakartapost.com/world/2024/11/12/beijing-draws-baselines-around-shoal-in-manilas-jurisdiction-to-fortify-claims.html. Accessed on 16 Aug 2025

Reuters (2025 Jan 25) Philippines suspends South China Sea survey after China's 'harassment', from https://www.reuters.com/world/asia-pacific/philippines-accuses-china-harassing-its-fisheries-boats-south-china-sea-2025-01-25/. Accessed on 31 Jul 2025

Reuters (2025 Apr 21) China to import more Indonesian products, foreign minister says, from https://www.reuters.com/markets/emerging/china-import-more-indonesian-products-foreign-minister-says-2025-04-21. Accessed on 31 Jul 2025

Sakamoto S (n.d.) China's erosion of UNCLOS: distortion through domestic legislation and interpretation, from https://www.cas.go.jp/jp/ryodo_eg/kenkyu/assets/pdf/senkaku/column/sakamoto01_en.pdf. Accessed on 31 Jul 2025

Su H (2011) China's position and interests in the South China Sea: a rational choice in its cooperative policies (p 1). Center for Strategic and International Studies, from https://www.csis.org/analysis/chinas-positions-and-interests-south-china-sea-rational-choices-its-cooperative-policies. Accessed on 31 July 2025

Stokes M, Hsiao R (2018) The People's Liberation Army General Political Department—Political Warfare with Chinese characteristics, from https://project2049.net/wp-content/uploads/2018/04/P2049_Stokes_Hsiao_PLA_General_Political_Department_Liaison_101413.pdf. Accessed on 31 July 2025

Sugandha (2020 Aug 27) Maritime disputes tribunal now has a Chinese member, many call it 'Fox in the Henhouse'. India News Network, from https://www.indianewsnetwork.com/20200827/maritime-disputes-tribunal-now-has-a-chinese-member-many-call-it-fox-in-the-henhouse. Accessed on 31 Jul 2025

Strangio S (2022 May 27) Philippines' Marcos pledges to uphold landmark South China Sea ruling. The Diplomat, from https://thediplomat.com/2022/05/philippines-marcos-pledges-to-uphold-landmark-south-china-sea-ruling/. Accessed on 31 Jul 2025

Schultheiss C (2023 Jul 10) What has China's lawfare achieved in the South China Sea?. ISEAS Perspectives, from https://www.iseas.edu.sg/wp-content/uploads/2023/06/ISEAS_Perspective_2023_51.pdf. Accessed on 31 Jul 2025

Stiftung Wissenschaft und Politik (2023) The quadrilateral security dialogue between Australia, India, Japan and the United States. SWP Comment 2023/C 31, from https://www.swp-berlin.org/publikation/the-quadrilateral-security-dialogue-between-australia-india-japan-and-the-united-states. Accessed on 31 Jul 2025

Strangio S (2024 Nov) China declares baselines around disputed South China Sea shoal. The Diplomat, from https://thediplomat.com/2024/11/china-declares-baselines-around-disputed-south-china-sea-shoal/. Accessed on 31 Jul 2025

South China Morning Post (2025 Apr 9). Xi Jinping vows to boost strategic ties with neighbours as trade war escalates, from https://www.scmp.com/news/china/diplomacy/article/3305809/china-strengthen-strategic-ties-neighbours-xi-jinping-says. Accessed on 31 Jul 2025

解放军报 (2004 May 31) 战时政治工作的一项重要内容:西安政院开设法律战专题教学 法律战走进现代课堂 [An important aspect of political work in wartime: Xi'an Political Academy launches special courses on legal warfare—legal warfare enters the modern classroom], from https://news.sohu.com/2004/05/31/94/news220319483.shtml. Accessed on 31 Jul 2025

解放军报 (2004 Jul 16) 中国人民解放军开始"三战"的研究和训练 [The People's Liberation Army begins research and training on the "Three Warfares"], from https://mil.news.sina.com.cn/2004-07-16/1738210714.html. Accessed on 31 Jul 2025

The collection Ancient Chinese Maps, Available at https://www.viewofchina.com/ancient-chinese-maps. Accessed on 31 Jul 2025

乌元春 (2011) 中国首次指责菲律宾入侵南沙群岛 措辞强硬 [China accuses the Philippines of invading the Spratly Islands for the first time with strong wording]. Huan Qiu, from https://world.huanqiu.com/article/9CaKrnJqU7p. Accessed on 31 Jul 2025

百度百科 (2020) 700多年前, 中国人是如何将一回归年的时长精确到365.2425?, from https://baike.baidu.com/tashuo/browse/content?id=786fffe2b0cbfbf30978b9d1. Accessed on 31 Jul 2025

The Strategic Research Group (2016) Defining the relationship between China's "three wars" and its air power "three wars" case study, from https://www.mod.go.jp/asdf/meguro/center/arpw02/113memo3.pdf. Accessed on 31 Jul 2025

The Guardian (2016 Jul 12) South China Sea dispute: what you need to know about The Hague court ruling, from https://www.theguardian.com/news/2016/jul/12/south-china-sea-dispute-what-you-need-to-know-about-the-hague-court-ruling. Accessed on 31 Jul 2025

The Hong Kong Maritime Rescue Co-ordination Centre, from https://www.mardep.gov.hk/en/public-services/port-services/search-and-rescue/index.html or https://www.info.gov.hk/gia/general/200010/17/1017207.htm. Accessed on 31 Jul 2025

The Straits Times (2019 May 30) Xi broke promise on South China Sea: top US general, from https://www.straitstimes.com/asia/east-asia/chinas-president-xi-broke-promise-on-south-china-sea-says-top-us-general. Accessed on 31 Jul 2025

Taylor G (2019 Aug 22) State department accuses China of muscling Vietnam out of oil and gas exploration. The Washington Times, from https://www.washingtontimes.com/news/2019/aug/22/state-department-accuses-china-muscling-vietnam-ou/. Accessed on 31 Jul 2025

The Straits Times (2020 Jan 7) Indonesia deploys fighter jets in stand-off with China, from https://www.straitstimes.com/asia/se-asia/indonesia-deploys-fighter-jets-in-stand-off-with-china. Accessed on 31 Jul 2025

Tianjin High-end Equipment Research Institute (2021) Xi Jinping's diplomatic thought learning outline published. Tsinghua University, from https://en.tsinghua-tj.org/news/5409.html. Accessed on 31 Jul 2025

The Economist (2021) China is becoming more assertive in international legal disputes, from https://www.economist.com/china/china-is-becoming-more-assertive-in-international-legal-disputes/21804496. Accessed on 31 July 2025

人民网 (2012 Nov 23) 新护照上的中国锦绣山河 (组图) [China's beautiful rivers and mountains on the new passport (Photo series)], from http://world.people.com.cn/n/2012/1123/c1002-19678358.html. Accessed on 31 Jul 2025

Tran TT (2013 Mar 28) China, ASEAN, US in the South China Sea: Rebalancing the triangle. Nghiên cứu Biển Đông, from https://nghiencuubiendong.vn/tran-truong-thuy-china-asean-us-in-the-south-china-sea-rebalancing-the-triangle.6569.adata. Accessed on 31 Jul 2025

Tran HDM et al (2021 Sept 28) Beijing more than just a 'worse violator' in S China Sea. Asia Times, from https://asiatimes.com/2021/09/beijing-more-than-just-a-worse-violator-in-s-china-sea/. Accessed on 31 Jul 2025

Tsuruta J (2024 May 13) The China coast guard and Beijing's strategic ambiguity. The Diplomat, from https://thediplomat.com/2024/05/the-chinese-coast-guard-and-beijings-strategic-ambiguity/. Accessed on 31 Jul 2025

The Maritime Executive (2025 Jan 12) China begins patrolling boundary of its "nine-dash line" claim, from https://maritime-executive.com/article/china-begins-patrolling-boundary-of-its-nine-dash-line-claim. Accessed on 31 Jul 2025

VnExpress (2017 Mar 3) China launches new cruise ship tour to Vietnam's Paracel Islands, from https://e.vnexpress.net/news/news/china-launches-new-cruise-ship-tour-to-vietnam-s-paracel-islands-3549694.html. Accessed on 31 Jul 2025

Valencia M (2021 Sept 13) Vietnam's hypocrisy in South China Sea dispute. Asia Times, from https://asiatimes.com/2021/09/vietnams-hypocrisy-in-south-china-sea-dispute/. Accessed on 31 Jul 2025

Walton T (n.d.) China's three warfares, https://indianstrategicknowledgeonline.com/web/Three%20Warfares.pdf, Accessed on 31 Jul 2025

Wang Y (2021, Aug 6) "Four Respect" on the South China Sea issue. Ministry of Foreign Affairs, from http://eng.chinamil.com.cn/view/2021-08/06/content_10071930.htm, Aaccessed on 31 July 2025

Williams RD (2020) International law with Chinese characteristics: Beijing and the "rules-based" global order. Global China. Brookings Institution, from https://www.brookings.edu/wp-content/uploads/2020/10/FP_20201012_international_law_china_williams.pdf. Accessed on 31 Jul 2025

Xinhua (2016 Dec 18) China to hand over underwater drone to US in appropriate manner. China Daily, from https://www.chinadaily.com.cn/china/2016-12/18/content_27699934.htm

Xinhua (2020 Apr 1) China to launch law enforcement campaign for marine environmental protection, from http://www.china.org.cn/china/2020-04/01/content_75887143.htm. Accessed on 31 Jul 2025

Xinhua (2022 Oct 23) Xi Jinping elected general secretary of CPC Central Committee: Communiqué. People's Daily Online, from http://en.people.cn/n3/2022/1023/c90000-10162373.html. Accessed on 31 Jul 2025

Zhang X (2018 Oct 16) Respect the authority of international law and maintain international order. People's Daily, from http://theory.people.com.cn/n1/2018/1016/c40531-30344197.htm. Accessed on 31 Jul 2025

Zou W (2020) 【全民國防】抵禦中共「三戰」威脅 捍衛民主, from https://www.ydn.com.tw/news/newsInsidePage?chapterID=1216263. Accessed on 31 Jul 2025

Zumbrun J (2021) China wields new legal weapon to fight claims of intellectual property theft. Wall Street J, from https://www.wsj.com/articles/china-wields-new-legal-weapon-to-fight-claims-of-intellectual-property-theft-11632654001. Accessed on 31 Jul 2025

Chapter 3
Lawfulness of Malaysia, Philippines, and Vietnam in the South China Sea: An Overview

As smaller states and claimants in the South China Sea, these countries do not pursue a specific lawfare doctrine. Instead, they advocate for the full and good-faith implementation of international law. Their approach prioritizes lawfulness over lawfare, seeking to resolve disputes through peaceful means. However, depending on factors such as national capabilities, pragmatic policy choices, and the nature of their relationships with China and other external partners, each country demonstrates varying degrees and nuances in the implementation of this approach.

This chapter examines how Malaysia, the Philippines, and Vietnam pursue lawfulness rather than lawfare in addressing disputes in the South China Sea. Unlike China's systematic strategy of legal warfare, these smaller claimant states emphasize the good-faith implementation of international law, particularly UNCLOS, to safeguard sovereignty, maritime rights, and regional stability. Malaysia adopts a cautious and pragmatic approach, combining legal diplomacy, selective occupation of maritime features, and ASEAN-centered multilateralism while avoiding direct confrontation with China. The Philippines has embraced a legal resistance most directly, exemplified by the 2013 arbitration case against China and its continuing reliance on UNCLOS and the 2016 Arbitral Award, supplemented by new domestic legislation and transparency initiatives. Vietnam, meanwhile, underscores the peaceful settlement of disputes, relying on its 3P formula—Publicity, Public Opinion, and Public International Law—as a principled counterweight to China's Three Warfares, while strengthening both domestic and international legal frameworks. Together, these case studies reveal diverse but complementary strategies that prioritize lawfulness as a stabilizing alternative to lawfare. By leveraging international law and diplomatic engagement, these states reinforce the legitimacy of their maritime claims while resisting coercion and contributing to the maintenance of regional order.

H. T. Nguyen, T. K. N. Tran, *Lawfulness and Lawfare in the South China Sea*,
International Law in Asia,
https://doi.org/10.1007/978-981-95-4001-3_3

Malaysia's Lawfulness on the South China Sea

Malaysia entered the South China Sea disputes relatively late and, accordingly, its approach has emphasized the interpretation and application of international law—particularly UNCLOS—to legitimize its maritime claims, rather than to aggressively challenge those of other claimant states. Generally speaking, Malaysia does not maintain an official doctrine or strategic framework specifically focused on lawfare in the South China Sea. Its engagement with the concept has been limited and primarily confined to isolated discussions, such as in the context of fundamental rights, religious freedom, and public order.[1]

In the realm of maritime disputes, Malaysia adopts a "soft hedging" strategy—a nuanced balancing act that seeks to uphold national interests while preserving amicable relations with major powers, especially China.[2] This approach is defined by non-confrontational behavior, the use of legal diplomacy, and a focus on economic pragmatism. Rather than resorting to overt power projection, Malaysia emphasizes the protection of its maritime entitlements through diplomatic means, while simultaneously reinforcing bilateral and multilateral cooperation within ASEAN frameworks. This reflects a broader policy orientation aimed at preserving regional stability and ensuring that the South China Sea remains a zone of peace and constructive engagement.

Historical and Legal Background of Malaysia's Claims

Malaysia's assertions in the South China Sea are grounded in its 1979 publication of the Peta Baru Menunjukkan Sempadan Perairan dan Pelantar Benua Malaysia (New Map Showing the Territorial Waters and Continental Shelf Boundaries of Malaysia).[3] This map delineated Malaysia's maritime boundaries, including claims over parts of the Spratly Islands (Kepulauan Spratly), based on its interpretation of rights to the continental shelf and EEZ under UNCLOS. Relying on the 1979 map, Malaysia progressively established a presence on several maritime features, Swallow Reef (Layang-Layang) in 1983, Ardasier and Mariveles Reefs in 1986, Dallas and Louisa Reefs in 1987, Erica Reef in 1993, and Navigator Reef in 1999. These actions elicited diplomatic protests from other claimant states, notably Vietnam and the Philippines.

Malaysia's position, as reflected in the 1979 map, rests on two principal legal foundations:

---

[1] St Antony's College, University of Oxford (2019).

[2] Nguyen Huu Tuc (2015).

[3] Country Profile from the Maritime Awareness Project: Malaysia, from https://www.nbr.org/publication/malaysia/, accessed on 31 July 2025.

First, it asserts entitlement to the continental shelf and a 200-nautical-mile EEZ, measured from both its mainland and insular baselines, in accordance with the provisions of UNCLOS.

Second, Malaysia claims sovereignty over maritime features located within these maritime zones, operating under the assumption that geographic proximity and continental shelf entitlements can reinforce its sovereign claims over such features.

However, this interpretation faces legal challenges. UNCLOS, particularly Article 77, affirms that rights over the continental shelf exist ipso facto and ab initio, independent of occupation or explicit proclamation. Thus, Malaysia cannot use continental shelf entitlements to justify sovereignty over land features. Moreover, Article 121 stipulates that maritime zones are generated from land territory (including islands), not *vice versa*—occupying maritime zones does not, in itself, establish sovereignty over land features within them.

The features occupied by Malaysia in the South China Sea, though more modest in scale than the claims of China or Vietnam, hold significant strategic value. They provide a military and logistical foothold in contested waters, support national energy security due to potential hydrocarbon reserves, and ensure continued access to vital fisheries. Malaysia was among the earliest regional actors to expand the civilian use of its occupied features. Swallow Reef (Layang-Layang), located roughly 300 kilometers from the coast of Borneo, exemplifies this approach. Since the 1980s, Malaysia has maintained a military presence on the reef and gradually developed it into a semi-civilian facility, including an airstrip and modest tourism infrastructure. Rather than provoking confrontation, Malaysia's objective has been to seek recognition of the *status quo*. Malaysia's South China Sea policy is shaped by the dual imperatives of protecting sovereignty and preserving stable ties with major powers, especially China. While it consistently affirms its maritime claims through patrolling and limited development, it avoids public confrontation and prefers a restrained, low-profile diplomatic approach. This reflects Malaysia's broader strategic calculus: China is its largest trading partner and a key source of investment, making bilateral stability a core foreign policy priority. At the same time, Malaysia is a founding member of ASEAN and supports the bloc's central role in managing regional maritime disputes. Despite ASEAN's often slow, consensus-based processes, Malaysia continues to back its efforts to promote dialogue and finalize a Code of Conduct with China.

Beyond regional diplomacy, Malaysia maintains security cooperation with countries such as the U.S., Australia, and Japan through joint exercises and capacity-building programs. These partnerships help strengthen Malaysia's maritime capabilities without signaling alignment against China.

In essence, Malaysia's claims, while legally framed through UNCLOS, also reflect broader national interests in resource protection, territorial integrity, and regional influence. Although Malaysia does not assert a lawfare doctrine *per se*, its strategy illustrates a legalist posture aimed at reinforcing claims through international law and the selective occupation of geographically favorable features.

Malaysia's Approaches to Lawfare in the South China Sea Disputes

Since the early 1990s, Malaysia has sought to assert and safeguard its territorial claims and sovereign rights within its EEZ and Continental Shelf claim. While maintaining a modest but consistent military presence on several features in the Spratly Islands, Malaysia has strategically utilized international legal frameworks to reinforce its security and jurisdictional claims. Central to this effort is Malaysia's firm rejection of China's expansive Nine-dash Line, which it regards as a serious violation of international law and an encroachment on its maritime rights.

Malaysia's legal diplomacy has grown more assertive in recent years. In May 2009, Malaysia and Vietnam jointly submitted a claim to the CLCS, in accordance with Article 76(8) of UNCLOS. This move was aimed at extending the continental shelf beyond 200 nautical miles in parts of the South China Sea. In December 2019, leveraging the landmark 2016 Arbitral Award that found most features in the Spratlys incapable of generating EEZs, Malaysia submitted a partial claim to the CLCS for an extended continental shelf in the northern part of the South China Sea. Although this triggered strong objections from China and the Philippines, it also encouraged other claimants to clarify their own maritime claims, contributing to a more transparent legal discourse in the region.[4]

Following the ICJ rulings related to maritime disputes with Indonesia and Singapore,[5] Malaysia has become more cautious and prefers not to pursue high-profile legal challenges like the Philippines' 2013 arbitration case. Nevertheless, Malaysia consistently emphasizes that maritime entitlements should be determined in accordance with UNCLOS. While upholding this principle, it seeks to manage disputes primarily through diplomacy, particularly by engaging in quiet bilateral discussions aimed at conflict mitigation.

Malaysia's strategy for countering China's Three Warfares has been notably consistent across the administrations of Prime Ministers Mahathir Mohamad, Najib Razak, and Anwar Ibrahim, and can be summarized in three key points. First, Malaysia seeks to steadfastly assert and defend the country's territorial claims and sovereign rights within its EEZ, and, when necessary, is prepared to extend its continental shelf claims based on UNCLOS and the 2016 Arbitral Tribunal Award.

Second, Malaysia attempts to downplay the consequences of Chinese incursions into its waters and refrains from strong public condemnation when not necessary. This is to avoid decoupling the country's vital economic ties with China, its largest trading partner and an important source of investment.

---

[4] Nguyen (2019). See also Parameswaran (2015).

[5] Sovereignty over Pedra Branca/Pulau Batu Puteh, Middle Rocks and South Ledge (Malaysia/Singapore), Judgment, I.C.J. Reports 2008, from https://icj-cij.org/sites/default/files/case-related/130/130-20080523-JUD-01-00-EN.pdf, accessed on 31 July 2025; Sovereignty over Pulau Ligitan and Pulau Sipadan (Indonesia/Malaysia), Judgment, I.C.J. Reports1998, from https://icj-cij.org/case/102, accessed on 31 July 2025.

Third, the country supports the ASEAN-China conflict management process, namely the ongoing negotiations for a COC, and promotes a peaceful resolution of the dispute through bilateral negotiations.

Malaysia's three-pronged policy is quite pragmatic.[6] The country publicly rejected China's Nine-dash Line claim in 2019, calling it "ridiculous," but is also willing to remain quiet about the China Coast Guard's near-constant presence at Luconia Shoals and its regular harassment of Malaysian drilling rigs and survey ships in its EEZ in 2023. Kuala Lumpur deployed military personnel to the five atolls it occupies in the contested Spratly Islands in the 1990s, filed a joint continental shelf submission with Vietnam in 2009, and made an extended continental shelf claim in 2019. However, it tends to react to the presence of other foreign warships in the area, viewing them as a destabilizing factor. Unlike the Philippines, Malaysia is also willing to control media coverage to avoid transparency on maritime incidents, but is prepared to be firm when its interests are threatened. For instance, when Beijing raised "concerns" about Petronas' activities, Prime Minister Anwar responded that "Malaysia sees the area as Malaysian territory, therefore Petronas will continue its exploration activities there."[7]

Malaysia has adopted what scholars describe as "triadic maritime diplomacy"—a strategic blend of coercive, persuasive, and cooperative approaches in navigating maritime tensions in the South China Sea.[8] This framework reflects Malaysia's broader diplomatic posture, which emphasizes pragmatism, discretion, and the prioritization of national interest over confrontation. Despite rising regional tensions, Malaysia has pursued a measured response. For instance, although it filed diplomatic protests in response to China's 2023 map reasserting the Nine-dash Line and, more recently, against the Philippines' maritime submissions and new legislations in 2024—both perceived as infringing upon Malaysian maritime boundaries—it has largely downplayed incidents involving the China Coast Guard.[9] These include the regular harassment of Malaysian drilling operations and persistent patrols near the Luconia Shoals. Rather than escalate such events through the media or legal confrontation, Malaysia favors backchannel diplomacy and avoids overt conflict, reflecting its strategic effort to separate security concerns from its critical economic relationship with China—its largest trading partner and a major investor.[10]

Drawing on Malaysia's conduct from the 1970s to 2023, Emirza Syailendra (2024) argues that Kuala Lumpur's seemingly low-key posture in the South China Sea is not passivity but a calculated small-state strategy to avoid an "action–reaction spiral":[11] Malaysia asserts rights through law, quiet diplomacy and measured maritime

[6] Storey (2024).

[7] Amy Chew (2023).

[8] Putra (2024).

[9] Storey (2024).

[10] Strangio (2023).

[11] Syailendra (2024). See also Bentley (2023).

presence while calibrating responses to minimize escalation with larger powers, preserve economic ties and keep strategic options open—recasting apparent inertia as purposeful restraint. To reinforce its maritime position, Malaysia maintains a continuous naval and enforcement presence, notably in areas like the Luconia Shoals, while investing in modest but strategically placed infrastructure such as a new naval base in Bintulu and Spratly Island outposts,[12] enabling effective sovereignty assertion without provoking confrontation. These efforts are paired with calibrated responses—continuing energy exploration within its EEZ despite Chinese objections, and dispatching maritime patrols when foreign vessels encroach—all framed within a broader strategy of measured defense modernization and diplomatic restraint to safeguard territorial and resource interests while preserving political and economic stability.[13]

Malaysia's support for ASEAN-led dispute management is another key component of its approach. It remains committed to the development of a COC in the South China Sea and views ASEAN unity as essential for collective bargaining power.[14] However, Malaysian officials, including Foreign Minister Mohamad Hasan, have emphasized that the COC is strictly a framework for engagement between ASEAN and China. They assert that any resolution of sovereignty disputes in the South China Sea must ultimately be achieved through direct negotiations among the relevant claimants, without external involvement.[15]

In sum, Malaysia's approach to the South China Sea dispute differs notably from those of Vietnam or the Philippines. It does not embrace lawfare as a confrontational tool but instead engages in lawful behavior to the extent necessary to protect its national interests while avoiding serious violations of international law. Rather than using legal mechanisms as instruments of strategic warfare, Malaysia deploys legal diplomacy, quiet assertion, and multilateral engagement to uphold its claims in a manner that maximizes security and economic benefits while minimizing the risk of conflict.

The Philippines' Lawfulness on the South China Sea

Historical and Legal Background of the Philippines' Claims

The Philippines first became involved in the Spratly Islands sovereignty dispute in 1950. On May 17 of that year, President Elpidio Quirino asserted that, under international law, the Spratly Islands should belong to the nearest country—namely, the Philippines. This statement provoked strong protests from both China and

[12] Daniel (2024). See also Krishnan (2020).

[13] Sadi et al. (2024). See also Mahmud (2025).

[14] Ryan (2023).

[15] Bernama TV (2024, April 25).

Vietnam, particularly during the proceedings of the 1951 San Francisco Peace Treaty negotiations.[16]

The issue resurfaced on 15 May 1956, when Filipino national Thomas Cloma and his companions landed on several Spratly Islands. Cloma unilaterally claimed sovereignty over these islands, renaming them "Freedomland," based on assertions of discovery and occupation. Shortly afterward, he requested official Philippine protection over the territory he claimed to govern. Responding to this, Philippine Foreign Secretary Carlos P. Garcia held a press conference on 25 May 1956, declaring that the group of islands in the South China Sea—excluding seven islets internationally recognized as part of the Spratlys in France's 1933 declaration (Itu Aba, Spratly Island, Northeast Cay, Southwest Cay, Loaita, Amboyna Cay and Thitu)[17]—were *terra nullius* (land belonging to no one). Due to their proximity to the Philippine archipelago and their strategic relevance to national defense, Garcia claimed these islands rightfully belonged to the Philippines.[18] Both Vietnam and China strongly protested Garcia's statement. Nevertheless, in 1971, under the pretext of protecting national security, Philippine forces occupied several Spratly features—Likas (West York), Parola (Northeast Cay), Kota (Loaita), and Pag-asa (Thitu Island).[19] The occupation expanded in 1978 with the seizure of Panata Island (Lankiam Cay). That same year, Presidential Decree No. 1596 on 11 June 1978 established a new administrative unit named Kalayaan (Freedomland), which was annexed to the province of Palawan. The decree outlined specific geographic coordinates that enclosed the claimed area and asserted full Philippine sovereignty over its terrestrial, maritime, and aerial domains.[20] In 1980, the Philippines occupied another small feature, Commodore Reef, located approximately 180 nautical miles from the nearest previously occupied island.

Historical records and naming conventions indicate that, compared to Vietnam and China, the Philippines lacks longstanding historical ties to the Spratly Islands. The country's boundaries were initially defined under Article 3 of the 1898 Treaty of Paris between Spain and the U.S. and were further clarified by the 1900 U.S.—U.K. Treaty.[21] The maritime boundaries established under these treaties were reaffirmed by Philippine Republic Act No. 3046 (1961).[22] The Spratly Islands lie

[16] Central Intelligence Agency (1971).

[17] Asia Sentinel (2015, May 26).

[18] Rosen (2014), p. 12.

[19] Rosen (2014), p. 27.

[20] Presidential Decree No. 1596 (1978, June 11). Declaring certain area part of the Philippine territory and providing for their government and administration. The LawPhil Project, from https://www.lawphil.net/statutes/presdecs/pd1978/pd_1596_1978.html accessed on 31 July 2025

[21] Avalon Project (1898, December 10) Treaty of peace between the U.S. and Spain. Yale Law School, from https://avalon.law.yale.edu/19th_century/sp1898.asp accessed on 31 July 2025. See also Longley (2019).

[22] Republic Act No. 3046 (1961, June 17). An act defining the baselines of the territorial sea of the Philippines (as amended by RA 5446), from https://lawphil.net/statutes/repacts/ra1961/ra_3046_1961.html accessed on 31 July 2025.

outside the western boundaries defined in these treaties, placing them beyond the scope of Philippine territorial sovereignty as traditionally understood.

Consequently, the Philippines has largely relied on geographical proximity and legal reinterpretations to support its claims. Its legal argument rests on the notion *terra nullius* and could be claimed through discovery. The Philippines argued that after WWII, the islands were under *de facto* trusteeship of the Allied Powers, and Japan had renounced all claims to them. Lacking a formal postwar settlement for the islands, the Philippines contended that these features were open for settlement and economic exploitation by any Allied member on an equal-opportunity basis.[23]

The Philippines' legal claim to sovereignty over the Spratly Islands is weak for several reasons. First, the Spratly Islands—broadly defined to include reefs, rocks, and low-tide elevations—have long been subject to claims by Vietnam, China, France, the United Kingdom, and Japan. Therefore, they do not qualify as *terra nullius* under international law. Second, Thomas Cloma, a private citizen, unilaterally declared a claim to the area without legal authority or state endorsement. His actions cannot be interpreted as conferring sovereignty to the Philippine state, as they do not align with international legal principles governing territorial acquisition. Both Vietnam and China formally rejected his claims. Third, even if the islands had been under Allied trusteeship following World War II, the Philippines would have required explicit Allied consent to assert sovereignty. No such consent was ever granted, including during the occupation of Pag-asa (Thitu) Island in 1978 or the subsequent occupation of other features. Moreover, the Philippine government has never clearly distinguished between the Spratly Islands and the area known as "Freedomland." It appears to be a political effort to rebrand the area under a new name, "Kalayaan," but this does not alter the legal character of the sovereignty dispute. While the Philippines may legitimately claim an EEZ and continental shelf under UNCLOS, the legal regime governing maritime zones cannot serve as a basis for asserting sovereignty over islands.[24]

Despite its lack of strong historical or legal foundations for territorial acquisition in the Spratly Islands, the Philippines does have a valid basis for extending its EEZ and continental shelf in accordance with UNCLOS. This reality helps explain the country's recent pivot toward greater reliance on UNCLOS and the 2016 Arbitral Ruling in its maritime diplomacy.

Philippines' Approaches to Lawfare in the South China Sea Disputes

To assess the Philippines' perspective on lawfare and its implementation of international law, including UNCLOS, in the South China Sea, this analysis will examine both scholarly opinions and the actions of the Philippine government.

---

[23] National Bureau of Asian Research (n.d.). Philippines. Maritime Awareness Project, from https://www.nbr.org/publication/philippines/ accessed on 31 July 2025.

[24] Nguyen (2004), pp. 264–269.

Philippine Scholarly Views on Lawfare and Legal Resistance in the South China Sea

In his public statements, former Philippine National Security Adviser Roilo Golez consistently advocated for the use of "lawfare, not warfare"[25] as a strategic response to China's militarization of reclaimed reefs, atolls, and shoals in the South China Sea—many of which have been transformed into artificial islands. Golez emphasized that the 2016 Arbitral Ruling now forms part of international law and can be invoked by the Philippines, alongside the provisions of UNCLOS, to assert and protect its sovereign rights. He argued that all states—regardless of their size, including China, the U.S., and the Philippines—must comply with international law as responsible members of the international community.[26]

Renato Cruz De Castro, professor at De La Salle University, similarly underscores the Philippines' reliance on legal frameworks and international arbitration to address complex territorial disputes. He highlights lawfare as a strategic diplomatic tool in the South China Sea, particularly in response to Chinese assertiveness. De Castro views the filing of the South China Sea arbitration case and the subsequent ruling as acts of legal resistance aimed at defending Philippine sovereignty.[27]

Meanwhile, Jay L. Batongbacal of the University of the Philippines argues that China is actively engaging in lawfare—using legal tools strategically to legitimize and reinforce its maritime claims in the South China Sea. He contends that the Philippines and other affected states must counter these tactics by reinforcing their legal positions through international mechanisms such as UNCLOS. Batongbacal advocates for upholding the rule of law and pushing for China's compliance with the 2016 Arbitral Award, while also encouraging cooperation among ASEAN members and broader international partners to safeguard their interests and build resilience against the growing influence of the regional giant.[28]

In addressing China's historic claims, Philippine Supreme Court Senior Associate Justice Antonio Carpio has been leading a truth campaign to counter the People's Republic of China's expansive assertions over the South China Sea since 2019.[29] He stresses that the Philippines must educate the Chinese people on the true history of the South China Sea—that, as authoritatively ruled by The Hague tribunal, there is no historical evidence whatsoever that China owned, possessed, or controlled the South China Sea at any time in China's history. He has dubbed this ongoing effort, the South China Sea Truth Movement, a grassroots movement utilizing freedom of expression to clarify the historical facts about the South China Sea. Justice Carpio has invited the peoples of Vietnam, Malaysia, Indonesia, and Brunei—countries whose EEZs are also affected by China's nine-

[25] Villanueva (2018).

[26] Villanueva (2018).

[27] De Castro (2014). pp. 111–129. See also De Castro (2017), pp. 345–370.

[28] Batongbacal (2021).

[29] Institute for Maritime and Ocean Affairs (2019). See also Indo-Pacific Defense Forum (2019).

dashed line—to join this movement. Additionally, he has published a book, The South China Sea Dispute: Philippine Sovereign Rights and Jurisdiction in the West Philippine Sea, available online,[30] to further engage and promote the movement.

Although there remains some ambiguity in the use of the term lawfare—whether it carries a positive or negative connotation—there is a prevailing consensus among Philippine scholars that lawfare is a central element of China's regional strategy. They emphasize that international law, particularly UNCLOS, provides the most legitimate and peaceful means of response.

The Use of Judicial Mechanisms in Philippine Counter-Lawfare Strategy

After the Scarborough incident in 2012 and under increasing pressure from China on the ground, the Philippines decided to pursue a legal solution involving the participation of a third party. The decision to initiate legal proceedings was influenced by at least four key factors. First was the U.S.—Philippines alliance and renewed hopes for American support in the aftermath of the Scarborough Shoal standoff. Despite lingering doubts about the U.S.'s response during the crisis, the Philippines placed increased confidence in the 1951 U.S.—Philippines Mutual Defense Treaty, which was seen as a crucial element in deterring further aggressive actions by China in the South China Sea. Second, the Philippines grew increasingly disillusioned with DOC, viewing it as ineffective in restraining China's assertive behavior. As legal scholar Bernard Oxman noted, DOC lacks the status of a binding legal instrument, resulting in what he described as "the absence of a clear legal order" in the region—an absence that has contributed to both legal uncertainty and strategic instability.[31] Third, the Philippines' consistent and rigorous adherence to UNCLOS provided a solid legal foundation for its position in the arbitration case, allowing it to frame its arguments squarely within the framework of international law. Finally, the Philippines also explored peaceful means of engaging with China by pursuing a bilateral agreement for joint exploration and development in parts of the Spratly Islands—an approach that initially excluded Vietnam in 2003. However, due to Vietnam's strong objections and insistence on multilateralism in disputed areas, a tripartite agreement involving the Philippines, China, and Vietnam was eventually concluded. This was formalized in the 2005 Tripartite Joint Marine Seismic Undertaking (JMSU), which aimed to conduct seismic surveys in a designated area of the South China Sea. The JMSU, however, expired in 2008, and the Philippines later chose not to renew the agreement due to rising domestic concerns over sovereignty, transparency, and legal consistency with the Philippine Constitution.[32]

---

[30] Carpio (2017).

[31] Oxman (2017), pp. 235–256.

[32] Storey (2008). See also Dong (2024), pp. 921–926.

The country undertook thorough preparations to bring China to court in 2012, beginning with assembling the right personnel. Three key figures played pivotal roles in both the decision to file the case and the preparation process. Philippine Supreme Court Justice Antonio Carpio emerged as a leading advocate among Filipino scholars for using legal means to counter China's excessive claims in the South China Sea. He had long established a research team composed of prominent national and international maritime law experts. Meanwhile, Foreign Affairs Secretary Albert del Rosario, who took office in 2011 during a period of intensifying Chinese assertiveness, set up a task force on the West Philippine Sea at the Department of Foreign Affairs. This task force included key members from the Offices of Maritime and Ocean Affairs and Asia-Pacific and was tasked with crafting strategic responses to regional incidents. Former President Benigno Aquino III also played a decisive role. In the wake of the 2012 Scarborough incident, he convened a meeting with his cabinet and representatives from both the Senate and the House of Representatives.[33]

Regarding legal proceeding strategy, the Philippines consulted international legal experts, engaging four prominent international lawyers to provide preliminary opinions: W. Michael Reisman, a professor of international law at Yale University; Bernard Oxman, a law professor at the University of Miami; Carolyn Lamm from the law firm White & Case; and Paul Reichler of the Foley Hoag law firm. The Philippines ultimately decided to pursue arbitration under Annex VII of UNCLOS, relying on the Convention's compulsory dispute settlement procedures. This strategic choice enabled the Philippines to construct a strong argument affirming the tribunal's jurisdiction. It submitted 17 carefully framed questions requesting interpretations of relevant UNCLOS provisions while deliberately avoiding any request for the tribunal to resolve sovereignty disputes, which fall outside its jurisdiction.

The Philippines also decided to amend its domestic laws to address legal gaps and align with the provisions of UNCLOS. In 2009, the Philippines enacted the Baselines Law (RA 9522), which redrew the archipelagic baselines in accordance with UNCLOS provisions. This law explicitly excluded Scarborough Shoal and the Kalayaan Island Group—areas under Philippine sovereignty claims in the Spratlys—from the archipelagic waters established by the new baselines.[34] According to the Philippine Supreme Court, establishing archipelagic baselines in accordance with UNCLOS will (i) prevent other countries from freely entering and exploiting resources in Philippine waters, and (ii) help preserve the integrity of the national position in international disputes involving Philippine maritime rights. Therefore, the maritime zones calculated from Scarborough and Kalayaan will follow the "regime of islands," allowing each entity to maintain its own maritime zones, which are subject to the decisions of the court.[35]

---

[33] Vitug (2018).

[34] Supreme Court of the Philippines E-Library (2009, March 10) Republic Act No. 9522—An act to amend certain provisions of Republic Act No. 3046, as amended by Republic Act No. 5446, to define the archipelagic baseline of the Philippines and for other purposes, from https://elibrary.judiciary.gov.ph/thebookshelf/showdocs/2/2318 accessed on 31 July 2025.

[35] Mérueñas (2011).

Leveraging their experience in litigation before international courts and their expertise in maritime law, the legal advisors for the Philippine government anchored the arbitration case on two primary issues: (i) the rejection of China's Nine-dash Line claim as inconsistent with UNCLOS, and (ii) a request for the Arbitral Tribunal to determine the legal status of features in the Spratly Islands and their capacity to generate maritime zones. One of the most significant challenges was anticipating how the Tribunal would assess the legal status of Itu Aba (Taiping Island), the largest naturally formed feature in the Spratlys.

To support its position, the Philippines had to compile and present a wide array of technical documents, nautical charts, historical records, and expert legal and scientific opinions to argue that none of the features in the Spratly Islands—including Itu Aba—was capable of generating an EEZ or continental shelf beyond 12 nautical miles. During the hearings on 25 November 2015, Philippine counsel underscored the principle of equity, arguing that allowing small and insignificant entities that merely appear above water at high tide to generate full EEZs and continental shelves would be unreasonable and unfair to other coastal states.[36]

Should Itu Aba have been recognized as an island entitled to an EEZ and continental shelf, it would have created a substantial overlapping maritime area in the South China Sea, potentially undermining the Tribunal's jurisdiction over several of the Philippines' submissions. This legal uncertainty persisted until the deadline for oral submissions in March 2014, when President Benigno Aquino III ultimately endorsed the position that Itu Aba should not qualify for more than a 12-nautical-mile territorial sea. This stance was strongly supported by Foreign Affairs Secretary Albert del Rosario, Supreme Court Senior Associate Justice Antonio Carpio, and a dedicated team of international legal experts. Confident in their experience and jurisprudential strategy, the Philippine legal team believed that raising the issue proactively would persuade the Tribunal to adopt their interpretation.

The Philippines' meticulous preparation was one of the key factors contributing to the Tribunal's ruling in favor of legal norms over coercive strategies—lawfulness over lawfare. In its 2016 award, the Tribunal concluded that none of the maritime features in the Spratly Islands qualified as islands capable of generating an EEZ or continental shelf. This landmark decision enabled the Philippines to assert a broader EEZ extending up to 200 nautical miles, while simultaneously invalidating expansive maritime claims by other states, particularly China.

This legal triumph was the product of strategic foresight, rigorous documentation, and unwavering political will. However, while the arbitration represented a major legal milestone for the Philippines, it did not automatically translate into corresponding geopolitical gains. Under the Duterte administration, the legal victory was downplayed, primarily out of concern for maintaining economic ties

[36] "There was also much concern about the potential for insignificant insular features to intrude on the maritime entitlements of other States." See Final Transcript Day 2—Hearing on the Merits and Remaining Issues of Jurisdiction and Admissibility, 25 November 2015, lines 2–4, p. 64, from https://pcacases.com/web/sendAttach/1548, accessed on 31 July 2025.

with China. Furthermore, China's continued use of alternative strategies—including military, economic, and diplomatic tools—to counter the ruling further complicated efforts to operationalize the 2016 Award.[37]

Under the Marcos administration, the Philippines has continued to regard legal action as one of the central pillars of its comprehensive strategy to counter China's excessive and unlawful actions in the South China Sea. Successive senior officials—including Secretary of Justice Jesus Crispin Remulla (September 2023), Solicitor General Menardo Guevarra (November 2023), and former Supreme Court Justice Francis Jardeleza (May 2024)—have publicly advocated for filing a new lawsuit against China for the large-scale destruction of coral reefs. These officials underscored that "environmental destruction is a crime against humanity."[38] Scientific research conducted by Filipino marine experts has revealed that China's island-building activities have buried more than 4,600 acres (approximately 1,861 hectares) of coral reef ecosystems. This environmental degradation is estimated to cause an annual loss of approximately 33.1 billion pesos.[39] On 23 January 2025, the Philippine Secretary of Justice confirmed that the government plans to initiate legal proceedings before the Arbitral Tribunal within the year, targeting China's environmentally destructive actions in the South China Sea.[40]

This forthcoming case stems from several important considerations. The Philippines has been under increasing pressure from China in maritime features such as Second Thomas Shoal, Sabina Shoal, and Whitsun Reef. Over the past years, Philippine legal authorities have also devoted significant time and resources to compiling robust evidence to support a claim for environmental damages. The case is consistent with President Marcos's broader policy of transparency, which seeks to expose unlawful actions in the South China Sea and mobilize international opinion in support of the Philippines' position. In this context, the Philippine government has called upon China to open Bajo de Masinloc (Scarborough Shoal) for independent international inspections by UN bodies or credible environmental organizations to verify the extent of the damage and support efforts to protect the marine environment. Through the lawsuit, the Philippines also hopes to garner support from major powers and international environmental institutions.

Importantly, the timing of the lawsuit aligns with recent developments in international law, including the 2024 advisory opinion issued by ITLOS[41]

---

[37] Heydarian (2018), pp. 283–299.

[38] Magramo (2023). See also Partlow (2024).

[39] Reuters (2024, July 9).

[40] Cervantes (2024).

[41] International Tribunal for the Law of the Sea (ITLOS) (2024) Request for an advisory opinion submitted by the Commission of Small Island States on Climate Change and International Law, Advisory Opinion of 21 May 2024 (Case No. 31), from https://itlos.org/fileadmin/itlos/documents/cases/31/Advisory_Opinion/C31_Adv_Op_21.05.2024_orig.pdf, accessed on 31 July 2025.

on the protection of the marine environment and the 2025 advisory opinion of ICJ[42] on state obligations concerning climate change. These parallel legal efforts reinforce the legitimacy and urgency of the Philippines' case, and are likely to attract sympathy and solidarity from other states. Another significant motivation lies in the prospect of obtaining material compensation for the damage caused. Precedents for such reparations exist: Japan compensated the Philippines for the devastation of Manila during World War II, and the U.S. paid 87 million pesos after the USS Guardian damaged the Tubbataha Reef in the Sulu Sea.[43] The advisory opinions of the ITLOS[44] and ICJ[45] regarding the compulsory obligations of states concerning acts and omissions that cause significant harm to the environment may encourage the Philippines to pursue opportunities to bring major polluters before international courts and tribunals in future climate change–related cases.

However, relying on third-party intervention—such as the mediation role of President Obama during the 2012 Scarborough Shoal standoff and the 2016 Arbitral Award—has produced only limited results due to the lack of enforcement mechanisms, the absence of good faith among the disputing parties, and the failure to address the underlying issues of territorial sovereignty. Therefore, the Philippines must integrate these legal instruments into a broader strategy that effectively leverages international law in managing and resolving its disputes with China.

Other Measures Adopted by the Philippines in Response to China's Lawfare

Beyond initiating arbitration proceedings under Annex VII of UNCLOS, the Philippines has adopted a comprehensive counter-lawfare strategy combining legal, diplomatic, operational, legislative, and informational measures. These efforts are grounded in international law and seek to reinforce Philippine sovereignty claims and maritime entitlements in the South China Sea.

---

[42] International Court of Justice (ICJ) (2025) Obligations of States in respect of climate change, Advisory Opinion of 23 July 2025, from https://www.icj-cij.org/sites/default/files/case-related/187/187-20250723-adv-01-00-en.pdf, accessed on 27 July 2025.

[43] Philippine Daily Inquirer (2014, October 25).

[44] International Tribunal for the Law of the Sea (ITLOS) (2024) Request for an advisory opinion submitted by the Commission of Small Island States on Climate Change and International Law, Advisory Opinion of 21 May 2024 (Case No. 31), from https://itlos.org/fileadmin/itlos/documents/cases/31/Advisory_Opinion/C31_Adv_Op_21.05.2024_orig.pdf, accessed on 31 July 2025.

[45] International Court of Justice (ICJ) (2025) Obligations of States in respect of climate change, Advisory Opinion of 23 July 2025, from https://www.icj-cij.org/sites/default/files/case-related/187/187-20250723-adv-01-00-en.pdf, accessed on 27 July 2025.

(i) **'Unveiling the Truth' strategy**

In recent years, the Philippines has employed a transparency initiative—the use of legal norms and factual documentation to control the narrative of the dispute. The Philippine Coast Guard now actively publicizes incidents of Chinese aggression using videos, eyewitness accounts, and direct media engagement, in contrast to the earlier practice of delayed disclosures under the Duterte administration. This shift is exemplified by the efforts of Commodore Jay Tarriela, who emphasized that "Chinese actions in the shadows are now checked,"[46] compelling China to either desist or justify its conduct publicly. Western journalists have been invited aboard Philippine vessels to observe Chinese coercive tactics firsthand, increasing international awareness and support. This approach transforms each encounter at sea into documentary evidence that supports Manila's legal position under UNCLOS and the 2016 Arbitral Award, undermines China's narrative dominance, and mobilizes diplomatic pressure. By making incidents public rather than confined to bilateral channels, the strategy leverages global opinion as a form of lawfare, framing the Philippines' actions as rooted in lawfulness while portraying China's interference as contrary to established international norms.

Tensions on the ground between the Philippines and China in the South China Sea have escalated sharply in recent years, particularly around Second Thomas Shoal and Scarborough Shoal. The BRP Sierra Madre, intentionally grounded at Second Thomas Shoal in 1999 to assert Philippine sovereignty, serves as a constant physical assertion of Manila's maritime entitlements under UNCLOS.[47]

A major flashpoint occurred in August 2023, when China blocked a Philippine resupply mission to the Sierra Madre, citing an alleged agreement with former President Duterte permitting China to salvage the vessel. President Marcos Jr. publicly rejected the existence of such an agreement, declaring any such commitment null and void.[48] Between March and July 2024, the Chinese Coast Guard further intensified its tactics: deploying water cannons, laser beams, and even physical force using sharp tools and pliers, injuring personnel and damaging vessels.[49] Another significant incident unfolded on 11 August 2025 near Scarborough Shoal, an area within the Philippines' EEZ as recognized by the Arbitral Tribunal. While escorting vessels delivering aid to Filipino fishermen, the Philippine Coast Guard encountered aggressive blocking maneuvers by Chinese coast guard and naval ships. During the high-speed chase, the China Coast Guard cutter

---

[46] Goldenziel (2023). See also Alegre (2025).

[47] AP News (2016, July 12).

[48] Schultheiss (2024).

[49] Lariosa (2024).

CCG-3104 executed a dangerous maneuver and collided head-on with a Chinese Navy Type 052D destroyer—both in pursuit of the Philippine Coast Guard vessel BRP Suluan.[50] The China Coast Guard cutter CCG-3104 sustained major bow damage and was rendered "unseaworthy," while the destroyer suffered dents. Philippine authorities condemned the incident as reckless, stressing that their vessels were operating to protect traditional fishing grounds—a right affirmed by the Arbitral Award—and offered medical assistance via radio, which received no reply.[51] China accused the Philippines of "dangerous maneuvers"[52] but conspicuously omitted any acknowledgment of the collision in its public statements, a tactic that undermines transparency and evades direct legal responsibility.

In addition, China has increasingly framed the Philippines' approach as a deliberate "weak state narrative" designed to constitute a form of lawfare. The Xinhua News Agency Research Institute (2025) contends that Manila employs a "gray-zone strategy" in which it exaggerates maritime incidents—such as alleged "Chinese rammings" or "water-cannon attacks"—and dramatizes the continued presence of vessels like the grounded Sierra Madre to cast itself as a victim of great-power coercion.[53] By portraying itself as weak, the Philippines is said to manipulate international opinion, enlist external support, and secure diplomatic legitimacy for what China characterizes as unlawful occupations and provocations. Yet this depiction misinterprets lawful resistance as lawfare. For smaller states, emphasizing asymmetry and appealing to international law and global opinion are not manipulative acts but legitimate methods of safeguarding sovereign equality. Far from distorting the law, Manila's reliance on UNCLOS arbitration and public diplomacy reflects lawfulness, demonstrating how weaker states may invoke law and transparency to resist unilateral coercion and defend the principle that legal order, not power politics, must prevail in the South China Sea.

However, observers note a dangerous cycle in which "transparency fuels escalation rather than restraint."[54] Chinese authorities treat each public exposé as provocation, responding with heightened shows of force to avoid any perception of weakness. A fresh flashpoint erupted in 2025 at Scarborough Shoal (Bajo de Masinloc), where China unveiled plans to designate the disputed reef as a national "marine natural reserve."[55] By publicizing each Chinese infringement and pushing back against Beijing's "environmental" narrative, the Philippines reinforces the principle that rules—not coercion—must govern the South China Sea. Yet it also confronts a perilous reality: China is shifting from passive defense to active

[50] Shepherd (2025).

[51] Gomez (2025).

[52] China Daily (2025, August 15).

[53] Xinhua News Agency Research Institute [新华社研究院] (2025). pp. 10–11.

[54] Gutierrez (2025).

[55] Espenilla (2025).

"governing" of disputed features,[56] blurring the line between lawful governance and unlawful appropriation. The legal battle over Scarborough Shoal thus continues, with Manila's commitment to lawfulness and transparency serving as a counterweight to China's expanding arsenal of gray-zone tactics and lawfare in the maritime domain.

Diplomatically, the Philippines has been proactive in voicing opposition to China's expansive claims. Between 2016 and 2023, the Philippines lodged over 461 diplomatic protests against Chinese actions in the South China Sea demonstrating sustained diplomatic resistance to China's maritime assertiveness.[57]

Collectively, these incidents illustrate the Philippines' evolving lawfare strategy: combining operational presence with the legal authority of UNCLOS and the 2016 Arbitral Award, supported by proactive evidence-gathering to expose violations. The transparency initiative, in particular, transforms each encounter at sea into a legal and diplomatic asset, reinforcing Manila's rights while shaping the international narrative. In an environment where China's coercive actions are often justified through selective legal interpretations, the Philippines' reliance on a clear, adjudicated legal framework positions lawfulness as both shield and sword in the ongoing South China Sea dispute.

(ii) **National legal measures**

The Philippines has increasingly emphasized the use of domestic legal measures to reinforce its maritime claims and uphold international law. In November 2024, two landmark pieces of legislation were enacted: The Philippine Maritime Zones Act (PMZA)[58] and the Philippine Archipelagic Sea Lanes Act (PASLA).[59] These laws align the Philippines' domestic legal framework with the provisions of UNCLOS, as affirmed by the Supreme Court of the Philippines. The Philippine Maritime Zones Act (PMZA) provides a legal foundation for asserting the Philippines' sovereign rights and jurisdiction over its internal waters, territorial sea, contiguous zone, EEZ, and continental shelf. It codifies maritime entitlements and strengthens the country's legal position in disputes over marine resources and maritime boundaries. The Philippine Archipelagic Sea Lanes Act, on the other hand, designates specific sea lanes for international navigation within the Philippine archipelago, ensuring the right of innocent passage while simultaneously incorporating environmental safeguards and national security considerations.

These two legislative measures form a cohesive framework that enhances the Philippines' capacity to manage its maritime zones, protect its marine environment, facilitate global trade, and assert sovereign rights in accordance with international

[56] Fu Ting & Moritsugu (2025).

[57] Fernandez (2023).

[58] See the Philippine Maritime Zones Act, from https://legacy.senate.gov.ph/lisdata/4304339610!.pdf, accessed on 31 July 2025.

[59] See the Philippine Archipelagic Sea Lanes Act, from https://web.senate.gov.ph/lisdata/4233038515!.pdf, accessed on 31 July 2025.

law.[60] The Philippine Maritime Zones Act (PMZA) solidifies the legal basis for asserting sovereign rights over resources within internal waters, the territorial sea, the contiguous zone, the EEZ, and the continental shelf. Meanwhile, the Philippine Archipelagic Sea Lanes Act (PASLA) addresses international shipping lanes and balances trade facilitation with maritime environmental protection. Together, from the Philippines' view, these laws form a comprehensive framework for managing maritime jurisdiction, reinforcing both national sovereignty and international legal compliance.

In response to China's inclusion of the Nine-dash Line on its passports in 2016, the Philippines adopted a symbolic yet pointed countermeasure: it stamped visas on these passports that included a Philippine map asserting its EEZ and maritime entitlements. In coordination with Vietnam, it also enforced restrictions on the import of materials—such as films, posters, and merchandise—bearing the Nine-dash Line image, framing them as propaganda tools.[61]

Based on the above analysis, it is evident that since 2016, the Philippines has increasingly adopted a counter-lawfare strategy in response to China's legal maneuvers. This strategy underscores the Philippines' commitment to international law—particularly UNCLOS—and promotes the principle of lawfulness or counter-lawfare as a key pillar in safeguarding its maritime rights and entitlements in the South China Sea.

Vietnam's Lawfulness on the South China Sea

Since 2013, following the HD-981 oil rig incident, Vietnamese scholars have increasingly engaged in discussions surrounding the concept of lawfare. In his insightful article, *Nguyễn Tiến Đức* argues that instrumental lawfare appears to be dominant in Vietnam's approach to disputes in the South China Sea.[62] Trang (Mae) Nguyen, meanwhile, leans toward Tom Ginsburg's conceptualization of authoritarian international law,[63] which highlights how smaller or less powerful states utilize international legal tools in the geopolitical power game against stronger nations.[64]

In contrast, *Nguyễn Hồng Thao* and other contributors argue that the term lawfare is not suitable within the official perspective of Vietnam—a peace loving country that does not engage in warfare and consistently advocates for

[60] Senate of the Philippines. (2024, November 11). New maritime and sea lanes laws secure Philippines' waters and safeguard marine resources [Press release], from https://web.senate.gov.ph/press_release/2024/1111_legarda1.asp, accessed on 31 July 2025.

[61] Madarang (2019).

[62] Nguyen T D (2025), p.4.

[63] Ginsburg (2020), pp. 221–228.

[64] Nguyen (2020), pp. 237–241. See also section "Multiple approaches to the concept of lawfare".

the peaceful settlement of disputes. Vietnam employs international law as an effective tool to safeguard its legitimate interests, rather than to advance any militarized agenda. Instead of embracing the concept of lawfare, Vietnam promotes the lawfulness of international law—or what may be termed counter-lawfare strategies—to resist actions that constitute lawfare and undermine its rights under international law. The "3P formula"—Publicity, Public Opinion, and Public International Law—serves as a principled counter-framework to China's Three Warfares strategy. It emphasizes the fair, equitable, and good-faith implementation and interpretation of international law. Vietnamese scholars broadly agree on the central objective of leveraging international law as a means of self-preservation and strategic hedging. However, they diverge on terminology: while some adopt the term lawfare, others prefer lawfulness to characterize Vietnam's legal approach, highlighting its commitment to peaceful dispute resolution and international legal norms.[65]

Vietnam's Position on Resolving Disputes in the South China Sea

Vietnam's steadfast commitment to protecting its sovereignty and legal rights in the South China Sea is evident in its consistent adherence to international law, particularly the provisions of UNCLOS. Vietnam employs various peaceful measures within the framework of international law to refute and counter China's lawfare tactics in the region. First, Vietnam consistently asserts its legal position in the South China Sea based on UNCLOS and other relevant international legal instruments. By adhering to established international legal norms, Vietnam reinforces its claims to sovereignty, sovereign rights, and jurisdiction over maritime features in the region. As a developing country, Vietnam has high hopes in upholding the international legal order at sea and on the oceans, as created by UNCLOS.[66]

Second, Vietnam utilizes international law to engage in peaceful dispute resolution mechanisms and cooperative initiatives with China and other relevant parties. Through diplomatic channels and legal frameworks, Vietnam seeks to address maritime disputes while promoting mutual understanding and cooperation.

Third, Vietnam invokes international law to counter China's false allegations and narratives that are inconsistent with international legal principles. Through targeted diplomatic efforts and public diplomacy, Vietnam refutes disinformation and defends its lawful entitlements in the South China Sea.

Fourth, Vietnam leverages international law to foster a unified stance among regional and international actors regarding the South China Sea issue. By advocating for adherence to international legal norms and principles, Vietnam seeks to garner support for its positions and uphold the rule of law in the region. Vietnam's strategic

[65] See section "Lawfulness in international law".

[66] Nguyen (2021), p. 231. See also Nguyen (2022), pp. 229–272.

approach underscores the centrality of international law as a cornerstone for protecting its maritime interests. Through consistent legal advocacy and peaceful means, Vietnam aims to preserve its sovereignty and assert its legitimate rights in accordance with established international norms.

In parallel, Vietnam is actively working to strengthen its domestic legal framework on maritime issues in alignment with UNCLOS. This legal consolidation plays a critical role in rejecting external claims—particularly from China—that contravene international law. Key aspects of Vietnam's strategy include: (i) affirming its sovereignty over the *Hoàng Sa* (Paracel) and *Trường Sa* (Spratly) islands in accordance with international law; (ii) resolutely protecting its legitimate rights and interests as provided for under UNCLOS; and (iii) settling disputes in the South China Sea through peaceful means, without the use or threat of force, in strict compliance with international law, particularly UNCLOS.

Affirming Sovereignty Over the *Hoàng Sa* (Paracel) and *Trường Sa* (Spratly) Islands in Accordance With International Law

Vietnam has consistently and unequivocally affirmed its sovereignty over the Paracel and Spratly Islands through various official channels, including Vietnam's Communist Party documents, government white papers, diplomatic statements and notes verbales from the Ministry of Foreign Affairs, as well as spokesperson statements and dialogues, negotiations, and meetings with other countries. This steadfast position reflects Vietnam's enduring commitment to safeguarding its territorial integrity and maritime sovereignty in accordance with international law, particularly UNCLOS.

Historically, the name "*Hoàng Sa*" refers to both the Paracel and Spratly Islands. The term *Hoàng* translates to "yellow," a color traditionally associated with royal authority, often symbolizing the presence or ownership of a king. Naming a territory with the word *Hoàng* thus implies it is a "land with a sovereign" or "land of the King." The name *Hoàng Sa* also reflects the *Nguyễn* Lords' reverence for Lord *Nguyễn Hoàng*, the founder of Cochinchina—the southern region of Vietnam—who ruled during the 17th and much of the eighteenth century. This nomenclature highlights the cultural and historical importance attributed to these islands by Vietnamese rulers. Furthermore, *Hoàng Sa* was also the name of the *Hoàng Sa* Company, established by the *Nguyễn* Dynasty in the seventeenth century. This fleet was tasked with traveling to the Paracel and Spratly Islands (later by the Bac Hai Company, a detachment of the Hoang Sa Company) to collect artifacts and goods from foreign shipwrecks, serving both economic and administrative functions that reinforced Vietnam's longstanding presence and management over these maritime territories.[67] Notably, Imperial Archives of Nguyen

[67] Ministry of Foreign Affairs of the Socialist Republic of Vietnam, The Hoang Sa and Truong Sa Archipelagoes Vietnamese Territories 9–11 (1981) [Vietnam White Paper 1981]. See also Trinh (2014).

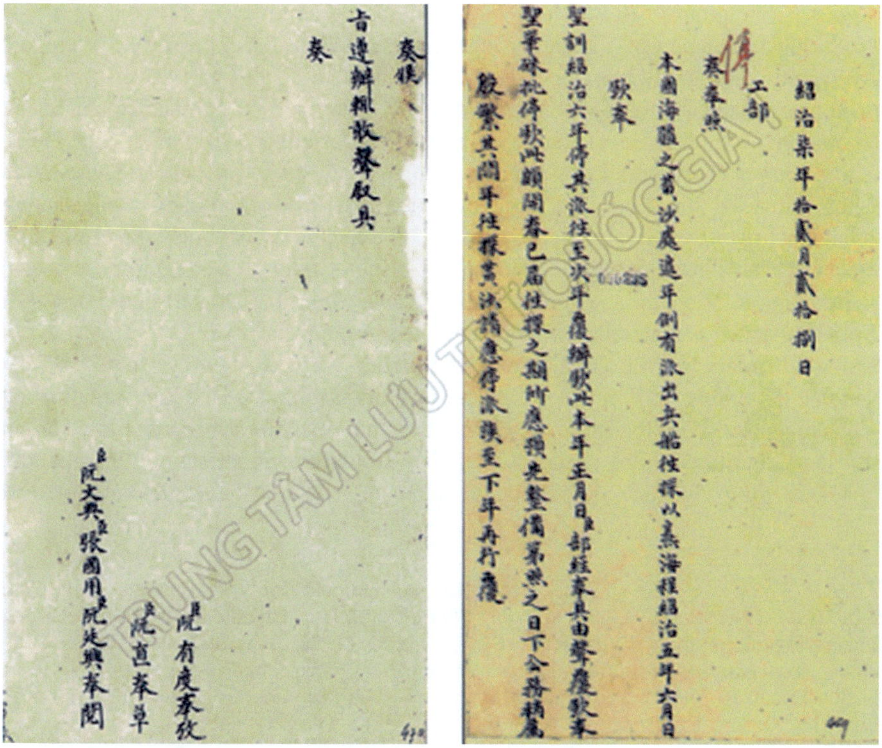

Fig. 3.1 Archive Record No. 18. *Source* National Archives Center No.1 of the State Records and Archives Department of Vietnam[70]

Dynasty [*Châu bản Triều Nguyễn*], which assert Vietnam's sovereignty over the Paracel and Spratly Islands,[68] have been recognized as UNESCO World Documentary Heritage since 2017 (see Fig. 3.1).[69]

Vietnam's sovereignty over the *Hoàng Sa* (Paracel) and *Trường Sa* (Spratly) Islands has been affirmed through numerous official documents issued by the Vietnamese Government across different periods and has been widely addressed in

[68] The Nguyen kings and the Nguyen dynasty explicitly recognized that "Hoàng Sa is the maritime border of our country" (本國海疆之黄沙處).

[69] See Imperial Archives of Nguyen Dynasty (1802–1945), from https://www.unesco.org/en/memory-world/imperial-archives-nguyen-dynasty-1802-1945?hub=1081. See also Bqp.vn. (2017, May 14).

[70] Trung tâm Lưu trữ Quốc gia 1 (2022, January 17). Châu bản triều Nguyễn—Những chứng cứ lịch sử, pháp lý về chủ quyền của Việt Nam đối với Hoàng Sa—Trường Sa [Imperial Archives of Nguyen Dynasty—Historical and legal evidence of Vietnam's sovereignty over Paracel and Spratly Islands], from https://archives.org.vn/gioi-thieu-tai-lieu-nghiep-vu/chau-ban-trieu-nguyen-nhung-chung-cu-lich-su-phap-ly-ve-chu-quyen-cua-viet-nam-doi-voi-hoang-sa-truong-sa.htm or https://archives.org.vn:2001/files/ecm/source_files/2022/01/17/anh-chup-man-hinh-2022-01-17-luc-21-21-01-220530-170122-35.jpg, accessed on 31 July 2025.

various publications.[71] Between 1979 and 1988, the Ministry of Foreign Affairs of the Socialist Republic of Vietnam published three White Papers asserting Vietnam's sovereignty over the two archipelagos. These include: "Vietnam's Sovereignty over the Hoang Sa and Truong Sa Archipelagos" (28 September 1979); "The Hoang Sa and Truong Sa Archipelagos: Vietnamese Territory" (December 1981); and "The Hoang Sa and Truong Sa Archipelagos and International Law" (25 April 1988). These White Papers provided historical and legal evidence to reaffirm Vietnam's longstanding sovereignty over the two archipelagos, based on effective occupation, while reiterating Vietnam's call for the peaceful settlement of disputes through negotiation.

In addition, Vietnam's sovereignty over the *Hoàng Sa* (Paracel) and *Trường Sa* (Spratly) Islands is reaffirmed in key national legislation, including the 2003 Law on National Borders and the 2012 Law of the Sea of Vietnam.[72] On 23 June 1994, the National Assembly of Vietnam adopted a resolution ratifying UNCLOS, reaffirming Vietnam's position on maritime issues and its commitment to contributing to a fair and just legal maritime order. Article 2 of the Resolution emphasizes: "By ratifying UNCLOS, the Socialist Republic of Vietnam expresses our determination to

---

[71] E.g. Chemillier-Gendreau, M. (1996). La souveraineté sur les archipels Paracels et Spratleys. L'Harmattan; Haller-Trost, R. (1990). The Spratly Islands: A study on the limitations of international law. Westview Press; Heinig, D. (1976). Disputed islands in the South China Sea: Paracels, Spratlys, Pratas, Macclesfield Bank. Institute of Asian Affairs; Kittichaisaree, K. (1987). The law of the sea and maritime boundary delimitation in South-East Asia. Oxford University Press; Luu, V. L. (1996). The Sino-Vietnamese difference on the Hoang Sa and Truong Sa archipelagos. National Political Publishing House; Prescott, V. (1999). Limits of national claims in the South China Sea. Oxford University Press; Samuels, M. (1982). Contest for the South China Sea. Methuen; Valencia, M, Van Dyke, J. M, & Ludwig, N. (1997). Sharing the resources of the South China Sea. Martinus Nijhoff; Kivimäki, T. (Ed.). (2002). War or peace in the South China Sea? Nordic Institute of Asian Studies; Nguyen, H. T (2004). Le Vietnam et ses différends maritimes dans la Mer de Bien Dong/Mer de Chine méridionale. Éditions L'Harmattan; Furtado, X. (1999). International law and the dispute over the Spratly Islands: Whither UNCLOS? Contemporary Southeast Asia, 21(3), 386–404; Gjetnes, M. (2001). The Spratlys: Are they rocks or islands? Ocean Development & International Law, 32(2), 191–204; Hamzah, B. A. (1990). Jurisdictional issues and conflicting claims in the Spratlys. Foreign Relations Journal, 1(1), 1–26; Joyner, C. (1998). The Spratly Islands dispute: Rethinking the interplay of law, diplomacy and geo-politics in the South China Sea. International Journal of Marine and Coastal Law, 13(2), 193–236; Hyer, E. (1994). Special issue: The South China Sea territorial disputes. American Asian Review, 12, 1–209; Nguyen, H. T, & Amer, R. (2007). Managing Vietnam maritime boundary disputes. Ocean Development & International Law, 38, 305–324; Nguyen, H. T, & Amer, R. (2009). A new legal arrangement for the South China Sea. Ocean Development & International Law, 40(4), 333–349; Nguyen, H. T (2012). Vietnam's position on the sovereignty over the Paracels & the Spratlys: Its maritime claim. Journal of East Asia and International Law, 5(1), 165–211; Zou, K. (2007). South China Sea studies in China: Achievements, constraints and prospects. Singapore Year Book of International Law, 11, 85–96.

[72] Vietnam Law and Legal Forum (2013, July 1) The 2012 Law of the Sea of Vietnam, Article 21: "The State of Vietnam exercises sovereignty over the islands and archipelagos of Vietnam". Vietnam Law and Legal Forum. https://vietnamlawmagazine.vn/the-2012-law-of-the-sea-of-vietnam-4904.htm, accessed on 31 July 2025.

coordinate with the international community to establish an equitable legal order for the seas and oceans and promote development and cooperation at sea."[73] The resolution affirmed Vietnam's sovereignty over its internal waters and territorial sea, as well as its sovereign rights and jurisdiction over the contiguous zone, EEZ, and continental shelf, in accordance with the provisions of UNCLOS and the principles of international law. It also demanded that other countries respect Vietnam's maritime rights and interests.

Moreover, the resolution explicitly affirms Vietnam's sovereignty over the *Hoàng Sa* (Paracel) and *Trường Sa* (Spratly) Islands and reaffirms Vietnam's policy of settling disputes and other differences in the South China Sea through peaceful dialogue, based on equality, mutual understanding, mutual respect, and adherence to international law.[74] Vietnam's position is to separate the issue of territorial sovereignty, which must be addressed in accordance with international law, from the resolution of maritime disputes within the framework of the law of the sea, particularly as provided under UNCLOS.

Resolutely Safeguarding Vietnam's Legitimate Rights and Interests Under UNCLOS

The National Assembly's resolution ratifying UNCLOS marked a significant milestone in affirming Vietnam's commitment to the international legal order governing the seas. By ratifying the Convention, Vietnam expressed its determination to contribute to shaping a legal framework that upholds fairness, justice, and equality in the use and governance of maritime spaces. The resolution also reflects Vietnam's recognition of the vital role of cooperation among coastal states and its commitment to the responsible and sustainable development of marine resources in collaboration with regional and global partners. As a State Party to the Convention, Vietnam is committed to fully implementing its provisions and using its dispute resolution mechanisms to address maritime issues in a lawful, peaceful, and constructive manner. Through this commitment, Vietnam seeks to advance a stable, equitable, and cooperative maritime environment that contributes to long-term peace and prosperity in the region.[75]

Resolution No. 36-NQ/TW of the Party Central Committee, dated 22 October 2018, on the Strategy for the Sustainable Development of Vietnam's Marine Economy to 2030, with a Vision to 2045 (Vietnam Marine Strategy 2018),

---

[73] Declarations and Reservations, from https://treaties.un.org/pages/ViewDetailsIII.aspx?src=TREATY&mtdsg_no=XXI-6&chapter=21&Temp=mtdsg3&clang=_en#EndDec, accessed on 31 July 2025.

[74] Vietnam Law and Legal Forum (2019, July 29) Vietnam respects, fully implements UNCLOS 1982. Vietnam Law and Legal Forum, from https://vietnamlawmagazine.vn/vietnam-respects-fully-implements-unclos-1982-16789.html, accessed on 31 July 2025.

[75] Le (2019).

articulates Vietnam's vision of becoming a strong maritime nation marked by sustainability, prosperity, security, and safety. Central to this strategy is the commitment to persistently foster a peaceful and stable maritime environment underpinned by a robust legal order at sea—an essential foundation for the safe and effective utilization of marine resources. The Strategy highlights the significance of international law in maintaining maritime peace and stability and reaffirms Vietnam's unwavering dedication to preserving a rules-based maritime order. This long-standing approach reflects Vietnam's consistent policy of promoting sustainable development and regional cooperation while safeguarding national interests at sea.

Resolution No. 36-NQ/TW explicitly affirms that Vietnam "resolutely and persistently fights to protect the country's sovereignty and legitimate interests at sea." As a coastal state and a State Party to UNCLOS, Vietnam's maritime rights and obligations are clearly defined in UNCLOS and further codified in the 2012 Law of the Sea of Vietnam.

In accordance with UNCLOS, Vietnam has the right to determine its maritime zones, including internal waters, territorial sea, contiguous zone, EEZ, and continental shelf. Vietnam exercises sovereignty over its internal waters and territorial sea, and holds sovereign rights for the exploration, exploitation, management, and conservation of natural resources within its EEZ. It also holds jurisdiction over activities such as the installation and use of artificial islands, marine scientific research, and environmental protection within this zone. Furthermore, Vietnam enjoys exclusive sovereign rights to explore and exploit the natural resources of its continental shelf, including the authority to permit and regulate oil and gas operations. On the high seas, Vietnam exercises freedoms related to navigation, overflight, fishing, the laying of submarine cables and pipelines, the construction of artificial islands and structures, and marine scientific research. The right of hot pursuit is also recognized for foreign vessels that violate Vietnamese laws and regulations. These rights are integral to Vietnam's comprehensive strategy to assert its maritime sovereignty, responsibly manage marine resources, and uphold the principles of international maritime law as established under UNCLOS.

In accordance with the spirit of the aforementioned Resolutions, Vietnam has demonstrated a sustained commitment over the past 30 years (1994–2025) since ratifying UNCLOS. With genuine goodwill, Vietnam has consistently endeavored to fully implement the rights and obligations enshrined in the Convention, thereby contributing to the establishment of a legal order at sea, ensuring effective maritime governance, maintaining peace and stability, and fostering cooperation and sustainable development. These efforts affirm that Vietnam is a responsible and proactive member of the Convention, as reflected in its numerous actions and initiatives over the years.

Firstly, Vietnam has applied the provisions of UNCLOS to enhance its legal system, creating a robust framework for marine management and economic activities. This framework facilitates international integration and cooperation, aiming to maintain and promote regional and international peace and stability. The Vietnam Law of the Sea in 2012, which comprises 7 chapters and 55 articles addressing various maritime issues. These include baselines, internal waters, territorial waters, contiguous zones, EEZs, continental shelves, islands, the Paracel Islands, the Spratly Islands, and other maritime features under Vietnam's sovereignty, sovereign rights, and national jurisdiction. The law also covers activities in Vietnamese waters, marine economic development, and the management and protection of seas and islands. The 2012 Law of the Sea developed, expanded, and revised the contents of the two Governmental Declarations made by Vietnam in 1977 and 1982, which had established Vietnam as the first country in Southeast Asia to declare a 200-nautical-mile EEZ and continental shelf, in accordance with the spirit of the then-final draft UNCLOS Texts of negotiations.

The provisions of the 2012 Vietnam's Law of the Sea align with those of UNCLOS, reflecting Vietnam's respect and responsibility in implementing the Convention. Additionally, Vietnam continuously researches, amends, and supplements other legal provisions related to the management and use of the sea to increasingly comply with international regulations and standards committed to in relevant international treaties. For instance, the 2017 Vietnam Fisheries Law was amended and supplemented to better align with recommendations from the European Commission for managing Vietnam's fisheries activities.

Secondly, Vietnam fully and in good faith implements the provisions of UNCLOS and actively participates in the activities of institutions established under the Convention. Vietnam has nominated qualified experts to serve as arbitrators and mediators under UNCLOS,[76] as well as representatives in the International Seabed Authority, reflecting its strong commitment to maintaining a peaceful and stable maritime environment and to promoting cooperation and sustainable development in the South China Sea region.[77]

This commitment is further evidenced by Vietnam's timely and comprehensive efforts to submit reports on the limits of its continental shelf beyond 200 nautical miles. These include: (i) a submission concerning the northern part of the South China Sea in May 2009 (VNM-N); (ii) a joint submission with Malaysia in May 2009 regarding the southern continental shelf; and (iii) a final submission in July 2024 covering the central portion of Vietnam's continental shelf (VNM-C).[78] All three submissions were prepared on solid scientific and legal foundations and in line with Article 76 (8) of UNCLOS and the guidelines provided by the CLCS in August 2009.

---

[76] Chapter XXI: Law of the Sea [Treaty Series No. XXI-6]. United Nations Treaty Collection, from https://treaties.un.org/Pages/ViewDetailsIII.aspx?src=TREATY&mtdsg_no=XXI-6&chapter=21&Temp=mtdsg3&clang=_en, accessed on 31 July 2025.

[77] Vietnam News Agency (2024, November 15) UNCLOS remains fully relevant for sea, ocean governance: Deputy FM. Vietnam Plus, from https://en.vietnamplus.vn/unclos-remains-fully-relevant-for-sea-ocean-governance-deputy-fm-post304111.vnp, accessed on 31 July 2025.

[78] United Nations (2024, July 17) CLCS-95-2024-LOS: Submission by Vietnam on the limits of the continental shelf beyond 200 nautical miles in respect of the Central Area [United Nations Convention on the Law of the Sea, Article 76 notification], from https://www.un.org/depts/los/clcs_new/submissions_files/vnm95_24/CLCS-95-2024-LOS.Eng.pdf, accessed on 31 July 2025.

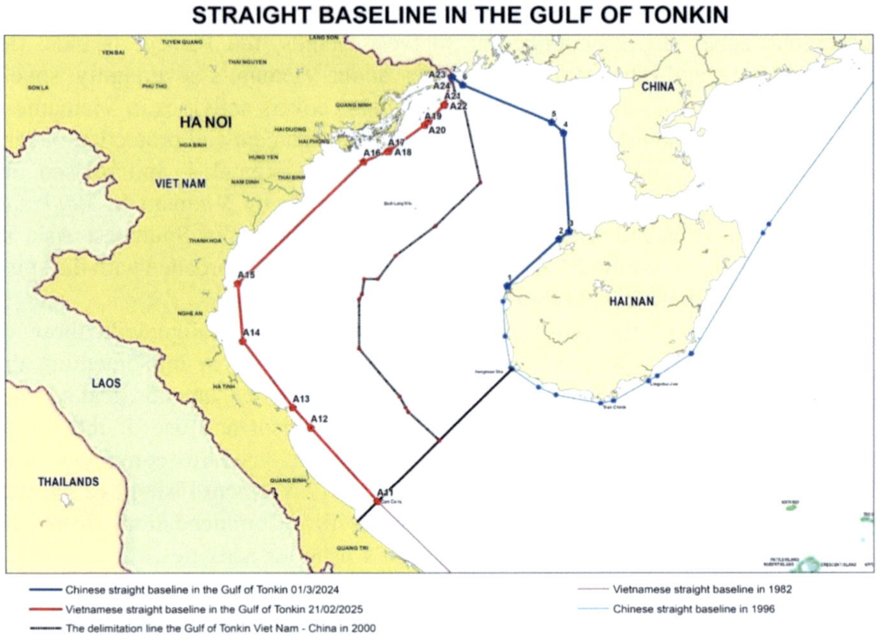

Fig. 3.2 Baseline in the Gulf of Tonkin. *Source* Nguyễn Duy Lương, Nguyễn Hồng Thao, 01 March 2025

Vietnam continues to improve its system of baselines in the Gulf of Tonkin. On 21 February 2025, the Government of Vietnam issued the Declaration on the Baseline for Determining the Breadth of the Territorial Sea in the Gulf of Tonkin (see Fig. 3.2 below). This declaration was promulgated pursuant to the 2012 Law of the Sea of Vietnam and Resolution No. 68/NQ-UBTVQH15, adopted by the Standing Committee of the National Assembly on 14 February 2025.[79] Vietnam's baseline system in the Gulf of Tonkin follows a hybrid approach, combining straight baselines with normal baselines, connecting Point A11 (*Cồn Cỏ* Island) to Point A24 (which corresponds to Point 1 of the 2000 Sino-Vietnamese Gulf of Tonkin Maritime Boundary Line) and a normal baseline, defined by the lowest low-water line along the coast of Bạch Long Vĩ Island UNCLOS allows for the use of both methods. The straight baseline system applies to a chain of islands generally aligned with the mainland coast. It links 12 islands and reefs, with the farthest feature, Thanh Lam Island, situated 21.59 nautical miles from the shore. Most of the islands are located

[79] Vietnam News Agency (2025, February 21) Việt Nam announces baseline for determining territorial sea width in the Gulf of Tonkin. VNN, from https://vietnamnews.vn/environment/1692631/viet-nam-announces-baseline-for-determining-territorial-sea-width-in-the-gulf-of-tonkin.html, accessed on 31 July 2025.

within 12 nautical miles of the mainland, closely following the general direction of the coastline and meeting the requirements of UNCLOS (Article 7).

Some scholars have suggested that Vietnam's baseline declaration in the Gulf of Tonkin was a response to China's baseline declaration in the same gulf in March 2024.[80] They argue that it may be a lawfare tactic aimed at gaining leverage in negotiations and pressuring Vietnam in the South China Sea.[81] However, Vietnam is well aware that the declaration of its baselines in the Gulf of Tonkin is a necessary measure for objective maritime management and international maritime cooperation needs.[82] Vietnam emphasizes that the establishment of these baselines is intended to affirm its rights and obligations under UNCLOS, while fully complying with the 2012 Law of the Sea of Vietnam. This serves as a firm legal foundation for the protection and exercise of Vietnam's sovereignty, sovereign rights, and jurisdiction. It also supports maritime management, economic development, and international cooperation.[83]

Both countries, China and Vietnam, have an interest in completing their baseline systems and clearly defining their maritime zones and their legal regimes in the Gulf of Tonkin, based on the Maritime Boundary Delimitation Agreement. Nevertheless, this does not prevent Vietnam from being concerned that China's March 2024 baseline system includes segments that extend about 50 nautical miles from the mainland and do not follow the general direction of the coast. This action effectively turns the international strait of Qiongzhou Strait into China's internal waters, thereby affecting the right of transit for Vietnam and other nations.[84] Vietnam's approach, applying both straight and normal baselines, demonstrates legal flexibility and strategic foresight. It reflects Vietnam's efforts to safeguard national interests in a manner consistent with international law, particularly Articles 5 and 7 of UNCLOS, and aligns with the state practice of other coastal nations.

In addition to its full and good-faith implementation of UNCLOS, Vietnam actively engages in the development, ratification, and implementation of regional and international legal instruments related to maritime affairs. These include numerous conventions adopted under the framework of the International Maritime Organization (IMO). Notable among them are: the International Convention for the Prevention of Pollution from Ships (1973), together with its 1978 Protocol (MARPOL); the International Regulations for Preventing Collisions at Sea (COLREGs, 1972); the International Convention for the Safety of Life at Sea (SOLAS, 1974); the Convention for the Suppression of Unlawful Acts Against the Safety of Maritime Navigation (SUA,

[80] Statement of the Government of the People's Republic of China on the Baseline of the Territorial Sea in the Northern Gulf of Tonkin, https://www.mfa.gov.cn/web/ziliao_674904/1179_674909/202403/t20240301_11252543.shtml, accessed on 31 July 2025.

[81] The PRC's Straight Baselines in the Gulf of Tonkin, USINDOPACOM J06/SJA TACAID SERIES, https://www.pacom.mil/Portals/55/Documents/Legal/J06%20TACAID%20-%20STRAIGHT%20BASELINE%20CLAIMS%20(FINAL).pdf?ver=_Kvu6zOzDglPEyY157gUhw%3d%3d, accessed on 31 July 2025.

[82] Anjaiah (2025, February 25).

[83] Nguyen H T (2025).

[84] VNExpress (2024, March 14).

1988); the International Convention on Civil Liability for Oil Pollution Damage (CLC, 1992); the Convention on the Facilitation of International Maritime Traffic (FAL, 1965); the International Convention on Maritime Search and Rescue (SAR, 1979); and the Convention on the International Maritime Satellite Organization (INMARSAT – 1976). Vietnam has also entered into several regional agreements under the ASEAN framework, demonstrating its commitment to enhancing maritime cooperation and connectivity. These include the Agreement on Facilitating the Search for Ships in Distress and the Rescue of Survivors from Distressed Ships (1975), the ASEAN Framework Agreement on the Facilitation of Goods in Transit (1998), and the ASEAN Framework Agreement on the Facilitation of Inter-State Transport (2009).

Peaceful Settlement of South China Sea Disputes in Full Compliance with UNCLOS and International Law

To resolve all types of disputes, Vietnam adheres to a consistent policy of employing peaceful measures, as outlined in international law. This commitment is one of the fundamental principles of international law, expressly recognized in Article 2(4) and Article 33 of the UN Charter. Peaceful dispute resolution methods include negotiation, mediation, investigation, conciliation, arbitration, and recourse to international courts. Moreover, the foundation for resolving disputes in the South China Sea is grounded in international law. For disputes concerning the sovereignty of the Paracels and Spratlys, the applicable legal framework is international law governing territorial acquisition. In addressing other types of disputes in Vietnam, UNCLOS serves as a comprehensive and authoritative legal instrument. It is utilized as a basis in negotiations with other countries and in employing legal measures as prescribed in Part XV of the Convention. Vietnam has also shifted from the position of emphasizing 'negotiations on the basis of mutual respect for independence and sovereignty, in accordance with international law and practices' as stated in the two Governmental Declarations of 1977 and 1982 and National Assembly's Resolution on the ratification of UNCLOS in 1994, to affirming the free choice of any 'peaceful means in conformity with UNCLOS, international law, and practices' as stipulated in Article 4(3) of the 2012 Law of the Sea.

Vietnam has been one of the leading countries in Southeast Asia in negotiating maritime boundary delimitation and resolving maritime disputes in accordance with the principles of equitable dispute settlement under UNCLOS. Vietnam has consistently regarded UNCLOS as an effective legal instrument for protecting its sovereignty, sovereign rights, and jurisdiction at sea. To date, Vietnam has primarily relied on negotiations to resolve maritime delimitation disputes with neighboring coastal states along the South China Sea. Many of these disputes have been peacefully settled through diplomatic negotiations, resulting in the conclusion of several delimitation and cooperation agreements. Notable agreements include the 1997 Agreement on Maritime Boundary Delimitation in the Gulf of Thailand between Vietnam and Thailand; the 2000 Agreement on the Delimitation of Territorial Waters, Exclusive Economic Zones, and Continental Shelves in the

Gulf of Tonkin between Vietnam and China; the 2000 Agreement on Fisheries Cooperation and the 2024 Protocol on Fisheries Cooperation in the Gulf of Tonkin between Vietnam and China; the 2003 Agreement on the Delimitation of the Continental Shelf between Vietnam and Indonesia; and the 2022 Agreement on the Delimitation of Exclusive Economic Zones between Vietnam and Indonesia.

Vietnam's practice in resolving maritime disputes has enriched and further affirmed the validity of UNCLOS provisions, while also contributing to their interpretation and clarification. This contribution can be seen in three main aspects.

First, Vietnam has applied the principle of equitable solutions in maritime delimitation in a creative and pragmatic manner. At the Third conference on the Law of the Sea, Vietnam was in the Group of 29 to support the equitable solutions versus to the equidistant (median) principle. Delimitation must be based, first and foremost, on mutual agreement grounded in international law. Any method of delimitation may be used, provided it leads to an equitable solution acceptable to the parties involved.

In its continental shelf delimitation with Indonesia, Vietnam initially invoked the principle of the natural prolongation of the continental shelf to identify the disputed area. It subsequently succeeded in persuading Indonesia to adopt a negotiated compromise, which narrowed the disputed zone and led to an agreed delimitation line acceptable to both sides.

In its negotiations over the EEZ and continental shelf with Thailand in 1997, and with China in the Gulf of Tonkin in 2000, the principle of equitable was reflected in the consideration of special circumstances—such as the presence and location of islands—which were taken into account to adjust the provisional equidistance line and reach mutually acceptable solutions.

In the delimitation with Thailand, *Thổ Chu* Island, located 50 nautical miles from *Phú Quốc* Island, was considered a special circumstance in relation to the Thai mainland and was given a 32.5% effect in the delimitation.[85] In the Gulf of Tonkin delimitation, *Bạch Long Vĩ* Island—located 130 nautical miles from Hainan and 110 nautical miles from *Hòn Dấu*—was similarly treated as a special circumstance. It was accorded a 25% effect, with a 15-nautical-mile arc drawn from the island.[86]

Second, the practice of Vietnam, along with that of other states, provided concrete examples that contributed to ICJ's formulation and recommendation of the three-step approach to maritime delimitation, as applied in the Maritime Delimitation in the Black Sea (Romania v. Ukraine) case in 2009. This approach involves first establishing a provisional equidistance line as a starting point, then considering special circumstances to adjust that line to achieve an equitable solution, and finally verifying the equitable result by comparing the ratio between the length of the coastlines and the maritime areas allocated to each party.[87] Vietnam

[85] Nguyen (1997), pp. 74–78.

[86] Nguyen (2005), pp. 25–45.

[87] Judgment, Maritime Delimitation in the Black Sea (Romania v. Ukraine), ICJ Reports 2009, paras. 115–122, pp. 101–103.

successfully applied this approach in its 2000 delimitation with China in the Gulf of Tonkin. The ratio of the Vietnamese and Chinese coastlines was approximately 730 km to 695 km, while the resulting maritime area was divided in a 53:47 ratio, favoring Vietnam—equivalent to a ratio of about 1.135:1.[88]

Third, Vietnam has demonstrated flexibility in its position on maritime delimitation with Indonesia. While Vietnam generally supports the use of a single delimitation line for both the continental shelf and the EEZ in areas where the sea is less than 400 nautical miles wide—due to its practical benefits for maritime management and its consistency with state practice—it remained open to Indonesia's position advocating separate delimitation lines, based on the distinct legal regimes that govern the EEZ and continental shelf under UNCLOS. Notably, UNCLOS does not mandate a uniform method for delimitation in all circumstances.[89] With the announcement of the conclusion of the EEZ delimitation negotiations in December 2022, Vietnam and Indonesia have set a new precedent under UNCLOS: it is entirely permissible to establish two separate delimitation lines for the EEZ and the continental shelf, even in areas where the distance between opposite coasts is less than 400 nautical miles.[90]

Vietnam is also the most successful country in the region in applying provisional arrangements pending final agreement, in accordance with Articles 74 and 83 of UNCLOS. A notable example is the 1995 joint petroleum development agreement signed between the national oil companies of Vietnam (PetroVietnam) and Malaysia (Petronas), covering a defined area in the Gulf of Thailand.[91]

Joint development initiatives have extended beyond hydrocarbons. In 2004, Vietnam and China signed a bilateral fisheries cooperation agreement in the Gulf of Tonkin, initially valid for 12 years and extendable for an additional 3 years unless either party objected. The agreement remained in effect until 2020, following a one-year extension.

Another example of joint development is the 1982 Agreement on Historic Waters between Vietnam and Cambodia, which established a jointly managed historic waters area.

In parallel, Vietnam and China are continuing negotiations aimed at either delimiting maritime boundaries or, in the interim, applying joint development arrangements in the waters beyond the mouth of the Gulf of Tonkin.

In addition to negotiations, Vietnam does not exclude the possibility of resorting to legal or other peaceful means for dispute resolution if necessary. The use of legal mechanisms is regarded as a civilized and legitimate approach, as enshrined in the UN Charter and UNCLOS. Although Vietnam was not a party to the arbitration case initiated by the Philippines against China, it submitted a Declaration dated

[88] Nguyen (2005), pp. 25–45.

[89] Maritime Delimitation in the Area between Greenland and Jan Mayen (Denmark v. Norway), ICJ Reports 1993, para. 42.

[90] Nguyen (2024), pp. 267 – 302.

[91] Nguyen (2003), pp. 137–150.

7 December 2014 affirming the Arbitral Tribunal's jurisdiction, thereby indirectly supporting the legal process. As a member of ASEAN, Vietnam does not stand apart from the regional trend of utilizing international judicial bodies to resolve disputes. In practice, seven out of ten ASEAN countries—including Cambodia, Indonesia, Malaysia, Myanmar, the Philippines, Singapore, and Thailand—have resorted to legal measures such as ICJ, ITLOS, or Arbitral Tribunals under Annex VII of UNCLOS to address disputes concerning sovereignty, territorial claims, or the interpretation and application of UNCLOS.

In its relations with other claimant states, Vietnam has proactively concluded agreements to elevate strategic partnerships with China (2008, upgraded to a comprehensive strategic partnership in 2013), the Philippines (2015), and Malaysia (2004, upgraded to a strategic partnership in 2015), reaffirming a commitment to peacefully resolving disputes based on international law and UNCLOS. Bilateral disputes are to be addressed through bilateral negotiations, while multilateral disputes will be resolved through multilateral frameworks.

Notably, in October 2011, Vietnam and China concluded the Agreement on Basic Principles Guiding the Settlement of Sea Issues. This agreement was intended to facilitate progress in negotiations over maritime issues and to seek fundamental and long-term solutions acceptable to both parties. It also encourages both sides to actively explore transitional and provisional measures that do not prejudice either side's legal positions or policies, including discussions and research on cooperative development initiatives.[92]

Vietnam's overarching viewpoint and stance on the South China Sea issue align with the provisions of international law, particularly UNCLOS. This perspective shares numerous similarities with those of other countries, both within the region and beyond. Countries such as the US, Australia, Japan, UK, France, Germany, New Zealand, South Korea, and India have voiced their support for Vietnam's position. This support is evidenced by various documents and joint statements issued at ASEAN summits, ministerial conferences, and related gatherings in 2020, including the ASEAN Regional Forum (ARF), the East Asia Summit (EAS), and the ASEAN Plus Three (APT) Foreign Ministers' Meeting. These documents affirm common points with Vietnam's views on the South China Sea issue, emphasizing the resolution of disputes through peaceful means in accordance with UNCLOS, the importance of respecting the legal order at sea, and the recognition of UNCLOS as the basis for determining the rights to maritime zones, sovereign rights, jurisdiction, and legitimate interests of countries in maritime zones.

[92] Vietnam News Agency (2011, October 16). Vietnam–China joint statement, from http://vna/Agrement15102011seaprinciples/vietnam-china-joint-statement-2011.htm, accessed on 31 July 2025.

Vietnam's Counter-Lawfare Measures in the South China Sea

As a neighboring country of China with maritime and sovereignty claims in the South China Sea, Vietnam has been significantly impacted by China's assertive lawfare, particularly since 2009 when China publicly asserted its Nine-dash Line claim before the UN. In response to China's strategic maneuvers, Vietnam has demonstrated unwavering resolve, deploying a range of diplomatic, political, field, legal, and propaganda measures to safeguard its interests and assert its legality and legitimacy in the South China Sea. In navigating maritime issues with China, Vietnam consistently upholds the Agreement on Basic Principles Guiding the Settlement of Maritime Issues between Vietnam and China, signed in October 2011. Vietnam maintains a steadfast and unwavering stance, persistently advocating for the peaceful resolution of disputes in the South China Sea based on international law, particularly UNCLOS.

In the pursuit of a fundamental and long-term solution to the disputes in the South China Sea, all relevant parties bear the obligation to refrain from further unilateral actions that escalate tensions and complicate the situation. Instead, they should collaborate to uphold peace and stability, abstain from the use or threat of force, avoid militarization, and strictly adhere to the principles outlined in the UN Charter, UNCLOS, and the standards of international law. This includes honoring the five principles of peaceful coexistence and effectively implementing DOC and ASEAN's 6-point principles on the South China Sea issue (2012), while working towards the expeditious establishment of a COC. Vietnam consistently reiterates these views at bilateral and multilateral fora, issuing statements and notes at various levels, and seeking support from like-minded countries both within and outside the region. By fostering a collective commitment to these principles, the parties involved can work towards a peaceful and cooperative resolution of the disputes in the South China Sea.

Notably, the establishment of the Friends of UNCLOS Group at the UN headquarters in New York, the US, on 30 June 2021, marked a significant diplomatic initiative led by the German Ambassador and the Vietnamese Ambassador to the UN.[93] This forum, attended by Deputy Secretary-General for Legal Affairs and Legal Advisor of the UN Miguel de Serpa Soares and representatives from 96 member countries, aims to facilitate open discussions on Law of the Sea issues. By providing a platform for member countries to engage in dialogue, the group seeks to address disagreements, foster better mutual understanding among nations, and tackle complex issues related to seas and oceans in their respective regions. Since its inception, the forum has seen participation from 115 countries, highlighting its growing importance as a venue for international cooperation and collaboration on maritime matters governed by UNCLOS.[94] Vietnam is the host country for the Cybersecurity Convention in October 2025. For the first time, an international convention has been named after Vietnam's capital, Hanoi. The UN's decision to designate Hanoi as the signing venue for a significant global multilateral treaty in

[93] Vu (2021).

[94] Vu (2021).

an area of great interest to the international community, including maritime cybersecurity enhances the city's status in the realm of international law, affirming Hanoi's identity as the City of Peace. This development further empowers Vietnam to actively promote multilateralism and take a leading role in shaping international law for the purposes of peace, stability, and prosperity.[95]

Vietnam has effectively employed and combined various legal tools—such as official statements, diplomatic notes, and white papers—to counter legal narratives and expose the unreasonableness of other States' claims. These instruments have also been crucial in rejecting China's defamatory accusations that seek to delegitimize Vietnam's lawful position, as well as in opposing foreign activities inconsistent with UNCLOS. This section will clarify a number of counter-lawfare measures adopted by Vietnam, demonstrating how its responses are consistent with those employed by other States and contribute to defending lawfulness in the South China Sea.

Rejecting Claims Inconsistent With UNCLOS

Refuting China's claims of first discovery, effective administration, and successor title over the Paracel and Spratly Islands

China is not the country that discovered and effectively controlled the two Paracels and Spratlys Islands. The white papers issued by the Ministry of Foreign Affairs of Vietnam in 1979, 1981, and 1988 provided substantial evidence to refute China's claims regarding the Paracels or Spratlys. These claims included: i) that the Chinese people were the earliest to discover the Paracels or Spratlys; ii) that China named the islands in the South China Sea; iii) that Chinese people were the earliest to exploit and conduct business on the Paracels or Spratlys; and iv) that the Chinese government was the first to manage and exercise sovereignty over these islands. According to international law, the activities of fishermen and seafarers do not establish territorial sovereignty. Territorial sovereignty is recognized through actual, continuous, and peaceful occupation by a state. Historical evidence from maps, books, and newspapers in China has never indicated that the Paracels or Spratlys were considered the southernmost territory of China.

Vietnam has also rejected China's arguments set forth in its 1980 White Paper regarding the alleged inheritance of sovereignty over the Paracel and Spratly

[95] The Convention comprises nine chapters and 71 articles, covering key topics such as General Provisions, Crimes, Jurisdiction, Procedural Measures and Enforcement Law, International Cooperation, Preventive Measures, Technical Assistance and Information Exchange, Enforcement Mechanisms, and Final Provisions. Scheduled for signing in Hanoi, Vietnam and registration at the United Nations in May 2025, the Convention will come into effect 90 days after the receipt of 40 ratification letters. Additionally, regional international organizations may also become parties to the Convention if at least one of their member states ratifies it. See United Nations. (2024, December 24). UN General Assembly adopts milestone cybercrime treaty. UN News, from https://news.un.org/en/story/2024/12/1158521, accessed on 31 July 2025.

Islands. Specifically, China claims: (i) inheritance based on the 1887 and 1895 Boundary Delimitation Treaties between France and the Qing Dynasty; and (ii) succession from Japan with international recognition following World War II.

However, the Franco-Qing boundary treaties only addressed the land boundaries between Tonkin (northern Vietnam) and the Chinese provinces of Guangdong and Yunnan, as well as offshore islands near the northern coast of the Gulf of Tonkin. These treaties did not govern the sovereignty over or maritime areas surrounding the Paracel and Spratly Islands. Moreover, France itself recognized Vietnam's sovereignty over the Paracel Islands, as reflected in official correspondence exchanged in 1925, thereby further refuting China's claim of succession.

China has argued that Japan recognized its sovereignty over the Paracel and Spratly Islands by invoking Article 2 of the Treaty of Peace between Japan and the Republic of China, concluded in 1952. However, this provision merely reiterates Japan's obligation under Article 2 of the Treaty of Peace with Japan, signed at San Francisco on 8 September 1951 (commonly referred to as the San Francisco Treaty). To properly understand the intent of the parties to the San Francisco Treaty, it is essential to consider the broader context of its negotiation, along with the preceding international conferences—namely the Cairo (1943), Potsdam (1945), and San Francisco (1951) Conferences. The Cairo Declaration, which included the Republic of China as a signatory, stated that:

> Japan shall be stripped of all the islands in the Pacific which she has seized or occupied since the beginning of the First World War in 1914, and that all the territories Japan has stolen from the Chinese, such as Manchuria, Formosa, and the Pescadores, shall be restored to the Republic of China. Japan will also be expelled from all other territories which she has taken by violence and greed.[96]

This spirit is reflected in Article 2(b) of the San Francisco Treaty, which provides that "Japan renounces all right, title and claim to Formosa and the Pescadores," thereby recognizing the return of these specific territories to China. However, the Paracel and Spratly Islands are not mentioned in Article 2(b) but fall under Article 2(f), which concerns other territories Japan acquired "by violence and greed."[97]

Notably, at the San Francisco Conference in 1951, A.A. Gromyko, First Deputy Foreign Minister of the USSR and head of the Soviet delegation, proposed a 13-point amendment on behalf of China. One of these amendments sought Japan's explicit recognition of Chinese sovereignty over several islands in the South China Sea, including the Paracels.[98] This proposal was overwhelmingly rejected, receiving 46 votes against, 3 in favor, and 2 abstentions. At the same San Francisco

---

[96] National Diet Library (n.d.) Cairo Communiqué, from https://www.ndl.go.jp/constitution/e/shiryo/01/002_46/002_46tx.html, accessed on 31 July 2025.

[97] Ministry of Foreign Affairs of Japan (n.d.) San Francisco Treaty, from https://www.mofa.go.jp/region/europe/russia/territory/edition92/period4.html, accessed on 31 July 2025.

[98] Ministry of Foreign Affairs of Japan (n.d.) San Francisco Treaty, from https://www.mofa.go.jp/region/europe/russia/territory/edition92/period4.html, accessed on 31 July 2025.

Conference, *Trần Văn Hữu*, then Prime Minister and concurrently Foreign Minister of the State of Vietnam, publicly reaffirmed Vietnam's sovereignty over the Paracel and Spratly Islands. No state present raised any objection to this statement.[99]

These facts clearly demonstrate that the majority of states did not recognize Chinese sovereignty over the Paracel and Spratly Islands. In 2014, the Permanent Mission of Vietnam to the UN submitted a letter to the UN Secretary-General, attaching Vietnam's official position on its sovereignty over the Paracel Islands, and publicly rejected China's assertion that its sovereignty over the Paracel and Spratly Islands had been widely recognized by the international community. Similarly, Vietnam's Note Verbale No. 22/HC-2020, dated 30 March 2020,[100] along with other subsequent communications, reaffirmed this position.

Vietnam's Ministry of Foreign Affairs White Papers also reject China's invocation of a suzerain-vassal relationship as a basis for its claims over Vietnam, including the Paracels and Spratlys Islands. This so-called suzerainty is fundamentally different from the Western concept of suzerainty and was largely ceremonial in nature, lacking legal substance. Chinese dynasties were under no obligation to protect Vietnam, and in fact, Vietnam had maintained its independence since 938 AD. Moreover, this argument is self-defeating for China. By claiming a suzerain-vassal relationship during the period when Vietnam had not yet regained independence, China implicitly acknowledges that it was Vietnam—not China—that established and exercised territorial sovereignty over the Paracel and Spratly Islands during that time.[101]

In addition to refuting China's claim of first discovery and occupation, Vietnam has consistently asserted and substantiated its sovereignty over the Paracel and Spratly Islands through both historical records and legal evidence. This includes the establishment of the Hoang Sa flotilla by the Vietnamese state and feudal State's activities such as shipwreck rescue missions, tax collection, and administration in the area—all of which are documented in official Vietnamese historical chronicles as well as international records.[102]

The Vietnamese Ministry of Foreign Affairs spokesperson's statement on 30 December 1978 reaffirmed Vietnam's sovereignty over both island groups. This was followed by the Ministry's official statement on 7 August 1979, and reiterated once more during an international press briefing on 23 April 2014, by Mr. *Lê Hải Bình*, then-spokesperson of the Ministry of Foreign Affairs, in relation to developments in the South China Sea. All these statements reaffirm the consistent position that Vietnam has full historical evidence and legal grounds to assert sovereignty over the Paracel and Spratly Islands, in accordance with international law. Vietnam's sovereignty over the two

---

[99] Le Monde (1951, September 9–10). San Francisco Conference, 7 September 1951.

[100] The Note Verbale No. 22/HC-2020 dated 30 March 2020 of The Permanent Mission of the Socialist Republic of Vietnam to the UN, from https://www.un.org/depts/los/clcs_new/submissions_files/mys_12_12_2019/VN20200330_ENG.pdf, accessed on 31 July 2025.

[101] Chemillier-Gendreau (2000), p. 74–81.

[102] Nguyen (2012), pp. 174–183.

islands conforms with international law on the acquisition of territory. Vietnam has exercised continuous, peaceful, and effective occupation over these islands for centuries.

Rejecting the Argument that China's Sovereignty Over the Xisha and Nansha Archipelagos has been Widely Recognized by the International Community
Vietnam's 1988 White Paper issued by the Ministry of Foreign Affairs presented arguments and evidence demonstrating that none of the three major international conferences—Cairo (1943), Potsdam (1945), or San Francisco (1951)—contained any provision recognizing China's sovereignty over the Paracel and Spratly Islands. The core legal and historical arguments supporting this position have been outlined in the preceding sections.

During the diplomatic note exchanges—often referred to as the "note verbale battles"—of 2009–2011 and 2019–2025, many countries publicly rejected China's claim that its sovereignty over the Paracels and Spratlys had been widely recognized by the international community. Notably, in its official communication during the 2020 note verbale exchange, Australia clearly stated:

> The Australian Government does not accept China's assertion in its note of 17 April 2020 that its sovereignty claims over the Paracel Islands and the Spratly Islands are 'widely recognized by the international community' (noting the protests by Vietnam [No. 22/HC-2020, No. 24/HC-2020 and No. 25/HC-2020] and the Philippines [No. 000192-2020] in this respect). The Australian Government also wishes to express its strong concern in relation to China's claims of 'continuously and effectively' exercising sovereignty over low-tide elevations, given that they do not form part of the land territory of a State.[103]

This statement reflects growing international pushback against China's historical narratives and legal assertions regarding sovereignty in the South China Sea.

Rejecting the claim of Nine-dash Line and Four Sha[104]
Vietnam has repeatedly affirmed its stance and rejected China's nine-dash line claim. Note Verbale No. 86/HC-2009 dated 8 May 2009, and Note Verbale No. 240/HC-2009 dated 18 August 2009, sent by Vietnam to the Secretary General of the UN, clearly stated that China's claims to the islands and adjacent waters in the South China Sea, as manifested in the map (Nine-dash Line) attached with Notes Verbale No. CML/17/2009 and No. CML/18/2009, have no legal, historical, or factual basis, therefore have null and void.[105]

Legally, the terms used by China in Note CML/17/2009 dated 7 May 2009, such as "adjacent waters" and "relevant waters," are not recognized in UNCLOS. When

---

[103] The Note Verbale No. N20/026 dated 23 July 2020 of the Permanent Mission of the Commonwealth of Australia to the UN, from https://www.un.org/depts/los/clcs_new/submissions_files/mys_12_12_2019/2020_07_23_AUS_NV_UN_001_OLA-2020-00373.pdf, accessed on 31 July 2025.

[104] See section "China's Maps".

[105] The Note Verbale No. 86/HC-2009 dated May 8, 2009 of the Permanent Mission of the Socialist Republic of Vietnam to the UN, from https://www.un.org/depts/los/clcs_new/submissions_files/vnm37_09/vnm_re_chn_2009re_vnm.pdf, accessed on 31 July 2025.

China issued the 2023 Standard Map, Vietnam continued to oppose all forms of expressing the dotted line claim in the South China Sea, a claim that is inconsistent with international law and violates the sovereignty and maritime rights of Vietnam. Vietnam's views and stance on China's Four Sha claim have been unequivocally expressed in Vietnam's Note No. 22/HC-2020 dated 30 March 2020, sent to the Secretary-General of the UN. In this note, Vietnam thoroughly rejected each argument presented by China in its Four Sha claim.

First, in Note CML/17/2019, China argued that its Four Sha claim is in accordance with international law and practice, implying that it is governed not only by UNCLOS but also by customary international law. In support of this argument, China referenced paragraph 8 of the Preamble to UNCLOS that "that matters not regulated by this Convention continue to be governed by the rules and principles of general international law." On this basis, China claimed that UNCLOS is not exhaustive and that issues not specifically addressed by the Convention—such as its Four Sha assertion—fall under the purview of customary international law. In response, Vietnam's Note Verbale No. 22/HC-2020, dated 30 March 2020, unequivocally affirms that UNCLOS provides "the sole legal basis for and defines in a comprehensive and exhaustive manner the scope of their respective maritime entitlements" in the South China Sea. This position directly refutes China's claim that UNCLOS is incomplete and challenges the attempt to justify the Four Sha concept through customary international law outside the scope of UNCLOS.

Second, the maritime entitlement of each high-tide feature in the *Hoàng Sa* (Paracel) Islands and the *Trường Sa* (Spratly) Islands shall be determined in accordance with Article 121(3) of UNCLOS. Under this provision, low-tide elevations or submerged features are not capable of appropriation and do not, in and of themselves, generate entitlements to any maritime zones. Vietnam asserts sovereignty solely over high-tide features (*terra firma*) in the South China Sea. Submerged banks and low-tide elevations are not subject to territorial acquisition. This position is entirely consistent with international law, as first affirmed in the Qatar v. Bahrain case (2001) by ICJ, and subsequently reaffirmed by other international judicial bodies, including the ICJ in the Malaysia v. Singapore (2008) and Nicaragua v. Colombia (2012) cases, as well as by the Arbitral Tribunal in the South China Sea Arbitration (2016).

This means that only naturally formed land features that are above water at high tide in the South China Sea may generate maritime zones. Furthermore, only those high-tide features that are capable of sustaining human habitation or an economic life of their own may be entitled to a full suite of maritime zones, including internal waters, territorial sea, EEZ, and continental shelf, as per Article 121(3). This position, consistently upheld by Vietnam, rejects China's claims that seek to generate maritime zones from low-tide elevations or fully submerged features, which do not meet the legal criteria under international law.

Third, Vietnam maintains that the baselines of the groups of islands in the South China Sea, including the *Hoàng Sa* (Paracel) and *Trường Sa* (Spratly) Islands, cannot be drawn by joining the outermost points of their respective outermost features. This position explicitly rejects China's approach, which involves drawing baselines similar to archipelagic baselines around the outermost features of the offshore archipelagos over which it claims sovereignty in the South China Sea. China has argued that, since UNCLOS does not contain provisions permitting continental States to draw archipelagic baselines, such baselines may instead be justified under customary international law. However, Vietnam asserts that this claim is inconsistent with international law, particularly UNCLOS, which explicitly limits the right to draw archipelagic baselines to "archipelagic States" as defined under Article 46 of UNCLOS.

According to the South China Sea Arbitral Tribunal, in its 2016 Award, China does not meet the criteria under Article 46 to be recognized as an archipelagic State. Furthermore, the Tribunal found that the water-to-land ratio in the Truong Sa (Spratly) archipelago exceeds the threshold of 9:1, rendering the archipelagic baseline method inapplicable.[106] Article 7 of UNCLOS permits the use of straight baselines only in specific circumstances—namely, where "the coastline is deeply indented and cut into" or where "there is a fringe of islands along the coast in its immediate vicinity." These provisions do not extend to situations involving offshore islands or remote archipelagos. Although UNCLOS does not explicitly forbid the use of straight baselines in other contexts, the Arbitral Tribunal in the South China Sea Arbitration concluded that the criteria under Article 7, when read in conjunction with Articles 46 and 47—which govern the use of archipelagic baselines—implicitly prohibit the use of straight baselines for offshore archipelagos that do not meet the definitional threshold for archipelagic States. Moreover, the Tribunal held that no consistent and established international practice exists that would support the application of any alternative baseline regime beyond those clearly outlined in the Convention.

In addition, the formal objections by States such as the United Kingdom, Australia, and France,[107] which China had previously cited in an attempt to support the formation of a customary international law allowing the application of archipelagic baselines to offshore islands, in fact reinforce the opposite conclusion. These objections underscore the absence of an established international custom permitting continental States to draw archipelagic-style baselines around their offshore island groups. Accordingly, China's claims lack legal validity and contradict both the provisions of UNCLOS and the consistent practice of the international community.

Fourth, Vietnam opposes any maritime claims in the South China Sea that exceed the limits provided in UNCLOS, including claims to historic rights; these claims are without lawful effect. Vietnam's position aligns with the 2016 Award of the Arbitral Tribunal in the South China Sea Arbitration, which clearly found that

[106] PCA Case No. 2013–19, South China Sea Arbitration, Award of 12 July 2016, paras. 573–574, from https://docs.pca-cpa.org/2016/07/PH-CN-20160712-Award.pdf, accessed 30 March 2025.

[107] France, Germany and the United Kingdom emphasize the specific and exhaustive conditions set forth in the Convention for the application of straight and archipelagic baselines which are defined in Part II and Part IV of UNCLOS. Therefore, there is no legal ground for continental States to treat archipelagos or marine features as a whole entity without respecting the relevant provisions in Part II of UNCLOS or by using those in Part IV applicable only to archipelagic States. See The Note Verbale BF N° 2020–0343647 dated September 16, 2020 from the Permanent Missions of France, Germany and the United Kingdom to the UN, from https://www.un.org/depts/los/clcs_new/submissions_files/mys_12_12_2019/2020_09_16_FRA_NV_UN_001_EN.pdf, accessed on 31 July 2025.

any assertion of historic rights beyond the scope of the Convention is incompatible with UNCLOS and, therefore, unlawful under international law.

Vietnam's positions as articulated in Note Verbale No. 22/HC-2020 dated 30 March 2020 are consistent with its longstanding and coherent stance, and fully in conformity with UNCLOS, the 2012 Law of the Sea of Vietnam, and the findings and interpretations of the Arbitral Tribunal in the South China Sea Arbitration Award of 12 July 2016. This Note also serves as a comprehensive restatement of Vietnam's previously publicized views on the South China Sea issue, including its Note dated 6 June 1996 circulated at the UN protesting China's drawing of straight baselines around the Paracel Islands, its submissions on the extended continental shelf to CLCS on 6 May and 7 May 2009 which reflect Vietnam's EEZ and continental shelf measured from its mainland thereby indicating that the Paracel and Spratly Islands do not possess independent continental shelves, and its Declaration dated 7 December 2014 submitted to the Arbitral Tribunal in the South China Sea Arbitration affirming that the features in the Spratly Islands referred to by the Philippines in its Memorial are not entitled to an EEZ or a continental shelf.

Vietnam has also rejected China's assertion that the bank is located in waters adjacent to the so-called "Nansha" (Spratly) archipelago and therefore constitutes part of Chinese "territory." On 19 May 1992, the Permanent Mission of Vietnam to the UN circulated a note to UN Member States affirming that the *Bãi Tư Chính* (Vanguard Bank) area "is located on the continental shelf of Vietnam, outside the periphery of the *Trường Sa* (Spratly) Archipelago."[108] This position was reaffirmed in the statement by the Spokesperson of the Vietnamese Ministry of Foreign Affairs dated 3 October 2019 and other official statements issued thereafter.

Affirming Vietnam's Sovereignty Over *Hoàng Sa* (Paracel) and *Trường Sa* (Spratly) Islands Consistently and Continuously Over Time

During the Third UN Conference on the Law of the Sea (1973–1982), the Government of the Republic of Vietnam (South Vietnam),[109] followed by the Socialist Republic of Vietnam (reunified Vietnam)[110] affirmed that *Hoàng Sa*

[108] Statement of the Ministry of Foreign Affairs of the Socialist Republic of Vietnam on the Agreement between Chinese and U.S. Oil Companies for the Exploration and Exploitation of Oil and Gas on the Continental Shelf of Vietnam, Press Release No. 08/BC, Vietnamese Permanent Mission to the United Nations, May 19, 1992.

[109] United Nations (1974) Third United Nations Conference on the Law of the Sea, Official Records, Volume 1: Summary Records of Plenary Meetings of the First and Second Sessions, and of Meetings of the General Committee, Second Session: New York, 3–15 December 1973; Caracas, 20 June—29 August 1974, from https://digitallibrary.un.org/record/858066?ln=en&v=pdf, accessed on 31 July 2025.

[110] United Nations (1980) Third United Nations Conference on the Law of the Sea, Official Records, Volume 13: Summary Records, Plenary, General Committee, First and Third Committees, as well as Documents of the Conference, Ninth Session, New York, 3 March—4 April 1980, from https://digitallibrary.un.org/record/19737?ln=en&v=pdf, accessed on 31 July 2025. See also United

(Paracel) and *Trường Sa* (Spratly) Islands are part of the territory of Vietnam and that Vietnam holds undisputed sovereignty over these archipelagos, regardless of unlawful claims and the illegal occupation of certain islands by China.

Vietnam's consistent protest against China's unlawful occupation of the Paracel Islands in 1974 is evidenced by a series of official communications submitted to the UN. These include the note dated 16 January 1974, followed by Note S/11200 dated 21 January 1974, and Note S/11202 dated 25 January 1974, all addressed to the UN Security Council. These communications condemned China's blatant violation of Vietnam's sovereignty through the seizure of the features *Hữu Nhật*, *Quang Hòa*, and *Duy Mộng* features in the Paracel Islands.[111] The notes laid out Vietnam's historical, legal, and factual grounds for its sovereignty over the Paracel Islands.

The correspondence and diplomatic notes of the Socialist Republic of Vietnam —such as the letter to the UN Secretary-General dated 19 October 1979 enclosing the White Paper titled "Vietnam's Sovereignty over the Hoang Sa and Truong Sa Archipelagos" (A/34/541, S/13565); the letter dated 5 February 1982 enclosing the White Paper "The Paracel and Spratly Archipelagos: Vietnamese Territories" (A/37/83, S/14861); the letter dated 9 July 2014 from the Permanent Mission of Vietnam to the UN (Doc. A/68/942); and Note Verbale No. 22/HC-2020 dated 30 March 2020—all firmly and consistently reaffirmed Vietnam's sovereignty over the Paracel and Spratly Islands.

Documents submitted to the UN affirm that Vietnam holds sovereignty over the *Hoàng Sa* (Paracel) and *Trường Sa* (Spratly) Islands since the time they were *terra nullius* (land belonging to no one), and that such sovereignty was established in accordance with the principle of effective occupation under international law on territorial acquisition. Vietnam effectively, continuously, and peacefully administered both the *Hoàng Sa* (Paracel) and *Trường Sa* (Spratly) Islands prior to their unlawful occupation by China.

China's use of force in 1974 to seize the Paracel Islands from Vietnam constituted a violation of international law. Under international law governing territorial acquisition, the use of force to occupy territory cannot confer sovereignty. In other words, China has no lawful sovereignty over the Paracel Islands.

Nations. (1982). Third United Nations Conference on the Law of the Sea. Official Records. Volume 17: Plenary Meetings, Summary Records and Verbatim Records, as well as Documents of the Conference, Resumed Eleventh Session and Final Part Eleventh Session and Conclusion, Montego Bay, 6 to 10 December 1982, from https://digitallibrary.un.org/record/81862?ln=en&v=pdf, accessed on 31 July 2025.

[111] Security Council Document S/11199, dated 18 January 1974, including Vietnam's Note dated 16 January 1974 to the President of the UN Security Council, from http://daccess-ods.un.org/access.nsf/get?open&DS=S/11199&Lang=E, accessed on 31 July 2025.

Assessing the Implications of Foreign Domestic Laws on Maritime Claims in the South China Sea

Regarding China's Coast Guard Law (2021), Vietnam expressed a clear and principled stance: Countries are obliged to comply with international laws and international treaties to which they are a signatory, especially the 1982 United Nations Convention on the Law of the Sea (UNCLOS), when they issue and implement national legal documents relating to the sea.[112] This statement underscores Vietnam's position that China cannot enact domestic legislation that exceeds or contradicts the provisions of UNCLOS.

According to the provisions of UNCLOS, maritime law enforcement forces may only conduct enforcement activities within maritime zones established in accordance with the Convention, and such activities must conform to the legal regime of each respective maritime zone and be limited to matters permitted by the Convention. In areas beyond national jurisdiction—or even in overlapping maritime zones where no agreement exists between the concerned parties—maritime law enforcement forces are not permitted to carry out enforcement measures, except in cases involving vessels flying their own flag or when exercising universal jurisdiction over specific acts such as piracy, as defined under the Convention.

Accordingly, enforcement measures by the Chinese Coast Guard against foreign warships under Articles 21, 22 of China's Coast Guard Law are inconsistent with UNCLOS. The Convention provides that warships and government vessels operated for non-commercial purposes enjoy complete immunity in the EEZ of coastal States and on the high seas. Even within the territorial sea, the coastal State may only require a foreign warship to leave if it violates the laws and regulations adopted by the coastal State in accordance with UNCLOS.

In contrast, China's Coast Guard Law authorizes its coast guard to take measures such as warning, inspection, expulsion, or even coercive towing of foreign warships in the so-called "waters under China's jurisdiction." Even if these waters were defined in accordance with UNCLOS, they would include the EEZ and territorial sea—zones in which foreign warships are entitled to full immunity. The combination of China's ambiguous Four Sha and Nine-dash Line claims with the vague concept of "waters under national jurisdiction," along with the authorization to use force as referenced in Article 22 of the Coast Guard Law, further complicates the situation. This legal framework effectively authorizes the Chinese Coast Guard to use force across nearly the entire South China Sea, raising serious concerns about the legality and legitimacy of such enforcement actions under international law. Therefore, the enforcement measures authorized under Articles 21, 22 of China's Coast Guard Law are impermissible under UNCLOS.

[112] Response of Spokesperson of the Ministry of Foreign Affairs of Vietnam, Le Thi Thu Hang, on January 22, 2021, in reaction to the Standing Committee of the National People's Congress of China passing a law allowing the Chinese coast guard to use force. See Vietnam News Agency (2021, April 29). Int'l public opinion concerned over China's coast guard law. VietnamPlus, from https://en.vietnamplus.vn/intl-public-opinion-concerned-over-chinas-coast-guard-law-post200622.vnp, accessed on 31 July 2025.

Vietnam has responded similarly to China's Maritime Traffic Safety Law (2021), the 2023 Standard Map, China's notification standardizing names for 64 features in the South China Sea, referring to them as part of the "Southern Sea" (2024),[113] as well as the Philippine Maritime Zones Act and the Archipelagic Sea Lanes Act (2024).[114] Vietnam respects the rights of coastal states to promulgate domestic laws and regulations related to maritime affairs, as long as these laws are in alignment with UNCLOS.[115]

However, Vietnam asserts its sovereignty over the *Hoàng Sa* (Paracel) and *Trường Sa* (Spratly) archipelagos and its rights within the maritime zones established under international law, and calls for all nations to fully respect these rights. Vietnam is committed to safeguarding its sovereignty and legitimate interests through measures that are consistent with international law, particularly UNCLOS. Vietnam reaffirms its readiness to resolve disputes and differences peacefully, in full compliance with international law.[116]

Protesting China's Inappropriate Administrative Decisions in the South China Sea

In addition to using domestic legal regulations, China actively promotes administrative decisions related to the South China Sea to supplement its lawfare tactics, thereby contributing to the strengthening and realization of its claims, which are inconsistent with international law, in the South China Sea.

Regarding China's administrative decisions on "standard names" and the establishment of Xisha and Nansha districts within the so-called "Sansha city" in the South China Sea, Vietnam has issued a clear objection. Vietnam reaffirms its sovereignty over the Paracels and Spratlys Islands in accordance with international law, along with its national sovereign rights and jurisdiction over maritime zones established in accordance with UNCLOS. Vietnam states unequivocally that those moves of China are invalid and unrecognized, and they are not favorable for the friendship among nations and further complicate the situation in the South China Sea, the region and the world.[117]

[113] See section "Lawfare Techniques Through the Imposition of Domestic Law on the International Arena".

[114] See section "Other Measures Adopted by the Philippines in Response to China's Lawfare".

[115] Vietnam News Agency (2024, December 14).

[116] VietnamNet (2024, November 22).

[117] Statement by the Spokesperson of the Ministry of Foreign Affairs of Vietnam, Lê Thị Thu Hằng on 19 April, 2020 at the regular press conference. See Vietnam News Agency (2020, April 19).

Joint Development versus Cooperation for Mutual Development

Joint development is widely regarded as a pragmatic mechanism that enables parties to transcend deadlocked disputes and derive mutual benefits from natural resources in maritime areas with overlapping entitlements. Its legal basis lies in Articles 74(3) and 83(3) of UNCLOS, which provide for provisional arrangements pending maritime boundary delimitation. International tribunals have also acknowledged joint development as a practical interim solution.[118] Typically state-centric in nature, joint development agreements are concluded between disputing states to foster cooperation without prejudicing their respective legal positions. Crucially, joint development is applicable only to areas where maritime boundaries remain unresolved and must not undermine ongoing or future delimitation efforts.

However, attempts to implement joint development in the South China Sea—where maritime and territorial disputes are deeply intertwined—have produced limited outcomes. China first introduced the notion of "setting aside disputes and pursuing joint development" on 24 September 1975, when Vice Premier Deng Xiaoping raised the idea during a meeting with Vietnamese General Secretary *Lê Duẩn*. Acknowledging disputes over the Xisha (Paracel) and Nansha (Spratly) Islands, Deng proposed that these issues could be "discussed later."[119] The idea resurfaced publicly in August 1990, when Premier Li Peng reiterated China's willingness to pursue joint development in the South China Sea with Southeast Asian nations.[120]

Despite these declarations, China's actual conduct has often contradicted the cooperative spirit of joint development. In 1992, Beijing unilaterally authorized the China National Offshore Oil Corporation (CNOOC) to sign an oil exploration agreement with U.S.-based Crestone Energy Corporation in Vanguard Bank (*Bãi Tư Chính*), an area located within Vietnam's continental shelf. China justified this action by invoking its expansive nine-dash line claim, arguing that the area lay within 200 nautical miles of the Spratly Islands.[121] Simultaneously, it proposed a formula to Vietnam—"sovereignty belongs to China, set aside disputes, and pursue joint development" (搁置争议, 共同开发)[122]—but with the sovereignty claim hidden beneath the surface.

Vietnam rejected this proposal outright, perceiving it as a veiled attempt to legitimize the nine-dash line, a claim inconsistent with UNCLOS and detrimental

---

[118] North Sea Continental Shelf Judgement, ICJ Reports 1969: 53, p.101 (c) (2); Award in the arbitration regarding the delimitation of the maritime boundary between Guyana and Suriname, Award of 17 September 2007, Reports of International Arbitral Awards, Vol. XXX, pp. 1–144, (United Nations, 2012).

[119] "[. . .] between us there is still dispute on Xisha Islands and Nansha Islands . . . , of course this problem can be discussed later". See White Paper of Vietnam Ministry of Foreign Affairs "Paracel Islands—Spratly Islands and International Law", Hanoi, 1998, p. 28.

[120] Guoxing (1998), p. 101.

[121] Nordquist et al. (Eds.) (2006), p. 166.

[122] Ministry of Foreign Affairs of the People's Republic of China. (n.d.). 搁置争议, 共同开发 [Set aside dispute, pursue joint development], from https://www.mfa.gov.cn/ziliao_674904/wjs_674919/2159_674923/200011/t20001107_10250989.shtml, accessed on 31 July 2025.

to Vietnam's sovereign rights and jurisdiction.[123] Vietnam has identified several flaws in China's approach: it presupposes Chinese sovereignty, contradicting the principle of mutual respect; it extends disputes into areas where no lawful Chinese claims exist; it conflates territorial sovereignty with maritime delimitation, blurring critical legal distinctions; and it promotes joint activity in areas where China has no legitimate maritime entitlement, undermining the integrity of UNCLOS. At its core, China's version of joint development operates under the implicit assumption that the nine-dash line is valid, turning disputed areas into *de facto* non-disputed ones and nullifying the concept of temporarily setting aside disagreements.

To counter this, Vietnam has introduced the concept of "Cooperation for Mutual Development", which upholds legal principles while fostering equitable cooperation. Cooperation for mutual development distinguishes itself from joint development through five key characteristics: it is firmly grounded in international law, including the UN Charter and UNCLOS—particularly Articles 74, 83, 118, 119, and 123; it allows participation from non-state actors, such as private entities—as exemplified by the 2005 tripartite agreement among national oil companies of China, Vietnam, and the Philippines; it is flexibly applicable to various maritime zones, not limited to disputed areas; it encompasses a wide array of activities including resource exploration, environmental protection, search and rescue, anti-piracy efforts, and disaster response, aligning with regional instruments such as the DOC and the draft COC; and it promotes long-term, sustained cooperation aimed at de-escalating tensions and preventing unilateral actions.[124]

Cooperation for mutual development has also proven more viable than other joint initiatives. From 2005 to 2008, China, Vietnam, and the Philippines participated in the Tripartite Joint Marine Seismic Undertaking (JMSU) in parts of the Spratly Islands, but it eventually collapsed due to legal and political criticism.[125] Similarly, the Philippines' 2011 proposal for a "Zone of Peace, Freedom, Friendship and Cooperation" (ZoPFFC), which aimed to separate disputed from non-disputed areas, failed to gain traction due to lack of consensus and perceptions of bias.[126]

In contrast, Vietnam's promotion of Cooperation for mutual development underscores its commitment to lawful cooperation, sustainable development, and regional peace—without compromising sovereignty or endorsing unlawful maritime claims. Cooperation for mutual development also offers a constructive pathway for Vietnam to invite cooperation in oil exploration and exploitation in transboundary fields, such

---

[123] Statement of the Ministry of Foreign Affairs of the Socialist Republic of Vietnam on the Agreement between Chinese and US Oil Companies for the Exploration and Exploitation of Oil and Gas on the Continental Shelf of Vietnam, Press Release N^0 08/BC, Vietnamese Mission to the United Nations, 19 May 1992.

[124] Nguyen (2018), pp. 70–74. See also Nguyen and Ton (2018).

[125] Nguyen and Amer (2009), pp. 333–349.

[126] Del Rosario (2011, August 9). Philippine policy response and action. Department of Foreign Affairs, Republic of the Philippines, from https://www.philembassy.no/news-item/philippine-policy-response-and-action-by-department-of-foreign-affairs-secretary-hon. See also Storey (2012); G. H. (n.d.)

as those crossing the delimitation line in the Gulf of Tonkin. Vietnam has expressed openness to welcoming Chinese and other international oil companies to engage in exploration and development activities in its territorial sea, in accordance with UNCLOS and with full respect for Vietnam's sovereignty and sovereign rights.

A notable example is the 2000 Sino-Vietnamese Agreement on Fishery Cooperation in the Gulf of Tonkin, under which each side contributed maritime areas (post-delimitation) to form a joint fishery zone, overseen by a Joint Fishery Committee committed to sustainable development. This model, rooted in Cooperation for mutual development principles, could also be applied by the Philippines. The Joint Oceanographic and Marine Scientific Research Expedition in the South China Sea (JOMSRE-SCS) was initiated in 1994 by Vietnam and the Philippines to foster bilateral friendship and advance scientific understanding of the South China Sea. Between 1997 and 2007, four joint expeditions—mainly around the Spratly Islands—produced valuable data on marine biodiversity and the environment. Although both countries agreed in 2008 to expand the initiative to include ASEAN states, China, and international organizations, efforts to launch a second phase have so far been unsuccessful.[127] Continuing this initiative under the model of Cooperation for mutual development would enable both Vietnam and the Philippines to promote marine scientific cooperation in accordance with international law, while also garnering broader regional and international support—particularly from stakeholders involved in multilateral disputes such as those in the Spratly Islands.

References

Books

Carpio AT (2017) The South China Sea Dispute: Philippine Sovereign Rights and Jurisdiction in the West Philippine Sea. https://murillovelardemap.com/wp-content/uploads/2017/05/SCS-WPSDisputeNon-Interactive.pdf. Accessed 27 Aug 2025

Chemillier-Gendreau M (2018 May 25) Sovereignty over the Paracel and Spratly Islands. Kluwer Law International

Nguyen HT (2004) Le Vietnam et ses différends maritimes dans la mer de Bien Dong (Mer de Chine méridionale). Pedone, Paris

Nguyen HT (2021) Vietnam's South China Sea policy. In Zou K (ed) Routledge handbook of the South China Sea. Routledge, New York. https://doi.org/10.4324/9780367822217-16

Nguyen HT (2022) Vietnam's position on sovereignty over the Paracels and the Spratlys: its maritime claims. In: Lee EYJ (ed) ASEAN international law. Springer, pp 229–272. https://doi.org/10.1007/978-981-16-3195-5_14

Nguyen HT (2024) Indonesia-Vietnam maritime delimitation: from single-line to double-line. In Nguyen HT, Vu H D (eds) Asia and UNCLOS: 30 years' implementation–An assessment. Springer. DOI: https://doi.org/10.1007/978-981-97-1556-5_12

Nordquist MH et al (eds) (2006) Recent developments in the law of the sea and China. Center for Oceans Law and Policy. Leiden, Boston: Martinus Nijhoff Publishers

[127] Vu (2021).

Vitug MD (2018) Rock Solid: how the Philippines won its Maritime Case against China. Ateneo de Manila University Press, Quezon City

Xinhua News Agency Research Institute [新华社研究院] (2025). 碧波深处有中华—中国在南海领土主权海洋权益的历史和法理依据 [Deep in the blue waves lies China—historical and legal basis of China's territorial sovereignty and maritime rights in the South China Sea]. Xinhua News Agency Research Institute, from https://f2.xhinst.net/group1/M00/00/C0/CgoMm2ila0mEdzl1AAAAAF9urw4215.pdf. Accessed on 25 Aug 2025

Articles

Dong S (2024 Dec) The decision of the Supreme Court of the Philippines on the constitutionality of the JMSU. Chin J Int Law 23(4). https://doi.org/10.1093/chinesejil/jmae034. Accessed on 31 Jul 2025

GH (n.d.) An appraisal of the joint development approach to the South China Sea dispute: prospects and challenges, from http://jpinyu.com/wp-content/uploads/2015/05/6-South-China-Sea.pdf

Ginsburg T (2020) Authoritarian international law? Am J Int Law 114(2):221–228. https://www.proquest.com/docview/2390107547?sourcetype=Scholarly%20Journals. Accessed on 31 Jul 2025

Guoxing J (1998) China vs South China Sea security. Secur Dial 29:1

Heydarian RJ (2018) Mare Liberum: aquino, Duterte, and the Philippines' evolving lawfare strategy in the South China Sea. Asian Polit Policy 10(2):283–299. https://doi.org/10.1111/aspp.12392. Accessed on 31 Jul 2025

Nguyen HT, Amer R (2009) A new legal arrangement for the South China Sea? Ocean Dev Int Law 40(4):333–349, from. https://doi.org/10.1080/00908320903077200

Nguyen HT, Ton NTB (2018) Joint development from China's position and cooperation for mutual benefit from Vietnam's stance in the South China Sea. Asian J Leg Stud, 7, from https://asianjournaloflegalstudies.wordpress.com/wp-content/uploads/2018/07/joint-development-from-the-china_s-view-and-e2809ccooperation-for-mutual-agreement-at-seae2809d-from-the-vietnam_s-stance-in-the-south-china-sea.pdf. Accessed on 28 Aug 2025

Nguyen HT (1997) Vietnam's first maritime boundary agreement. Boundary Secur Bull 5(3)

Nguyen HT (2003) Vietnam and joint development in the Gulf of Thailand. Asian Yearb Int Law 8(1998–1999)

Nguyen HT (2005) Maritime delimitation and fishery cooperation in the Tonkin Gulf. Ocean Dev Int Law 36(1)

Nguyen HT (2012) Vietnam's position on the sovereignty over the Paracels & the Spratlys: its maritime claim. J East Asia Int Law 5(1)

Nguyen HT (2018) Khái niệm "Hợp tác cùng phát triển trên biển" [The concept of "cooperation for mutual development"]. Tạp Chí Nhà Nước Và Pháp Luật 1:70–74

Nguyen TD (2025) Vietnam's dynamic approach to lawfare. Asian J Int Law 15

Nguyen TM (2020) International law as hedging: perspectives from secondary authoritarian states. Am J Int Law 114(2), https://www.researchgate.net/publication/343692944_International_Law_as_Hedging_Perspectives_from_Secondary_Authoritarian_States. Accessed on 31 Jul 2025

Oxman BH (2017) The South China Sea arbitration award. Univ Miami Int Comp Law Rev 24(2), from https://repository.law.miami.edu/umiclr/vol24/iss2/4/. Accessed on 31 Jul 2025

Storey I (2012 Apr 27) ASEAN and the South China Sea: movement in lieu of progress. China Brief 12(9), from https://jamestown.org/program/asean-and-the-south-china-sea-movement-in-lieu-of-progress/. Accessed on 31 Jul 2025

Syailendra E (2024 June 25) Malaysia's strategic approach: unpacking the "action-reaction spiral" logic in the South China Sea. https://doi.org/10.1111/aspp.12751, from https://onlinelibrary.wiley.com/doi/10.1111/aspp.12751. Accessed on 19 Aug 2025

Trinh KM (2014). Vietnam's feudal state managed Paracel Islands and waters of Vietnam in the South China Sea for centuries. Vietnam J Soc Sci Inf Rev 8(3), from https://vjol.info.vn/index.php/ssirev/article/download/22031/18819/. Accessed on 31 Jul 2025

Internet Materials

Alegre P (2025 June 10) Manila's transparency initiative: a strategy for deterrence? Pacific Forum, from https://pacforum.org/publications/yl-blog-130-manilas-transparency-initiative-a-strategy-for-deterrence/. Accessed on 12 Aug 2025

Amy Chew A (2023 Apr 25) Malaysia's energy needs face Chinese pushback in South China Sea, Aljazeera, from https://www.aljazeera.com/economy/2023/4/25/malaysian-energy-needs-clash-with-china-claims-in-south-china-sea. Accessed on 31 Jul 2025

Anjaiah V (2025 Feb 25) Vietnam announces a baseline to determine its territorial waters in Gulf of Tonkin – opEd, from https://www.eurasiareview.com/25022025-vietnam-announces-a-baseline-to-determine-its-territorial-waters-in-gulf-of-tonkin-oped/. Accessed on 31 July 2025

AP News (2016 Jul 12) Timeline: the China-Philippines South China Sea dispute, from https://apnews.com/national-national-general-news-bcd47429a69240af81544554a78fd138. Accessed on 31 Jul 2025

Asia Sentinel (2015 May 26) Fact, fiction and the South China Sea, from https://www.asiasentinel.com/p/fact-fiction-south-china-sea. Accessed on 31 Jul 2025

Batongbacal JL (2021) The Philippines and the South China Sea arbitration award: external appeasement and internal dissension (ISEAS Perspective No. 2021/126). ISEAS – Yusof Ishak Institute, from https://www.iseas.edu.sg/articles-commentaries/iseas-perspective/2021-126-the-philippines-and-the-south-china-sea-arbitration-award-external-appeasement-and-internal-dissension-by-jay-l-batongbacal/. Accessed on 31 Jul 2025

Bentley S (2023) The maritime fulcrum of the Indo-Pacific: Indonesia and Malaysia respond to China's creeping expansion in the South China Sea. U.S. Naval War College, China Maritime Studies Institute, from https://www.andrewerickson.com/wp-content/uploads/2023/01/CMSI_China-Maritime-Study-17_Indonesia-Malaysia-Respond-to-Chinas-Creeping-Expansion-in-SCS_Bentley_2022.pdf. Accessed on 15 Aug 2025

Bernama TV (2024 Apr 25) Malaysia: all parties must adhere to international law on the South China Sea, from https://www.bernama.com/en/news.php?id=2321872. Accessed on 31 Jul 2025

Bqp.vn (2017 May 14) Nguyen dynasty documents honour Vietnam's sovereignty over sea and islands, from https://mod.gov.vn/en/event/detail?current=true&urile=wcm:path:/mod/sa-mod-en/sa-en-news/sa-en-news-vn/5d8c662a-8fa5-41b7-a5dd-d2b0bca111aa. Accessed on 31 Jul 2025

Central Intelligence Agency (1971 July 22) Islands of the South China Sea (declassified and approved for release December 24, 2024), from https://www.cia.gov/readingroom/docs/CIA-RDP08C01297R000300180019-2.pdf. Accessed on 31 Jul 2025

Cervantes FM (2024 May 30) PH to complete environmental case vs China in 'few weeks'—DOJ. Philippine News Agency, from https://www.pna.gov.ph/articles/1225935. Accessed on 31 Jul 2025

China Daily (2025 Aug 15) Philippine ships' dangerous maneuvers seriously endangered the safety of the Chinese ships and personnel in the South China Sea: china's defense ministry, from https://www.chinadaily.com.cn/a/202508/15/WS689eecd8a310b236346f1dfd.html?. Accessed on 15 Aug 2025

Country Profile from the Maritime Awareness Project: Malaysia, from https://www.nbr.org/publication/malaysia/. Accessed on 31 Jul 2025

Daniel T (2024 Oct 08) Malaysia eyes strengthened South China Sea defence with new naval base in Borneo, from https://www.isis.org.my/2024/10/08/malaysia-eyes-strengthened-south-china-sea-defence-with-new-naval-base-in-borneo/. Accessed on 15 Aug 2025

De Castro RC (2014) The 2012 Scarborough Shoal stand-off: from stalemate to escalation of the South China Sea dispute? In: Buszynski L, Roberts CB (eds) The South China Sea maritime dispute. Routledge, pp 111–129. https://doi.org/10.4324/9781315858029-6, from https://www.researchgate.net/publication/345611834_The_2012_Scarborough_Shoal_stand-off. Accessed on 31 Jul 2025

De Castro RC (2017) The 12 July 2016 permanent court of arbitration's (PCA) award: the Philippines' lawfare versus China's realpolitik in the South China Sea dispute. Int J China Stud 8(3):345–370, from https://www.academia.edu/36431166/The_12_July_2016_Permanent_Court_of_Arbitrations_PCA_Award_The_Philippines_Lawfare_versus_Chinas_Realpolitik_in_the_South_China_Sea_Dispute. Accessed on 31 Jul 2025

Espenilla J (2025 Nov 15) China's upgraded lawfare in the South China Sea: China is stepping up its legal narratives targeting the Philippines. The Diplomat, https://thediplomat.com/2025/11/chinas-upgraded-lawfare-in-the-south-china-sea/. Accessed on 27 Nov 2025

Fernandez D (2023 Jan 26) PH files 461 diplomatic protests vs China since 2016, says DFA. INQUIRER.net, from https://globalnation.inquirer.net/210063/ph-files-461-diplomatic-protests-vs-china-since-2016. Accessed on 15 Aug 2025

Fu Ting, Moritsugu K (2025 Sep 18) China says it wants to protect coral reefs in the South China Sea: Experts are doubtful. AP News. https://apnews.com/article/south-china-sea-scarborough-shoal-china-philippines-3b9e648e72573794a71ab35d320306 11. Accessed on 27 Nov 2025

Goldenziel J (2023 Sept 1) Water cannon reveals Philippine transparency strategy against China needs reinforcement. Forbes, from https://www.forbes.com/sites/jillgoldenziel/2023/09/01/water-cannon-reveals-philippine-transparency-strategy-against-china-needs-reinforcement/. Accessed on 31 Jul 2025

Gomez J (2025 Aug 15) Philippines blames China for ship collision in disputed South China Sea, from https://apnews.com/article/south-china-sea-philippines-scarborough-shoal-0164b204d780052482c18a0876811266. Accessed on 15 Aug 2025

Gutierrez P (2025 Sep 2) China's Pushback Against the Philippines' Maritime Strategy: The Limits of Transparency. The Diplomat, https://thediplomat.com/2025/09/chinas-pushback-against-the-philippines-maritime-strategy-the-limits-of-transparency/. Accessed on 27 Nov 2025

Indo-Pacific Defense Forum (2019 June 25) Truth movement to debunk PRC claims in the South China Sea, from https://ipdefenseforum.com/2019/06/truth-movement-to-debunk-prc-claims-in-the-south-china-sea/. Accessed on 31 Jul 2025

Institute for Maritime and Ocean Affairs (2019 June 9) A call for a South China Sea truth movement. Institute for Maritime and Ocean Affairs, from https://imoa.ph/opinion-a-call-for-a-south-china-sea-truth-movement-4/. Accessed on 31 Jul 2025

Krishnan T (2020 Nov 12) Malaysia in the South China Sea: a growing mismatch between threat and capabilities. Asia Maritime Transparency Initiative, from https://amti.csis.org/malaysia-in-the-south-china-sea-a-growing-mismatch-between-threat-and-capabilities/. Accessed on 15 Aug 2025

Lariosa AM (2024 June 17) Philippine sailor severely injured, vessels damaged as Chinese block South China Sea mission. USNI New, from https://news.usni.org/2024/06/17/philippine-sailor-severely-injured-vessels-damaged-as-chinese-block-south-china-sea-mission. Accessed on 31 Jul 2025

Le TTM (2019 Aug 9) UNCLOS 1982—overarching framework for establishing legal order for seas and oceans, promoting development cooperation at sea. Vietnam Plus, from https://en.vietnamplus.vn/unclos-1982-overarching-framework-for-establishing-legal-order-for-seas-and-oceans-promoting-development-cooperation-at-sea-post157548.vnp. Accessed on 31 Jul 2025

Longley R (2019 Jul 29) Treaty of Paris 1898: the end of the Spanish-American War. ThoughtCo, from https://www.thoughtco.com/treaty-of-paris-1898-4692529. Accessed on 31 Jul 2025

Madarang CRS (2019 Oct 24) What happened to the policy of refusing to stamp visas on China passports with 9-dash line? PhilStar, from https://interaksyon.philstar.com/politics-issues/2019/10/24/156530/philippines-china-passport-visa-9-dash-line-stamp/. Accessed on 31 Jul 2025
Magramo K (2023 Sept 22) The Philippines accuses China's shadowy maritime militia of destroying coral reefs in South China Sea. CNN, from https://abc17news.com/news/national-world/cnn-world/2023/09/22/the-philippines-accuses-chinas-shadowy-maritime-militia-of-destroying-coral-reefs-in-south-china-sea/. Accessed on 31 Jul 2025
Mahmud AH (2025 Aug 12) Malaysia steps up ways to 'confront threats' in South China Sea, but will this rock the boat? Channel News Asia, from https://www.channelnewsasia.com/asia/malaysia-south-china-sea-claim-defence-anwar-ibrahim-5288436. Accessed on 15 Aug 2025
Merueñas M (2011 Aug 16) Supreme court upholds PHL 2009 Baselines law. GMA News, from https://www.gmanetwork.com/news/topstories/nation/229617/supreme-court-upholds-phl-2009-baselines-law/story/#goog_rewarded. Accessed on 31 Jul 2025
National Bureau of Asian Research (n.d.) Philippines. Maritime Awareness Project, from https://www.nbr.org/publication/philippines/. Accessed on 31 Jul 2025
Nguyen HT (2019 Dec) Malaysia's new game in the South China Sea. The Diplomat, from https://thediplomat.com/2019/12/malaysias-new-game-in-the-south-china-sea/. Accessed on 31 Jul 2025
Nguyen HT (2025) Thêm một bước tiến trong việc khẳng định các vùng biển thuộc chủ quyền của Việt Nam [One more step in affirming Vietnam's sovereignty over its maritime zones]. VietnamNet, from https://vietnamnet.vn/buoc-tien-trong-viec-khang-dinh-cac-vung-bien-thuoc-chu-quyen-cua-viet-nam-2383608.html. Accessed 27 Aug 2025
Nguyen Huu Tuc (2015 Jan 5) Malaysia and the South China Sea: will KL abandon its hedging strategy? RSIS Commentary, No. 003, from https://www.files.ethz.ch/isn/187038/CO15003.pdf. Accessed on 31 Jul 2025
Parameswaran P (2015 Feb) Playing It Safe: Malaysia's Approach to the South China Sea and Implications for the United States. Maritime Strategy Series, from https://www.files.ethz.ch/isn/189746/CNAS%20Maritime%206_Parameswaran_Final.pdf. Accessed on 19 August 2025
Philippine Daily Inquirer (2014 Oct 25) What went before: USS guardian running aground Tubbataha reefs, from https://globalnation.inquirer.net/113430/what-went-before-uss-guardian-running-aground-tubbataha-reefs. Accessed on 31 Jul 2025
Putra BA (2024 Mar 25) Malaysia's "triadic maritime diplomacy" strategy in the South China Sea. All Azimuth, from https://www.allazimuth.com/2024/03/25/malaysias-triadic-maritime-diplomacy-strategy-in-the-south-china-sea/. Accessed on 31 Jul 2025
Reuters (2024 Jul 9) Philippines rejects China's accusation of environmental damage in South China Sea, from https://www.reuters.com/world/asia-pacific/philippines-rejects-chinas-accusation-environmental-damage-south-china-sea-2024-07-09/. Accessed on 31 Jul 2025
Rosen ME (2014 Aug) Philippine claims in the South China Sea: a legal analysis (a CNA occasional paper). CNA, from https://www.cna.org/archive/CNA_Files/pdf/iop-2014-u-008435.pdf. Accessed on 31 Jul 2025
Ryan SEKZ (2023 May 15) Malaysia: securing sovereignty in the South China Sea through ASEAN centrality. Yale J Int Aff, from https://www.yalejournal.org/publications/malaysia-securing-sovereignty-in-the-south-china-sea-through-asean-centrality. Accessed on 15 August 2025
Sadi CMH et al (2024 July) South China Sea maritime disputes and Malaysia international integrative relations as a jihad strategy in balancing the World's authoritative powers. Eur Chem Bull 2(7):5290–5305, from https://www.researchgate.net/publication/382111906_South_China_Sea_Maritime_Disputes_and_Malaysia_International_Integrative_Relations_as_a_Jihad_Strategy_in_Balancing_the_World%27s_Authoritative_Powers. Accessed on 15 Aug 2025
Schultheiss C (2024 June 11) There is no 'secret agreement' between China and the Philippines on Second Thomas Shoal. The Diplomat, from https://thediplomat.com/2024/06/there-is-no-secret-agreement-between-china-and-the-philippines-on-second-thomas-shoal/. Accessed on 12 Aug 2025

Shepherd C (2025 Aug 11) Footage shows two Chinese ships colliding while chasing Philippine boat. The Washington Post, from https://www.washingtonpost.com/world/2025/08/11/south-china-sea-collision/. Accessed on 15 August 2025

St Antony's College, University of Oxford (2019 Apr 30) Fundamental rights lawfare: religious freedom and public order in Pakistan and Malaysia [Talk]. Oxford Talks. Speaker: Matthew Nelson (SOAS); Organising department: Asian Studies Centre, from https://talks.ox.ac.uk/talks/id/e8df4228-91ac-4cf5-80b9-391265c43b9e/. Accessed on 31 Jul 2025

Storey I (2008) Conflict in the South China Sea: China's relations with Vietnam and the Philippines. The Asia-Pacific Journal: Japan Focus, from https://apjjf.org/ian-storey/2734/article. Accessed on 31 Jul 2025

Storey I (2024 Aug 28) Malaysia and the South China Sea Dispute: a sea change under Prime Minister anwar? Fulcrum, from https://fulcrum.sg/malaysia-and-south-china-sea-dispute-a-sea-change-under-prime-minister-anwar/. Accessed on 31 Jul 2025

Strangio S (2023 Apr 11) Malaysia clarifies South China Sea policy following PM's comments. The Diplomat, from https://thediplomat.com/2023/04/malaysia-clarifies-south-china-sea-policy-following-pms-comments/. Accessed on 31 Jul 2025

The South China Sea Dispute: philippine Sovereign Rights and Jurisdiction in the West Philippine Sea, from https://imoa.ph/philippine-sovereign-rights-and-jurisdiction-in-the-west-philippine-sea/. Accessed on 31 Jul 2025

Trinh KM (2014) Vietnam's feudal state managed Paracel Islands and waters of Vietnam in the South China Sea for centuries. Vietnam J Soc Sci Inf Rev 8(3), from https://vjol.info.vn/index.php/ssirev/article/download/22031/18819/. Accessed on 31 Jul 2025

Vietnam Law and Legal Forum (2019 Jul 29) Vietnam respects, fully implements UNCLOS 1982. Vietnam Law and Legal Forum, from https://vietnamlawmagazine.vn/vietnam-respects-fully-implements-unclos-1982-16789.html. Accessed on 31 Jul 2025

Vietnam News Agency (2020 Apr 19) Vietnam strongly protests establishment of so-called Sansha city. VietnamPlus, from https://en.vietnamplus.vn/vietnam-strongly-protests-establishment-of-so-called-sansha-city-post172004.vnp. Accessed on 12 Aug 2025

Vietnam News Agency (2021 Apr 29) Int'l public opinion concerned over China's coast guard law. VietnamPlus, from https://en.vietnamplus.vn/intl-public-opinion-concerned-over-chinas-coast-guard-law-post200622.vnp. Accessed on 31 July 2025

Vietnam News Agency (2024 Dec 14) Vietnam calls for full adherence to UNCLOS legal standards, obligations. Nhân Dân online, from https://en.nhandan.vn/vietnam-calls-for-full-adherence-to-unclos-legal-standards-obligations-post142256.html. Accessed on 12 Aug 2025

VietnamNet (2024 Nov 22) Vietnam responds to Philippines and China actions in East Sea (Press briefing on November 21, by Ministry of Foreign Affairs spokesperson Pham Thu Hang), from https://vietnamnet.vn/en/vietnam-responds-to-philippines-and-china-actions-in-east-sea-2344557.html. Accessed on 31 Jul 2025

Villanueva MA (2018 May 25) Lawfare, not warfare in South China Sea. The Philippine Star, from https://www.philstar.com/opinion/2018/05/25/1818339/lawfare-not-warfare-south-china-sea, https://www.bernama.com/en/news.php?id=2321872. Accessed on 31 Jul 2025

VNExpress (2024 Mar 14) Vietnam requests China to respect Gulf of Tonkin delimitation agreement, https://e.vnexpress.net/news/news/vietnam-requests-china-to-respect-gulf-of-tonkin-delimitation-agreement-4722407.html. Accessed on 31 Jul 2025

Vu M (2021 Jul 1) Group of Friends launched to promote UNCLOS. Hanoi Times, from https://hanoitimes.vn/group-of-friends-launched-to-promote-unclos-317916.html. Accessed on 31 Jul 2025

Vu HD (2021 Dec 8) Resumption of JOMSRE-SCS: practical suggestions to move forward. Asia Maritime Transparency Initiative (AMTI), from https://amti.csis.org/resumption-of-jomsre-scs-practical-suggestions-to-move-forward/. Accessed on 31 Jul 2025

Chapter 4
Lawfulness versus China's Lawfare in the South China Sea

This chapter analyzes how the clash between lawfare and lawfulness has unfolded through the 2016 Arbitral Award, diplomatic note verbale exchanges, cartographic battles, ASEAN–China COC negotiations, and broader struggles to shape the rules of the regional and international order. It begins with the 2016 Arbitral Award, which invalidated China's nine-dash line and clarified the status of maritime features under UNCLOS. The ruling reshaped the legal landscape and became a reference point for subsequent state practice. China rejected the Award and escalated its lawfare through the Four Sha and Nanhai Zhudao doctrines, new domestic legislation, and persistent gray-zone tactics.

The chapter then examines the two rounds of note verbale battles triggered by Malaysia, the Philippines, and Vietnam's submissions to the CLCS. These exchanges expanded into a broader confrontation, drawing in external powers such as the U.S., Australia, Japan, and European states. It next turns to the cartographic battle, where China's maps sought to entrench excessive claims. Malaysia, Vietnam, and the Philippines firmly rejected these maps across multiple fronts where they appeared. The discussion also covers the ASEAN–China COC negotiations, marked by disputes over scope, binding enforcement, and restrictions on external actors. The Philippines and Vietnam insist that any COC must align with UNCLOS and the 2016 Award, while China favors ambiguous commitments that preserve unilateral flexibility. Finally, the chapter highlights the struggle to "shape the rules." China seeks to reinterpret or selectively apply UNCLOS to shift the normative framework, while Malaysia, Vietnam, and the Philippines counter by upholding lawfulness, insisting that both the COC and broader settlements remain firmly rooted in UNCLOS and the Award.

Taken together, these confrontations demonstrate how lawfare and lawfulness are continually tested. China adapts its lawfare to entrench control, while regional claimants and external partners advance lawfulness to reinforce UNCLOS and the rules-based order.

H. T. Nguyen, T. K. N. Tran, *Lawfulness and Lawfare in the South China Sea*,
International Law in Asia,
https://doi.org/10.1007/978-981-95-4001-3_4

Legal Confrontation Surrounding the 2016 South China Sea Arbitral Award

Conclusions and Impact of the 2016 South China Sea Arbitration Award

After failed negotiations and mediation efforts surrounding Scarborough Shoal, the Philippines decided to turn to legal remedies to counter China's pressure and lawfare activities. On 22 January 2013, the Philippines submitted a Note Verbale to China along with its Notification and Statement of Claims in the West Philippine Sea,[1] thereby initiating arbitration against China under Annex VII of UNCLOS. In this case, the Philippines requested the Tribunal to clarify the legal status of certain maritime features in the Spratly Islands and to assess the validity of the nine-dash line.

China repeatedly declared that it "does not accept and does not participate in the arbitration unilaterally initiated by the Philippines."[2] However, in its 2015 Award on Jurisdiction and Admissibility, which was later confirmed by the 2016 Award on the Merits, the Tribunal held that it had jurisdiction over the case even in the absence of a party.

On 12 July 2016, the Tribunal rendered its final award.[3] First and foremost, it held that the maritime rights and obligations of the Philippines and China in the South China Sea are governed solely by UNCLOS, and it rejected all maritime claims that were incompatible with the Convention.

The Convention's provisions supersede any historical rights that conflict with its provisions.[4] On this basis, the Arbitration Tribunal dismissed China's nine-dash line claim and historical rights in the South China Sea. Within the scope of China's historical rights to resources in the waters of the South China Sea, these rights are nullified as they are inconsistent with the EEZ regime of the Convention. The Tribunal also determined that historically, seafarers and fishermen from China, as well as from other countries, utilized the islands in the South China Sea, but there was insufficient evidence to demonstrate that China alone exercised control over

---

[1] Department of Foreign Affairs of the Republic of the Philippines (2013, January 22) Notification and statement of claim in the West Philippine Sea by the Philippines, from https://www.officialgazette.gov.ph/2013/01/22/dfa-notification-and-statement-claim-on-west-philippine-sea-january-22-2013/, accessed on 31 July 2025.

[2] Permanent Court of Arbitration (2014, December 17) Press release: Arbitration regarding the South China Sea (Republic of the Philippines v. People's Republic of China), from https://pcacases.com/web/sendAttach/1297, accessed on 31 July 2025.

[3] PCA Case No. 2013–19, the matter of the South China Sea Arbitration (Philippines v. China), Award of 12 July 2016, from https://pcacases.com/web/sendAttach/2086, accessed on 31 July 2025.

[4] PCA Case No. 2013–19, the matter of the South China Sea Arbitration (Philippines v. China), Award of 12 July 2016, pp. 116–117, from https://pcacases.com/web/sendAttach/2086, accessed on 31 July 2025.

the waters and resources in the South China Sea. Consequently, the Tribunal concluded that there is no legal basis for China to claim historic rights to resources in the sea areas enclosed by the nine-dash line.[5]

Second, the Tribunal extensively elucidated Article 121(3) concerning the legal status conditions of islands and rocks. Relying on historical records and the natural condition of maritime features in the South China Sea prior to land reclamation and artificial island construction activities, the Tribunal determined the legal status of these maritime features. The Tribunal concluded that five features cited by the Philippines in its claim—Hughes Reef, Gaven Reef (South), Subi Reef, Mischief Reef, and Second Thomas Shoal—are low-tide elevations, which do not generate any maritime zones of their own and cannot be subject to appropriation by any State.

Regarding the legal status of high-tide features, including Scarborough Shoal, Cuarteron Reef, Fiery Cross Reef, Johnson Reef, McKennan Reef, and Gaven Reef (North), the Tribunal found that they qualify as "rocks" under Article 121(3) of UNCLOS, which means they are not entitled to an EEZ or continental shelf. The Tribunal emphasized that the determination of a feature's status must be based on its natural capacity to sustain either a stable human community or economic life of its own, without reliance on external resources or artificial enhancements. The current presence of official personnel on many features is maintained through external support and does not reflect the natural capacity of those features.

Moreover, the Tribunal determined that no feature in the Spratly Islands is capable of generating extensive maritime zones. Specifically, it concluded that there is no legal basis for any Chinese historic rights or other sovereign rights and jurisdiction beyond those provided in the Convention, in the waters of the South China Sea encompassed by the "nine-dash line." None of the high-tide features in the Spratly Islands qualifies as a fully entitled island under Article 121 of the Convention. Therefore, there is no maritime feature in the Spratly Islands that can generate entitlement to an EEZ or continental shelf. Furthermore, the Spratlys cannot collectively generate maritime zones as a single unit.[6]

Third, the Tribunal declared that low-tide elevations cannot be subject to territorial appropriation. They are not capable of generating a territorial sea, except in cases where they are located wholly or partially within the 12-nautical-mile territorial sea measured from land or islands and serve as internationally recognized base points. Submerged features are also not subject to territorial appropriation. Furthermore, since a low-tide elevation or a seabed area cannot legally be transformed into an island through human intervention, the Tribunal held that

[5] Notice of the Philippines' lawsuit against China, p. 9, https://pca-cpa.org/wp-content/uploads/sites/175/2016/07/PH-CN-20160712-Press-Release-No-11-English.pdf, accessed on 31 July 2025.

[6] PCA Case No. 2013–19, the matter of the South China Sea Arbitration (Philippines v. China), Award of 12 July 2016, paras. 643–645, from https://pcacases.com/web/sendAttach/2086, accessed on 31 July 2025.

a rock cannot be turned into a fully entitled island through land reclamation. The legal status of a maritime feature must be assessed based on its natural condition.[7]

Fourth, the Tribunal rejected any possibility of applying the archipelagic baseline to features in the Spratly Islands[8]

Fifth, the Tribunal determined that China had violated a number of provisions of the Convention and other rules of international law concerning the protection of the marine environment and the safety of navigation.[9]

Sixth, The Tribunal stated that Scarborough Shoal was a traditional fishing ground for fishermen of many nationalities, including those from the Philippines, China (including from Taiwan), and Vietnam.[10]

The ruling not only affected the main parties to the case but also had implications for many other countries in the region and beyond, in the context of the implementation and development of the law of the sea. Regarding the maritime zones in the Spratlys, the Tribunal's conclusions have six major implications:

First, the relevant coastal States may only claim up to 12 nautical miles (NM) of territorial sea and 24 NM of contiguous zone, measured from the baselines of each high-tide feature in the Spratlys.

Second, the EEZ and continental shelf of coastal States can only be generated from their mainland territories. These zones are no longer subject to overlap from the nine-dash line claim or from any EEZ or continental shelf claims originating from the Spratlys. Coastal States such as Vietnam, the Philippines, Malaysia, Brunei, and even China retain the full rights to their 200 NM EEZs measured from their respective mainland coasts.

Third, the Tribunal dismissed any prospect of applying the archipelagic baseline to features in the Spratly Islands.

Fourth, Coastal States such as China, the Philippines, Brunei, Malaysia, and Vietnam are encouraged to extend the outer limits of their continental shelf beyond 200 NM from the mainland baselines, in accordance with UNCLOS provisions.

Fifth, there will be a high seas area in the central part of the South China Sea, where all States enjoy the freedoms of the sea—such as freedom of navigation, overflight, fishing, marine scientific research, and the construction of artificial islands and installations. In other words, the South China Sea

---

[7] PCA Case No. 2013–19, the matter of the South China Sea Arbitration (Philippines v. China), Award of 12 July 2016, para. 508, p. 214, from https://pcacases.com/web/sendAttach/2086, accessed on 31 July 2025.

[8] PCA Case No. 2013–19, the matter of the South China Sea Arbitration (Philippines v. China), Award of 12 July 2016, para.575, from https://pcacases.com/web/sendAttach/2086.

[9] PCA Case No. 2013–19, the matter of the South China Sea Arbitration (Philippines v. China), Award of 12 July 2016, para. 992–993, 1181, from https://pcacases.com/web/sendAttach/2086, accessed on 31 July 2025.

[10] PCA Case No. 2013–19, the matter of the South China Sea Arbitration (Philippines v. China), Award of 12 July 2016, para. 805, from https://pcacases.com/web/sendAttach/2086, accessed on 31 July 2025.

becomes more multilateral and international rather than strictly bilateral or regional.[11]

Sixth, fishing rights in certain areas are recognized as traditional—such as in Scarborough Shoal, where Filipino, Chinese, and Vietnamese fishermen may engage in fishing. The Award creates the possibility for a joint fisheries development mechanism in the central South China Sea, where the high seas exist.

Seventh, there will be an Area—common heritage of mankind—in the center of the South China Sea, where "No State shall claim or exercise sovereignty or sovereign rights over any part of the Area or its resources; no State or natural or juridical person shall appropriate any part of the Area or its resources. No such claim or exercise of sovereignty or sovereign rights nor such appropriation shall be recognized."[12]

The Award opens the possibility for ASEAN countries that do not claim sovereignty over the Paracel or Spratly Islands to directly participate in the management processes of the high seas and the Area—common heritage of mankind—in the central South China Sea.

Eighth, the ruling sets a precedent by leveraging the compulsory dispute resolution mechanism under UNCLOS to interpret the Convention, thereby promoting its precise and equitable implementation. This mechanism allows appropriate legal remedies to be pursued even in the absence of one party before the Arbitral Tribunal, thus encouraging the use of peaceful and lawful avenues to resolve disputes in the South China Sea.

Overall, the Award significantly reduces the overlapping claims in the South China Sea. It affects the politics, economy, and security of the countries bordering the South China Sea, the internal solidarity of ASEAN, the U.S.—China strategic competition, and the foreign policies of States with interests in the region. This decision is also a test of the credibility of international law, the commitment to its implementation, and the goodwill of the parties involved. The impact of this award will be felt across many generations.[13]

The Arbitral Ruling in the South China Sea: Lawfulness Affirmed, Lawfare Intensified

The ruling has had an impact not only on the directly involved parties, namely the Philippines and China, but also on the attitudes of countries both within and outside the region, particularly as reflected in the diplomatic note exchanges during the legal battle over submissions on extended continental shelves in the South China Sea.

---

[11] Nguyen and Nguyen (2021).

[12] UNCLOS, Article 137.

[13] Nguyen H T (2022), pp. 245–273.

China's Lawfare Strategy in Response to the 2016 Award

In essence, the 2016 South China Sea Arbitral Award has served as a catalyst for many countries to reassess their policies in the region, with the notable exception of China. Rather than simply responding to Western criticisms, China has leveraged the ruling to proactively enhance its lawfare strategies, complemented by Psychological warfare and media manipulation. This strategic shift marks China's transition from a reactive posture to active engagement in shaping the narrative, setting the rules from the outset, and influencing public discourse to its advantage.

China's response to the 2016 Arbitral Award exemplifies a sophisticated, multi-layered lawfare strategy aimed at discrediting the ruling while reasserting its maritime claims. Before the Tribunal's hearing, the Chinese Ministry of Foreign Affairs issued a Position Paper in 2014, outlining legal arguments against the Philippines' lawsuit at the International Arbitral Tribunal.[14] In this paper, China argued that the Tribunal lacked jurisdiction and that its claims were based on historical rights, asserting a superior legal basis over UNCLOS. This preemptive action represented the first step in China's broader lawfare campaign, designed to avoid international scrutiny and potential legal consequences.

Following the Tribunal's decision, which overwhelmingly rejected China's nine-dash line and its historical rights claims, Beijing launched an extensive campaign to delegitimize both the process and the outcome of the arbitration. The Chinese government deployed a range of legal, diplomatic, and media tools to create a counter-narrative aimed at undermining the authority of the Tribunal and discrediting its findings. Central to this effort was the 2016 White Paper published by the State Council Information Office, in which China reiterated its refusal to recognize the Arbitral Award and defended its territorial claims as a matter of historical and sovereign right. The 20,000-word document formalized China's legal stance by emphasizing its non-participation in the arbitration process, including the failure to nominate arbitrators, submit counter-submissions, accept the Tribunal's jurisdiction, or recognize its decision—while continuing to assert China's historical rights, despite the Tribunal's clear ruling that these claims were incompatible with UNCLOS.[15] Moreover, China's lawfare strategy extended into the academic sphere.[16] In 2018, the Chinese Society of International Law released a 500-page critique titled South China Sea Arbitration Awards: A Critical Study, which systematically challenged the legal reasoning and conclusions of the Arbitral Award.[17] This publication sought not only to dispute the

---

[14] The Position Paper of the Government of the People's Republic of China on the Matter of Jurisdiction in the South China Sea Arbitration Initiated by the Republic of the Philippines, issued on December 7, 2014, from https://english.www.gov.cn/archive/press_briefing/2014/12/07/content_281475020441708.htm, accessed on 31 July 2025.

[15] Speech by Professor Beckman at the 10th South China Sea International Conference (November 2018 in Da Nang, Vietnam).

[16] See section "Academic Lawfare: How China internationalizes disputed claims through scholarly influence".

[17] Chinese Society of International Law (2018), pp. 207–748.

legitimacy of the Tribunal but also to undermine the legal principles upon which the ruling was based. By mobilizing legal scholars, China attempted to lend academic credibility to its political stance and reinforce its narrative on the global stage.[18]

In parallel, state-controlled media outlets[19]—such as Global Times, Xinhua News Agency, and People's Daily—were actively deployed to disseminate narratives discrediting the arbitral process. For instance, Xinhua described the Tribunal as a "farce" and a "puppet of the Peace Palace," attempting to decouple it from the UN system. It also amplified inflammatory remarks from figures like Mr. Wu Shicun, who accused the Tribunal of bias and manipulation through Philippine funding.[20] Similarly, People's Daily portrayed the ruling as widely rejected by international public opinion, often citing dubious or unofficial sources to create the illusion of global consensus against the Award.[21]

Beyond domestic efforts, China also sought to influence international opinion by supporting foreign academics who published commentaries favorable to its position. Think tanks such as the South China Sea Strategic Situation Probing Initiative (SCSPI) further contributed to this strategy through studies that selectively framed facts to support China's maritime claims.

Diplomatically, China issued a series of notes verbales to the UN, particularly in response to submissions regarding the extended continental shelf in the South China Sea. These notes reaffirmed China's position that the Arbitral Tribunal had acted *ultra vires* (beyond its powers), arguing that its jurisdiction did not extend to the matters at hand. This legal rejection was framed within the broader context of China's steadfast "three no's" policy: no participation in the arbitration process, no acceptance of the Tribunal's jurisdiction, and no recognition of the Tribunal's decision (see Table 4.1 below).[22]

Table 4.1 China's Arguments versus the Arbitral Tribunal's Decisions on Jurisdiction and Admissibility

China's arguments	The Arbitral Tribunal's decision
1. The essence of the Philippines' lawsuit concerns sovereignty disputes over features in the Spratlys, which fall outside UNCLOS. Therefore, China argues the Tribunal lacks jurisdiction	The Tribunal found that the Philippines' submissions did not require a ruling on sovereignty; rather, it explicitly urged the Tribunal to refrain from adjudicating on sovereignty matters. Consequently, although there exists a sovereignty dispute between the parties, the dispute that the Tribunal is tasked

(continued)

[18] Treves (2016).

[19] See section "Combining Legal Warfare with Psychological Warfare and Public Opinion Warfare".

[20] 新华社 [Xinhua News Agency] (2016, July 21).

[21] 宦佳 [Huan J] (2016).

[22] See the next section on the submission of claims regarding the outer limits of continental shelves and the subsequent exchange of diplomatic notes.

Table 4.1 (continued)

China's arguments	The Arbitral Tribunal's decision
	with resolving is unrelated to this issue, focusing solely on the interpretation and application of UNCLOS. Thus, the dispute falls within the Tribunal's jurisdiction[23]
2. Arbitration requires the consent of both parties.China claims the Philippines' unilateral action is invalid under international law.China asserts that the international arbitration mechanism necessitates the consent of both disputing parties. As the Philippines unilaterally initiated the lawsuit, China contends that it contravenes international law and thus holds no validity for China	Under Article 9 of Annex VII of UNCLOS, a party's non-participation does not impede the Tribunal's authority. The Tribunal's decisions are final and binding regardless of China's absence[24]
3. Existing agreements (e.g., DOC, TAC, joint statements) obligate negotiation as the sole method of dispute resolution. China argues that various agreements such as DOC, the Southeast Asia Treaty of Amity and Cooperation (TAC), joint statements, meeting minutes, exchanges, and consultations between the two nations explicitly stipulate the employment of negotiation as the sole method to address South China Sea disputes. Therefore, the Philippines' unilateral lawsuit is deemed a breach of its commitments to both China and ASEAN nations	The Tribunal held that such agreements are non-binding political declarations or lack enforceable dispute resolution mechanisms. The Philippines was not precluded from initiating arbitration under UNCLOS. The Arbitral Tribunal ruled that neither DOC nor the bilateral declarations between the Philippines and China held legal binding force. Consequently, these agreements did not establish obligatory negotiations between the parties. Even if considered binding, such as the Treaty of Friendship and Cooperation, these agreements lacked specific dispute resolution mechanisms and did not preclude the parties from utilizing UNCLOS's dispute settlement mechanisms. Additionally, the Tribunal noted that negotiations between the Philippines and China regarding South China Sea disputes had been ongoing for a considerable period. Despite discussions on potential dispute resolutions, no conclusive agreement had been reached prior to the Philippines initiating the lawsuit. Therefore, the Tribunal determined that China could not prevent the Philippines

(continued)

[23] PCA Case No. 2013–19, the matter of the South China Sea Arbitration (Philippines v. China), Judgment on Jurisdiction and Admission of Case dated 29 October 2015, paras. 148–178, from https://pcacases.com/web/sendAttach/2579, accessed on 31 July 2025.

[24] PCA Case No. 2013–19, the matter of the South China Sea Arbitration (Philippines v. China), Judgment on Jurisdiction and Admission of Case dated 29 October 2015, paras. 179–188, from https://pcacases.com/web/sendAttach/2579, accessed on 31 July 2025.

Table 4.1 (continued)

China's arguments	The Arbitral Tribunal's decision
	from pursuing the case before the Arbitral Tribunal on the basis of ongoing negotiations[25]
4. The "obligation to exchange views" was not satisfied. China contends no meaningful dialogue occurred. China asserts that there has been no substantial and specific exchange between China and the Philippines regarding the dispute. Thus, the "obligation to exchange views"—a prerequisite for the application of UNCLOS jurisdiction—has not been fully satisfied. Consequently, China contends that the Philippines cannot resort to arbitration	The Tribunal concluded that a party's unilateral initiation of proceedings before the Arbitral Tribunal under Part XV of UNCLOS does not amount to an abuse of rights. The Tribunal emphasized that Article 286 grants a UNCLOS state party the unilateral right to commence proceedings without the necessity of negotiation or obtaining consent from the opposing party, provided it adheres to the procedural provisions outlined in the convention[26]
5. China invoked Article 298 of UNCLOS to exclude jurisdiction over certain disputes. China points out that it has invoked the exclusion of the Tribunal's jurisdiction under Article 298 of UNCLOS. As a result, China argues that it is not obligated to participate in the proceedings and is not bound by any decision rendered by the Arbitral Tribunal	Concerning the limitations and exceptions to jurisdiction under Articles 297 and 298 of UNCLOS, the Arbitral Tribunal deemed it pertinent to assess whether these provisions preclude the Tribunal's jurisdiction, as contended by China, a determination hinging largely on the Tribunal's resolution of several substantive issues. For instance, the Philippines sought a declaration from the Tribunal asserting that China's claims of historic rights based on the nine-dash line are incompatible with UNCLOS, while Article 298 excludes from the Tribunal's jurisdiction disputes involving historic titles and historic bays. To ascertain whether the Philippines' request falls within the purview of Article 298's exclusion, the Tribunal must delineate the nature of the "historic rights" upon which China relies, assessing whether they share the same essence as "historic title or historic bay." Determining the essence and scope of China's historic rights claim constitutes a substantive aspect of the case. Consequently, the Tribunal opted to defer the jurisdictional issue for

(continued)

[25] PCA Case No. 2013–19, the matter of the South China Sea Arbitration (Philippines v. China), Judgment on Jurisdiction and Admission of Case dated 29 October 2015, part VII, from https://pcacases.com/web/sendAttach/2579, accessed on 31 July 2025.

[26] PCA Case No. 2013–19, the matter of the South China Sea Arbitration (Philippines v. China), Judgment on Jurisdiction and Admission of Case dated 29 October 2015, paras. 332–353, from https://pcacases.com/web/sendAttach/2579, accessed on 31 July 2025.

Table 4.1 (continued)

China's arguments	The Arbitral Tribunal's decision
	consideration during the merits phase of certain submissions by the Philippines related to these exceptions. It is essential to note that the Tribunal's decision neither signifies a denial of jurisdiction over these submissions, as some analysts have implied, nor does it indicate a confirmation of jurisdiction or any conclusions regarding the legality of the Philippines' requests. Instead, it merely denotes that the Tribunal cannot reach a determination at present and must await the adjudicatory session on the substance of the matter to render a decision[27]

Source Author's compilation

During the public hearings on climate change at the ICJ, held from 02 to 13 December 2024,[28] the Philippines strategically invoked the 2016 Arbitral Award to reaffirm its legal authority under UNCLOS. This move aimed to underscore the continued relevance of the Tribunal's findings, particularly the invalidation of China's expansive Nine-dash Line claim and the clarification of maritime entitlements in the South China Sea. In contrast, China argued that climate change challenges the applicability and scope of UNCLOS, pointing to the Convention's lack of explicit references to "greenhouse gas emissions" or "climate change." By seeking an advisory opinion from the ICJ, the Philippines seeks to elevate the legal principles articulated in the Arbitral Award to a broader global context. While an advisory opinion would not carry binding legal force, it would nonetheless possess substantial persuasive authority, potentially reinforcing the Award's legitimacy in international legal discourse. China, however, has advanced a counter-narrative by framing the issue within the context of environmental change. By doing so, it seeks to shift attention from sovereignty and legal obligations toward a more fluid interpretation of maritime rights in light of evolving ecological conditions.

This approach serves to dilute the impact of the 2016 Ruling by embedding it in a dynamic framework wherein maritime features—and their associated legal entitlements—are portrayed as increasingly uncertain due to climate-induced transformations. Moreover, it enables China to present itself as a cooperative actor engaging with global environmental concerns, while continuing to reject the binding nature of the arbitral outcome. This diplomatic repositioning underscores

[27] PCA Case No. 2013–19, the matter of the South China Sea Arbitration (Philippines v. China), Judgment on Jurisdiction and Admission of Case dated 29 October 2015, part VIII, from https://pcacases.com/web/sendAttach/2579, accessed on 31 July 2025.

[28] Public hearings to be held from Monday 2 to Friday 13 December 2024, from https://www.icj-cij.org/node/204312, accessed on 31 July 2025.

China's broader lawfare strategy—leveraging legal ambiguity and global challenges to contest unfavorable legal decisions without direct confrontation.

The Arbitral Ruling, though dismissed by Beijing, had tangible effects on China's behavior. In response, China intensified its physical presence in disputed waters, expanded maritime surveys, and unilaterally assigned Chinese names to maritime features situated on the continental shelves of other coastal states. More subtly, China recalibrated its legal rhetoric by advancing the concept of the Four Sha.[29] As Julian Ku and Chris Mirasola argue, the Four Sha claim repackages old arguments in new legal form, but remains fundamentally inconsistent with international law principles.[30] Further signaling its rejection of the Arbitral Award, China's 2016 announcement of plans to establish straight baselines around Scarborough Shoal directly contradicted the Tribunal's conclusion that such features do not qualify for baseline construction under UNCLOS. This comprehensive deployment of lawfare tactics was intended to prevent the Arbitral Award from gaining broader acceptance in international law and to pressure other states—particularly those in Southeast Asia—to dismiss the Ruling in favor of China's claims. China has continued to maintain its historical claims over the South China Sea, framing these claims as superior to those recognized under international law. This remains a central element of China's strategy to assert its dominance in the region, while simultaneously undermining the international legal framework that opposes its objectives.

Lawfulness Prevailing Over Lawfare: The Philippines and the 2016 Arbitral Ruling

The 2016 Arbitral Award represents a significant legal victory for the Philippines in its longstanding maritime dispute with China. The tribunal unanimously upheld nearly all of Manila's claims, confirming that China's actions violated UNCLOS, and declared the ruling legally binding on Beijing.[31]

However, under the pressure of lawfare tactics and appealing promises of economic investment from China, the administration of President Rodrigo Duterte distanced itself from the ruling. Duterte publicly dismissed it as "a piece of paper"[32] fit only for the wastebasket,[33] citing the futility of implementation in the face of China's economic power and its unwillingness to comply. He warned that pushing the ruling could jeopardize vital trade and investment relations with China—then one of the Philippines' largest economic partners. As a result, the Philippines effectively shelved the ruling for nearly eight years.

---

[29] See section China's Maps.

[30] Ku and Mirasola (2017).

[31] Medina (2017).

[32] Duterte (2021, May 5).

[33] Duterte (2021, May 5).

Nevertheless, legal principles have re-emerged under the administration of President Ferdinand Marcos Jr., who has pursued a proactive strategy to revive and operationalize the ruling. While the formal renaming of maritime areas within the Philippines' jurisdiction as the "West Philippine Sea" was actually initiated under President Benigno Aquino III in 2012,[34] Marcos has continued to reinforce and emphasize this designation throughout his administration. This move served both legal and political purposes: to assert the Philippines' sovereign identity and to counter the notion–reinforced by the term "South China Sea"–that China holds historical title over the area. Vietnam has similarly long referred to these waters as the "East Sea," underscoring how terminology and mapping are themselves contested arenas in the broader struggle for maritime legitimacy.

The Philippines has sought to transform it into a foundational legal instrument in asserting its maritime entitlements and defending its sovereign rights in the South China Sea. While the decision lacks an enforcement mechanism under international law, it has evolved into a potent diplomatic and legal asset—reinforcing the Philippines' position in bilateral engagements, shaping global discourse on maritime rights, and mobilizing support for a maritime rules-based order grounded in UNCLOS.

Operational enforcement has also been stepped up. The Marcos administration has enhanced the presence of the Philippine Navy and Coast Guard around maritime features such as Ayungin Shoal and Bajo de Masinloc, which lie within the Philippines' 200-nautical-mile EEZ. These actions—ranging from patrols to the installation of buoys, navigational aids, and lighthouses—are interpreted as tangible means of asserting control and implementing the arbitral decision. They directly challenge China's continuing presence and infrastructure-building in these areas, which the tribunal had declared as unlawful. These efforts have led to increasingly frequent confrontations between Philippine and Chinese coast guard vessels, particularly around Second Thomas Shoal, Sabina Shoal and other flashpoints in the West Philippine Sea.

President Marcos has also adopted a strategy of transparency, highlighting Chinese incursions to international audiences and aligning with likeminded partners. This approach has garnered broad support from the U.S., Japan, Australia, the European Union, India, and South Korea—nations that share an interest in upholding international law and freedom of navigation in the region.[35]

At the legislative level, the Philippines has embedded references to the 2016 Arbitral Ruling into new laws enacted in 2024, further reinforcing its legal authority within the domestic legal framework. The ruling has also stimulated a broader legal imagination among Filipino officials and scholars, sparking growing interest in launching new environmental or jurisdiction-based legal actions against China's

[34] Philippine Government (2012). Administrative Order No. 29—Naming the West Philippine Sea of the Republic of the Philippines, and for other purposes. Official Gazette, from https://www.officialgazette.gov.ph/2012/09/05/administrative-order-no-29-s-2012/ accessed on 31 July 2025.

[35] Mogato (2024).

activities in the South China Sea. Precedents such as Mauritius v. United Kingdom (Chagos Archipelago), Nicaragua v. U.S., and The Arctic Sunrise case (Netherlands v. Russia) demonstrate how smaller states can leverage UN General Assembly resolutions, international arbitration, and global diplomatic pressure to secure partial compliance—even from more powerful adversaries.

Within this context, Manila may consider pursuing non-binding resolutions through the UN General Assembly or seeking an advisory opinion from ICJ to further internationalize the ruling and pressure China through legal and normative channels.[36]

Ultimately, this strategic legal posture aims to increase the Philippines' credibility, while simultaneously exposing the gap between China's professed commitment to international law and its actions on the ground. By embedding the Arbitral Ruling into a variety of legal and multilateral fora, Manila is not merely defending its own claims but also contributing to the defense of the international legal order in the South China Sea.

This evolving legal strategy demonstrates the Philippines' intent to convert a single arbitral ruling into a durable diplomatic asset—capable of shaping global narratives, influencing third-party states, and reinforcing the legitimacy of UNCLOS as the cornerstone of maritime governance.

In the case of the Philippines and the 2016 Arbitral Ruling, the concept that lawfulness has prevailed over lawfare is a highly accurate and compelling assessment of the long-term outcome. The Philippines' journey from shelving the ruling to actively enforcing it highlights a crucial point: while lawfare can exert short-term influence, the authority and legitimacy of international law can endure and ultimately reassert themselves. This case has become a powerful testament to the idea that a legal victory, once secured, remains a permanent asset that can be leveraged over time, reaffirming that the rule of law can indeed triumph over political pressure. The Philippines' efforts once again affirm that lawfulness is being consolidated and is prevailing over lawfare.

Position of Other States to the Ruling

While the Arbitral Ruling is legally binding only on the parties to the case—namely the Philippines and China—it nonetheless holds significant value for the international community. In particular, it serves as an important subsidiary means for determining and clarifying the meaning of provisions under UNCLOS, as recognized in Article 38(1)(d) of the Statute of ICJ.

Several countries, including Australia, France, Germany, Japan, Indonesia, New Zealand, the United Kingdom, and the U.S., voiced support for the Award and called on China to respect the tribunal's decision. In contrast, Cambodia has consistently supported China's position regarding the South China Sea disputes

[36] Poling (2025).

and has openly rejected the 2016 Arbitral Tribunal's Ruling. Prior to the Tribunal's decision, Cambodian Prime Minister Hun Sen declared that the ruling Cambodian People's Party would not support the arbitration court's forthcoming decision, labeling it as "the worst political collusion in the framework of international politics".[37] Following the tribunal's ruling, Cambodia maintained its stance, with Prime Minister Hun Sen reiterating that the South China Sea issue should be resolved bilaterally between the concerned parties and not through ASEAN.[38]

Within ASEAN, while the Philippines and Vietnam both advocated for the inclusion of the Arbitral Ruling and the need to respect international law in the joint communiqué issued by ASEAN foreign ministers, Cambodia opposed the proposed language. Cambodia expressed a preference for resolving disputed claims through bilateral negotiations rather than multilateral or legal approaches. Singapore underscored its neutral position and urged all parties to "fully respect legal and diplomatic processes, exercise self-restraint and avoid any activities that may raise tensions in the region." Ultimately, ASEAN released a joint communiqué that emphasized the need to avoid actions that could escalate tensions in the South China Sea and reaffirmed the commitment to the peaceful resolution of disputes in accordance with international law, particularly UNCLOS.[39]

The divergent positions of states have been most clearly reflected in the so-called "note verbale battle"—an intensifying diplomatic battle of formal notes submitted to the UN regarding extended continental shelf claims in the South China Sea.

The Legal Note Verbale Confrontation Over Continental Shelf Submissions in the South China Sea

The note verbale battles in the South China Sea illustrate how diplomatic correspondence can be transformed into a powerful lawfare tactic. Under Paragraph 5(a) of Annex I to the Rules of Procedure of the CLCS, even a single note verbale alleging the existence of a dispute is sufficient to block the CLCS from considering a coastal state's submission.[40]

The joint submission by Malaysia and Vietnam, along with Vietnam's separate partial submission on the outer limits of their continental shelves beyond 200 nautical miles from the baselines used to measure the breadth of the territorial sea, submitted to the CLCS on 06 and 07 May 2009, respectively, triggered the first major diplomatic note exchange in the South China Sea—commonly referred to as Note Verbale Battle 1.0. Between 2009 and 2011, a total of 12 diplomatic notes

[37] Xinhua (2016, July 4).

[38] Zhang (2016).

[39] Storey (2016).

[40] Tran (2023), pp. 124–145.

were exchanged: China (3 notes), Malaysia (2 notes), The Philippines (3 notes), Vietnam (3 notes), and Indonesia (1 note). China responded strongly by officially submitting its Nine-Dash Line claim to the UN on 07 May 2009. The Philippines submitted a separate diplomatic protest on 4 August 2009, reaffirming its claims over the Kalayaan Island Group (part of the Spratlys) and North Borneo (under dispute with Malaysia). Although Indonesia is not a claimant state, it also lodged a diplomatic note rejecting the legality of China's Nine-Dash Line. This prolonged standoff eventually contributed to the Philippines' initiation of arbitral proceedings against China under Annex VII of UNCLOS in 2013, culminating in the 2016 Arbitral Award, which declared the Nine-Dash Line unlawful and determined that none of the features in the Spratlys generate more than a 12-nautical-mile territorial sea.

A second, more expansive round of diplomatic note exchanges—Note Verbale Battle 2.0—emerged in response to the 2019 submission by Malaysia to the CLCS. Unlike the first wave, this phase involved broader international participation, including non-claimant and extra-regional states. Between 2019 and August 2025, a total of 32 diplomatic notes were submitted in relation to Malaysia's 2019 submission: Claimant States: Malaysia (3 notes), China (13 notes), Philippines (3 notes), Vietnam (3 notes), Indonesia (2 notes); Extra-regional States: U.S. (2 notes), United Kingdom (1 note), France (1 note), Germany (1 note), New Zealand (1 note), Australia (1 note), Japan (1 note). In relation to the Philippines' submission on 14 June 2024, 12 diplomatic notes were issued by: Claimant States: Philippines (2), Malaysia (1), Vietnam (1), China (4); Extra-regional States: U.S. (1), United Kingdom (1), Germany (1), France (1). For Vietnam's 17 July 2024 submission, 11 diplomatic notes were exchanged: Claimant States: Vietnam (2), China (5); Extra-regional States: U.S. (1), United Kingdom (1), Germany (1), France (1). Altogether, in the span of six years, these three rounds of continental shelf-related submissions have resulted in 55 diplomatic notes—reflecting intensifying legal confrontation and growing international engagement over the South China Sea.[41]

Some authors argue that there have been three waves of diplomatic note exchanges in the South China Sea, from 2009–2011, 2013–2016, and 2019–2024.[42] Others contend that the three waves were 2009–2011, 2019–2023 with Malaysia's submission for an extended continental shelf, and 2024–2025 with the extended continental shelf submissions by the Philippines and Vietnam.[43] However, for the purposes of this book, we are of the view that the first wave of diplomatic notes was related to the extension of the continental shelf before the 13 May 2009, deadline set by the Meeting of States Parties to the Convention on the Law of the Sea, and the public release of China's nine-dash line. The second wave was a consequence of the 2016 Arbitral Award and the subsequent extended

[41] CLCS, Submissions, https://www.un.org/depts/los/clcs_new/commission_submissions.htm, accessed on 31 July 2025.

[42] Nguyen and Nguyen et al (2025), pp. 35–41. See also Agusman (2025), pp 163–177.

[43] Nguyen (2024).

continental shelf claims made by all claimant states except Brunei and China. Brunei has no intention of extending its claims, while China cannot make an extended continental shelf claim as it would contradict its nine-dash line claim. Regardless, the diplomatic note exchanges and extended continental shelf submissions have brought more clarity to the parties' positions and the specific coordinates of their claims than ever before.

Note Verbale Battle 1.0 (2009–2011)[44]

The Note Verbale Battle 1.0 was brief in duration, limited in the number of submissions, and involved only a few states—yet it was no less intense in its legal and diplomatic implications. This phase was triggered by the Joint Submission made by Malaysia and Vietnam on 6 May 2009, followed by Vietnam's Partial Submission concerning the outer limits of the continental shelf in the northern area of the South China Sea on 7 May 2009.

The legal basis for these actions was the call made by the Meeting of States Parties to UNCLOS, requiring submissions regarding extended continental shelves to be made by 13 May 2009, for those states with potential entitlement to natural prolongations beyond 200 nautical miles from their baselines.[45] These submissions were made in accordance with Article 76(8) of UNCLOS, which governs the delineation of the outer limits of the continental shelf, and in conformity with the Rules of Procedure of the CLCS.[46]

Both Malaysia and Vietnam regarded their submissions as genuine efforts to fulfill obligations under international law. These moves prompted other claimant states to gradually clarify their own positions regarding the legal status of maritime features and the scope of their claims in the South China Sea. As such, this phase marked a significant turning point in the legal discourse surrounding the South China Sea, helping to bring greater transparency to competing claims.

Notably, in making the joint submission, both Malaysia and Vietnam deliberately based their claims on extensions from their mainland territories, rather than on maritime features in the Spratly Islands. This approach implicitly reflects a shared legal position that such features do not, in themselves, generate entitlement to a continental shelf. The submission may thus be considered a noteworthy instance of subsequent practice relevant to the interpretation of Article 121(3) of UNCLOS in the South China Sea context. By excluding the Spratly features, the two states effectively supported the interpretation that rocks incapable of sustaining

[44] Nguyen D T and Nguyen H T (2012), pp. 35–56. See also Nguyen H T (2021), pp. 165–191.

[45] Convention on the Continental Shelf, Commission on the Limits of the Continental Shelf. Oxford Public International Law, from https://opil.ouplaw.com/display/10.1093/law:epil/9780199231690/law-9780199231690-e455, accessed on 31 July 2025.

[46] See Rules of Procedure of the Commission, https://www.un.org/depts/los/clcs_new/commission_rules.htm, accessed on 12 August 2025.

human habitation or economic life of their own cannot give rise to an EEZ or continental shelf. Consequently, this joint submission represents significant state practice that contributes to the evolving interpretation of Article 121(3), in accordance with Article 31(3)(b) of the Vienna Convention on the Law of Treaties, which recognizes subsequent practice by parties as a valid tool for treaty interpretation.

On 7 May 2009, China submitted diplomatic Note CML/17/2009 in protest against the joint submission by Malaysia and Vietnam to the Commission on the Limits of the Continental Shelf. This note was accompanied by a map featuring the nine-dash line, marking the first time this map was officially presented within the UN framework. In the note, China asserted that the maritime areas enclosed by the nine-dash line—including archipelagos and adjacent waters—fall under its jurisdiction. This demarcation effectively challenges the maritime entitlements of neighboring South China Sea states, particularly efforts to extend the outer limits of their continental shelves.

Vietnam promptly dispatched a diplomatic communication to the UN condemning the nine-dash line claim. Simultaneously, Malaysia reiterated that "the Joint Submission is without prejudice to the position of States which are parties to a land or maritime dispute"[47] in the South China Sea.

On 4 August 2009, the Philippines issued a separate diplomatic protest, reaffirming its stance on the Kalayaan Island Group (part of the Spratly Islands claimed by the Philippines) and North Borneo (in dispute with Malaysia). Scarborough Reef and the Kalayaan Island Group were not encompassed within the new archipelagic baseline defined by Act 9522 of 10 March 2009, which amended Act 3046 of 1961. A note dated 5 April 2009, from the Philippines provided a robust legal basis, grounded in the principle of "the land dominates the sea," to contest the legality of China's nine-dash line.[48]

China's position was comprehensively expressed in Note Verbale CML/8/2011, in response to the Philippines.[49] This document laid the foundation for many of China's subsequent diplomatic communications, especially during the Note Verbale exchanges from 2019 to 2025. In this note, China asserted its indisputable sovereignty over the islands in the South China Sea and the adjacent waters, claiming sovereign rights and jurisdiction over the relevant maritime zones, seabed, and subsoil. These claims, it argued, are supported by abundant historical and legal evidence. China also maintained that in a series of international treaties and the domestic legislation of the Philippines prior to the 1970s, the Philippines had

[47] The Note Verbale HA 24/09 dated 20 May 2009 of the Permanent Mission of Malaysia to the UN, from https://www.un.org/depts/los/clcs_new/submissions_files/mysvnm33_09/mys_re_chn_2009re_mys_vnm_e.pdf, accessed on 12 August 2025.

[48] The Note Verbale No. 000819 dated 4 August 2009 of the Permanent Mission of the Republic of the Philippines to the UN, from https://www.un.org/depts/los/clcs_new/submissions_files/mysvnm33_09/clcs_33_2009_los_phl.pdf, accessed on 12 August 2025.

[49] The Note Verbale CML/8/2011 dated 14 April 2011 of the Permanent Mission of the People's Republic of China to the UN, from https://www.un.org/depts/los/clcs_new/submissions_files/mysvnm33_09/chn_2011_re_phl_e.pdf, accessed on 12 August 2025.

never asserted sovereignty over the Nansha Islands or any of their components. It further invoked the principle of *la terre domine la mer*, stating that a coastal state's entitlement to an EEZ or continental shelf cannot infringe upon the territorial sovereignty of other states. Lastly, China emphasized that since the 1930s, its government had publicly defined the geographical scope and the names of features within the Nansha Islands, asserting that these features are entitled to a territorial sea, EEZ, and continental shelf, in accordance with its interpretation of international law.

During the Note Verbale Battle 1.0, Indonesia stood out as the only non-claimant state to formally articulate its position. In 2010, despite not being a party to the territorial disputes in the South China Sea, Indonesia explicitly challenged China's nine-dash line, asserting that it lacked any legal basis under UNCLOS.[50] Indonesia's position stemmed primarily from concerns that China's vague historical claims might infringe upon maritime zones surrounding the Natuna Islands, where Indonesia exercises sovereign rights over natural resources. By proactively voicing its objections, Jakarta emphasized the need to uphold a rules-based maritime order consistent with UNCLOS and reaffirmed its stance that overlapping claims in the region must be resolved through international legal norms, rather than through historical assertions or faits accomplis.

To assert its nine-dash line claim, China has intensified its presence on the ground in the South China Sea through provocative actions, including a standoff with the Philippines at Scarborough Shoal in 2012 and extensive island reclamation on several shoals in the Spratly Islands archipelago since 2014. China's pressure tactics led to the exclusion of the South China Sea dispute from the Declaration of the 2012 ASEAN Summit. The threat posed by China and the diplomatic exchanges of notes battle version 1.0 prompted the Philippines to initiate arbitration proceedings against China under Annex VII of UNCLOS in 2013.

Indeed, the extension of the continental shelf in 2009 served as a catalyst for a significant debate regarding the legal validity of the nine-dash line and the status of entities within the Spratly Islands archipelago. The subsequent arbitration ruling and China's assertive reactions have intensified both regional and international scrutiny on the perspectives of involved nations concerning these matters. Specifically, two overarching questions have emerged: firstly, how can states safeguard their rights within the framework of international law? And secondly, how should smaller states navigate and respond to the demands of a powerful nation? The diplomatic exchanges of note verbal battle 1.0 have left a legacy of unresolved inquiries that warrant ongoing examination and deliberation.

---

[50] The Note Verbale No. 480/POL-703/VII/10 dated 8 July 2010 of Indonessia Permanent Mission to the UN, https://www.un.org/depts/los/clcs_new/submissions_files/mysvnm33_09/idn_2010re_mys_vnm_e.pdf, accessed on 31 July 2025.

Note Verbale Battle 2.0 (2019–2025)

Two key catalysts that triggered the second round of diplomatic note exchanges were the South China Sea Arbitration Award and Malaysia's strategic move to leverage the ruling by advancing its extended continental shelf claim further northward. The "Note Verbale Battle 2.0" saw the widest participation to date, with not only regional claimants but also non-regional states weighing in. These exchanges focused primarily on the legal weight of the Arbitral Award, the right to extend the continental shelf, emerging concepts such as Nanhai Zhudao and Four Sha, and the broader principles of freedom of navigation, as well as the duty to respect and uphold the rule-based international order. This phase may be regarded as the pinnacle of the contest between **lawfulness** and **lawfare** in the South China Sea.

Malaysia's Extended Continental Shelf Submission: A Direct Challenge to the Nine-dash Line Claim

On 12 December 2019, Malaysia submitted a partial claim for an extended continental shelf (ECS) in the northern part of the South China Sea.[51] This move was seen as a continuation of its earlier joint submission with Vietnam in 2009. Accordingly, Malaysia framed this 2019 submission as a legitimate exercise of its rights and obligations under UNCLOS, in conformity with its relevant provisions and the Rules of Procedure of the CLCS.

Malaysia has reiterated this legal basis in multiple diplomatic notes, including its December 2019 note and Note Verbale HA 26/20 dated 29 July 2020. In these communications, Malaysia emphasized that the partial submission was made "without prejudice" to ongoing maritime boundary delimitation processes between states with opposite or adjacent coasts, as well as to the positions of the concerned parties regarding unresolved land and maritime disputes in the South China Sea.

In reality, the legal basis for this submission rests heavily on the 2016 Arbitral Tribunal Award in the case between the Philippines and China, which determined that all insular features in the Spratly Islands possess only a 12-nautical-mile territorial sea and do not generate EEZs or continental shelves. Malaysia's position is that, since the features in the Spratlys lack entitlement to continental shelves, there is no legal obstacle preventing Malaysia from extending its continental shelf northward. The submission essentially builds upon and expands the claim outlined in Malaysia's 1979 map issued by the Department of Mapping and Survey, covering both the southern and northern parts of the South China Sea. This new

[51] See more details at the Commission on the Limits of the Continental Shelf (CLCS). Outer limits of the continental shelf beyond 200 nautical miles from the baselines: Submissions to the Commission: Partial Submission by Malaysia in the South China Sea, from https://www.un.org/depts/los/clcs_new/submissions_files/submission_mys_12_12_2019.html. accessed on 31 July 2025.

claim potentially doubles Malaysia's continental shelf entitlement compared to its original 1979 position.[52]

Notably, Malaysia's submission also implicitly applies the Tribunal's legal reasoning to the Paracel Islands by stating that "the subject of this Partial Submission is not located in an area which has any land or maritime dispute between Malaysia and any other coastal State." Through this phrasing, Malaysia avoids acknowledging any Chinese claim and indirectly signals its alignment with the 2016 Award's legal reasoning.

Although Malaysia was not a party to the Philippines v. China arbitration, its submission is widely interpreted as a tacit endorsement of the 2016 Award. By excluding any reference to China's nine-dash line, Malaysia effectively rejects the line's validity. At the same time, Malaysia respects the rights of other coastal states to extend their continental shelves in areas beyond 200 nautical miles, including in the vicinity of the Spratlys.

Importantly, the submission also acknowledges the possibility of overlapping claims, stating that "there are areas of possible overlapping entitlements in respect of the continental shelf beyond 200 nm of the area of the subject of this Partial Submission." This opens the door to future negotiations and potential cooperation. In this regard, the Philippines may join Malaysia and Vietnam in making a tripartite submission on the extended continental shelf beyond 200 nautical miles—a move that would further consolidate regional alignment against China's expansive maritime claims.

The Philippines' Notes and Actions[53]

The Philippines leveraged diplomatic notes as a formal mechanism to challenge other nations' claims, affirm its national interests, and seek international acknowledgment and support for its positions [54]in 2020, the Philippines provided increased clarity on its maritime position through a series of diplomatic notes and legal actions. The 2009 Philippines notes verbale had previously laid out two principal objections to the Vietnam—Malaysia joint submission to the CLCS. First, the Philippines noted that the proposed Joint Defined Area overlapped with its continental shelf. The absence of any reference to the Kalayaan Island Group (KIG) in that note suggested a certain hesitation from Manila due to the uncertain legal status of the Kalayaan Island Group (KIG) at that time. The physical constraints of the Palawan Trough limited the extent of the continental margin from the main Philippine islands to within 200 nautical miles, implying that only high-tide

[52] Nguyen H T (2019).

[53] Nguyen (2024).

[54] Bautista (2021), pp 66–113.

features in the Kalayaan Island Group (KIG)—if they were capable of generating their own EEZ and continental shelves—could create any meaningful overlap with the Joint Defined Area. Second, the Philippines objected on the grounds that the area overlapped with disputed territory arising from claims over several islands, including North Borneo—today's Sabah, a Malaysian-administered territory also claimed by the Philippines. Though the territorial dispute over Sabah could hinder maritime delimitation, a mutually agreed decision by the involved States to set aside this issue could facilitate the definition of extended continental shelves from opposite coasts.

On 6 March 2020, the Philippines issued a diplomatic note in response to Malaysia's partial submission to the CLCS from December 2019. This note expanded upon the Philippines' 2009 objections, presenting three principal grounds for protest. First, the submission encompassed maritime features within the Kalayaan Island Group (KIG), which the Philippines claims as part of its sovereign territory. Second, it overlapped with areas of the continental shelf beyond 200 nautical miles from the Philippine archipelagic baselines—zones for which the Philippines intended to submit its own claims in the future. Third, Malaysia's submission was based on projections from parts of North Borneo, over which the Philippines has maintained its sovereign claim and never relinquished its position. These second and third points echoed the concerns outlined in the 2009 diplomatic note, particularly with respect to the North Borneo dispute.

However, the 2020 note also reflected a significant evolution in the Philippines' legal position, shaped in large part by the authoritative findings of the 2016 South China Sea Arbitral Tribunal Award. The Tribunal had determined that none of the high-tide features in the Spratly Islands, in their natural condition, are capable of sustaining human habitation or an economic life of their own, as required under Article 121(3) of UNCLOS, and thus cannot generate EEZs or continental shelves. This legal interpretation was reiterated in Note No. 0929–2020, dated 9 October 2020, in which the Philippines explicitly declared that it asserts no maritime entitlements beyond those defined under UNCLOS, as interpreted by the Tribunal's Award.

Accordingly, the Philippines shifted its position from asserting potential EEZ and continental shelf entitlements from features in the Kalayaan Island Group (KIG) to affirming that any high-tide features within the Kalayaan Island Group (KIG) may only generate a 12-nautical-mile territorial sea. The Philippines would only extend its continental shelf beyond 200 nautical miles from its archipelagic baselines, rather than from any Kalayaan Island Group (KIG) features. In this context, the Philippines also expressed its willingness to engage with Malaysia in discussions aimed at delimiting their respective maritime entitlements.

This position by the Philippines was operationalized on 14 June 2024, when the Philippines submitted to the CLCS information concerning the limits of its continental shelf beyond 200 nautical miles from its baselines in the West Palawan

Region, pursuant to Article 76(8) of UNCLOS.[55] The submission took place during the 34th Session of the States Parties to UNCLOS, which marked the 30th anniversary of the Convention's entry into force. Although the formal deadline for extended continental shelf submissions was 13 May 2009, the Philippines delayed its South China Sea-related filing by 15 years. This delay stands in contrast to its 2009 submission regarding Benham Rise (now Philippine Rise), which received a favorable CLCS recommendation in 2012. The belated timing of the West Palawan submission is significant, reflecting a shift under President Ferdinand Marcos Jr. toward greater transparency and assertiveness in defending the Philippines' maritime rights.

The Philippines' submission for an extended continental shelf (ECS) in the Western Pacific Region (WPR) marks a significant legal and scientific effort to secure maritime entitlements under UNCLOS. Grounded firmly in Article 76 of UNCLOS and supported by comprehensive geological, hydrographic, and geophysical data, the submission aims to demonstrate the natural prolongation of the Philippines' continental margin beyond 200 nautical miles, measured from its archipelagic baselines. This has substantial implications for regional maritime boundaries, potentially altering dynamics in the South China Sea by asserting the Philippines' rights over seabed areas beyond its EEZ, thereby enhancing its resource exploration capabilities and sovereignty. Reactions from other claimant states have been varied: China and Malaysia have formally objected, while Vietnam has also opposed but expressed openness to negotiations. These responses reflect the complex interplay of legal, historical, and diplomatic considerations in the region. The U.S., ASEAN, and the EU emphasize the importance of a rules-based order and the peaceful resolution of disputes, supporting the Philippines' adherence to UNCLOS procedures. However, procedural challenges persist within the CLCS, especially regarding the need for prior consent from disputing states,

[55] A partial submission of data and information on the outer limits of the continental shelf of the Republic of the Philippines in the West Palawan Region pursuant to Article 76 of the United Nations convention on the Law of the Sea, from https://www.un.org/depts/los/clcs_new/submissions_files/phl1/2023PhlEsDoc001Secured.pdf, accessed on 16 August 2025. See also the Note Verbale No. D.167/2024 dated 18 June 2024 of the Permanent Mission of the People's Republic of China to the UN, from https://www.un.org/depts/los/clcs_new/submissions_files/phl1/20240618ChnNvUnEng.pdf, accessed on 13 August 2025; the Note Verbale HA. 37/2024 dated 27 June 2024 of the Permanent Mission of Malaysia to the UN, from https://www.un.org/depts/los/clcs_new/submissions_files/phl1/20240627MysNvUn001.pdf, accessed on 31 July 2025; the Note Verbale 136/ CH-2024 dated 17 July 2024 of the Permanent Mission of Vietnam to the UN, from https://www.un.org/depts/los/clcs_new/submissions_files/phl1/20240717VnmNvUn001VietNamese.pdf, accessed on 31 July 2025; the Note Verbale No. 512–2024 dated 29 July 2024 of the Permanent Mission of the Philipines, from https://www.un.org/depts/los/clcs_new/submissions_files/phl1/20240729PhlNvUnEng.pdf, accessed on 31 July 2025; The Note Verbale No. D.240/2024 dated 19 August 2024> of the Permanent Mission of the People's Republic of China to the UN, from https://www.un.org/depts/los/clcs_new/submissions_files/phl1/20240819ChnNvUn002eng.pdf, accessed on 31 July 2025; The U.S. Communication LEGAL 2024–173 dated 5 December 2024, from https://www.un.org/depts/los/clcs_new/submissions_files/phl1/20241205UsaNvUn001.pdf, accessed on 31 July 2025.

which can delay or hinder the review process. While diplomatic exchanges could facilitate acceptance among the Philippines, Malaysia, and Vietnam—since UNCLOS guarantees the CLCS's recommendations are without prejudice to delimitation—the likelihood of approval diminishes significantly in the case of China, given its firm stance and extensive claims in the South China Sea. The Philippines' strategic legal approach underscores its commitment to a rules-based order and demonstrates that lawful, diplomatic means are effective for asserting maritime rights. By meticulously adhering to UNCLOS and presenting a scientifically rigorous case, the Philippines aims to strengthen its position in future negotiations, promote lawful dispute resolution, and set a precedent for regional and international maritime governance.[56]

Several motivations underlie this strategic move. First, the submission supports the 2016 Arbitral Award, which found that features in the Spratlys are legally entitled to no more than 12 nm of territorial sea. By basing its ECS claim on its mainland rather than disputed features, the Philippines reaffirms the legal limits set by the Tribunal, implicitly challenging the legitimacy of China's expansive Nine-dash Line. Second, this step strengthens the Philippines' legal posture *vis-à-vis* China's historical rights claim, which the Tribunal declared to be inconsistent with UNCLOS. Third, the submission reinforces the Philippine Baselines Law of 2012, which excluded the KIG from the archipelagic baseline, further emphasizing a rules-based. The Philippines has chosen **lawfulness** over **lawfare** to correctly understand and properly apply UNCLOS.

Despite Manila's renewed resolve, the submission faces multiple challenges. First, the Palawan Trench disrupts the natural prolongation of the Philippine continental shelf, making it more difficult to qualify for an extended continental shelf under the "natural prolongation" criterion outlined in Article 76 of UNCLOS. Consequently, the Philippines relies on the arcs-not-exceeding-60-nautical-miles formula in Paragraph 4(a)(ii) of Article 76, rather than the sediment thickness method—an approach partly justified by insufficient sediment data in the West Palawan Region (WPR).

Second, the southern extent of the Philippine claim originates near Sabah, a territory administered by Malaysia but historically claimed by the Philippines. This longstanding dispute introduces the risk of further controversy, particularly since Malaysia unequivocally reaffirmed its sovereignty over Sabah in a note verbale dated 27 June 2024. Additionally, potential overlaps with Vietnam's existing extended continental shelf submissions in the central South China Sea may necessitate bilateral negotiations. Although Vietnam reserved its sovereign rights in its December 2019 statement, it has also expressed a willingness to engage diplomatically with the Philippines, as indicated in its statement of 20 June 2024 affirming readiness for negotiations.

A third complicating factor involves unresolved sovereignty over certain Spratly features. While the 2016 Arbitral Ruling significantly limits the maritime

[56] Bautista and Schofield (2024), pp. 317–343.

entitlements of these features, lingering disputes over sovereignty could complicate whether these features affect the outer limits of an extended continental shelf. Moreover, if international law ultimately finds that Spratly features do not generate EEZs or continental shelves, parts of the South China Sea may qualify as high seas—a scenario that would raise complex questions regarding marine resource governance in an already contentious region.

The new Philippine submission comes at a time of heightened tensions. Malaysia maintains a firm stance on Sabah and notes its own overlapping extended continental shelf claim. China, for its part, has not submitted an extended continental shelf claim in the South China Sea but continues to assert "indisputable sovereignty" over the so-called Nanhai Zhudao (South China Sea Islands) and their adjacent waters. On 17 June 2024, Beijing strongly criticized the Philippine action as contrary to Chinese rights and international law, further alleging that Manila's move undermines DOC.[57]

Vietnam's Notes and Actions

In the 2.0 round of Notes Verbales exchanges, Vietnam reaffirmed its consistent stance on sovereignty, emphasizing that "Vietnam has ample historical evidence and legal basis to assert its sovereignty over the *Hoàng Sa* (Paracel) and the *Trường Sa* (Spratly) Islands in accordance with international law."[58] However, in interpreting and applying UNCLOS, Vietnam has also taken into account the impact of the 2016 South China Sea Arbitral Award to reinforce its legal position. This approach is clearly reflected in Vietnam's submissions to the UN Secretary-General, notably the note dated 30 March 2020 responding to China's note of 23 March 2020, and the note dated 10 April 2020 in response to the submissions by Malaysia.

First, Vietnam remains steadfast in its position that "UNCLOS provides the sole legal basis for and defines in a comprehensive and exhaustive manner the scope of their respective maritime entitlements"[59] in the South China Sea. Accordingly, Vietnam opposes any maritime claims in the region that exceed the limits established by UNCLOS, including claims based on so-called historic rights—claims that lack lawful effect. This stance reflects Vietnam's consistent rejection of the Nine-dash Line and the associated claim of historic rights. Vietnam's opposition is evident in a series of official communications, including its note dated 6 August 1998 protesting Article 14 of China's 1998 Law on the Exclusive

---

[57] Dey (2024).

[58] The Note Verbale No. 22/HC-2020 dated 30 March 2020 of the Permanent Mission of the Socialist Republic of Viet Nam to the UN, from https://www.un.org/depts/los/clcs_new/submissions_files/mys_12_12_2019/VN20200330_ENG.pdf, accessed on 31 July 2025.

[59] The Note Verbale No. 22/HC-2020 dated 30 March 2020 of the Permanent Mission of the Socialist Republic of Vietnam to the UN, from https://www.un.org/depts/los/clcs_new/submissions_files/mys_12_12_2019/VN20200330_ENG.pdf, accessed on 31 July 2025.

Economic Zone and Continental Shelf, the note dated 8 May 2009 objecting to China's 7 May 2009 submission, and its rejection of China's 2012 notification calling for bids on nine petroleum blocks located entirely within Vietnam's EEZ and continental shelf.

Second, the note affirms that the maritime entitlements of each high-tide feature in the *Hoàng Sa* (Paracel) and the *Trường Sa* (Spratly) Islands must be determined in accordance with Article 121(3) of UNCLOS. Vietnam has, on at least two occasions, demonstrated its interpretation and application of Article 121(3) prior to the Arbitral Ruling—an interpretation entirely consistent with the Tribunal's decision.

During the preparation of its joint submission with Malaysia, Vietnam extended its continental shelf beyond 200 nautical miles from the mainland, on the basis that the features in the Spratly Islands did not generate their own continental shelf. Second, in its 2014 note to the Arbitral Tribunal supporting jurisdiction, Vietnam emphasized that none of the features cited by the Philippines could generate an EEZ or continental shelf, as they were either low-tide elevations or rocks incapable of sustaining human habitation or economic life of their own under Article 121(3) of the Convention.[60]

The Tribunal's ruling merely reinforced Vietnam's already consistent and legally sound position in interpreting UNCLOS. Furthermore, the legal status of the Paracel Islands is to be determined not only under Article 121(3) of UNCLOS, but also pursuant to Article 20 of Vietnam's 2012 Law of the Sea.[61] According to this law, islands that can sustain human habitation or economic life of their own are entitled to internal waters, territorial seas, contiguous zones, EEZs, and continental shelves. In contrast, rocks that cannot sustain such habitation or life are not entitled to either an EEZ or a continental shelf.

Third, the note maintains Vietnam's opposition to the application of archipelagic baselines to groups of islands in the South China Sea, including the Paracel and Spratly Islands. It reads "the baselines of the groups of islands in the East Sea, including the Hoang Sa Islands and the Truong Sa Islands, cannot be drawn by joining the outermost points of their respective outermost features", reconfirming Vietnam's objection to China's baseline drawn around the Paracel Islands in 1996[62] and any similar attempt for the Spratly Islands in the future.

Fourth, the note asserts that low-tide elevations or submerged features are not capable of appropriation and do not, in and of themselves, generate entitlements to any maritime zones.

---

[60] PCA Case No. 2013–19, the matter of the South China Sea Arbitration (Philippines v. China), Judgment on Jurisdiction and Admission of Case dated 29 October 2015, https://pcacases.com/web/sendAttach/2579, accessed on 31 July 2025.

[61] Law of the Sea of Vietnam 2012.

[62] U.S. Department of State, Bureau of Oceans and International Environmental and Scientific Affairs. (1996). Straight baseline claim: China (Limits in the Seas, No. 117), from http://www.state.gov/documents/organization/57692.pdf, accessed on 31 July 2025.

To clarify the legal status of maritime features and low-tide elevations in the Spratly Islands, Vietnam reserves the right to further extend its continental shelf in the central part of the South China Sea. This right is important because the extended continental shelf from Vietnam's central coast may overlap with areas in Malaysia's partial submission, and potentially with the Philippines' submission dated 14 June 2024. As a result, Vietnam has adopted a moderate approach toward neighboring states' submissions, maintaining its sovereign rights while signaling openness to cooperation.

In its 10 April 2020 note, Vietnam reaffirmed its 2009 Joint Submission with Malaysia and its Partial Submission (from 6 May 2009 and 7 May 2009) concerning the continental shelf beyond 200 nautical miles. Vietnam reserved all rights to submit additional information in other areas, suggesting a flexible and forward-looking stance.

Regarding the Philippines' submission, in Note No. 136/CH-2024 dated 17 July 2024, Vietnam pointed out that parts of the Philippines' claim encroach upon Vietnam's 200-nautical-mile continental shelf as set out in the Joint and Partial Submissions made since 2009. Vietnam firmly rejected the Philippines' claim to those overlapping areas, deeming it inconsistent with international law, including UNCLOS, and a violation of Vietnam's sovereign rights and jurisdiction. Nonetheless, Vietnam emphasized that it reserves all rights concerning these overlapping areas and expressed its willingness to discuss and negotiate with the Philippines based on the Convention. This approach not only reaffirms Vietnam's legal position but also stimulates future cooperation with other coastal states in the region.

On 17 July 2024, Vietnam submitted to the CLCS, pursuant to Article 76(8) UNCLOS, information on the limits of the continental shelf beyond 200 nautical miles from the baselines from which the breadth of the territorial sea is measured, in respect of the Central Area (VNM-C).[63] This submission marks the completion of Vietnam's efforts to clearly define and publicly announce the outer limits of its extended continental shelf in the South China Sea (see Fig. 4.1 below). This action follows similar submissions by Malaysia and the Philippines.[64] These three moves challenge the Nine-dash Line claim and are viewed as efforts to promote regional cooperation among claimant states, encourage transparent resolution of overlapping claims, and foster a rules-based order in the South China Sea.[65]

Vietnam's move followed similar submissions by Malaysia and the Philippines, reinforcing a collective push by coastal states to assert their legal entitlements in

---

[63] UN Notification, https://www.un.org/depts/los/clcs_new/submissions_files/vnm95_24/CLCS-95-2024-LOS.Eng.pdf, accessed on 31 July 2025 See also Vietnam's Continental Shelf Submission, https://www.un.org/depts/los/clcs_new/submissions_files/vnm95_24/Vnm952024-EXECUTIVE_SUMMARY.pdf, accessed on 31 July 2025.

[64] Reyes (2024).

[65] Reyes (2024).

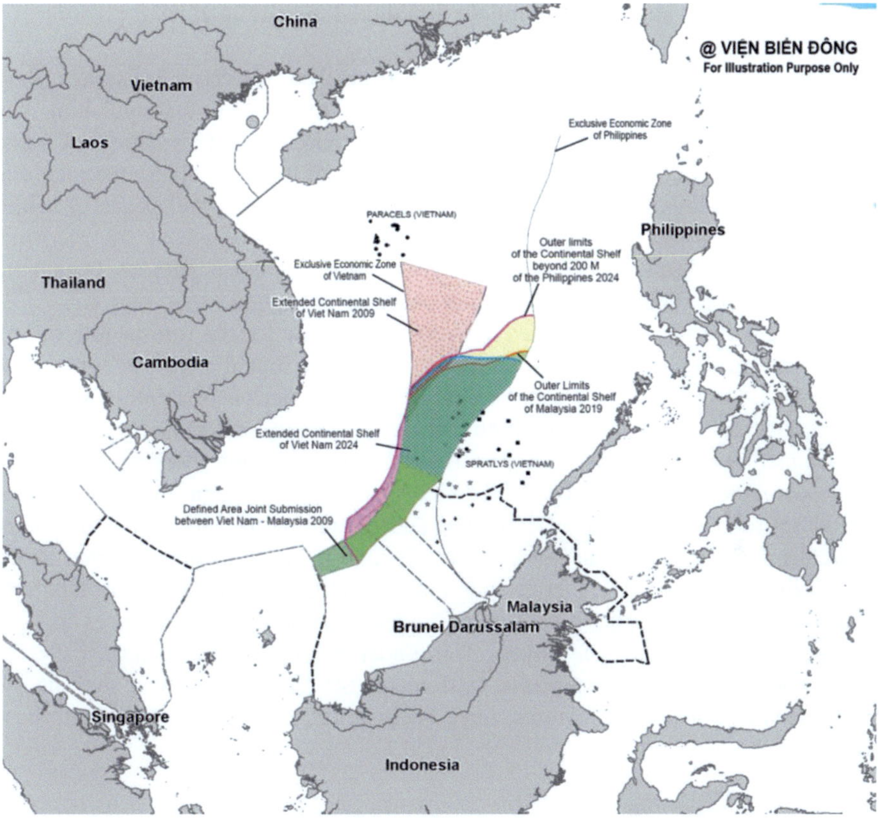

Fig. 4.1 Map of outer continental shelf claim lines in the South China Sea. *Source* East Sea Institute, Diplomatic Academy of Vietnam, 18 July 2024[66]

accordance with UNCLOS.[67] These three actions represent a coordinated challenge to the Nine-dash Line, and are widely viewed as encouraging greater regional cooperation. By clarifying and submitting their respective claims transparently, claimant states are contributing to efforts to resolve overlapping claims and promote a rules-based order in the South China Sea.

The continuing exchange of notes verbales among claimant states is likely to persist, especially in the aftermath of the 2016 South China Sea Arbitral Tribunal award. This ruling has catalyzed a wave of formal legal communications, ending a period of relative diplomatic silence. In what some scholars have called a "battle

[66] The illustration is available at: https://cdn-glx-9.galaxycloud.vn/tool/media/static.lib?sid=94&db681=1&type=mg&id=rf300570&media=image&name=%E1%BA%A3nh_Viber_2024-07-18_16-52-17-236.jpg, accessed on 31 July 2025.

[67] Reyes (2024).

of notes verbales," states have publicly articulated their refined legal positions on maritime entitlements and sovereignty.[68]

Although these diplomatic notes do not resolve the underlying disputes, their importance lies in clarifying the legal nature of the claims, distinguishing key issues, and untangling complex legal and factual narratives. This increased transparency is vital. It not only sharpens understanding of the legal divergences among parties but also lays the groundwork for future negotiations and peaceful settlement. Through these exchanges, important legal aspects—such as the maritime status of specific features—have been significantly elucidated, thereby enhancing the prospects for a legally grounded and peaceful resolution in the region.

The exchange of notes verbales is likely to continue for the foreseeable future, particularly in the wake of the South China Sea Tribunal's award, which has prompted a surge of legal clarifications following a period of relative silence.[69] In this ongoing "battle," many claimants have formally and publicly articulated their refined legal positions regarding their claims. Although these exchanges do not resolve the dispute outright, the importance of these legal communications should not be underestimated. They have successfully helped to clarify the nature of the disputes, organize the issues distinctly, and begin to dismantle some of the complexities involved. The increased transparency and clarification of each party's claims are expected to facilitate a better understanding of the differences in legal perspectives among those involved. This understanding could, in turn, pave the way toward negotiating a peaceful settlement. Several legal issues, such as the maritime status of certain features, have been significantly clarified through these notes verbales.

Non Claimants' Notes and Actions

Indonesia contributed two diplomatic notes dated 26 May 2020[70] and 12 June 2020.[71] These notes emphasize Indonesia's sovereign rights and clarify its positions regarding maritime boundaries, particularly rejecting overlapping maritime claims and insisting on compliance with international law of the sea. Therein, Indonesia explicitly rejects China's assertions of overlapping maritime claims and interests in the South China Sea. The country firmly protests any negotiations on maritime

[68] Agusman (2025), pp. 174–175.

[69] Agusman (2025), pp. 174–175.

[70] The Note Verbale No. 126/POL-703/V/20 dated 26 May 2020 of the Permanent Mission of the Republic of Indonesia to the UN, from https://www.un.org/depts/los/clcs_new/submissions_files/mys_12_12_2019/2020_05_26_IDN_NV_UN_001_English.pdf, accessed on 31 July 2025.

[71] The Note Verbale No. 148/POL-703/VI/20 dated 12 June 2020 of the Permanent Mission of the Republic of Indonesia to the UN, from https://www.un.org/depts/los/clcs_new/submissions_files/mys_12_12_2019/2020_06_12_IDN_NV_UN_002_ENG.pdf, accessed on 31 July 2025.

boundaries or related issues that conflict with international law, reaffirming its commitment to upholding legal principles in the region.[72]

The U.S. communicated its position on 01 June 2020[73] and again on 5 December 2024.[74] The U.S. clearly reaffirmed its commitment to freedom of navigation and overflight, criticized excessive maritime claims, and advocated adherence to the rules-based international maritime order outlined in UNCLOS. Additionally, the U.S. has strongly opposed China's maritime claims, deeming them inconsistent with international law as outlined in UNCLOS. It also emphasizes that the tribunal's ruling on the matter is final and binding, underscoring the importance of respecting international legal decisions.[75] As the former Secretary of State Mike Pompeo asserted in July 2020, "America stands with our Southeast Asian allies and partners in protecting their sovereign rights to offshore resources … and [we] reject any push to impose 'might makes right' in the South China Sea or the wider region."[76]

Australia similarly dismisses China's claims of widespread sovereignty over the Paracel and Spratly Islands. It stresses that such claims are incompatible with UNCLOS and that any historical rights or jurisdiction exceeding the treaty's limits are invalid.[77] Australia's communication dated 23 July 2020[78] highlighted its concern for maintaining international maritime order and legal stability. Australia supported the peaceful resolution of disputes through established international legal mechanisms.

France, Germany, and the United Kingdom jointly reaffirm the importance of maintaining freedom of the high seas. They reject claims of historic rights over South China Sea waters that do not adhere to international law and UNCLOS provisions, reaffirming their commitment to the rule of law in maritime affairs. The United Kingdom submitted its note on 16 September 2020,[79] reaffirming its

[72] Nguyen H T (2023), pp. 128–154.

[73] Letter A/74/874–S/2020/483 dated 1 June 2020 from the Permanent Representative of the U.S. of America to the UN, from https://docs.un.org/en/a/74/874, accessed on 31 July 2025.

[74] Letter A/79/674 dated 5 December 2024 from the Permanent Representative of the U.S. of America to the UN, from https://docs.un.org/en/A/79/674, accessed on 31 July 2025.

[75] Nguyen (2023), pp. 128–154.

[76] U.S. Embassy in Georgia (2020, July 22). U.S. rejects China's 'unlawful' claims in South China Sea, from https://ge.usembassy.gov/u-s-rejects-chinas-unlawful-claims-in-south-china-sea-july-22/, accessed on 15 August 2025.

[77] Nguyen (2023), pp. 128–154.

[78] The Note Verbale No. 20/026 dated 23 July 2020 of the Permanent Mission of the Commonwealth of Australia to the UN, from https://www.un.org/depts/los/clcs_new/submissions_files/mys_12_12_2019/2020_07_23_AUS_NV_UN_001_OLA-2020-00373.pdf, accessed on 31 July 2025.

[79] The Note Verbale UK NV No. 162/20 dated 16 September 2020 of the Permanent Mission of the United Kingdom of Great Britain and Northern Ireland to the UN, from https://www.un.org/depts/los/clcs_new/submissions_files/mys_12_12_2019/2020_09_16_GBR_NV_UN_001.pdf, accessed on 31 July 2025.

commitment to international maritime law, freedom of navigation, and the importance of peaceful dispute resolution. France issued a diplomatic note on the same day, 16 September 2020,[80] similarly emphasizing adherence to UNCLOS and the rejection of excessive maritime claims not based on international law. Germany also contributed a note on 16 September 2020,[81] underlining the importance of international maritime law, notably UNCLOS, in resolving territorial disputes and maintaining regional stability.

Japan has expressed support for the positions of these non-claimant states, further disapproving of China's stance on the South China Sea. This stance highlights Japan's alignment with international legal norms and principles. Japan's note dated 19 January 2021[82] reiterated its stance on the peaceful resolution of disputes and adherence to international law, particularly UNCLOS, expressing concern over actions that could escalate tensions in the region.

New Zealand communicated its position on 3 August 2021,[83] stressing the importance of upholding international maritime law, particularly UNCLOS, and maintaining peace and stability through legal channels and negotiations. New Zealand has voiced its opposition, rejecting China's claims of historic rights, archipelagic straight baselines around island groups, and artificial modifications of underwater features in the South China Sea.

China's Notes and Actions

China has been particularly active in issuing diplomatic notes, accounting for over one-third of all communications across the three submissions. In response to Malaysia's 2019 submission, China issued 13 of the 32 notes recorded, dated

[80] The Note Verbale BF No. 2020–0343647 dated 16 September 2020 of the Permanent Mission of France to the UN, from https://www.un.org/depts/los/clcs_new/submissions_files/mys_12_12_2019/2020_09_16_FRA_NV_UN_001_EN.pdf, accessed on 31 July 2025.

[81] The Note Verbale No. 324/2020 dated 16 September 2020 of the Permanent Mission of the Federal Republic of Germany to the UN, from https://www.un.org/depts/los/clcs_new/submissions_files/mys_12_12_2019/2020_09_16_DEU_NV_UN_001.pdf, accessed on 31 July 2025.

[82] The Note Verbale SC/21/002 dated 19 January 2021 of the Permanent Mission of Japan to the UN, from https://www.un.org/depts/los/clcs_new/submissions_files/mys_12_12_2019/20210119JpnNvUn001OLA202000373.pdf, accessed on 31 July 2025.

[83] The Note Verbale No. 08/21/02 dated 3 August 2021 of the Permanent Mission of New Zealand to the UN, from https://www.un.org/depts/los/clcs_new/submissions_files/mys_12_12_2019/20210803NzNote.pdf, accessed on 31 July 2025.

12 December 2019,[84] 23 March 2020,[85] 17 April 2020,[86] 2 June 2020,[87] 9 June 2020,[88] 18 June 2020,[89] 29 July 2020,[90] 7 August 2020,[91] 18 September 2020,[92] 28 January 2021,[93] 16 August 2021,[94] 25 July 2022,[95] and 28 February 2025.[96] Regarding the Philippines' 2024 submission, China issued 4 of

[84] The Note Verbale CML/14/2019 dated 12 December 2019 of the Permanent Mission of the People's Republic of China to the UN, from https://www.un.org/depts/los/clcs_new/submissions_files/mys85_2019/CML_14_2019_E.pdf, accessed on 31 July 2025.

[85] The Note Verbale CML/11/2020 dated 23 March 2020 of the Permanent Mission of the People's Republic of China to the UN, from https://www.un.org/depts/los/clcs_new/submissions_files/mys_12_12_2019/China_Philippines_ENG.pdf, accessed on 31 July 2025.

[86] The Note Verbale CML/42/2020 dated 17 April 2020 of the Permanent Mission of the People's Republic of China to the UN, from https://www.un.org/depts/los/clcs_new/submissions_files/mys_12_12_2019/2020_04_17_CHN_NV_UN_003_EN.pdf, accessed on 31 July 2025.

[87] The Note Verbale CML/46/2020 dated 02 June 2020 of the Permanent Mission of the People's Republic of China to the UN, from https://www.un.org/depts/los/clcs_new/submissions_files/mys_12_12_2019/2020_06_02_CHN_NV_UN_eng.pdf, accessed on 31 July 2025.

[88] Letter A/74/886 dated 09 June 2020 from the Permanent Representative of China to the UN, from https://docs.un.org/en/a/74/886, accessed on 31 July 2025.

[89] The Note Verbale CML/48/2020 dated 18 June 2020 of the Permanent Mission of the People's Republic of China to the UN, from https://www.un.org/depts/los/clcs_new/submissions_files/mys_12_12_2019/2020_06_18_CHN_NV_UN_006_English.pdf, accessed on 31 July 2025.

[90] The Note Verbale CML/54/2020 dated 29 July 2020 of the Permanent Mission of the People's Republic of China to the UN, from https://www.un.org/depts/los/clcs_new/submissions_files/mys_12_12_2019/20200729_CHN_NV_UN_e.pdf, accessed on 31 July 2025.

[91] The Note Verbale CML/56/2020 dated 07 August 2020 of the Permanent Mission of the People's Republic of China to the UN, from https://www.un.org/depts/los/clcs_new/submissions_files/mys_12_12_2019/20200807_CHN_NV_UN_Eng.pdf, accessed on 31 July 2025.

[92] The Note Verbale CML/63/2020 dated 18 September 2020 of the Permanent Mission of the People's Republic of China to the UN, from https://www.un.org/depts/los/clcs_new/submissions_files/mys_12_12_2019/2020_09_18_CHN_NV_UN_009_e.pdf, accessed on 31 July 2025.

[93] The Note Verbale CML/1/2021 dated 28 January 2021 of the Permanent Mission of the People's Republic of China to the UN, from https://www.un.org/depts/los/clcs_new/submissions_files/mys_12_12_2019/20210128ChnNvUn009OLA202000373e.pdf, accessed on 31 July 2025.

[94] The Note Verbale CML/32/2021 dated 16 August 2021 of the Permanent Mission of the People's Republic of China to the UN, from https://www.un.org/depts/los/clcs_new/submissions_files/mys_12_12_2019/20210816ChnNvUNen.pdf, accessed on 31 July 2025.

[95] The Note Verbale CML/96/2022 dated 25 July 2022 of the Permanent Mission of the People's Republic of China to the UN, from https://www.un.org/depts/los/clcs_new/submissions_files/mys_12_12_2019/20220725EN.pdf, accessed on 31 July 2025.

[96] The Note Verbale No. D.034/2025 dated 28 February 2025 of the Permanent Mission of the People's Republic of China to the UN, from https://www.un.org/depts/los/clcs_new/submissions_files/mys_12_12_2019/20250228E.pdf, accessed on 31 July 2025.

the 12 notes, dated 18 June 2024,[97] 19 August 2024,[98] 28 February 2025,[99] and 08 April 2025.[100] In response to Vietnam's 2024 submission, China accounted for 5 of the 11 notes, those included the Note Verbales dated 29 July 2024,[101] 14 October 2024,[102] 28 February 2025,[103] 08 April 2025,[104] and 10 June 2025.[105]

Those documents consistently emphasize China's sovereignty claim, citing three primary factors: (i) Asserting sovereignty over the islands in the South China Sea, including Pratas, Paracels, Macclesfield Bank, and Spratlys. China claims internal waters, territorial seas, contiguous zones, EEZs, and continental shelf rights in these areas, along with historical rights. (ii) Addressing specific archipelagos separately when necessary, such as Spratlys and Scarborough Shoal, to reiterate China's claims over these territories and adjacent waters. (iii) Utilizing both the collective term "Nan Hai islands" and the individual names of the archipelagos like Paracels and Spratlys to reinforce China's territorial assertions.

China actively engages in the note battles, increasingly leveraging international law to advance its interests. This is evident through three key strategies: (i) Leveraging pre-UNCLOS international customs to justify purported historical rights within the Nine-dash Line and mainland archipelagos. (ii) Employing deliberate ambiguity by combining sovereignty over islands with historical rights claims

[97] The Note Verbale No. D.167/2024 dated 18 June 2024 of the Permanent Mission of the People's Republic of China to the UN, from https://www.un.org/depts/los/clcs_new/submissions_files/phl1/20240618ChnNvUnEng.pdf, accessed on 13 August 2025.

[98] The Note Verbale No. D.240/2024 dated 19 August 2024 of the Permanent Mission of the People's Republic of China to the UN, from https://www.un.org/depts/los/clcs_new/submissions_files/phl1/20240819ChnNvUn002eng.pdf, accessed on 13 August 2025.

[99] The Note Verbale No. D.035/2025 dated 28 February 2025 of the Permanent Mission of the People's Republic of China to the UN, from https://www.un.org/depts/los/clcs_new/submissions_files/phl1/CHINA_No.D.035_2025_E.pdf, accessed on 13 August 2025.

[100] The Note Verbale No. D.061/2025 dated 08 April 2025 of the Permanent Mission of the People's Republic of China to the UN, from https://www.un.org/depts/los/clcs_new/submissions_files/phl1/D-0612025ChinaEN.pdf, accessed on 13 August 2025.

[101] The Note Verbale No. D.229/2024 dated 29 July 2024 of the Permanent Mission of the People's Republic of China to the UN, from https://www.un.org/depts/los/clcs_new/submissions_files/vnm95_24/20240729ChnNvUn001E.pdf, accessed on 13 August 2025.

[102] The Note Verbale No. D.272/2024 dated 14 October 2024 of the Permanent Mission of the People's Republic of China to the UN, from https://www.un.org/depts/los/clcs_new/submissions_files/vnm95_24/20241014ChnNvUn002E.pdf, accessed on 13 August 2025.

[103] The Note Verbale No. D.035/2025 dated 28 February 2025 of the Permanent Mission of the People's Republic of China to the UN, from https://www.un.org/depts/los/clcs_new/submissions_files/vnm95_24/CHINA_No.D.035_2025_E.pdf, accessed on 13 August 2025.

[104] The Note Verbale No. D.612/2025 dated 08 April 2025 of the Permanent Mission of the People's Republic of China to the UN, from https://www.un.org/depts/los/clcs_new/submissions_files/vnm95_24/D-0612025ChinaEN.pdf, accessed on 13 August 2025.

[105] The Note Verbale No. D.612/2025 dated 10 June 2025 of the Permanent Mission of the People's Republic of China to the UN, from https://www.un.org/depts/los/clcs_new/submissions_files/vnm95_24/CHINANV12520250610Eng.pdf, accessed on 13 August 2025.

within the Nine-dash Line. This strategy aims to extend China's jurisdiction over the entire South China Sea, effectively transforming areas claimed by other countries into disputed territories. (iii) Using claims of sovereignty enforcement in the South China Sea to justify actions that contravene international law. Notably, China's response to the U.S. on 28 February 2025, was the most severe, where China accused the U.S. of misinterpreting UNCLOS, alleging "hypocrisy" and "double-standard" stance.

It can be observed that the second battle of notes highlighted two contrasting perspectives. All notes, except China's, consistently advocate the following positions: (1) There are no high-tide features in the Spratly Islands capable of generating a maritime zone exceeding 12 nautical miles, as they fail to sustain human habitation or economic activity on their own under Article 121(3) of UNCLOS. (2) The archipelagic baseline method is applicable only to archipelagic nations and cannot be improperly applied to offshore islands of mainland states. (3) Activities such as island reclamation and construction cannot alter the legal status of a feature under UNCLOS. (4) Claims based on the exercise of "historic rights" over South China Sea waters are inconsistent with international law and UNCLOS provisions. Additionally, the countries reaffirm their commitment to upholding freedom of navigation and overflight in the South China Sea.

The second battle of diplomatic notes, in contrast to the first, saw a significant increase in the number of participating countries and addressed a wider range of issues arising from the South China Sea dispute. This inclusive approach allowed both regional and non-regional countries to express their perspectives. The active engagement of opposing views aims to foster a comprehensive understanding of UNCLOS and its applicability. This battle serves as a forum for constructive discussions on the peaceful resolution of South China Sea disputes, rather than resorting to displays of military power at sea. By encouraging dialogue and promoting a shared understanding of international law, it facilitates a collaborative approach to addressing contentious issues in the region.

Legal Confrontation on the Code of Conduct

For over two decades, China and the ASEAN have been negotiating a Code of Conduct (COC) for the South China Sea, with the goal of reducing tensions in this disputed maritime region.

The idea for a COC was first conceived in the 1992 ASEAN Declaration on the South China Sea in response to China's 1988 occupation of low-tide elevations in the area, which had destabilized the region. In 1996, the idea was raised again at the ASEAN Foreign Ministers' Meeting in Jakarta, following Vietnam's admission to the bloc and China's occupation of Mischief Reef in 1995. ASEAN member states desired a code of conduct for the South China Sea that would lay the foundation for long-term regional stability and promote mutual understanding among claimant states.[106]

In 1999, based on drafts from the Philippines and Vietnam, ASEAN worked to discuss and agree upon a common COC draft to be negotiated with China. However, China initially refused to negotiate, causing the COC-building process to face significant difficulties and even reach a stalemate. China only changed its position when it began to view the COC negotiations as a potential bargaining chip to control ASEAN and exclude all outside interference, especially from the U.S. In November 2002, ASEAN and China signed the Declaration on the Conduct of Parties in the South China Sea (DOC) at the 8th ASEAN Summit in Cambodia. The DOC was a temporary compromise measure, bridging ASEAN's desire for specific regulations with China's preference for general principles. Both sides agreed to continue COC negotiations while adhering to the DOC to create a political environment conducive to dispute resolution, conflict prevention, and the maintenance of peace and stability in the South China Sea.[107]

After 10 years of implementation, the DOC failed to prevent parties from strengthening their foothold in the South China Sea, including expanding and building military bases on low-tide elevations in violation of the 1982 UN Convention on the Law of the Sea (UNCLOS) and the principle of self-restraint. In November 2012, at the ASEAN-China Summit in Cambodia, ASEAN leaders proposed that China restart the COC negotiation process. However, despite expressing a willingness to consult with ASEAN on the COC, China declined, citing reasons such as "the time is not yet ripe" or "waiting for a suitable moment."

ASEAN-China negotiations on the COC only truly resumed in 2014 when China needed this forum to deter the Philippines from bringing its South China Sea case to an arbitral tribunal under UNCLOS Annex VII and to curb the interference of the U.S. and its allies in the South China Sea. Nevertheless, the negotiation process remained very slow. After three years, in August 2017, the parties only managed to agree on a framework document to guide future discussions, which was less than one A4 page long. A year later, the parties approved a 19-page Consolidated Document containing each country's submissions on what should be included in the COC. In November 2018, Premier Li Keqiang expressed a desire for the COC to be finalized by 2021. However, the COVID-19 pandemic once again slowed the process. In 2022, the parties intended to adopt the COC in Cambodia, the same location where the DOC was adopted 20 years prior, but they did not succeed. To date, the parties have completed the third reading of the Single Draft Negotiating Text, and the possibility of reaching a COC remains if all parties demonstrate goodwill.

---

[106] Nguyen (2001), pp. 105–130.

[107] Nguyen (2003), pp. 279–287.

Although DOC established general political principles, a legally binding COC has yet to be finalized. As of July 2025, talks have accelerated—with parties "politically committed" to finalize a code by 2026[108]—yet fundamental legal disagreements persist. These negotiations have become a legal confrontation pitting ASEAN's insistence on rules-based norms against China's more flexible, sovereignty-driven approach. Key points of contention include whether the COC will be legally binding or merely political, its geographic and substantive scope, how it will be enforced, and its compatibility with international law (especially UNCLOS).

Binding Nature of the Code: Legal versus Political Commitments

One central dispute is whether the COC will carry legally binding force or serve only as a political guideline. ASEAN (particularly claimant states like the Philippines, Vietnam, and Malaysia) has long argued that the code must be a legally binding agreement to be effective.[109] ASEAN leaders stress that only a binding code—with clear obligations—can hold parties accountable and deter aggressive behavior. This reflects a desire for a rules-based order in the South China Sea, where commitments are enforceable rather than left to unilateral interpretation. In contrast, China historically favored a "flexible, non-binding" COC, viewing it as a diplomatic understanding rather than a strict legal regime.[110]

Beijing has been wary that a binding pact could constrain its extensive claims and activities at sea. Indeed, China has "never accepted" the notion of a legally binding code, treating ASEAN's demand on this point as unacceptable.[111] The clash is clear: ASEAN sees legal bindingness as crucial for compliance and credibility, whereas China prefers voluntary commitments that preserve its freedom of action. Negotiators have yet to bridge this gap. Notably, by April 2025 Chinese and ASEAN officials publicly professed a shared political commitment to making the COC legally binding by 2026.[112] But given China's past reluctance, skepticism remains over whether any final text will truly impose legal constraints. Absent a binding character, ASEAN fears the COC would be an "impotent document" with little practical impact, whereas China is careful to avoid any agreement that could be invoked against its interests in international tribunals or other legal fora.

---

[108] Philippine News Agency (2025, May 2).

[109] Epstein (2023).

[110] Lee (2024).

[111] Liu and Spangler (eds) (2016).

[112] Mendez (2020).

Geographic and Substantive Scope of the COC

Defining the COC's scope has proven "fundamental and contentious."[113] This encompasses both the geographical areas covered and the activities regulated. China seeks to narrowly delineate the code's reach. It has insisted the COC apply only to parts of the South China Sea where Beijing does not already exercise full control.[114] In practice, this could exclude areas like the Paracel Islands and other zones China considers its sovereign territory. Reports even indicate that China wanted its expansive Nine-dash Line claim to be tacitly acknowledged within the COC's scope—a proposition firmly rejected by ASEAN states, since the Nine-dash Line encroaches on their own maritime zones.[115] ASEAN, especially its claimant members, takes the opposite view: the code must cover all disputed features and waters in the South China Sea to be meaningful. Countries such as the Philippines and Vietnam argue that no contested area should be exempt, given China's claim spans almost 90% of the sea.[116] They fear a limited scope would allow Beijing to fortify or behave as it pleases in excluded areas. There is also friction over the substantive scope—what conduct the code will govern.[117]

This ongoing COC negotiation also reflects China's strategic interest in limiting "external interference" in the South China Sea.[118] One of China's proposals states that parties in the South China Sea should establish a notification system for military activities, requiring them to inform each other of major military operations if necessary. Additionally, the proposal stipulates that joint military exercises with countries outside the region should not proceed without prior notification and the absence of objection from the involved parties. If implemented, this provision would effectively prevent any bilateral or multilateral military exercises—such as those involving ASEAN nations and countries like the U.S. or Japan—unless Beijing grants its approval. Reaching consensus on this point proves challenging within ASEAN. For instance, Vietnam has expressed disagreement with China's stance and submitted its own alternative. Vietnam recommends that only a notification be required for upcoming joint or combined military drills within the South China Sea, with such notices given at least 60 days prior to the exercises. Other countries like the Philippines and Singapore are also likely to oppose the Chinese proposal.[119]

To bolster its territorial claims and exert greater influence, China suggested that oil and gas exploration in disputed areas should be coordinated and conducted collectively by the littoral states of the South China Sea. It also emphasized that

---

[113] Lee (2024).

[114] Lee (2024).

[115] Seow (2024).

[116] Lee (2024).

[117] Lin and Sothirak (2025).

[118] Emmers (2014), pp. 61–77.

[119] Panda (2024).

such activities should not involve companies from outside the region. Malaysia, however, opposed this stance and responded with a counter-proposal, proposing that nothing in the Code of Conduct (COC) should restrict the rights or obligations of parties under international law—specifically, their ability to engage in activities with foreign nations or private companies of their choosing. These issues remain highly contentious, making it unlikely that consensus or a common position will be reached. It appears that China included the oil exploration provision as a way to pressure other claimant states into agreeing to joint development projects with Chinese firms. Many neighboring nations see this tactic as a breach of their sovereign rights under UNCLOS. Should China agree to remove this clause, it would significantly weaken its own territorial and jurisdictional claims. Consequently, reaching an agreement on the Code of Conduct continues to seem out of reach.[120]

Overall, these dueling proposals on exercises and resource development underscore how scope is a legal battleground: China's clauses aim to solidify its claims and exclude outside influence, while ASEAN claimants insist the COC must not legitimize any curtailment of their rights. So far, these issues remain unresolved, and they epitomize the broader struggle to delineate a scope acceptable to both sides.

Enforcement and Dispute Settlement Mechanisms

Another challenge is whether the COC will include any mechanism to enforce its provisions or resolve alleged breaches. Past regional instruments, like the 2002 DOC, lacked enforcement teeth—a shortcoming ASEAN is keen to address. ASEAN's position (particularly among claimant states) is that the code should establish clear compliance and dispute-resolution procedures to ensure accountability.[121] This could mean regular consultations on implementation, reporting of incidents, or even a neutral mediation/arbitration process if parties accuse each other of violations. ASEAN officials argue that without rules and mechanisms to encourage compliance and accountability, any agreement would be ineffective.[122] For instance, experts have suggested adding hotlines and incident-prevention protocols to manage encounters at sea[123] as well as joint oversight committees.

[120] Panda (2024).

[121] Le, L. M. (2015, June 26). Remarks by H.E. Le Luong Minh, Secretary-General of ASEAN, High-Level International Workshop 2015: Managing South China Sea Conflict from ASEAN Perspective. Hotel Borobudur, Jakarta. ASEAN, from https://asean.org/wp-content/uploads/images/2015/July/SG_Remarks/SG%20remarks%20at%20SCS%20conference%2026%20June%202015_FIN.PDF, accessed on 31 July 2025. See also Hu (2021), pp. 119–147.

[122] Lee (2024).

[123] South China Sea Expert Working Group (2018, October 11). A blueprint for a South China Sea Code of Conduct. Asia Maritime Transparency Initiative, from https://amti.csis.org/blueprint-for-south-china-sea-code-of-conduct/, accessed on 31 July 2025.

However, China's stance makes robust enforcement unlikely. Beijing strongly prefers that disputes be handled bilaterally and opposes third-party adjudication or oversight that could constrain its actions. In fact, China's government has explicitly stated it "does not accept any means of third party dispute settlement or any solution imposed on China"[124] regarding territorial or maritime delimitation issues. This policy was evident in China's refusal to participate in the 2013–2016 arbitral proceedings initiated by the Philippines, and its 2006 declaration under UNCLOS Article 298 rejecting compulsory arbitration on maritime boundary disputes.[125] Consistent with that view, China is unlikely to agree to a COC enforcement clause that could lead to binding arbitration or sanctions for non-compliance. At most, China may accept a joint consultative mechanism that allows diplomats to discuss complaints—a diplomatic solution rather than a legal one. The lack of consensus on a dispute settlement mechanism was identified early on as a "significant hurdle" in the Single Draft Negotiating Text.[126]

Compatibility With UNCLOS and International Law

Both ASEAN and China publicly say the COC should align with international law, but they diverge sharply on what that means in practice. UNCLOS—often called the "constitution of the oceans"—is central to this debate. ASEAN countries view UNCLOS as the baseline for any regional code: the code's terms must not contradict UNCLOS rights and duties, and it should reinforce established legal principles like freedom of navigation and the EEZ regime.[127] Indeed, ASEAN statements emphasize that the COC must be in accordance with UNCLOS, and several ASEAN members have formally rejected China's extra-legal claims in UN fora by reaffirming that no maritime entitlements can exist beyond UNCLOS limits.[128] The 2016 Arbitral Award under UNCLOS is a touchstone in this context.[129] This ruling, while not about the COC *per se*, set a legal precedent that any future code would ideally respect. ASEAN's

---

[124] Ministry of Foreign Affairs of the People's Republic of China (2016, July 12) Statement of the Ministry of Foreign Affairs of the People's Republic of China on the Award of 12 July 2016 of the Arbitral Tribunal in the South China Sea Arbitration Established at the Request of the Republic of the Philippines, from https://www.mfa.gov.cn/eng/zy/gb/202405/t20240531_11367334.html, accessed on 31 July 2025.

[125] Seow (2024).

[126] South China Sea Expert Working Group (2018, October 11). A blueprint for a South China Sea Code of Conduct. Asia Maritime Transparency Initiative, from https://amti.csis.org/blueprint-for-south-china-sea-code-of-conduct/, accessed on 31 July 2025.

[127] Lee (2024).

[128] Pham N M T (2025). See also Delegation of the European Union to the Philippines, Press and Information Team (2025, July 12).

[129] See Section "Legal Confrontation Surrounding the 2016 South China Sea Arbitral Award".

position leans toward upholding this outcome: the Philippines has even codified the 2016 Award in its domestic law[130] as binding policy, and multiple ASEAN members (Indonesia, Malaysia, Vietnam, among others) have signaled alignment with the 2016 Award's findings in their official notes verbales and statements.[131] By contrast, China's position on compatibility is colored by its disputation of UNCLOS findings that go against its interests. China prefers to frame issues in terms of ambiguous "historical" rights and bilateral deals, sidelining unfavorable UNCLOS rulings.[132] Crafting a COC text that is acceptable to China yet does not dilute UNCLOS is therefore a delicate task. Any compromise wording must paper over, rather than resolve, this fundamental legal confrontation.

Legal Confrontation on Maps and the Rectification of Information

China's Maps

Currently, Chinese map applications for digital devices, the map of China displays a Nine-dash Line encompassing the entire South China Sea. Callahan (2020) introduces the concept of "map-fare," a neologism combining elements of "warfare" and "lawfare" to describe how maps are used strategically to shape political narratives and influence policy. The visual representation of territory, especially in contexts of imperial expansion and territorial disputes, can be a tool for promoting national pride, asserting sovereignty, and justifying political actions. Maps are not simply neutral representations of reality but actively participate in shaping political discourse and influencing policy outcomes. Objective cartographic elements can be utilized to create subjective and contested narratives regarding national identity, territorial sovereignty, and historical legitimacy.[133]

Nine-dash Line or Ten-dash Line? Solid Lines to Replace Dotted Lines?

The Nine-dash Line, Nine-dotted Line, Cow Tongue Line, U-shaped Line, or Ten-dash Line are various terms used by international scholars to refer to China's territorial claims depicted on maps, which run in close proximity to the coastlines of countries bordering the South China Sea.

According to information from China, the U-shaped Line first emerged around 1947, initially appearing in a privately published atlas rather than an official state publication.

[130] Such as Philippine Maritime Zones Act 2024 and Philippine Archipelagic Sea Lanes Act 2024.

[131] See section "The Legal Note Verbale Confrontation over Continental Shelf Submissions in the South China Sea".

[132] U.S.-China Economic and Security Review Commission (2020).

[133] Callahan (2020).

Subsequently, it was depicted on a "Map of South China Sea Islands" and a "Comparison Table of the Old and New Names of the South China Sea Islands", issued by the Department of Territorial Administration under the Ministry of the Interior of the Republic of China in February 1948. The line originates from the Vietnam-China border in the Gulf of Tonkin, extending southward along Vietnam's eastern coast to the southern extremity of James Shoal at approximately 4°N latitude. From there, it turns northward, running parallel to the western coastlines of Sabah (Malaysia), Palawan (Philippines), and the Luzon Archipelago, ultimately terminating approximately midway through the Bashi Channel between Taiwan and the Philippines.[134]

Initially, the U-shaped line comprised 11 segments. However, in 1953, then-Chinese Premier Zhou Enlai approved the removal of two segments: one between Hainan Island and the coast of Vietnam in the Gulf of Tonkin, and the other between Taiwan and Ryukyu Island of Japan. In 2014, China silently added a segment east of Taiwan, expanding the line from a nine-dash to a ten-dash configuration, covering an area of up to 5,500 kilometers.[135] China's introduction of the solid U-shaped line, as advocated by a group of scholars in early April 2018, represents another attempt to shape public opinion and assert maritime claims in the South China Sea.[136] This concept suggests that the U-shaped line serves as China's maritime border, implying sovereignty over the encompassed sea area akin to territorial land. The proposed line is envisioned to extend from the mouth of the Gulf of Tonkin, traversing southward through the EEZs and continental shelves of Vietnam, Indonesia, Malaysia, and the Philippines, before terminating southeast of Taiwan island. Notably, this solid line includes various structures in the South China Sea, such as the Spratlys, Paracels, James Shoal, and Scarborough Shoal.

On 28 August 2023, the Ministry of Natural Resources of China issued the 2023 edition of its "Standard Map," which officially modified the previously drawn Nine-dash Line by adding another dash to encompass Taiwan, thus creating a Ten-dash Line (see Fig. 4.2 below).[137] This expanded line now covers more than 90% of the South China Sea, including maritime territories also claimed by Vietnam, the Philippines, Brunei, Malaysia, and Taiwan. The new map also includes India's Arunachal Pradesh and the Aksai Chin plateau under Chinese territory. In response to strong opposition and protests from the concerned States,[138] Chinese Foreign Ministry spokesperson Wang Wenbin stated that the map was released to "raise public awareness of the standardized use of maps" and called on the concerned parties to view it "in an objective and rational light."[139] This is evidence that "mapfare" has been skillfully employed to gradually increase the legitimacy and value of the Nine-dash Line in the South China Sea.

[134] Li and Li (2003), p. 209.

[135] Kazianis (2014).

[136] South China Morning Post (2018).

[137] China Daily Online (2023, August 29).

[138] See the section "Legal Confrontation Surrounding the 2016 South China Sea Arbitral Award".

[139] Basilan (2023). See also Sakamoto (n.d.)

Fig. 4.2 China's Ten-dash Line map. *Source* Japan Forward website[140]

China's perspective on the Nine-dash Line is articulated through three key points. Firstly, China maintains that the Nine-dash Line represents a historical claim predating UNCLOS, and therefore, its provisions do not govern this claim. Secondly, Article 14 of China's 1998 Law on the Exclusive Economic Zone and Continental Shelf reinforces its assertion of historical rights in the South China Sea, although it does not clearly define the nature of these rights. By incorporating this provision, China prioritizes its historical claims over the framework established by UNCLOS. Lastly, China asserts that these historical rights validate its sovereignty over maritime features and their adjacent waters in the South China Sea.

---

[140] The 2023 Version of China's Map of Its Territory, from https://japan-forward.com/wp-content/uploads/2023/09/The-2023-Version-of-Chinas-Map-of-Its-Territory-2.jpg, accessed on 31 July 2025

Chinese Foreign Ministry spokesman Jiang Yu, during a press conference in Beijing on 15 September 2011, underscored China's unwavering sovereignty over the South China Sea and its islands. Jiang Yu maintained that China's position is rooted in historical events and international law. She argued that UNCLOS does not contain provisions permitting a country to extend its EEZ or continental shelf into the "territory/territorial waters" of other nations. Moreover, Jiang Yu asserted that the convention does not negate a country's sovereignty, which has been established through historical evolution and continuously reaffirmed by that nation.[141]

China's Nine-dash Line exemplifies its use of legal warfare, following the strategy of "turning nothing into something, turning something into belief, and turning belief into imposition." However, this claim lacks historical and international legal foundation for six key reasons.[142]

Firstly, China asserts "sovereign rights and jurisdiction" over the entire area encompassed by the Nine-dash Line, which covers approximately 80% of the South China Sea. This claim far exceeds China's legitimate maritime entitlements under UNCLOS, which stipulates that EEZs cannot extend beyond 200 nautical miles from the baseline, while continental shelves are limited to either 350 nautical miles or 100 nautical miles from the 2,500-meter isobath.[143] The outermost reaches of the Nine-dash Line stretch thousands of kilometers from China's mainland, placing them well beyond these legal limits. As a result, they cannot be classified as part of China's EEZ or continental shelf under UNCLOS provisions.

Secondly, the Nine-dash Line was never articulated or codified in any Chinese legal documents until China's official claim in May 2009. Prior to this declaration, the line was absent from foundational Chinese legal texts, including the 1958 Declaration of the Government of the People's Republic of China on China's Territorial Sea, the 1992 Law on Territorial Sea and Contiguous Zones, and the 1998 Law on the Exclusive Economic Zone and Continental Shelf. This absence underscores that the Nine-dash Line was not historically recognized by China itself as a formal legal boundary within its own domestic legal framework.

Thirdly, China's assertion of the Nine-dash Line encroaches upon the EEZs and continental shelves of other countries along the South China Sea coast, including Vietnam, the Philippines, Indonesia, Malaysia, and Brunei, all of which are members of the UNCLOS Convention.

Fourthly, there is no consensus among Chinese scholars regarding the exact origin of the Nine-dash Line. Some suggest it dates back to 1948, while others propose it may have emerged as early as 1947 or even 1914. The origin of this line is only documented in privately published materials from later years, appearing in

---

[141] Press conference of the Spokesperson of the Ministry of Foreign Affairs of China, September 15th, 2011, from http://www.fmprc.gov.cn/eng/xwfw/s2510/t860126.htm, accessed on 31 July 2025.

[142] Nguyen (1997).

[143] UNCLOS, Articles 57 and 76.

various forms such as the Eleven-dash Line, Nine-dash Line, or Ten-dash Line, with unclear and indeterminate coordinates. The Chinese government has yet to provide a precise explanation of the coordinates of the dashed lines in the claim.

Fifthly, China has failed to provide evidence demonstrating that its governments have effectively, consistently, and peacefully exercised "sovereignty" within the Nine-dash Line throughout history. In fact, countries surrounding the South China Sea continue to assert their sovereignty, sovereign rights, and national jurisdiction in accordance with the provisions of UNCLOS. Both regional and international entities persist in conducting routine aviation and navigation activities within the Nine-dash Line area, including regions beyond the sea areas and continental shelves that fall under the sovereignty, sovereign rights, and national jurisdiction of the countries bordering the South China Sea.

Finally, the ongoing dispute between Vietnam and China regarding sovereignty over the Paracel and Spratly Islands, along with similar claims from the Philippines, Malaysia, and Brunei over all or parts of the Spratly Islands, clearly indicates that China's Nine-dash Line claim in the South China Sea lacks recognition from other nations.

Four Sha or Nanhai Zhudao—A Supplement or Replacement for the Nine-dash Line Claim?

To counter the rejection of the Nine-dash Line by the 2016 Arbitral Tribunal's Ruling, China has introduced a new concept known as the Foursha island groups. The new lawfare narrative, called the Four Sha (literally meaning Chinese four sands) was revealed by Ma Xinmin, Deputy Director General in the Foreign Ministry's department of treaty and law, at a closed-door meeting during the 8th annual US-China Dialogue on the Law of the Sea and Polar Issues in Boston, U.S., on 28 August 2017.

The Four Sha concept encompasses four island groups: Tungsha (Pratas), Xisha (Paracels), Nansha (Spratlys), and Zhongsha (Macclesfield Bank).[144] China claims these island groups as historical territorial bodies and asserts that they fall within China's 200 nautical mile EEZ. China presents three key arguments to support its Four Sha claim. First, China asserts indisputable sovereignty over the islands in the South China Sea, including the four island groups referred to as the archipelago, consisting of Tungsha, Xisha, Nansha, and Zhongsha. Second, China contends that these island groups qualify as archipelagos, thereby entitling them to utilize archipelagic baselines for delineating maritime boundaries. Third, China claims that these island groups have associated maritime zones, including archipelagic waters, territorial waters, an EEZ extending to 200 nautical miles, and a continental shelf measured from the baseline of the aforementioned archipelagos.

[144] Gertz (2017).

By asserting the claim of the 'Four Sha,' China has altered its tactics, merging the Nine-dash Line claim with provisions related to maritime zones and archipelagic baselines under UNCLOS. This strategy effectively expands the definition of 'adjacent waters' in Chinese laws to include all geographical features in the Pratas, Paracels, Macclesfield Bank and Spratly Islands, treating each of them as possessing island status. From a legal standpoint, similar to the earlier Nine-dash Line claim, the assertion of maritime zones based on sovereignty over the Four Sha or Nanhai Zhudao lacks clarity and is not grounded in a robust legal framework. This claim demonstrates a lack of logical consistency and fails to present a convincing legal argument.

Firstly, regarding the legal basis of China's sovereignty claims over the Four Sha, China still relies on its old arguments that Chinese fishermen were the first to discover and name the features in the South China Sea since ancient times. However, this assertion lacks concrete evidence. There is no substantial proof demonstrating that China historically exercised sovereignty over the Paracel and Spratly island groups as a state. Additionally, the Zhongsha islands are submerged features, not land territories that could be occupied.

Secondly, concerning the establishment of archipelagic baselines, China lacks a legal basis to delineate archipelagic baselines for any island group purportedly belonging to the Four Sha or Nanhai Zhudao. According to UNCLOS provisions, China does not qualify as an archipelagic state and, therefore, cannot employ the method of drawing archipelagic baselines. This issue will be analyzed further in the next section.

Thirdly, regarding the claim to a vast sea area generated from the Four Sha or Nanhai Zhudao, the geographical features in the South China Sea share common characteristics such as coral formations, small size, and pristine natural conditions, which render them unsuitable for human habitation and lacking economic viability. Consequently, the by the 2016 Arbitral Tribunal's Ruling in the Philippines versus China case affirmed that features in the Spratlys and Scarborough Islands do not generate their own EEZs or continental shelves. Given the similar natural attributes of these features, this Tribunal ruling is likely applicable to other island groups in the Four Sha argument, including the Paracels and Pratas.

Moreover, China itself acknowledged in its 2016 White Paper that many features within these islands exhibit varying natural conditions, such as reefs, shoals, and sand dunes.[145] Consequently, certain features can only generate a maximum sea area of 12 nautical miles in accordance with UNCLOS regulations—significantly smaller than the expanse China seeks to claim. Thus, China's assertion of a 200-nautical-mile EEZ for the Four Sha, encompassing the Spratlys, contradicts the Tribunal's legally binding conclusion, thereby undermining its validity.

[145] 中国坚持通过谈判解决中菲在南海争议白皮书 [China adheres to negotiating a solution to the China-Philippines dispute in the South China Sea: White paper], from http://www.scio.gov.cn/37236/38180/Document/1626701/1626701.htm, accessed on 31 July 2025.

From an international strategic and legal perspective, the Four Sha claim represents a strategic maneuver aimed at revisiting old arguments under the guise of legal interpretation. By leveraging the terminology of UNCLOS, China seeks to distort its provisions to align with its longstanding objective of asserting dominance over the South China Sea. However, this tactic amounts to repackaging old arguments rather than presenting new legal justifications. Ultimately, the Four Sha claim underscores China's persistent efforts to control and monopolize the South China Sea, albeit through evolving tactics.

In terms of territorial scope, the EEZ and continental shelf claimed under the Four Sha concept would encompass a vast maritime area, potentially exceeding the expanse outlined by China's Nine-dash Line in the South China Sea. This extensive claim extends China's maritime jurisdiction over significant portions of the sea, reflecting its broader territorial ambitions in the region. By asserting control over an EEZ and continental shelf, China seeks to manipulate public perception and justify its claim to both biological and non-living resources within these maritime areas.

However, under UNCLOS, the establishment of such zones is reserved for coastal states, in accordance with the convention's provisions. China's attempt to extend its jurisdiction over the entire South China Sea through this claim effectively transforms the region into a zone of contention, compelling neighboring countries to engage in resource cooperation under Chinese oversight. Contrary to the principles established by UNCLOS and the 2016 Arbitral Tribunal ruling, this claim represents an unreasonable and hazardous escalation—surpassing even the audacity of the Nine-dash Line assertion.

Importantly, the Four Sha claim does not supersede or negate China's continued advocacy of the Nine-dash Line, which remains in play as circumstances dictate.

Furthermore, the Four Sha claim exemplifies the sophistication of China's lawfare. Unlike the Nine-dash Line claim, which is supported by a specific map and defined boundaries, China does not provide a map or clarify how archipelagic baselines apply to the individual islands within the South China Sea or to the South China Sea Islands as a whole. This ambiguity, arising from the use of two distinct claims with different implications, serves a unified objective: asserting control over the South China Sea. The strategy underscores China's adaptability and its willingness to evolve its legal approaches to further its territorial ambitions.

The Rectification of Information on the South China Sea Issues

China's use of the Nine-dash Line map in asserting its South China Sea claims has been a persistent source of conflict and controversy from 2009 to the present. Over this period, Malaysia, the Philippines, Vietnam, Indonesia, and other affected states have developed a range of responses—diplomatic, legal, and symbolic—to counter what they perceive as Chinese propaganda and unlawful encroachment. These states, though varying in their approaches and intensity, share a common denominator: none have accepted the Nine-dash Line. On the contrary, each has taken concrete steps to resist it and to assert their own rights under international law.

Malaysia

Malaysia had been avoiding overt confrontation for many years,[146] preferring negotiation and downplaying disputes. However, since the late 2010s, Malaysia has shifted to a more assertive stance as China's actions (and propaganda maps) encroach further into Malaysian-claimed areas. The evolution of Malaysia's response illustrates the growing regional resolve against the Nine-dash Line.

By 2023, Malaysia demonstrated an unequivocal stance against China's map claims.[147] When China released the new Ten-dash Line map in August 2023, Malaysia's Foreign Ministry promptly declared it "does not recognize China's claims in the South China Sea"[148] as shown in that map. The Ministry went further, publicly affirming that the Chinese map's claims "encroach" into Malaysia's maritime areas off Sabah and Sarawak, and stressed that the map has no binding authority over Malaysia. On Malaysia's Foreign Minister announced a formal protest note would be sent to Beijing—which he said was "the practice" whenever such claims are made. This swift protest was significant: Malaysia was aligning with fellow ASEAN claimants in outright rejection, rather than demurring. Domestically, Malaysian officials and analysts also invoked Malaysia's own 1979 maritime map (which shows Malaysia's claimed boundaries) as the basis, implying any foreign map (like China's) that contradicts it is unacceptable.[149]

Malaysia's response has transformed from a low-profile handling of China's map claims to an openly critical and law-based opposition. By engaging in UN diplomacy and publicly denouncing the Nine-dash Line as unfounded, Malaysia contributes to the regional pushback. This is epitomized by the Malaysian Foreign Minister's remark that claiming the whole South China Sea for China is "ridiculous."[150] Coming from a country that once shunned open conflict with China, that statement highlights how untenable China's propaganda map has become, even for the more reserved players. Malaysia now stands with its Southeast Asian neighbors in insisting that only UNCLOS-defined rights—not historical arcs on a map—can be recognized.[151]

[146] Sutter and Huang (2011).

[147] Al Jazeera (2023, August 31). See also Channel News Asia (2023, August 31).

[148] Channel News Asia (2023, August 31).

[149] Channel News Asia (2023, August 31).

[150] Regencia (2019).

[151] Channel News Asia (2023, August 31).

The Philippines

Among the disputants, the Philippines has been one of the most vocal and proactive in challenging China's Nine-dash Line claim. The Philippine government's responses can be characterized by a combination of legal action, diplomatic protest, and symbolic assertion of its own territorial map.

The Philippines has lodged numerous diplomatic protests against specific Chinese actions that reflect Nine-dash Line assertions. Every year, notes verbale and statements are issued protesting Chinese incursions or the presence of Chinese ships in areas the Philippines considers within its EEZ (for example, around Reed Bank or Scarborough Shoal). Each protest reiterates that China's Nine-dash Line has no validity and that China is violating Philippine rights. When China started using the Nine-dash Line image in its passports (2012), the Philippines was quick to react. The Philippines treated stamping a visa on those passports as potentially implying recognition of the map. Thus, from 2012 until 2019, Philippine visa stickers for Chinese nationals were issued on a separate paper insert rather than stamped into the passport itself.[152] This policy underscored the Philippines' protest—it refused to "legitimize" the Chinese map by even a simple immigration procedure.[153] By 2019, however, the Philippines decided on a clever twist: instead of avoiding the Chinese passport map, use it as an opportunity to imprint the Philippine perspective. In August 2019, President Duterte approved a proposal to resume stamping visas in Chinese passports but with a new design that features the Philippine map, including its entire EEZ and offshore territories. Presidential Spokesman Salvador Panelo explained that the visa stamp itself would display the Philippine map covering "all our territory ... even those that are disputed."[154] Foreign Secretary Teodoro Locsin, who championed this idea, tweeted that the stamp would show the Philippines' EEZ "to its widest extent"—a "tit for tat" response to the Chinese passport. In short, every Chinese visitor's passport would then carry a Philippine visa stamp drawing Philippine boundaries, which include areas China wrongly claims. This move both resolves a practical issue (keeping track of Chinese entrants by stamping passports) and makes a political statement. Panelo stated the measure was meant to assert the Philippines' ownership of West Philippine Sea areas on equal footing: "The good thing ... is [the stamp] will have the map of the Philippines where all our territory is included" .[155] By late 2019, the Philippines indeed began implementing this, effectively stamping Chinese passports with a repudiation of the Nine-dash Line.[156]

---

[152] Coconuts Manila (2019, August 7).

[153] Reuters (2012, November 28).

[154] Coconuts Manila (2019, August 7).

[155] Coconuts Manila (2019, August 7).

[156] 2019 (2019, August 7).

Notably, in the wake of the 2023 Chinese standard map release, the Philippines filed a formal protest,[157] labeling the new map as China's "latest attempt to legitimize" its untenable claims and explicitly stating it "has no basis under international law."[158] On 28 February 2025, the Nine-dash Line has been reported to expand and include Palawan in the Philippines. The National Historical Commission of the Philippines condemned a false claim circulating on Chinese social media that asserted Palawan once belonged to China. The National Historical Commission of the Philippines emphasized that historical evidence clearly demonstrates Philippine sovereignty over Palawan, with no other state contesting this fact. Furthermore, there is no evidence of a permanent Chinese settlement on the island, which has been continuously inhabited for 50,000 years.[159]

It is worth noting that throughout these maneuvers, the Philippine public and media have largely supported a firm stance. There have been patriotic campaigns, for example, widespread support for using the name West Philippine Sea, and outrage at Chinese activities like the 2019 sinking of a Filipino fishing boat by a Chinese vessel. Domestic sentiment has at times criticized leaders (like Duterte) for being too soft on China; this pushed even Duterte to occasionally harden his tone. In his 2019 State of the Nation speech, he insisted "the West Philippine Sea is ours, no ifs and buts,"[160] even as he argued against provoking China militarily. By 2021, the Philippines under Duterte filed a barrage of diplomatic protests as Chinese maritime militia swarmed Philippine-claimed reefs,[161] indicating that even the more China-friendly administration could not ignore the Nine-dash Line incursions.

Vietnam

Vietnam's proactive approach to fostering dialogue and collaboration on international law issues is evident through the organization of scientific conferences aimed at sharing insights and practices. Notably, the Diplomatic Academy has been hosting the South China Sea Conference annually for the past 15 years, providing a platform for robust discussions among international experts and practitioners. Furthermore, Vietnam has assembled a team of esteemed scholars who contribute significantly to legal discourse and representation in international courts. These scholars play a crucial role in researching and disseminating information about

[157] Philippine Embassy in Singapore (2023, August 31) Philippine statement on the 2023 version of China's standard map, from https://www.philippine-embassy.org.sg/philippine-statement-on-the-2023-version-of-chinas-standard-map/ accessed on 31 July 2025.

[158] Channel News Asia (2023, August 31).

[159] Mendoza (2025).

[160] Panganiban (2019).

[161] Trajano (2021). See also Yabes (2021); Morales (2021).

Vietnam's stance on key issues, particularly regarding the South China Sea disputes. Through their work, they produce valuable analyses and arguments to counter China's misleading claims and actions, thereby bolstering Vietnam's position on the international stage. Their efforts contribute to shaping a more informed and nuanced understanding of legal complexities surrounding maritime disputes in the region.

Before the incident involving China's Haiyang Dizhi 8 exploration ship and associated vessels illegally encroaching on Vietnam's waters from 02 July 2019, to 24 October 2019, *Nguyễn Bá Sơn*, President of the International Law Association Vietnam, issued two open letters to Huang Jin, President of the Chinese Association of International Law. The first letter was dated 24 August 2019, and the second was on 29 October 2019, serving as a response to an open letter from the President of the China International Law Association dated 19 September 2019. In the 24 August 2019 letter, the President of the Vietnam International Law Association presented a robust legal argument to challenge China's erroneous claims regarding the South China Sea, particularly concerning the activities of the Haiyang Dizhi 8 vessel and the disputed Nine-dash Line. These letters were instrumental in articulating Vietnam's legal position and refuting China's unfounded assertions in the South China Sea dispute.

Vietnamese scientists are proactively identifying and reporting instances of printing Nine-dash Line maps for political purposes in professional scientific publications to foreign journals. By doing so, they contribute to raising awareness internationally about the misuse of cartographic materials to advance geopolitical agendas. This proactive engagement helps to ensure that accurate and unbiased information is disseminated in academic circles, countering any attempts to manipulate scientific discourse for political ends.

China has ingeniously blended legal warfare with information warfare through various mass media channels, including books, newspapers, movies, and other mediums. Notably, the controversial nine dash line has been intentionally incorporated into a wide array of materials such as books, newspapers, children's books, textbooks, globes, video games, travel publications, clothing, consumer products, and more. For instance, this illicit delineation was discovered in a series of books titled "Chinese for Children" (3 volumes) published by *Thời đại* Publishing House in Ho Chi Minh City (March 2013), a booklet titled "Wow! Magical Secrets for Students" jointly translated and published by *Thế Giới* Publishing House and *Đinh Tỵ* Book Company (March 2018), and a Chinese textbook presented to Hanoi University of Business and Technology (November 2019). Numerous incidents have been reported, such as dozens of Chinese tourists wearing T-shirts printed with a map featuring the Nine-dash Line entering Vietnam at Cam Ranh airport in May 2018. Upon arrival, airport authorities promptly requested these individuals to change their attire before proceeding. Additionally, satellite navigation map installed in cars imported through Dinh Vu port—Hai Phong (October 2019) have also been found to feature this contentious demarcation.

The infiltration of the Nine-dash Line or its semblance is pervasive across various media platforms, including movies, games, and websites associated with major Chinese productions or events. For example, its appearance in films like "The Lost Tomb" (June 2015), "Operation Red Sea" (March 2018), "Abominable" (September 2019), "Put Your Head on My Shoulder" on Netflix (July 2020), "Madam Secretary" on Netflix (October 2020), "Pine Gap" on Netflix (July 2021), "You Are My Glory" on WeTV Vietnam (August 2021), and "One Life, One Life" broadcast on iQiyi Vietnam (September 2021). Moreover, the cow tongue line imagery extends to the realm of gaming, such as the game "Trip Panda's Travel Around the World" available on Google Play and Apple Store (November 2020). Even websites associated with significant international events have not been immune, as evidenced by its presence on the website of the Organizing Committee of the Oceanman International Swimming Tournament in Nha Trang (April 2023), and on the website of the Korean music group BlackPink (July 2023). Notably, the release of the Barbie movie in May 2023 faced a ban in Vietnam, while the Philippines requested the removal of any imagery that could be linked to the Nine-dash Line in the South China Sea before its release. A significant concern is that the Nine-dash Line image is increasingly targeting younger demographics through its incorporation into toys Babythree[162] and beverages (Chagee Milk Tea)[163] that are popular among this age group.

The incorporation of the Nine-dash Line imagery into movies, games, and other forms of entertainment distributed through online platforms can indeed foster false perceptions about national sovereignty. Take, for instance, the movie "The Lost Tomb," where images featuring the Nine-dash Line are presented alongside idol actors. The significance of this inclusion becomes more apparent when considering the context of "The Lost Tomb 2: The Wrath of the Sea 2019," particularly its connection to the Paracels, referred to as Xisha by China. The plot revolves around the excavation of an ancient tomb belonging to a Ming dynasty engineer located near Yong Xing Island (known as *Phú Lâm* Island in Vietnamese). Notably, numerous Vietnamese island names are impersonated throughout the series. For example, Chapter 8 is titled "Yong Xing Island," while Chap. 14 provides detailed descriptions of the grave-finding group's encounters in Xi Sha (Paracels). The consistent reference to Xisha in various chapters further solidifies its association with the events depicted in the narrative.

It is commendable that Vietnamese social network users were vigilant in sharing the map image featuring the Nine-dash Line on Huawei Vietnam's customer care website. The prompt action taken by authorities to address this issue is also noteworthy. The closure of the link to Huawei Vietnam's warranty center page and the removal of the map containing the illegal Nine-dash Line demonstrate a commitment to upholding national sovereignty and territorial integrity. Additionally, the review and inspection conducted by the General Department of Vietnam Customs in 2019 to prevent the installation of the Nine-dash Line on phones imported from China reflects proactive measures to safeguard against such

---

[162] An (2025).

[163] VOV (2025).

attempts. By addressing these incidents swiftly and decisively, Vietnam reinforces its stance on rejecting any attempts to assert illegitimate territorial claims in the South China Sea.

Other States' Responses to China's Maps

Indonesia

Although Indonesia is not a claimant to any Spratly or Paracel island, it has emerged as a staunch opponent of China's Nine-dash Line due to its implications for Indonesia's maritime rights. Parts of China's drawn line loop into Indonesia's exclusive economic zone north of the Natuna Islands (in the southernmost sector of the South China Sea).[164] Over the past decade, China has asserted that these waters are within its "traditional fishing grounds," leading to incursions by Chinese fishing boats and coast guard. Indonesia has responded by forcefully rejecting the Nine-dash Line, reinforcing its sovereignty around Natuna, and even re-mapping the area.

One of Indonesia's boldest responses came in July 2017. To visibly assert sovereignty and counter Chinese naming of waters, Jakarta announced that it was renaming the northern part of its EEZ in the South China Sea as the "North Natuna Sea."[165] The area in question lies northeast of the Natuna Islands, overlapping the southernmost dash of China's line. By renaming it on official maps, Indonesia sent a signal that this is Indonesian sovereign water, not disputed "South China Sea" waters. At a public ceremony, a new Indonesian map was unveiled showing the label "North Natuna Sea" in place of what China would call its southern South China Sea. An Indonesian maritime official described this as updating names "in line with usual practice" and highlighting oil and gas activity there under Indonesian jurisdiction. Chinese officials reacted coolly, calling the renaming "meaningless" and insisting the international community recognizes the area as part of the South China Sea. But Indonesia's intent was clear: to send "a clear message" of Indonesian sovereignty.[166] The act was political-diplomatic, underscoring to Indonesians and to China that Jakarta will defend its maritime boundaries. The renaming was accompanied by concrete actions—Indonesia stepped up naval patrols and even built up a military presence on Natuna Besar island. It also detained multiple Chinese fishing boats in its waters, undeterred by Chinese protests.[167]

Indonesia's response to the Nine-dash Line has been unequivocal: a blanket rejection of the claim's validity, consistent diplomatic pressure for clarification (which China evades), and concrete measures like renaming the sea and enhancing

[164] National University of Singapore (n.d.)

[165] Allard and Munthe (2017).

[166] Allard and Munthe (2017).

[167] Allard and Munthe (2017).

military vigilance. As the Indonesian foreign ministry stated plainly, "we do not recognize the Nine-dash Line" because it contravenes international law.[168] This Southeast Asia's largest state thus acts as an important bastion for the principle that UNCLOS-based entitlements (like Indonesia's 200 NM EEZ) cannot be unilaterally negated by another country's ancient map. Indonesia's firm position also provides political cover for ASEAN to discuss the issue more openly, since it cannot be dismissed as self-interested (Indonesia has no ambition to claim distant islands—its only interest is defending the UNCLOS order). In the broader narrative, Indonesia underscores that China's Nine-dash Line is not just a bilateral issue with a few neighbors, but a challenge to the entire region's adherence to international law.[169]

A joint statement issued during Indonesian President Prabowo Subianto's visit to Beijing in November 2024 presents a case of tension between lawfulness and lawfare. Many commentators interpreted the joint statement as a concession by Indonesia to China, particularly when it mentioned that the two countries had "reached important common understanding on joint development in areas of overlapping claims."[170] However, once again, lawfulness prevailed over lawfare, as Indonesia's Foreign Ministry repeatedly stated—immediately after the statement—that Indonesia is a non-claimant state in the South China Sea and has no overlapping jurisdiction with China.

India

While not involved in the South China Sea, India also had issues with Chinese maps. As noted earlier, in 2012 India angrily objected to the Chinese passport maps that showed disputed Indian territories as part of China. Indian border officials began stamping Chinese passports with India's own map (a tactic similar to the Philippines).[171]

This "stamp diplomacy" signaled that India too would not accept China's cartographic assertions. More directly regarding the South China Sea, India has supported freedom of navigation and UNCLOS compliance. In 2014, India's state-owned oil company OVL continued energy exploration in a Vietnamese-licensed block in the South China Sea despite Chinese displeasure—a sign of India tacitly rejecting China's exclusion claims. And after the 2023 standard map from China (with the extra dash and claims on Indian land), India's protest was vociferous: The External Affairs Ministry said it lodged a strong protest and that such claims "have no basis" and only complicate disputes.[172] This mirrored language used by others against the Nine-dash Line, creating diplomatic symmetry in rejecting China's maps whether on land or sea.

---

[168] Fabi and Blanchard (2015).

[169] Fabi and Blanchard (2015).

[170] Widianto (2024).

[171] Reuters (2012, November 28).

[172] Channel News Asia (2023, August 31).

Legal Confrontation on "Shaping the Rules"

China's Pragmatic Approach to Law

China's proactive and confident approach extends to organizing its administration and enacting internal laws to bolster its sovereignty claims. This includes efforts to refine its legal framework, particularly laws related to national security and defense, to provide a solid legal basis for enforcing China's claims in the region. Through these measures, China aims to assert its authority and strengthen its position in the South China Sea dispute.

China has been actively engaged in legislative activities, promulgating numerous new laws and amending existing ones to strengthen its maritime law enforcement capabilities and assert its jurisdiction in the South China Sea. Some key legislative actions include: (1) Amendment to the People's Armed Police Law (effective from June 2020): This amendment likely grants expanded powers to China's armed police forces, potentially including maritime law enforcement activities; (2) 2020 Rules on Inland Waterway Vessel Engineering (effective from 01 August 2020): These rules may involve regulations governing the construction and operation of vessels, including those used for maritime law enforcement purposes; (3) China Coast Guard Law Enforcement Certificate: This certificate likely outlines the legal authority and responsibilities of China's coast guard in enforcing maritime laws and regulations; (4) Regulations on Ocean Fisheries Management (amended): These regulations likely pertain to the management and regulation of fishing activities in China's maritime jurisdiction, including the South China Sea; (5) China's Maritime Management and Surveillance Mechanism: This mechanism likely encompasses a comprehensive framework for monitoring and managing maritime activities within China's jurisdiction, including law enforcement measures; (6) Amendment to the National Defense Law: This amendment may include provisions related to maritime defense and security, potentially enhancing China's capabilities to safeguard its maritime interests; (7) China Coast Guard Law (effective from 01 February 2021): This law likely delineates the powers and responsibilities of China's coast guard, including their authority to enforce maritime laws and regulations; (8) Revised Maritime Safety Law 2021 (effective from 01 September 2021): This revision likely updates regulations related to maritime safety, including provisions for enforcing safety measures in China's maritime territories; (9) Discretionary Standards for Administrative Sanctions on Marine Fisheries: These standards likely outline the procedures and criteria for imposing administrative sanctions on fisheries-related activities in China's maritime jurisdiction. These legislative initiatives reflect China's commitment to enhancing its maritime law enforcement capabilities and asserting its sovereignty and jurisdiction in the South China Sea.

Oriana (2021) highlights several points of divergence between Chinese law and the prevailing interpretation of UNCLOS.[173] Chinese law classifies the waters between islands and other geographical entities as internal waters, requiring prior authorization for commercial transit, a position explicitly applied to the Paracel Islands. This approach contrasts with UNCLOS Articles 46–54, which limit the archipelagic regime to a small number of designated archipelagic states, excluding the disputed islands of the South China Sea. China further asserts that its territorial sea extends 12 nautical miles from the outer perimeter of entire island groups, and that artificial islands as well as most geographical features are capable of generating territorial waters. By contrast, UNCLOS Article 121 requires that the breadth of the territorial sea be measured from each legally recognized geographical feature, and it excludes artificial islands from generating territorial seas. In this regard, most of the maritime features claimed by China do not meet the criteria of islands or even rocks and therefore cannot produce territorial waters. A final area of divergence arises in relation to the EEZ, where China claims the right to regulate military activities. The common understanding, consistent with UNCLOS Article 56, is that coastal states may only regulate economic activities within the EEZ, leaving military operations beyond their jurisdiction.[174]

China has taken several steps to solidify its legal basis for civil-military projects in the South China Sea: (1) Standardizing Island and Rock Names: China announced documents standardizing the names of 25 islands and rocks in the South China Sea, as well as 55 geographical entities at the bottom of the South China Sea. These entities are primarily located in the western part of the South China Sea, along the Nine-dash Line, with many in close proximity to Vietnam. This action follows China's earlier standardization of the names of 132 islands and reefs in the South China Sea in December 1934.[175] (2) Establishment of Xisha and Nansha Districts: China approved the establishment of the "Xisha District" and "Nansha District" under Sansha City, Hainan Province on 18 April 2020. The Xisha District, located on Woody Island, manages the Paracel Islands, Macclesfield Bank, and surrounding waters. The Nansha District, located on Fiery Cross Reef, manages the Spratly Islands and surrounding waters.[176] By standardizing names and delineating administrative districts, China aims to assert its jurisdiction and control over various features and territories in the region.

The shift in emphasis from the 13th Five-Year Plan to the 14th Five-Year Plan reflects China's increasing focus on legal and judicial measures to assert its maritime rights and interests. In the 13th Five-Year Plan, there was a general mention of improving the capacity of maritime law enforcement agencies and conducting research on maritime issues. However, the 14th Five-Year Plan specifically highlights the importance of strengthening legal research and struggles, as

[173] Oriana (2021).

[174] Oriana (2021).

[175] Zhao (2020).

[176] Wang (2020).

well as enhancing the construction of maritime jurisdiction agencies. This change in language suggests that China is actively preparing its legal infrastructure to handle maritime disputes more effectively.[177] By emphasizing the need to protect China's maritime rights and interests through legal means, China is signaling its intention to use its legal system to address maritime disputes with other countries. Xi Jinping's remarks at the 20th Congress of the Communist Party of China further underscore this emphasis on legal governance. By emphasizing the importance of adhering to the path of socialist rule of law with Chinese characteristics and building a socialist rule of law system, Xi Jinping is reaffirming the centrality of law in China's governance framework.[178] These developments indicate China's growing readiness to leverage legal mechanisms, both domestically and internationally, to assert its maritime claims and protect its interests in the South China Sea and beyond.

Responses to China's Pragmatic Approach to Law

China's nationalist interpretations of UNCLOS have raised concerns among many international observers. Rather than treating UNCLOS as a universal legal framework designed to balance the rights and obligations of all states, China often invokes historical narratives and sovereign interests in the South China Sea to justify expansive maritime claims. This tendency to blend domestic nationalism with international legal interpretation undermines the uniform application of UNCLOS and raises concerns about selective compliance. Many observers argue that this approach not only challenges the legitimacy of dispute resolution mechanisms under international law but also threatens regional stability by emboldening unilateral actions under the guise of legal justification. As a result, China's stance is widely perceived as an attempt to reshape maritime norms to align with its strategic interests rather than adhere to a rules-based international order.

By asserting expansive sovereignty claims and reinterpreting UNCLOS provisions to suit its own interests, China undermines the principles of international law and challenges the established norms governing maritime disputes. These interpretations not only create tensions in the South China Sea region but also have

[177] 国民经济和社会发展第十四个五年规划和2035年远景目标纲要(草案) [Outline of the 14th Five-Year Plan for National Economic and Social Development and the Long-Range Objectives Through the Year 2035 (Draft)]. (2021, March 6). Ministry of National Defense of the People's Republic of China, from http://www.mod.gov.cn/topnews/2021-03/06/content_4880496.htm, accessed on 31 July 2025.

[178] 习近平 [Xi, J.] (2022). 高举中国特色社会主义伟大旗帜 为全面建设社会主义现代化国家而团结奋斗—在中国共产党第二十次全国代表大会上的报告 [Hold high the great banner of socialism with Chinese characteristics and strive in unity for the comprehensive construction of a modern socialist country—Report to the 20th National Congress of the Communist Party of China]. 中国政府网, from http://www.gov.cn/xinwen/2022-10/25/content_5721685.htm, accessed on 31 July 2025.

broader implications for international order. By disregarding the legal rights of other countries and disregarding established legal norms, China's actions risk destabilizing the global rules-based order and eroding trust among nations.[179] Indeed, China's increasing participation in the formation of new legal norms reflects its ambition to reshape aspects of the international order according to its own interests and standards. By engaging in the development of legal norms, China seeks to challenge existing norms that may be perceived as constraining its actions while promoting alternative principles that align with its strategic objectives. This strategy allows China to assert its influence within the international system and shape the rules governing various areas of international relations, including trade, security, and territorial disputes. By leveraging its growing economic and diplomatic clout, China aims to establish itself as a key player in shaping the future direction of global governance.[180] China's active participation in multilateral fora reflects its strategic approach to shaping the "rules of the game" in its favor. By engaging in these fora, China seeks to influence the development of new norms and interpretations of existing rules that align with its interests. This approach allows China to assert its influence and ensure that its perspectives are considered in the formulation of rules and agreements governing maritime affairs. By doing so, China can advance its strategic goals while also maintaining a veneer of cooperation and engagement within the international community.

China's actions, though often inconsistent with UNCLOS, reveal a pattern of prioritizing its own interests and pushing the boundaries of established rules. Kardon (2023) argues that "there is no viable pathway for China to produce wholesale change to the legal rules of maritime order—but there are distinct signs of extra-legal change to maritime order in East Asia".[181] This is evident in China's claims to extensive maritime zones and its assertive approach to resource management and dispute resolution. While China's actions may not create completely new, universally accepted rules, they're creating a distinctly regional maritime order that is characterized by ambiguity, a decline in the consistent application of UNCLOS rules, and a prioritization of state sovereignty. The resulting maritime order is therefore neither entirely global nor entirely regional but rather a hybrid system with significant regional deviations from existing international norms.[182]

The Philippines' Archipelagic Sea Lanes Act and Maritime Zones Act in November 2024 aim to clarify and solidify its maritime claims in accordance with international law, specifically UNCLOS.[183] These laws are presented as a necessary step to prevent future administrations from potentially disregarding the 2016 Arbitral Ruling against China's expansive claims. In retaliation, China

---

[179] Jorgensen (2020).

[180] Jorgensen (2020). See also He (2019), pp. 469–480.

[181] Kardon (2023), p. 257.

[182] Kardon (2023), p. 257–269.

[183] Prétat and Poling (2024).

intensified its own lawfare strategy, publishing baselines around Scarborough Shoal, renamed various maritime features, and issued public legal assertions to reinforce its claims. Beijing also protested both laws, summoning Manila's ambassador and framing the measures as a "whitewash" of "illegal claims."[184] These actions, coupled with its continued refusal to fully comply with UNCLOS, are portrayed as a blatant disregard for international law and an escalation of the ongoing dispute. China's actions, including the drawing of baselines around Scarborough Shoal, represent a strategic use of lawfare. While the baselines themselves may appear less expansive than previous Chinese claims, their timing and context highlight a deliberate attempt to undermine the Philippines' legal maneuvers and assert its own sovereignty. This is contrasted with the Philippines' attempt to align its claims with UNCLOS and the 2016 arbitration findings. The document notes that while China's legal arguments have previously been based on the concept of "offshore archipelagos," a notion rejected by much of the international community, its current actions suggest a more pragmatic approach, though this does not necessarily lessen the immediate tension or the long-term implications of the dispute. The U.S.'s public support for the Philippines' new laws and call for other nations to adhere to UNCLOS is highlighted as a crucial element in countering China's actions. However, the potential for future conflict remains due to ongoing disagreements and the risk of China escalating its activities, particularly around Scarborough Shoal. The Philippines' legal approach, while potentially setting a positive precedent, faces significant challenges in achieving a lasting resolution to the dispute, given China's continued disregard for international law and its ongoing assertive actions in the region.[185]

The U.S. Department of State's press statement expresses strong support for the Philippines' Maritime Zones Act, emphasizing its alignment with the 1982 Law of the Sea Convention and the 2016 Arbitral Tribunal Ruling. The statement highlights that the Act is a routine clarification of Philippine maritime law, similar to legislation enacted by many other nations, including ASEAN members. The U.S. commends the Philippines' leadership in upholding international law, particularly in the South China Sea, and urges all states to align their maritime claims with the Law of the Sea Convention.[186]

The Chinese Ministry of Foreign Affairs' statement strongly rejects the Philippines' newly enacted Maritime Zones Act and Archipelagic Sea Lanes Act. The core argument centers on the assertion that these laws illegally incorporate

---

[184] Ministry of Foreign Affairs People's Republic of China (2024, November 08). Statement of the Ministry of Foreign Affairs of the People's Republic of China On the Enactment by the Republic of the Philippines Of Its "Maritime Zones Act" and "Archipelagic Sea Lanes Act", from https://www.mfa.gov.cn/mfa_eng/zy/gb/202412/t20241218_11498201.html, accessed on 12 August 2025.

[185] Prétat and Poling (2024).

[186] Miller, M. (2024, November 8). On the Philippines Maritime Zones Act. Press Statement. U.S. Department of State, from https://www.state.gov/on-the-philippines-maritime-zones-act/, accessed on 31 July 2025.

Chinese territory, specifically Huangyan Dao (Scarborough Shoal) and features within the Nansha Qundao (Spratly Islands), into the Philippines' maritime zones.[187] China vehemently denies the legitimacy of these territorial claims, emphasizing its own historical and legal basis for sovereignty over these areas, citing UNCLOS and various historical treaties. The statement forcefully contends that the Philippines' actions violate China's territorial sovereignty and maritime rights and interests in the South China Sea. A significant portion of the statement refutes the legal basis of the Philippines' claims, arguing that the 2016 Arbitral Award, which the Philippines attempts to enshrine in its domestic law, is invalid and lacks binding power. China reiterates its non-participation and non-recognition of this award. The statement further alleges that the Philippines' actions violate previous agreements, specifically referencing DOC, and accuses the Philippines of illegal occupation of various islands and reefs within the Nansha Qundao. The statement underscores that China's sovereignty and maritime rights are not affected by the Philippine laws and calls for the Philippines to immediately withdraw its personnel and facilities from the disputed areas.[188] The Chinese statement frames the Philippines' actions as illegal and provocative, representing a direct challenge to China's territorial integrity and maritime rights. It uses strong language to reiterate its claims, dismisses the 2016 Arbitral Ruling, and calls on the Philippines to respect Chinese sovereignty and cease its actions. The statement serves to solidify China's position on the South China Sea dispute and underscores the potential for further escalation of tensions between the two nations.

The Philippine Maritime Zones Act and the Philippine Archipelagic Sea Lanes Act formally assert and clarify the Philippines' maritime claims, aligning them with the 2016 international arbitration ruling that invalidated China's expansive claims. China's response to the Philippine laws is characterized by immediate condemnation and further assertive actions in the disputed waters.[189] Smaller countries like Malaysia, which also have overlapping claims in the South China Sea, express concerns about the Philippines' newly defined boundaries, particularly its implications for the Malaysian state of Sabah. This regional friction complicates any unified front against China's assertiveness and highlights the challenges of building a cohesive regional response to China's actions in the South China Sea. Competing national interests and economic considerations, specifically Malaysia's significant trade ties with China, may hinder the formation of such a unified opposition.[190]

---

[187] Ministry of Foreign Affairs of the People's Republic of China. (2024, November 8). Statement of the Ministry of Foreign Affairs of the People's Republic of China on the enactment by the Republic of the Philippines of its "Maritime Zones Act" and "Archipelagic Sea Lanes Act", from https://www.fmprc.gov.cn/eng/zy/gb/202411/t20241108_11523786.html, accessed on 31 July 2025.

[188] Ministry of Foreign Affairs of the People's Republic of China. (2024, November 8). Statement of the Ministry of Foreign Affairs of the People's Republic of China on the enactment by the Republic of the Philippines of its "Maritime Zones Act" and "Archipelagic Sea Lanes Act", from https://www.fmprc.gov.cn/eng/zy/gb/202411/t20241108_11523786.html, accessed on 31 July 2025.

[189] Walker and Rahn (2024).

[190] Walker and Rahn (2024).

In general, from 2009 up to date, the South China Sea has exemplified a clash between unilateral assertions of might and multilateral adherence to law. China's promulgation of sweeping domestic laws and its aggressive maritime enforcement operations have sought to entrench its claims, but they have also galvanized responses that invoke the authority of UNCLOS and international norms. Malaysia, the Philippines, Vietnam, and other states—each in their own way—have reinforced that UNCLOS is the ultimate basis of maritime rights and that China's expansive claims and coercive tactics are illegitimate. These states have used diplomatic protests, legal actions like the Philippines' arbitration, and security enhancements (both unilateral and with partners) to counter China's moves. Extra-regional powers including the U.S., Japan, and Australia have lent support by condemning violations of the law of the sea and by maintaining a presence to deter the use of force. Together, these reactions form a patchwork defense of the international maritime order. The legal perspective is clear: many of China's activities in the South China Sea—from claiming "historic" rights, to authorizing force in others' EEZs, to creating exclusion zones around artificial islands—conflict with UNCLOS and other international legal norms.

References

Books

Agusman DD (2025) The battle of notes verbales and the future of the South China Sea: an Indonesia's perspective. In Nguyen TLA, Vu HD (eds) Viability of UNCLOS amid Emerging Global Maritime Challenges. Springer, Singapore, https://doi.org/10.1007/978-981-97-5838-812. Accessed on 31 July 2025, pp 163–177

He Y (2019) China and its participation in global governance in the new era. In Social and Political Science 2019. Edward Elgar Publishing, pp 469–480. https://doi.org/10.4337/9781785366086.00037

Kardon IB (2023) China's law of the sea: the new rules of maritime order. Yale University Press

Nguyen HT (2022) La sentence du Tribunal d'arbitrage en 2016 sur les problèmes de la Mer de Chine méridionale, et ses conséquences. In La Mer de Chine méridionale au prisme du soft power – nouvelles approches franco-vietnamiennes d'un vieux conflit maritime. L'Harmattan 245–273

Articles

Bautista L, Schofield C (2024) The Philippines' submission for an extended continental shelf in the West Palawan Region: legal analysis, implications and reactions. Asia Pac J Ocean Law Policy 9(2):317–343, from https://doi.org/10.1163/24519391-090200010. Accessed on 31 Jul 2025

Bautista L (2021) Diplomatic notes and the South China Sea disputes. Philippine Yearb Int Law 20:66–113, from https://law.upd.edu.ph/wp-content/uploads/2023/04/04-Diplomatic-Notes-and-the-South-China-Sea-Disputes-.pdf. Accessed on 31 Jul 2025

Chinese Society of International Law (2018) South China Sea arbitration awards: a critical study. Chin J Int Law 17(2):207–748, from https://www.researchgate.net/publication/326070025_The_South_China_Sea_Arbitration_Awards_A_Critical_Study. Accessed on 31 Jul 2025

Emmers R (2014) ASEAN's search for neutrality in the South China Sea. Asian J Peacebuilding, 2(1):61–77. https://doi.org/10.18588/201405.000019, from https://ipus.snu.ac.kr/eng/wp-content/uploads/sites/2/2017/11/04_Ralf-Emmers_DOI.pdf, accessed on 31 Jul 2025

Li J, Li D (2003) The dotted line on the Chinese map of the South China Sea: a note. Ocean Dev Int Law 34(3–4):287–295

Lin J, Sothirak P (2025 Mar 18) The elusive code: why ASEAN needs a new playbook for the South China Sea. ISEAS Perspective, from https://www.iseas.edu.sg/articles-commentaries/iseas-perspective/2025-39-the-elusive-code-why-asean-needs-a-new-playbook-for-the-south-china-sea-by-joanne-lin-and-pou-sothirak/. Accessed on 31 Jul 2025

Nguyen BD et al (2025) The note verbale battle over the East Sea (2019–2024): an unprecedented legal-diplomatic fight in modern world history, Int J Law 11(5):35–41. https://www.lawjournals.org/assets/archives/2025/vol11issue5/11104.pdf. Accessed on 31 July 2025. ISSN: 2455-2194

Nguyen DT, Nguyen HT (2012) China's nine dotted lines in the South China Sea: the 2011 exchange of diplomatic nnotes between the Philippines and China. Ocean Dev Int Law 43(1):35–56. https://doi.org/10.1080/00908320.2012.647490

Nguyen HT, Nguyen TLH (2021 Jul 12) The South China Sea arbitration award: 5 years and beyond. The Diplomat, from https://thediplomat.com/2021/07/the-south-china-sea-arbitration-award-5-years-and-beyond/. Accessed on 31 Jul 2025

Nguyen HT (2001) Vietnam and the code of conduct for the South China Sea. Ocean Dev Int Law 32(2):105–130

Nguyen HT (2003) The 2002 declaration on the conduct of parties in the South China Sea – a note. Ocean Dev Int Law 34(3-4):279–287

Nguyen HT (2021) New battle of the diplomatic notes among claimants in 2019–2021. Asia Pac J Ocean Law Policy 6:165–191

Nguyen HT (2023) South China Sea: battle of the diplomatic notes among China and non-claimant states. Asia Pac J Ocean Law Policy 8(2023):128–154, from https://doi.org/10.1163/24519391-08010007,. Accessed on 31 Jul 2025

Tran HDM (2023) The approach of the commission on the limits of the continental shelf to submissions involving unresolved disputes: should it be modified? Asian J Int Law 13(1):124–145. https://doi.org/10.1017/S2044251322000224

Treves T (2016) China and the South China Sea arbitration: non-acceptance and non-participation. China-US Focus, from https://www.chinausfocus.com/peace-security/china-and-the-south-china-sea-arbitration-non-acceptance-and-non-participation. Accessed on 31 Jul 2025

Internet Materials

Al Jazeera (2023 Aug 31) Malaysia rejects new China map claiming entire South China Sea, from https://www.aljazeera.com/news/2023/8/31/malaysia-rejects-new-china-map-claiming-entire-south-china-sea. Accessed on 31 Jul 2025

Allard T, Munthe BC (2017 Jul 14) Asserting sovereignty, Indonesia renames part of South China Sea. Reuters, from https://www.reuters.com/article/world/asserting-sovereignty-indonesia-renames-part-of-south-china-sea-idUSKBN19Z0XZ/. Accessed on 31 Jul 2025

An N (2025 Mar 12) Dư luận tố Baby Three có 'đường lưỡi bò' trên mặt: Cục Quản lý và Phát triển thị trường kiểm tra (Public opinion accuses Baby Three of having a 'cow tongue line' on his face: department of market management and development inspects). TUOI TRE ONLINE. https://tuoitre.vn/du-luan-to-baby-three-co-duong-luoi-bo-tren-mat-cuc-quan-ly-va-phat-trien-thi-truong-kiem-tra-2025031216132456.htm. Accessed on 31 July 2025

Basilan M (2023 Jul 9) China upgrades its infamous 9-dash line to a 10-dash line: here's what it means. International Business Times, from https://www.ibtimes.com/china-upgrades-its-infamous-9-dash-line-10-dash-line-heres-what-it-means-3711039. Accessed on 31 Jul 2025

Callahan WA (2020) Map-fare. Sensible Politics, from https://sensiblepolitics.net/map-fare. Accessed on 31 July 2025

Channel News Asia (2023 Aug 31) Malaysia, Philippines join India in protesting China's new map staking claims over disputed territories, from https://www.channelnewsasia.com/asia/china-new-map-south-china-sea-territory-claim-protest-malaysia-india-indonesia-3736831. Accessed on 31 July 2025

China Daily Online (2023 Aug 29) 2023 Edition of national map released, from https://www.chinadaily.com.cn/a/202308/28/WS64ec91c2a31035260b81ea5b.html. Accessed on 31 Jul 2025

CLCS S, https://www.un.org/depts/los/clcs_new/commission_submissions.htm. Accessed on 31 Jul 2025

Coconuts Manila (2019 Aug 7) Philippines to stamp Chinese passports with controversial 9-dash line using design that shows 'all' PH territories. Strategic Front, from https://www.strategicfront.org/forums/threads/philippines-to-stamp-chinese-passports-with-controversial-9-dash-line-using-design-that-shows-all-ph-territories.3340. Accessed on 31 Jul 2025

Delegation of the European Union to the Philippines, Press and Information Team (2025 Jul 12) 9th Anniversary of the 2016 Arbitral Award on the South China Sea, from https://www.eeas.europa.eu/delegations/philippines/9th-anniversary-2016-arbitral-award-south-china-sea_en. Accessed on 31 Jul 2025

Dey S (2024 Aug 6) Submissions on the limits of continental shelf in the South China Sea. Modern Diplomacy, from https://moderndiplomacy.eu/2024/08/06/submissions-on-the-limits-of-continental-shelf-in-the-south-china-sea/. Accessed on 31 Jul 2025

Duterte R (2021 May 5) Arbitral ruling against China just a piece of paper. Rappler, from https://www.rappler.com/nation/duterte-speech-arbitral-ruling-china-just-piece-paper-may-5-2021/. Accessed on 31 Jul 2025

Epstein AK (2023 Sept 4) ASEAN's divisions weaken its stance on regional security. GIS Reports, from https://www.gisreportsonline.com/r/asean-issues/. Accessed on 31 Jul 2025

Fabi R, Blanchard B (2015 Nov 12) Indonesia asks China to clarify South China Sea claims. Reuters, from https://www.reuters.com/article/world/indonesia-asks-china-to-clarify-south-china-sea-claims-idUSKCNOT10KK/. Accessed on 31 Jul 2025

Gertz B (2017 Sept 21) Beijing adopts new tactic for S. China Sea claims. The Washington Free Beacon, from http://freebeacon.com/national-security/beijing-adopts-new-tactic-s-china-sea-claims/

Hu L (2021) Examining ASEAN's effectiveness in managing South China Sea disputes. Pac Rev 36(1):119–147. https://doi.org/10.1080/09512748.2021.1934519,. Accessed on 31 Jul 2025

Jorgensen M (2020) China is overturning the rules-based order from within. Lowy Institute, from https://www.lowyinstitute.org/the-interpreter/china-overturning-rules-based-order-within. Accessed on 31 Jul 2025

Kazianis H (2014 Jul 1) China's 10 red lines in the South China Sea. The Diplomat, from https://thediplomat.com/2014/07/chinas-10-red-lines-in-the-south-china-sea/. Accessed on 31 Jul 2025

Ku J, Mirasola C (2017 Sept 25) The South China Sea and China's "Four Sha" claim: new legal theory, same bad argument. Lawfare, from https://www.lawfareblog.com/south-china-sea-and-chinas-four-sha-claim-new-legal-theory-same-bad-argument. Accessed on 31 Jul 2025

Lee S (2024 Nov 21) ASEAN's elusive code of conduct for the South China Sea. East Asia Forum, from https://eastasiaforum.org/2024/11/21/aseans-elusive-code-of-conduct-for-the-south-china-sea/. Accessed on 31 Jul 2025

Liu FK, Spangler J (eds) (2016 Jan) South China Sea lawfare: legal perspectives and international responses to the Philippines v. China arbitration case. South China Sea Think Tank 南海智庫, Taiwan Center for Security Studies 臺灣安全研究中心, from http://en.nanhai.org.cn/uploads/file/file/South-China-Sea-Lawfare.pdf. Accessed on 31 Jul 2025

Medina CP (2017 Feb) Legal victory for the Philippines against China: a case study. Global Challenges, Geneva Graduate Institute, from https://globalchallenges.ch/issue/1/legal-victory-for-the-philippines-against-china-a-case-study/. Accessed on 31 Jul 2025

Mendez C (2020 Jan 28) DFA says China 'politically committed' to having COC on South China Sea, from https://globalnation.inquirer.net/274151/dfa-says-china-politically-committed-to-having-coc-on-south-china-sea. Accessed on 31 Jul 2025

Mendoza JE & Ggaviola (2025 Mar 1) Palawan was never part of China – NHCP, from https://www.inquirer.net/430724/palawan-was-never-part-of-china-nhcp/. Accessed on 31 Jul 2025

Mogato M (2024 May 5) Enforcing the arbitral ruling. PressOne, from https://pressone.ph/enforcing-the-arbitral-ruling/. Accessed on 31 Jul 2025

Morales NJ (2021 Apr 5) Philippines turns up heat on China over boats massing in South China Sea, from https://www.reuters.com/world/china/philippine-presidents-aide-warns-unwanted-hostilities-over-chinese-boats-2021-04-05/. Accessed on 31 Jul 2025

National University of Singapore (n.d.) Why Indonesia Has Stake in Fight to Defend UNCLOS. NUS Centre for International Law, from https://cil.nus.edu.sg/publication/why-indonesia-has-stake-in-fight-to-defend-unclos/. Accessed on 31 Jul 2025

Nguyen HT (1997) China's "nine broken lines" in the Bien Dong Sea (South China Sea) in the light of international law. Vietnam New 7(2073):265

Nguyen HT (2019 Dec) Malaysia's new game in the South China Sea. The Diplomat, from https://thediplomat.com/2019/12/malaysias-new-game-in-the-south-china-sea/. Accessed on 31 Jul 2025

Nguyen HT (2024 June 29) The Philippine submission: third round of note-verbal battle? Vietnamnet Global, from https://vietnamnet.vn/en/the-philippine-submission-third-round-of-note-verbal-battle-2296557.html. Accessed on 31 Jul 2025

Oriana SM (2021) How China is bending the rules in the South China Sea, Lowy Institute, from https://www.lowyinstitute.org/the-interpreter/how-china-bending-rules-south-china-sea. Accessed on 31 Jul 2025

Panda R (2024 Mar 26) Why a code of conduct on South China Sea remains elusive? Vivekananda International Foundation, from https://www.vifindia.org/print/12522?ref=tayohelp.com. Accessed on 31 Jul 2025

Panganiban AV (2019 Jul 28) WPS is ours … no ifs and buts. Philippine Daily Inquirer, from https://opinion.inquirer.net/122903/wps-is-ours-no-ifs-and-buts. Accessed on 31 Jul 2025

Pham NMT (2025 Jul 11) The 2016 South China Sea Ruling at Nine: where Does ASEAN Stand? ISEAS—Yusof Ishak Institute, from https://fulcrum.sg/the-2016-south-china-sea-ruling-at-nine-where-does-asean-stand/. Accessed on 31 Jul 2025

Philippine News Agency (2025 May 2) ASEAN, China 'politically committed' to conclude COC by 2026, from https://www.pna.gov.ph/articles/1248629. Accessed on 31 Jul 2025

Poling GB (2025 Jan 10) How to slay a giant: reviving the South China Sea Arbitration. Center for Strategic and International Studies (CSIS), from https://www.publicnow.com/view/0B69E5749E8498D5AA3415855187CF9ACFA6FFE5?1736538523. Accessed on 31 Jul 2025

Press conference of the Spokesperson of the Ministry of Foreign Affairs of China, September 15th, 2011, from http://www.fmprc.gov.cn/eng/xwfw/s2510/t860126.htm. Accessed on 31 Jul 2025

Prétat H, Poling GB (2024 Nov 21) Manila and Beijing clarify select South China Sea claims. Critical questions. Center for Strategic and International Studies, from https://www.csis.org/analysis/manila-and-beijing-clarify-select-south-china-sea-claims. Accessed on 31 Jul 2025

Regencia T (2019 Dec 21) Malaysia FM: China's 'nine-dash line' claim 'ridiculous'. Al Jazeera, from https://www.aljazeera.com/news/2019/12/21/malaysia-fm-chinas-nine-dash-line-claim-ridiculous. Accessed on 31 Jul 2025

Reuters (2012 Nov 28) China decries attempts to “read too much into” passport map row, from https://www.reuters.com/article/world/china-decries-attempts-to-read-too-much-into-passport-map-row-idUSBRE8AQ18P/. Accessed on 31 Jul 2025

Reyes MT (2024 Aug 14) Vietnam joins Philippines in continental shelf claim, challenging PRC assertiveness in South China Sea. IP Defense Forum, from https://ipdefenseforum.com/2024/08/vietnam-joins-philippines-in-continental-shelf-claim-challenging-prc-assertiveness-in-south-china-sea/. Accessed on 31 Jul 2025

Sakamoto S (n.d.) What are China’s aims with the Ten-dash Line in the South China Sea? Senkakus sites, from https://www.cas.go.jp/jp/ryodo_eg/kenkyu/senkaku/chapter04_column_04.html. Accessed on 31 Jul 2025

Seow J (2024 May 9) What’s next if the South China Sea code of conduct negotiations fail? NUS Centre for International Law, from https://cil.nus.edu.sg/blogs/whats-next-if-the-south-china-sea-code-of-conduct-negotiations-fail/. Accessed on 31 Jul 2025

South China Morning Post (2018) China’s claims South China Sea proposed continuous boundary first, from http://www.scmp.com/news/china/society/article/2141323/chinas-claims-south-china-sea-proposed-continuous-boundary-first. Accessed on 31 Jul 2025

Storey I (2016) Assessing responses to the Arbitral Tribunal’s ruling on the South China Sea (ISEAS Perspective, No. 43). ISEAS - Yusof Ishak Institute, from https://www.iseas.edu.sg/wp-content/uploads/pdfs/ISEAS_Perspective_2016_43.pdf. Accessed on 31 Jul 2025

Sutter RG, Huang CH (2011) Managing rising tensions in the South China Sea. Comp Connect 13(2), from https://cc.pacforum.org/2011/09/managing-rising-tensions-south-china-sea/. Accessed on 31 July 2025

The 2023 version of China’s map of its Territory, from https://japan-forward.com/wp-content/uploads/2023/09/The-2023-Version-of-Chinas-Map-of-Its-Territory-2.jpg. Accessed on 31 Jul 2025

Trajano JC (2021 Apr 19) Whitsun reef incident: duterte’s China strategy sinking? RSIS commentary, from https://dr.ntu.edu.sg/bitstream/10356/152544/3/CO21063.pdf. Accessed on 31 Jul 2025

U.S.-China Economic and Security Review Commission (2020) A ‘China model?’ Beijing’s promotion of alternative global norms and standards: hearing before the U.S.-China economic and security review commission, from https://www.uscc.gov/sites/default/files/2020-10/March_13_Hearing_and_April_27_Roundtable_Transcript_0.pdf. Accessed on 31 Jul 2025

VOV (2025) Trà sữa Chagee gỡ bỏ ứng dụng chứa “đường lưỡi bò” sau phản ứng của cư dân mạng (Chagee milk tea removes app containing “Cow tongue line” after Netizens’ reactions), https://vov.vn/thi-truong/tra-sua-chagee-go-bo-ung-dung-chua-duong-luoi-bo-sau-phan-ung-cua-cu-dan-mang-post1161448.vov. Accessed on 31 Jul 2025

Walker T, Rahn W (2024 Dec 4) Philippine laws up tension on South China Sea. Deutsche Welle, from https://www.dw.com/en/maritime-laws-in-philippines-up-tension-on-south-china-sea/a-70957095. Accessed on 31 Jul 2025

Wang X (2020) China’s Sansha City establishes Xisha, Nansha districts in major administrative move. China Military Online, from http://eng.chinamil.com.cn/view/2020-04/18/content_9795211.htm. Accessed on 31 Jul 2025

Widianto S (2024 Nov 11) Indonesia says it has no overlapping South China Sea claims with China, despite deal. Reuters, from https://www.reuters.com/world/asia-pacific/indonesia-says-it-has-no-overlapping-south-china-sea-claims-with-china-despite-2024-11-11/. Accessed on 31 Jul 2025

Xinhua (2016 Jul 4) Cambodia, Myanmar back negotiations over South China Sea by all parties concerned. Xinhua, from http://www.xinhuanet.com/english/2016-07/04/c_135488167.htm. Accessed on 12 Aug 2025

Yabes C (2021 Apr 16) Chinese maritime vessels spark tension in The Philippines. Australian Institute of International Affairs, from https://www.internationalaffairs.org.au/australianoutlook/chinese-maritime-vessels-spark-tension-in-the-philippines/. Accessed on 31 Jul 2025

Zhang P (2016 June 28) Cambodia's ruling party not to support arbitration court's decision over South China Sea. Xinhua, from https://english.cctv.com/2016/06/28/ARTIFHApSkSRx9UyfrABwNGE160628.shtml. Accessed on 31 Jul 2025

Zhao L (2020) Ministries release official names for South China Sea entities. China Daily, from https://www.chinadaily.com.cn/a/202004/20/WS5e9d3404a3105d50a3d176e8.html. Accessed on 31 Jul 2025

新华社 [Xinhua News Agency] (2016 Jul 21) 新华社发布系列调查起底临时仲裁庭 [Xinhua releases investigative series exposing the ad hoc arbitral tribunal], from http://www.xinhuanet.com/zgjx/2016-07/21/c_135529358.htm. Accessed on 31 Jul 2025

Chapter 5
Conclusion

The South China Sea remains one of the most contested and consequential maritime regions in the world, where legal claims, political ambitions, and strategic rivalries intersect. Over the course of this book, we have explored the evolving nature of lawfare—the deliberate use or manipulation of legal instruments to secure political, military, or economic advantage—and how it has reshaped the dynamics of regional maritime disputes. In parallel, we have advanced the concept of lawfulness as a normative and strategic response to lawfare, rooted in our proposed "3P formula": Publicity, Public Opinion, and Public International Law. This initiative underscores the belief that transparency, public legal discourse, and fidelity to internationally accepted legal norms are essential for preserving the integrity of international law and preventing its erosion through coercive reinterpretation.

The rise of lawfare in the South China Sea has illuminated both the potential and the vulnerability of international legal frameworks. On the one hand, legal instruments such as UNCLOS and the 2016 South China Sea Arbitral Award provide a clear, rules-based foundation for maritime entitlements and dispute resolution. On the other hand, the strategic deployment of legal ambiguity, distortion of historical narratives, and weaponization of domestic laws have exposed how easily international law can be subverted when state power overrides legal obligation. This duality raises urgent questions: can international law still serve as a stabilizing force, or is it at risk of becoming a pliable tool for national agendas?

China's multifaceted lawfare strategy exemplifies this dilemma. Underpinned by its Three Warfares doctrine—encompassing Legal, Psychological, and Public Opinion warfare—Beijing's actions in the South China Sea have tested the boundaries of lawful behavior in international relations. China asserts its maritime claims through a combination of historical reinterpretation, institutional influence, and operational control, often invoking international law selectively while rejecting adverse rulings, such as the 2016 Arbitral Award. Tactics include: misinterpreting or selectively applying UNCLOS provisions, promulgating domestic laws that conflict with international obligations, conducting coercive operations under the

H. T. Nguyen, T. K. N. Tran, *Lawfulness and Lawfare in the South China Sea*,
International Law in Asia,
https://doi.org/10.1007/978-981-95-4001-3_5

guise of law enforcement, and leveraging numerical dominance in international fora to shape legal narratives. These practices—ranging from "turning nothing into something" to discrediting opposing legal experts—aim not only to assert sovereignty but to reshape the normative structure of maritime law itself.

Faced with this challenge, ASEAN claimant states have developed varying approaches that reflect their national interests, legal traditions, and diplomatic constraints. Malaysia, for instance, has embraced a soft-hedging strategy that seeks to maintain constructive relations with China while quietly defending its legal positions. It emphasizes UNCLOS as the basis for its maritime entitlements—specifically its 200-nautical-mile EEZ and extended continental shelf claims—and favors legal diplomacy over confrontation. Malaysia avoids public escalation, mindful of its economic interdependence with China, yet strengthens its maritime posture through joint exercises with partners such as the U.S., Japan, and Australia. Its "triadic maritime diplomacy"—a calibrated mix of coercive, persuasive, and cooperative tools—demonstrates a sophisticated approach to managing legal and strategic tensions.

The Philippines, by contrast, has taken a more assertive and proactive path. It places international law at the heart of its maritime strategy, relying heavily on the 2016 Arbitral Ruling to challenge China's expansive Nine-dash Line claims. While historical and legal weaknesses persist in some of its sovereignty claims, the Philippines has adopted a comprehensive counter-lawfare approach—blending legal action, legislative reform, diplomatic engagement, operational assertiveness, and information campaigns. The launch of its transparency initiative, which allows domestic and international media to document Chinese actions at sea, reflects a strategic use of publicity and public opinion as integral components of its legal resistance. Through these measures, the Philippines not only reinforces its legal narrative but also mobilizes international support and reshapes the discourse around maritime law and sovereignty.

Vietnam presents another model—one that combines steadfast legal positioning with regional coalition-building. Vietnam has consistently asserted its rights under UNCLOS and uses international law as a shield for self-preservation and as a tool for strategic hedging. Its maritime policy, framed under the principle of "Cooperation for Mutual Development", prioritizes peaceful dispute resolution and lawful cooperation without sacrificing sovereignty or conceding to unlawful claims. Vietnam actively promotes legal unity among ASEAN states and fosters international partnerships to reinforce the rule of law at sea. This legal consistency—grounded in UNCLOS and supported by diplomatic outreach—enables Vietnam to counter China's lawfare through a strategy of principled persistence and collective legitimacy.

Collectively, these state practices demonstrate that lawfare is not a one-sided phenomenon. While China may dominate in scale and audacity, ASEAN claimant states are increasingly adaptive, using law not only defensively but as a proactive means of shaping maritime governance. The contest is as much about competing legal interpretations as it is about control of territory or resources. In this environment, the concept of lawfulness becomes especially significant—not merely as an ethical aspiration, but as a strategic framework for navigating complexity without capitulating to legal distortion.

Our initiative of lawfulness, encapsulated in the 3P formula, responds to this reality. By insisting on Publicity, we affirm the power of transparency and open legal reasoning as safeguards against covert coercion and legal ambiguity. Through Public Opinion, we recognize the importance of shaping domestic and global narratives that uphold justice, equity, and rule-based order. And by grounding our strategy in Public International Law, we commit to a legal order based on universally accepted norms, not power-driven reinterpretations. Lawfulness, then, is both a legal posture and a strategic doctrine: it empowers smaller states to defend their rights through principled legal action, and it offers a vision of international order anchored in fairness, predictability, and peace.

The broader context in which this struggle unfolds cannot be ignored. While the 2016 Arbitral Award was a landmark for the rule of law, its non-enforcement reflects the structural limitations of international adjudication in the absence of compliance mechanisms. Meanwhile, note verbale exchanges between claimant and non-claimant states highlight the persistent legal confrontation and the growing recognition among global actors—such as the U.S., the European Union, and Australia—of the South China Sea's legal and strategic significance. Negotiations over the ASEAN—China COC continue, but unresolved disputes over its binding nature, geographic scope, and enforcement mechanisms cast doubt on its potential to restrain coercive behavior or resolve the underlying legal challenges. China's persistent efforts to institutionalize its own legal narratives threaten to displace international legal norms with state-centric interpretations unless counterbalanced by a collective commitment to lawful conduct.

Ultimately, the confrontation between lawfulness and lawfare in the South China Sea reflects a deeper choice about the kind of international order we wish to build. Lawfare, while expedient, erodes trust, destabilizes norms, and prioritizes power over principle. Lawfulness, by contrast, offers a durable foundation for peace: it insists that disputes be resolved not through manipulation or intimidation, but through reason, dialogue, and respect for shared rules. As the region faces increasing geopolitical uncertainty and legal complexity, the path forward lies not in conceding to legal cynicism, but in affirming our commitment to lawful governance.

This book does not claim to resolve the South China Sea disputes. Instead, it offers a framework—grounded in legal analysis and regional practice—for understanding how law can be misused, and how it can be redeemed. The authors hope that the principle of lawfulness, as developed through the 3P formula, will inspire scholars, policymakers, and practitioners to engage more critically with the legal dimensions of international conflict and to work toward a maritime order where justice and legality prevail.

Our initiative of lawfulness, encapsulated in the 3P formula, responds to this reality. By insisting on Publicity, we affirm the power of transparency and open legal reasoning as safeguards against covert coercion and legal ambiguity. Through Public Opinion, we recognize the importance of shaping domestic and global narratives that uphold justice, equity, and rule-based order. And by grounding our strategy in Public International Law, we commit to a legal order based on universally accepted norms, not power-driven reinterpretations. Lawfulness, then, is both a legal posture and a strategic doctrine: it empowers smaller states to defend their rights through principled legal action, and it offers a vision of international order anchored in fairness, predictability, and peace.

The broader context in which this struggle unfolds cannot be ignored. While the 2016 Arbitral Award was a landmark for the rule of law, its non-enforcement reflects the structural limitations of international adjudication in the absence of compliance mechanisms. Meanwhile, note verbale exchanges between claimant and non-claimant states highlight the persistent legal confrontation and the growing recognition among global actors—such as the U.S., the European Union, and Australia—of the South China Sea's legal and strategic significance. Negotiations over the ASEAN—China COC continue, but unresolved disputes over its binding nature, geographic scope, and enforcement mechanisms cast doubt on its potential to restrain coercive behavior or resolve the underlying legal challenges. China's persistent efforts to institutionalize its own legal narratives threaten to displace international legal norms with state-centric interpretations unless counterbalanced by a collective commitment to lawful conduct.

Ultimately, the confrontation between lawfulness and lawfare in the South China Sea reflects a deeper choice about the kind of international order we wish to build. Lawfare, while expedient, erodes trust, destabilizes norms, and prioritizes power over principle. Lawfulness, by contrast, offers a durable foundation for peace: it insists that disputes be resolved not through manipulation or intimidation, but through reason, dialogue, and respect for shared rules. As the region faces increasing geopolitical uncertainty and legal complexity, the path forward lies not in conceding to legal cynicism, but in affirming our commitment to lawful governance.

This book does not claim to resolve the South China Sea disputes. Instead, it offers a framework—grounded in legal analysis and regional practice—for understanding how law can be misused, and how it can be redeemed. The authors hope that the principle of lawfulness, as developed through the 3P formula, will inspire scholars, policymakers, and practitioners to engage more critically with the legal dimensions of international conflict and to work toward a maritime order where justice and legality prevail.

MIX
Papier aus verantwortungsvollen Quellen
Paper from responsible sources
FSC® C105338

If you have any concerns about our products, you can contact us on
ProductSafety@springernature.com

In case Publisher is established outside the EU, the EU authorized representative is:
Springer Nature Customer Service Center GmbH
Europaplatz 3, 69115 Heidelberg, Germany

Printed by Libri Plureos GmbH
in Hamburg, Germany